The House in the Garden

The House in the Garden

The Bakunin Family and the Romance of Russian Idealism

John Randolph

Cornell University Press
Ithaca and London

First published 2007 by Cornell University Press

Printed in the United States of America

Library of Congress Cataloging-in-Publication Data

Randolph, John, 1967–
  The house in the garden : the Bakunin family and the romance of Russian idealism / John Randolph.
      p.   cm.
  Includes bibliographical references and index.
  ISBN 978-0-8014-4542-2 (cloth : alk. paper)
  1. Bakunin, Mikhail Aleksandrovich, 1814–1876—Political and social views.   2. Stankevich, N. V. (Nikolai Vladimirovich), 1813–1840—Political and social views.   3. Belinsky, Vissarion Grigorye-vich, 1811–1848—Political and social views.   4. Bakunin, Mikhail Aleksandrovich, 1814–1876—Family.   5. Stankevich, N. V. (Nikolai Vladimirovich), 1813–1840—Family.   6. Belinsky, Vissarion Gri-goryevich, 1811–1848—Family.   7. Family—Russia—Philosophy—History—19th century.   8. Idealism, Russian—History—19th century.   9. Russia—Intellectual life—1801–1917.   I. Title.

  HQ637.R36   2007
  306.85086'31094709034–dc22

                                                      2006035550

Cornell University Press strives to use environmentally responsible suppliers and materials to the fullest extent possible in the publishing of its books. Such materials include vegetable-based, low-VOC inks and acid-free papers that are recycled, totally chlorine-free, or partly composed of nonwood fibers. For further information, visit our website at www.cornellpress.cornell.edu.

Cloth printing   10 9 8 7 6 5 4 3 2 1

To Larisa Ivanova,
in gratitude and memory

CONTENTS

ACKNOWLEDGMENTS

Looking back on the writing of this book, I am humbled by the number of people who have helped me along. It is my great pleasure to thank at least some of them here. I am deeply grateful to the Andrew W. Mellon Foundation, the International Research and Exchanges Board, the University of California at Berkeley, and the University of Illinois at Urbana–Champaign for their generous financial support, without which this book could not have been written and published. In Russia, the scholars of numerous institutions gave generously as well, of their time and expertise. I thank the State Archive of the Russian Federation (Moscow); the State Archive of Ancient Acts (Moscow); the Tver State Regional Archive (Tver); the Saltykov-Shchedrin Museum (Tver); and the Russian National Library (St. Petersburg) for their assistance and their stewardship of the historical materials on which this book is based. My deepest gratitude goes to the archivists and scholars of the Manuscript Division of St. Petersburg's Institute of Russian Literature (Pushkin House). I was constantly amazed and encouraged by their scholarly devotion and collegial hospitality, even as I showed up, day after day, to consult the Priamukhino archive. My time at Pushkin House was, as we have joked since, my university. It is to one of their colleagues, the dearly missed Larisa Ivanova, that I dedicate this book.

I thank as well my academic mentors at Berkeley for their advice and support: Irina Paperno, Nicholas V. Riasanovsky, and the late Reggie Zelnik. Many other friends and colleagues have also contributed to this book. In St. Petersburg, I thank Dmitrii Mil'kov, Ksana Kumpan, and Al'bin Konechnyi.

Konstantin Lappo-Danilevskii provided numerous materials from his ongoing work on Nikolai Lvov. In Tver, Vladimir Sysoev gave generously of his extensive knowledge of the Bakunin family; I hope to repay the favor some day. Here in Champaign–Urbana, I have had wonderful, supportive colleagues, both in and out of the Department of History: in particular, I thank Diane Koenker, Mark Steinberg, Antoinette Burton, Harry Liebersohn, Harriet Murav, Lilya Kaganovsky, and my research assistants Erica Fraser, Rebecca Mitchell, and Randy Dills. Thanks as well to the many friends who helped me through this book: Jay Rubenstein, Gary Barth, Christine Kulke, Evgenii Bershtein, Francine Hirsch, Hazel Hahn, Arthur McKee, Victoria Frede, Konstantine Klioutchkine, Tom Newlin, Rebecca Friedman, Gregory Stroud, and Robin Breeding.

Last, but not least, let me thank my family: Michael and Ardith Fogarty; my grandmother Cathryn and father, John Randolph (now both deceased); my sisters, Gretchen, Sarah, and Erin; and my brothers, Ben, David, Matthew, John, and Nick. My wife, Kim Curtis, is probably as surprised as I am that all this is done, while my daughter, Lula, now nine months old, reminded me it was time to finish. My deepest gratitude to both of them: the one for waiting for me, the other for her arrival.

Portions of this book have appeared previously. Parts of chapter 9 were published in my article "'That Historical Family': The Bakunin Archive and the Intimate Theater of History in Imperial Russia, 1780–1925," *Russian Review* 63, no. 4 (October 2004): 574–93. Parts of chapter 8 appeared in "The Emancipation of Varvara Dyakova: Hegel, Sex, and the Call to Actuality in Imperial Russian Social Thought," *Gender and History* 18, no. 2 (Summer 2006):335–59. I thank the publishers of these journals for their kind permission to use this material. I thank the Institute of Russian Literature for its permission to reproduce images from its collection.

NOTE ON SOURCES

Archival Sources

Rossiiskaia natsional'naia biblioteka, Division of Manuscripts (RNB). St. Petersburg
    f. 542 (A. N. Olenin)

Institut russkoi literatury (Pushkinskii Dom), Manuscript Division (IRLI). St. Petersburg
    f. 16 (Bakunins)

Rossiiskii gosudarstvennyi arkhiv drevnikh aktov (RGADA). Moscow
    fonds 1341, 1354, 1355, 1356 (Materials of the General Survey)

Gosudarstvennyi arkhiv Tverskoi oblasti (GATO). Tver
    f. 103 (Tver Archive Commission)
    f. 1407 (Bakunin family papers)

Gosudarstvennyi arkhiv Rossiiskoi Federatsii (GARF). Moscow
    f. 825 (Bakunin family papers)

In my notes, I have followed the Russian convention of identifying documents by their *fond* (holding), *opis'* (register), *delo* (file), and *list* (page). These are abbreviated f., op., d., and l. (or ll. for pages), respectively. *Oborot* or ob. indicates the reverse side of the page. Note that at the Institute of Russian Literature files (*dela*) are titled by numbers, abbreviated as no. here.

Much of this book is based on previously unpublished material and in particular correspondence. Quite often, these manuscripts are either undated or bear only partial dates. Accordingly, dates that are my attribution occur in square brackets and are followed by a question mark. Dates indicated on the manuscript itself are given without brackets. Thus, the note "L. A. Bakunina to N. A. Beyer, letter of 24 January [1831?]" means that the original letter bears the date of 24 January, while I have attributed it to the year 1831. The notation "24 January 1831" means the entire date is on the original, whereas "24 [January 1831?]" means both the month and the year are my assumption. In those rare cases where my argument depends on precise dating, I will explain my attributions, though it has not proven practicable to do so throughout.

Except as noted, all dates are given according to the Julian, or "Old Style" (OS), calendar in use in Russia until 1917.

Last, in the main text I have simplified my spellings of Russian names, substituting *-sky* for *-skii* and eliminating hard and soft signs. In bibliographic citations, I retain the full spellings, according to the Library of Congress transliteration system.

Published Primary Sources
For multivolume works, I indicate volume number using a Roman numeral, followed by page number (e.g., Bakunin, *Sobranie*, I:24, means volume 1, page 24).

Bakunin, *Oeuvres [CD-ROM]:* International Institute of Social History. *Bakounine. Oeuvres complètes.* Amsterdam: Royal Netherlands Academy of Arts and Sciences, 2000. CD-ROM.

Bakunin, *Sobranie:* Bakunin, M. A. *Sobranie sochinenii i pisem, 1828–1876.* Edited by Iu. M. Steklov. 4 vols. Moscow: Izdatel'stvo Vsesoiuznogo obshchestva politkatorzhan i ssyl'no-poselentsev, 1934–1935.

Belinskii, *PSS:* Belinskii, V. G. *Pis'ma, 1829–1840. Polnoe sobranie sochinenii.* 13 vols. Moscow: Izdatel'stvo Akademii Nauk SSSR, 1953–1959.

Gertsen, *Sobranie:* Gertsen, A. I. *Sobranie sochinenii.* 30 vols. Moscow: Izdatel'stvo Akademii Nauk SSSR, 1956–1960.

Lehning, *Archives:* Internationaal Instituut Voor Sociale Geschiedenis Amsterdam. *Archives Bakounine. Bakunin-Archiv.* Edited by A. Lehning. 7 vols. Leiden: E. J. Brill, 1961–.

Pushkin, *PSS:* Pushkin, A. S. *Polnoe sobranie sochinenii.* 16 vols. Moscow-Leningrad: Izdatel'stvo Akademii Nauk SSSR, 1937–1949.

Stankevich, *Perepiska:* Stankevich, N. V. *Perepiska Nikolaia Vladimirovicha Stankevicha.* Edited by A. Stankevich. Moscow: Tipografiia A. I. Mamontova, 1914.

Despite more than a century of editorial attention, there exists no fully satisfactory scholarly edition of Mikhail Bakunin's works. In 2000, the International Institute of Social History (Amsterdam) released the most complete edition yet on CD-ROM. Among its many virtues, this edition is the first to publish Bakunin's writings in their original languages. I have consulted this edition heavily in interpreting Mikhail's early education and development, documented (for the most part) in a fascinating mix of French, Russian, and German. Unfortunately, this electronic edition is beginning to malfunction on the latest versions of Microsoft Windows, and I worry that it may soon be inaccessible. For this reason, in my notes I provide primary reference to paper editions where possible. When necessary—for example, when there are significant differences between Steklov's translation and the original—I will also provide a parallel reference to the *Oeuvres [CD-ROM]*. Please note that since the CD-ROM is organized by work and has no running pagination, my references are by title, date, and the internal pagination of each document. Thus, "*Oeuvres [CD-ROM]*, 2" indicates page 2 of the document in question.

The House in the Garden

INTRODUCTION

Ivan Ivanovich Lazhechnikov (1792–1869) was an Imperial Russian censor and educational official, but he was best known to his contemporaries as the "Russian Walter Scott." In the 1830s he published a series of wildly popular historical novels that mimicked Scott's technique of imagining the past through carefully chosen scenes from private life. Under his guidance, the Russian reading public traveled to the sixteenth and eighteenth centuries and overheard the personal conversations of Russia's rulers. In 1859, Lazhechnikov published a memoir that applied this technique to contemporary Russian history, with enduring if somewhat puzzling results.[1]

The subject of Lazhechnikov's memoir was the literary critic Vissarion Belinsky. Born in 1811, dead by 1848, Belinsky had a reputation as a brash outsider: a son of the provinces who broke into Russia's literary establishment and denounced it for ignoring social questions.[2] Yet Lazhechnikov sought to

---

[1] See I. I. Lazhechnikov, "Zametki dlia biografii Belinskogo," in *Polnoe sobranie sochinenii*, vol. 12 (St. Petersburg: Tovarishchestvo M. O. Vol'f, 1900), 228–60; V. A. Viktorovich, "Ivan Ivanovich Lazhechnikov," in *Russkie pisateli: Biograficheskii slovar'*, ed. P. A. Nikolaev, vol. 3 (Moscow: Sovetskaia entsiklopediia, 1989), 273–77. On the role of Scott's work in establishing private life as a prism on the past in nineteenth-century culture, see James Chandler, *England in 1819: The Politics of Literary Culture and the Case of Romantic Historicism* (Chicago: University of Chicago Press, 1998), 127–35, 147–50.

[2] On Belinsky's legend, see Isaiah Berlin, "A Remarkable Decade," in *Russian Thinkers*, ed. Henry Hardy (London: Penguin, 1994), 181–85; on his social style of criticism, see Victor Terras, *Belinskij and Russian Literary Criticism: The Heritage of Organic Aesthetics* (Madison: University of Wisconsin Press, 1974), 77–127.

offer his readers a fuller understanding of Belinsky's intellectual development by describing its private circumstances in more detail. (Lazhechnikov first met Belinsky in the early 1820s, while traveling as a school inspector.) He recalled Belinsky's birth to an impoverished rural family; his grinding education at the hands of old-school pedagogues; his move to Moscow, where Belinsky won admission to university but ran afoul of his superiors. Expelled in 1832, Belinsky quickly made a name for himself as a journalist but no money. When Lazhechnikov dropped by Belinsky's apartment in the mid-1830s, he was stunned to find the critic's room wedged underground between a laundry and a smithy. (From one side came a foul-smelling steam, from the other, the "hammers of Russian cyclopses.") Friends got Belinsky a job as personal secretary to a Russian aristocrat who had a beautiful house, an open table, and a musically inclined daughter. But Belinsky lasted only a short while in this heaven, deciding it was preferable to return to poverty than to pander to the vanity of a man he despised. He left, Lazhechnikov concludes with pride, "because he felt it was his *duty.*"[3]

Suddenly and without explanation, Lazhechnikov shifts scenes to a distant provincial home. "There is a corner of a district in Tver Province," he continues,

> on which nature has focused all her loving care, adorning it with the greatest gifts she could collect in a land of seven-month snows. The river in this picturesque locale seems to flow more playfully, flowers and trees grow more luxuriously, and there is more warmth there than in other places.

Here in this idyll there lived a large family that was "particularly awarded with spiritual gifts" and renowned for its unusual contentment. ("Never has a family lived more harmoniously," Lazhechnikov remarks.) "The spirit of the home" was its patriarch, a seventy-year-old man with "blue, unseeing eyes like Homer's" who had been educated at Italian universities and who loved to be surrounded by young people. He sponsored an unusually liberal atmosphere in his home, and as a result it was always crowded with guests. "Visitors streamed from all ends of Russia!" Lazhechnikov exclaims, adding, as if it were inevitable, that "Belinsky could not fail to come there as well."[4]

And when he did, Lazhechnikov finally concludes, the benighted critic en-

---

[3] Lazhechnikov, "Zametki," 255–56. Emphasis in the original.
[4] Ibid., 256–57.

tered an intimate world of intellectual activity that greatly stimulated his spiritual development and fostered the formation of his mature worldview. At this remote provincial home Belinsky found a society of philosophical young people—many of them students and ex-students of Moscow University—who were passionately committed to the study of German Idealist philosophy. "This was during the time," Lazhechnikov explains romantically, "when Hegel's teaching caught fire among us, when his adepts walked about in such an ecstatic rapture that they tried to recruit even old men, youths, and maidens into his school." One young man even used Hegelian aesthetics to write love letters "to a certain beautiful young lady, to whom he was not indifferent." And while the young man "laughed about this much later," Lazhechnikov believed that there was something profoundly progressive about this unusual combination of philosophy and private life. "It promoted the development of the younger generation's intellectual ability," he claimed. In Belinsky's case, it prepared him to write his provocative essays of the 1840s— "steeped in Hegelian philosophy," Lazhechnikov observes—that won him a place in history as modern Russia's boldest, most socially minded critic.[5]

Imperial Russian readers of the nineteenth century were renowned for their ability to read between the lines, yet there is much about Lazhechnikov's story that must have baffled them. Who was this unnamed provincial family, and what explained their unusual domestic distinction? What sort of support did their home life offer for intellectual activity in early-nineteenth-century Russia? Why, in particular, did it foster the unusual merger of intimacy and Idealist philosophy Lazhechnikov describes—and with what results? In the mid-nineteenth century, some readers would have been better equipped than others to answer these questions, but to this day no one has answered them all. That, in short, is the aim of this book.

The House in the Garden is a case study of the role played by home life in the making of Imperial Russian social thought. My aim has been to examine home life's function as a theater of intellectual activity in early-nineteenth-century Russia by reconstructing the history of one particularly distinguished and important home. My book tells the story of Priamukhino, the provincial manor house that stands at the center of Lazhechnikov's memoirs. It is based on the archive of Priamukhino's former owners, a Russian noble family named the Bakunins, and it is divided into two parts. Part 1, "Idyll," describes how the Bakunins first came to Priamukhino in the late eighteenth century and seeks to understand the distinguished, experimental character their family life ac-

[5] Ibid., 257–58.

quired when placed into this new domestic frame. Part 2, "Romance," explores the role this home played in the making of a charismatic tradition in Imperial Russian social thought that I call the romance of Russian Idealism. In particular, I examine how the Bakunin home supported the ambitions and reputations of three particularly influential young men: the radical critic Belinsky, the student icon Nikolai Stankevich (1813–1840), and the young Mikhail Bakunin (1814–1876).

Such an approach, I believe, opens a fundamentally new perspective on the making of Imperial Russian intellectual traditions. Most works of Russian intellectual history take the form of philosophical romances: tales of development that seek to explain how this or that thinker was transformed by an encounter with some idea, most commonly of European origin.[6] There can be a certain exclusive, incantatory quality to these narratives, however, as if ideas themselves were magical formulas that gave their possessors a special distinction and agency as "thinkers" in imperial society. "I even think that a man who has not *lived through* Hegel's *Phenomenology* and Proudhon's *Contradictions of Political Economy*, who has not passed through that furnace and been tempered by it, is not complete, not modern," the socialist Aleksandr Herzen (1812–1870) writes, evidently quite serious, in his memoir *Past and Thoughts*.[7]

Yet aspiring thinkers, like any other actors, require a stage for their performance and an audience to help give their actions distinction and meaning. To be made durable and influential, their charismatic stories have to be framed by supporting ideals, practices, and institutions. And if today—thanks to generations of scholarship based on nationalized private archives—the biographies of the Empire's most famous thinkers have a comfortable platform in modern Russia's printed record, scholars have yet to explore fully the intimate context surrounding their activities in the early nineteenth century. There is, as a result, a certain homeless quality to our understandings of Imperial Russian culture which I hope this history of one extremely productive home will help us correct. I seek to recontextualize the Russian intellectual history of this period—heretofore dominated by psychological approaches centered on alienation—within a cultural history that focuses on the domes-

---

[6] On the predominance of biography in Russian intellectual history and the relative neglect of the subject recently see Terence Emmons, "Russia Then and Now in the Pages of the American Historical Review and Elsewhere: A Few Centennial Notes," *American Historical Review* 100, no. 4 (1995): 1144, 1149.

[7] Alexander Herzen, *My Past and Thoughts*, ed. Dwight Macdonald, trans. Constance Garnett, introduction by Isaiah Berlin (Berkeley: University of California Press, 1973), 236; cf. Gertsen, *Sobranie*, IX:23.

tic realm's positive development as a sphere of distinction, agency, and memory in imperial society.

But what should a history of home life entail? Why have historians been fascinated by the Idealist tradition Lazhechnikov portrays, and what can Priamukhino's story help us understand about it? Before beginning my inquiry, a few more comments on its methods and historiographical context are in order.

❀❦❀

Both the English word "home" and the Russian word *дom* can mean any space of residence, but it is their more specific designation of a familial residence that I have in mind here. The eighteenth and nineteenth centuries in Europe saw an intensive elaboration of the social, political, and cultural space occupied by family life; and historians have analyzed this phenomenon in several different ways. First, they have seen the home as a social institution, as the bearer and producer of certain practices and ideals. A large body of literature, for example, speaks of the urban townhouse as the cradle of middle-class sociability and values.[8] Alternatively, historians speak of domesticity as an ideal produced in public discourse. In particular, some scholars have seen the robust interest in home life that characterized the early part of the nineteenth century as an attempt to contain the realm of politics and reestablish paternal authority after the French Revolution.[9] Last but not least, historians have described the home as a capacious stage for modern self-creation and performance. Above all, write Inga Bryden and Janet Floyd, "the home was imagined, in nineteenth-century domestic discourse, to provide a powerfully influential space for the development of character and identity."[10] Increasingly, historians are interested in domesticity's archival role in society as well and seek to understand how the home has both framed our understandings of the recent past and documented it.[11]

---

[8] On homes as producers of values, see, e.g., Leonore Davidoff and Catherine Hall, *Family Fortunes: Men and Women of the English Middle Class, 1780–1850* (Chicago: University of Chicago Press, 1987).

[9] See, for example, Michelle Perrot, "The Family Triumphant," in *From the Fires of Revolution to the Great War,* ed. Michelle Perrot, vol. 4 of *A History of Private Life,* ed. Phillipe Ariès and Georges Duby, trans. Arthur Goldhammer (Cambridge, Mass.: Belknap Press, 1990), 99–129, esp. 99–100; see also Lynn Hunt, *The Family Romance of the French Revolution* (Berkeley: University of California Press, 1991).

[10] Inga Bryden and Janet Floyd, introduction to *Domestic Space: Reading the Nineteenth-Century Interior,* ed. Inga Bryden and Janet Floyd (Manchester: Manchester University Press, 1999), 2.

[11] See, for example, Antoinette Burton, *Dwelling in the Archive: Women Writing House, Home, and*

It would be wrong to say that Russian history has no tradition of writing about the phenomenon of private life. Relatively early in the nineteenth century—because they feared that Russia's officious public record had ignored and suppressed important historical phenomena—Imperial Russian historians began to exploit personal archives. They created pioneering biographical studies of Russian thinkers, revealing an entire world of intimate intellectual activity that had heretofore escaped the public's attention. Yet historical interest in this intimate world was constrained by both political and polite pressures. Informants asked them to be discreet; censors blocked the discussion of certain names; and scholars themselves sometimes worried that their "excessive familiarity" with the personal lives of Russian thinkers was degrading the rights of privacy in Russia and the gender conventions built around them. Scholars were particularly careful to avoid injuring the domestic sensibilities of their era and used a variety of contortions to keep the names and reputations of women in particular out of the public eye.[12] In the end, the function of the histories of private life written in the nineteenth century was to justify and support the reputations of famous men, rather than to understand the genesis and function of the intimate theater of intellectual activity in Imperial Russia.

One effect of this historical reticence was to yield a bit too easily to a rapidly developing belief in modern Russia's homelessness. Russian literature throughout the imperial period expressed anxiety about Russian home life. To begin with, there was a tendency—very strongly expressed in eighteenth- and early-nineteenth-century memoir—to present the home as a bastion of patriarchy and backwardness in Russian life.[13] By the middle of the

---

History in Late Colonial India (New York: Oxford University Press, 2003); John R. Gillis, *A World of Their Own Making: Myth, Ritual, and the Quest for Family* (New York: Basic Books, 1996), 81–109.

[12] For leading examples of nineteenth-century intellectual biography, see P. V. Annenkov, *Nikolai Vladimirovich Stankevich: Perepiska ego i biografiia* (Moscow: Tipografiia Kat'kova, 1857); A. N. Pypin, *Belinskii, ego zhizn' i deiatel'nost', 1814–1876*, 2 vols. (St. Petersburg: Tipografiia M. M. Stasiulevicha, 1876); P. Miliukov, "Liubov' u 'idealistov tridtsatykh godov,'" in *Iz istorii russkoi intelligentsii: Sbornik statei* (St. Petersburg: Tipografiia A. E. Kolpinskogo, 1902), 73–168; A. Kornilov, *Molodye gody Mikhaila Bakunina: Iz istorii russkogo romantizma* (Moscow: M. and S. Sabashnikov, 1915). With the exception of Kornilov, all of these authors avoid identifying the female protagonists of their story directly. I discuss this literature in John Randolph, "'That Historical Family': The Bakunin Archive and the Intimate Theater of History in Imperial Russia, 1780–1925," *Russian Review* 63 (October 2004): 583–91. Miliukov expresses his concerns about his contemporaries' "excessive familiarity" in "Liubov' u 'idealistov,'" 73–74. M. Gershenzon notes his contemporaries' "complete neglect" of women's history during the Idealist period in "Russkaia zhenshchina 30-x godov," *Russkaia mysl'* 12 (1911): 54–73, esp. 54–56.

[13] Studies based on gentry memoir tend to draw the home in dark, traditional terms: see Jes-

nineteenth century, this tradition was counterbalanced in Russian belles lettres by what Andrew Baruch Wachtel has called the "myth" of the happy noble home (whose function, he contends, was to shore up noble distinction in
an era when that class's primacy in Russian life was being threatened). At
least partly in reply to this noble myth, however, harsher, more critical visions
continued to thrive. Many of Russia's most famous novels thematize familial
conflict, for example, Ivan Turgenev's *Fathers and Sons* (1862).[14] "We do not
even have homes," Petr Chaadaev announced dismally in his famous "First
Philosophical Letter" of 1829, arguing that Russia's cruel history had rendered it a nomad nation.[15]

One should be cautious, however, about taking such anxieties too literally.
It is important to draw a distinction between the intensity of domestic conflict—real or imagined—and the absence of domestic values in a culture. To
critique a home for falling short of the ideal, after all, is to pay indirect homage
to some other, dearly held domestic norm. Increasingly, scholars are turning
their attention to the familial, domestic frame surrounding much of Imperial
Russian social thought.[16] From the moment Russian noblemen were given
their liberty from obligatory service in 1762, the production of fancy homes
became a distinguishing hallmark of noble culture.[17] Through advice manu-

---

sica Tovrov, *The Russian Noble Family: Structure and Change* (New York: Garland, 1987); Marc
Raeff, *Origins of the Russian Intelligentsia: The Eighteenth-Century Nobility* (New York: Harcourt
Brace Jovanovich, 1966), 122–47.

[14] On the powerful myth of the unhappy, as well as happy, family in Imperial Russian literature, see Andrew Baruch Wachtel, *The Battle for Childhood: Creation of a Russian Myth* (Stanford:
Stanford University Press, 1990).

[15] See also Petr Iakovlevich Chaadaev, "Letters on the Philosophy of History: First Letter,"
in *Russian Intellectual History: An Anthology*, ed. and trans. Marc Raeff (Atlantic Highlands, NJ:
Humanities Press, 1986), 162.

[16] See, e.g., Wachtel, *The Battle for Childhood*; Priscilla Roosevelt, *Life on the Russian Country Estate: A Social and Cultural History* (New Haven: Yale University Press, 1995); Mary Wells Caven-
der, "'Kind Angel of the Soul and Heart': Domesticity and Family Correspondence Among the
Pre-Emancipation Russian Gentry," *The Russian Review* 61 (July 2002): 391–408; Rebecca
Friedman, *Masculinity, Autocracy, and the Russian University, 1804–1863* (New York: Palgrave
Macmillan, 2005), esp. chapter 5; Elise Kimerling Wirtschafter, *The Play of Ideas in Russian En-
lightenment Theater* (DeKalb, Illinois: Northern Illinois University Press, 2003), 53–83; and Irina
Paperno, ed., "Intimacy and History: The Herzen Family Drama Reconsidered," forthcoming
in 2007 as a special issue of *Russian Literature*. I review the wave of interest in estate life in post-
Soviet Russia in John Randolph, "The Old Mansion: Revisiting the History of the Russian
Country Estate," *Kritika* 1, no. 4 (2000): 729–49.

[17] On this theme, discussed in more detail in chapter 1, see Priscilla Roosevelt, "Russian Estate Architecture and Noble Identity," in *Architectures of Russian Identity 1500 to the Present*, ed.
James Cracraft and Daniel Rowland (Ithaca: Cornell University Press, 2003), 66–79; Roosevelt, *Russian Country Estate*.

als, law codes, and sentimental novels imported from abroad, belief in the "natural" virtues of domesticity—and their normative role as guides for the lives of modern men and women—began to be a commonplace of imperial culture in the early nineteenth century.[18] Political writers advanced the notion that the family was the basis of the imperial order, a point of view that both had some root in reality and was supported by the crown at the time.[19] Family chronicles, correspondences, and diaries began to accumulate in the spaces of home life, creating the materials from which later scholars would try to imagine the history of modern Russian society, independent of the records preserved by the state.[20]

After its purchase by the Bakunin family in 1779, Priamukhino became a particularly productive participant in this imperial domestic culture. Though the Bakunins had spent most of the eighteenth century living in the imperial capital of St. Petersburg, Mikhail Bakunin's grandfather and grandmother decided to take their chances on country life. At first it does not seem to have gone particularly well. The family's fortunes nearly collapsed under a combination of illness and debt. But in the 1790s the Bakunins recalled their youngest son, Aleksandr Mikhailovich Bakunin (1768?–1854), from imperial service; and thereafter Priamukhino became one of the most elaborately enlightened visions of home life the empire had yet seen.

Part 1 of my book explores the blossoming of this new domestic existence. Heretofore, scholars have relied on Aleksandr Kornilov's *Young Years of Mikhail Bakunin* (1915)—a monumental work of prerevolutionary scholarship—for their understandings of the early years of Bakunin family life. Kornilov worked closely with the Bakunins themselves as he wrote his book, the first of a planned trilogy on the Bakunin family's life. His explicit intention was to explore Priamukhino's history as an "embryo of culture and society."[21]

---

[18] See Barbara Alpern Engel, *Women in Russia, 1700–2000* (Cambridge: Cambridge University Press, 2004); Barbara Alpern Engel, *Mothers and Daughters: Women of the Intelligentsia in Nineteenth-Century Russia* (Cambridge, Mass.: Cambridge University Press, 1983), 8–42; and Catriona Kelly, *Refining Russia: Advice Literature, Polite Culture, and Gender from Catherine to Yeltsin* (Oxford: Oxford University Press, 2001).

[19] Alexander M. Martin, "The Family Model of Society and Russian National Identity in Sergei N. Glinka's Russian Messenger (1808–1812)," *Slavic Review* 57, no. 1 (Spring 1998): 28–49; Richard Wortman, "The Russian Imperial Family as Symbol," in *Imperial Russia: New Histories for the Empire*, ed. Jane Burbank and David Ransel (Bloomington: Indiana University Press, 1998), 60–86.

[20] For examples of this, see Thomas Newlin, *The Voice in the Garden: Andrei Bolotov and the Anxieties of Russian Pastoral, 1738–1833* (Evanston: Northwestern University Press, 2001), 168–78; Randolph, "'That Historical Family,'" as well as chapter 4.

[21] Kornilov, *Molodye gody*, 29.

Even so, he devoted only a short amount of space—a few pages—to the earliest years of the Bakunins' existence at Priamukhino in the late eighteenth century. (Most of his portrait of family life before 1820 is based on poetry written later.)[22]

Fortunately, enough materials survive from these years to sketch the public ideals and private practices behind Priamukhino's initial development. Sometimes noble interest in estate life in the late eighteenth century is seen as a demonstrative withdrawal from imperial society—or even a theatrical display of alienation. Based on the materials in the Bakunin archive, I argue that this phenomenon is better understood as a state-sponsored theater of distinction: a privatization of the power and charisma heretofore associated with the imperial court.[23] Some of the earliest papers produced at Priamukhino document the Bakunins' desire to be seen as an exemplary family. In particular, as his numerous poems and projects show, young Aleksandr Bakunin sought to fashion his home as a laboratory for the production of useful social truths. Though far from unopposed within his own family, Aleksandr's idyllic, and ideological, vision of Priamukhino's role in society stimulated the family's development as a theater for intellectual activity and helped win the Bakunins a wide-ranging reputation as an ideal family.[24] When his children forged ties with an ambitious group of Moscow youths in the early 1830s, this studiously enlightened home soon participated in the creation of a new and radical tradition in Russian social thought: the romance of Russian Idealism.

❀⁄❀

Until the early nineteenth century, as Richard Wortman has shown, Imperial Russian notions of history and historical agency were dominated by epic "scenarios of power" produced by the imperial court. According to these narratives, the pace and direction of Russia's development were set by Russia's

[22] See ibid., 1–81, of which the first ten pages are devoted to the late eighteenth century proper. The second volume of Kornilov's trilogy is A. Kornilov, *Gody stranstvii Mikhaila Bakunina* (Leningrad: Gosudarstvennoe izdatel'stvo, 1925), while he died before he could complete the third. On Kornilov's life and interest in the Bakunins, see especially A. A. Levandovskii, *Iz istorii krizisa russkoi burzhuazno-liberal'noi istoriografii: A. A. Kornilov* (Moscow: Izdatel'stvo Moskovskogo gosudarstvennogo universiteta, 1982).

[23] See chapters 1–2, below. This interpretation builds off of the insights of Richard Wortman's study of imperial political culture, *Scenarios of Power: Myth and Ceremony in Russian Monarchy* (Princeton: Princeton University Press, 1995–2000), and trenchant observations about estate culture made by Priscilla Roosevelt in "Russian Estate Architecture and Noble Identity," 66–67.

[24] See chapters 1–4, below.

emperors and empresses, who presented themselves as transcendent forces standing outside society.[25] By the middle of the nineteenth century, however, a new kind of modern history began to emerge in Russian literature. It took the form of a philosophical romance and surrounded a group of students and ex-students of Moscow University, sometimes called the "Idealists of the 1830s."[26] If the epic narratives surrounding the Romanov dynasty presented Russia's rulers as transcendent forces, the romance surrounding the Idealists emphasized their emergence from—and influence on—Russia's evolving social consciousness. These Idealists included in their number such radical celebrities as Aleksandr Herzen, Vissarion Belinsky, Mikhail Bakunin, and an independent-minded group of friends known loosely in Russian history as the "Stankevich circle," named after their charismatic leader, Nikolai Stankevich, who died in 1840.[27]

Where had this bold new group of men come from, and how had they become so distinguished and self-possessed? Why had they rejected imperial authority and tradition, in the name of their own social convictions? Almost none of these Idealists participated in the army or the court, Russia's traditional loci of power and distinction. Rather, they claimed to have been transformed and matured by philosophical studies they conducted first as students at Moscow University and then on their own private time. Central to this process was the startling practice of conducting their intimate affairs according to principles derived from German Idealist philosophy.

German Idealism was a philosophical movement that claimed to continue

---

[25] Wortman, *Scenarios of Power,* 1:1–10.

[26] Beginning in the 1840s, versions of this Idealist romance appeared in Russian fiction, criticism, memoir, and biography. For a sample from fiction, see the story "Andrei Kolosov" (1844) by Ivan Turgenev (I. S. Turgenev, *Polnoe sobranie sochinenii i pisem,* vol. 4 (Moscow: Nauka, 1980), 7–33; in criticism see N. G. Chernyshevskii, "Ocherki gogolevskogo perioda russkoi literatury," *Polnoe sobranie sochinenii,* ed. V. Ia. Kirpotin, vol. 3 (Moscow: OGIZ Gosudarstvennoe izdatel'stvo khudozhestvennoi literatury, 1947), 8–9 and 177–226, esp. 206–26. This essay was originally published in 1855–56. For memoir, see Herzen's *Past and Thoughts,* especially 229–53 (cf. Gertsen, *Sobranie,* IX:9–46); for biography see Annenkov, *N. V. Stankevich.* For examples of formal, scholarly use of the phrase "idealists of the 1830s" to describe this group, see, e.g., P. V. Annenkov, "Idealisty tridtsatykh godov," in *P. V. Annenkov i ego druz'ia* (St. Petersburg: A. S. Suvorin, 1892), 1–111 (this is about Herzen and Ogarev); Miliukov, "Liubov'."

[27] For stimulating portraits of the "men of the 1840s" as a group, see Berlin, "A Remarkable Decade"; Martin Malia, "What is the Intelligentsia?" *The Russian Intelligentsia,* ed. Richard Pipes (New York: Columbia University Press, 1961), 448–53; Michael Confino, "On Intellectuals and Intellectual Traditions in Eighteenth- and Nineteenth-Century Russia," *Daedalus* (Spring 1972): 125–28. Berlin and Malia emphasize alienation as their founding feature, while Confino develops the interpretation advanced below: that their esprit de corps was rooted in social conventions of their time.

the work of the Königsberg philosopher Immanuel Kant (1724–1804). Con-
tending that previous philosophers had attempted things that exceeded the
capacities of human reason, Kant sought to make the study of cognition, not
the study of being, philosophy's foundational concern. Though he acknowledged the power of empirical observation, he felt it needed to be undergirded
by an understanding of reason's formal limits and capabilities. "My question
is," he announced in his famous *Critique of Pure Reason* (1781), "what we can
hope to achieve with reason, when all the material and assistance of experience is taken away."[28] Though his language was notoriously technical and his
methods abstract, Kant was profoundly interested in moral questions. He
hoped to use his philosophy to establish firm principles that could guide humanity to the good life.

In particular, he believed that by determining the capabilities of human
reason, he could help usher in a more mature era in human existence. Kant
imagined a world populated by conscious, autonomous, and active people,
united into a harmonious community by their reasoned willingness to follow
the same moral law. Though Kant doubted that such an "ethical community"
could ever be built on earth, given human frailty, he described it as a governing norm toward which people should strive. As a model of what such a
perfect society would look like, he picked the paternal household.[29]

Already in the 1790s, however, the authority of Kant's methods was chal-
lenged by a series of self-proclaimed successors. They felt it was possible to
invent still clearer and more certain visions of reason's life in the world, over-
coming areas of uncertainty that Kant had left behind. They have been called
Idealists, because they placed the study of mind, rather than matter, at the
center of their philosophy and also because they believed—albeit for different reasons—that reality correlates to reason. The most illustrious authors
within this post-Kantian tradition were Johann Gottlieb Fichte (1762–1814),
Friedrich Wilhelm Joseph Schelling (1775–1854), and Georg Wilhelm Friedrich Hegel (1770–1831).[30] All of these men were prominent academicians,

[28] Immanuel Kant, "Preface [to the First Edition, 1781]," trans. F. Max Müller, *Basic Writings
of Kant*, ed. Allen W. Wood (New York: Modern Library, 2001), 6.

[29] On Kant's ideal of an "ethical community," and his proposal of the paternal household as
model, see Immanuel Kant, "Religion Within the Boundaries of Mere Reason," *Religion and Ra-
tional Theology*, trans. and ed. Allen W. Wood and George di Giovanni (Cambridge: Cambridge
University Press, 1996), 135–36; Terry Pinkard, *German Philosophy, 1760–1860: The Legacy of
Idealism* (Cambridge: Cambridge University Press, 2002), 63–65; and Isabel V. Hull, *Sexuality,
State, and Civil Society in Germany 1700–1815* (Ithaca: Cornell University Press, 1996), 301–14.

[30] On Kant and German Idealism in general, see Dieter Henrich, *Between Kant and Hegel: Lectures on German Idealism*, ed. David S. Pacini (Cambridge, Mass.: Harvard University Press,

in addition to being brilliant philosophers. In the early 1800s, their students began to establish a foothold in Russian universities and seminaries. Russian official tolerance of post-Kantian philosophy rested on the notion that its philosophical methods were less dangerous to religious orthodoxy and imperial authority than the rebellious, empirical reason championed by the French.[31]

The philosophical romance surrounding Russia's Idealists of the 1830s, however, soon threw doubt on this proposition. Not only did these charismatic students show a dangerously independent streak, they also seemed oblivious to the conventional limits of philosophical activity. In its native Germany, post-Kantian Idealism was practiced in public institutions, such as university lecture halls and scientific publications.[32] Russian analogues to this institutionalized Idealism existed, inside of the Imperial Academy; yet the most famous and charismatic traditions surrounding Russian Idealism were produced more intimately, on the stage of private life. Comic stories such as Lazhechnikov's—of a young man who wrote love letters in the language of Hegel—laced the growing literature about Idealism's development in Russia, and contemporaries were not entirely sure what to make of this phenomenon. On the one hand, this private cult of philosophy seemed to violate what many regarded to be the proper limits of abstract thought by pulling it so deeply into the sphere of intimate relations.[33] On the other hand, in Herzen's authoritative judgment, as in Lazhechnikov's, there was something progressive—if comical—about this idealistic habit of "living through" philosophy. It had allowed its practitioners to break their subservience to the Empire's

2003); Pinkard, *German Philosophy;* Frederick C. Beiser, *German Idealism: The Struggle against Subjectivism, 1781–1801* (Cambridge, Mass.: Harvard University Press, 2002); idem, *The Fate of Reason: German Philosophy from Kant to Fichte* (Cambridge, Mass.: Harvard University Press, 1987). On the definition of "Idealism," see especially Beiser, *German Idealism,* 5–6.

[31] On the arrival of Kantian and post-Kantian philosophy in Russia, see especially V. V. Zen'kovskii, *Istoriia russkoi filosofii,* vol. 1 (Paris: YMCA-Press, 1948); Z. A. Kamenskii and V. A. Zhuchkov, *Kant i filosofiia v Rossii* (Moscow: Nauka, 1994); Z. A. Kamenskii, *Russkaia filosofiia nachala XIX veka i Shelling* (Moscow: Nauka, 1980); V. F. Pustarnakov, ed. and comp., *Filosofiia Fikhte v Rossii* (St. Petersburg: Russkii Khristianskii gumanitarnyi institut, 2000); D. I. Chizhevsky, *Gegel' v Rossii* (Paris: Dom knigi i Sovremennye zapiski, 1939).

[32] Recent scholarship presents the Idealist movement as a phenomenon of public and civic institutions: see Theodore Ziolkowski, *German Romanticism and Its Institutions* (Princeton: Princeton University Press, 1990); Hull, *Sexuality, State, and Civil Society,* 300–323; Anthony J. La Vopa, *Fichte: The Self and the Calling of Philosophy, 1762–1799* (Cambridge: Cambridge University Press, 2001), esp. 230–68.

[33] For an extended example of this critique, see chapter 9, below. See also the unsettling judgments of this phenomenon in the stories of Ivan Turgenev, as analyzed by Jane Costlow, *Worlds within Worlds: The Novels of Ivan Turgenev* (Princeton: Princeton University Press, 1990), 11–29.

religious and political dogmas. In the process it made them independent, "complete," and fully "modern" men (to borrow Herzen's phrases) and prepared their subsequent, autonomous role in Russian life.[34]

Until the end of the imperial period, the comic but heroic romance surrounding the "Idealists of the 1830s" was broadly accepted by liberal and radical opinion. In the early twentieth century, Pavel Miliukov expressed a common sentiment among historians when he pictured the Idealists as the "best people of their time" and the "spiritual fathers and grandfathers of the best people of our own time."[35] After the October Revolution, however, scholarly opinion began to have doubts about how to evaluate the private practice of philosophical Idealism among this small group of educated Russians in the 1830s. Broadly speaking, one may say that scholarly opinion has been divided into two camps. The predominant current of scholarly thought holds that Russia's Idealists are best understood as psychological types, whose biographies illustrate the political and social processes at work in the formation of modern Russian social thought.[36] For others, however, the historical romance surrounding this small group of individuals is simply a charismatic myth, whose effect is to take the intimate activities of a few talented but exceptional men and present them as milestones in the development of educated Russia as a whole.[37]

---

[34] See Herzen, *My Past and Thoughts*, 236; cf. Gertsen, *Sobranie*, IX:23. On the broad influence of Herzen's judgments of this tradition, see Irina Paperno, "Sovetskii opyt, avtobiograficheskoe pis'mo i istoricheskoe soznanie: Ginzburg, Gertsen, Gegel'," *Novoe Literaturnoe Obozrenie* 68 (2004): 102–27.

[35] Miliukov, "Liubov'," 73.

[36] See Berlin, "Remarkable Decade," 114–17, 119–21, 136–49, esp. 119; Martin Malia, *Alexander Herzen and the Birth of Russian Socialism* (New York: Grosset & Dunlap, 1965); Andrzej Walicki, *The Slavophile Controversy: History of a Conservative Utopia in Nineteenth-Century Russian Thought*, trans. Hilda Andrews-Rusiecka (Notre Dame: University of Notre Dame Press, 1975); Aileen Kelly, *Mikhail Bakunin: A Study in the Psychology and Politics of Utopianism* (New Haven: Yale University Press, 1987). On Idealism as a form of modern mysticism, see Isaiah Berlin, "The Pursuit of the Ideal," in *The Proper Study of Mankind: An Anthology of Essays*, ed. Henry Hardy and Roger Hausheer (New York: Farrar, Straus, and Giroux, 1997), 14–16; Berlin, "The Apotheosis of the Romantic Will," in Hardy and Hausheer, *Proper Study of Mankind*, 560–61, 580. Written in this way, such interpretations accorded with postwar evaluations of the legacy of Idealism in German history, where Idealism was presented as a dangerous expression of social frustrations: see Henri Brunschwig, *La crise de l'état prussien à la fin du XVIII siècle et la genèse de la mentalité romantique* (Paris: Presses universitaires de France, 1947); J. L. Talmon, *The Origins of Totalitarian Democracy* (New York: Praeger, 1960); Karl Raimund Popper, *The Open Society and Its Enemies* (Princeton: Princeton University Press, 1963). See also Frederick Copleston's description of Idealism as a "metaphysics of reality" in *A History of Philosophy*, vol. 7, pt. 1, *Fichte to Hegel* (Garden City, NY: Image Books, 1963), 22.

[37] See Confino, "On Intellectuals and Intellectual Traditions," 117–49; Jane Burbank and

I myself tend to understand Russia's Idealists neither as exemplary men nor as myths but rather as myth makers. I believe that the romance of Russian Idealism was a charismatic tradition built in the 1830s, by an ambitious group of young men in and around Moscow University who sought to translate the central ambitions of post-Kantian thought — self-knowledge, autonomy, and progressive agency in society — into compelling Russian terms. Their explicit goal in doing so was to play a modern and inspirational role in Russia's intellectual development through the mastery of what they believed to be the most modern current of European social thought. In this sense, their common reputation in Russian history as the "best" (or at least the most illustrative) "people of their time" is a form of historical distinction they actively sought.

A history of the Bakunin home provides an excellent prism on this process of myth-construction because domestic society, ideals, and spaces proved integral to its operation. Perhaps no location in Imperial Russian culture is so closely associated with the history of Russian Idealism as the Bakunin family's estate Priamukhino. Reputed to be a temple of happiness within Moscow's student circles, it played a central role in the genesis of some of Idealism's most famous and influential historical romances — the stories of development surrounding Stankevich, Belinsky, and Bakunin.[38] Viewing the romance of Russian Idealism through the home offers us several potential insights. First, it shows the degree to which this romantic tradition participated in a charismatic culture of private life surrounding Russia's nobility. Second, it documents this tradition's engagement with — rather than alienation from — the official values of the Nicholaevan era, not least among them Kantian conceptions of manhood and paternalistic domestic norms. Last, it helps us understand why this charismatic intellectual tradition — the most crucial phase of which took place in private life and whose ideals, practices, and sub-

---

David Ransel, introduction to *Imperial Russia: New Histories for the Empire,* ed. Burbank and Ransel (Bloomington: Indiana University Press, 1998), xvi–xvii; Laurie Manchester, "The Secularization of the Search for Salvation: The Self-Fashioning of Orthodox Clergymen's Sons in Late Imperial Russia," *Slavic Review* 57, no. 7 (Spring 1998): 50–96.

[38] The only Idealists for whom Priamukhino was not a touchstone were Herzen and his close collaborator the poet Nikolai Ogarev; yet Herzen himself presents their interest in German Idealism as feeding off patterns established by the group just mentioned still earlier in the 1830s. Thus, in a famous passage from *Past and Thoughts,* Herzen presents his early intellectual development as having been predominantly "French" in orientation, as opposed to the "German" orientation of the Stankevich circle. It was only after his return from exile, in the late 1830s (and after the events discussed in this book) that he took up the study of the post-Kantian tradition in earnest. See Herzen, *My Past and Thoughts,* 231–36, esp. 231 (cf. Gertsen, *Sobranie,* IX:17–23, esp. 17).

sequent preservation depended on the agency of women — failed to recognize or distinguish their activity. (It also gives us a chance to rectify that situation, by understanding women's participation in this intimate intellectual culture and their thoughts about it.)

In short, I propose to broaden our intellectual histories of this period beyond the personal psychology of individual thinkers by attempting to reconstruct the history of the domestic realm in which they acted. Though most histories of Russian thought are romances of men and ideas, I will begin by considering the history of the stage on which these traditions depended, whose genesis lies in the late eighteenth century.

Idyll

CHAPTER ONE

A Prologue for the New Year 1790

At the end of the eighteenth century, numerous side routes laced the road between St. Petersburg and Moscow, linking provincial Russia's peasant communities to rivers, markets, towns, and eventually the capitals. Most of these roads led to villages with no resident landlords. A tiny few led to the pleasure palaces of imperial favorites, who would sweep down from the capital occasionally but who left their houses dark the rest of the year. Still other routes led to the full-time residences of full-time masters, nobles and serf-lords who lived on their estates. An eight-day journey in good weather from St. Petersburg, the manor house at Priamukhino was one of these.[1]

This mansion stood then where its ruins stand now, at the top of a gentle slope that rises from the Osuga River, one of the Volga's headwaters. Three peasant villages—home to some 280 men and women, all of whom were bound to the masters of this one house—surrounded it in a rough triangle. Two of these villages occupied the Osuga's far bank, across a bridge that led to the "big road," and from there to the district capital of Torzhok. The third village stood behind the master house, which in turn faced the view across the river. Today, Priamukhino's ruins consist of a stone neoclassical wing built by the Bakunin family in the early nineteenth century, but the original

---

[1] Priamukhino is roughly 250 miles to the southeast of St. Petersburg and 150 miles northwest of Moscow. On travel times between St. Petersburg and Moscow in the late eighteenth century, see Robert E. Jones, *Provincial Development in Russia: Catherine II and Jakob Sievers* (New Brunswick: Rutgers University Press, 1984), 75.

mansion, no longer visible, was much simpler. Like most estate houses in provincial Russia, it was made of wood: thick, round logs of fir, sided with rough-cut shingles. At its base was a large, one-story rectangle, one hundred feet long by fifty feet wide, supporting a steeply pitched roof. A windowed mezzanine on the western side let in light and housed servants; the owners, meanwhile, lived on the main floor. In these provinces, this would have been considered a large mansion in the old style, the home of rich and "real" masters, a home distinguished not so much by its construction or culture as by its capacity. Where most manor houses might have only one or two rooms for living, in the nineteenth century Priamukhino contained a dozen, not counting the servants' quarters.[2]

Even so, before the late 1780s we have no record at all of life inside Priamukhino's manor house and no windows onto the past between its four long walls. Using deeds and genealogical tables, it is possible to discover that Priamukhino belonged to the Shishkovs, a noble family whose men had served as local military commanders since the late sixteenth century. In 1779, the estate was purchased by Liubov Petrovna Bakunina (who would later be better known to history as Mikhail Bakunin's grandmother). Yet for a decade after 1779, as before, the interior of the manor house remains unilluminated by any records whatsoever.

The same thing can be said about the family life of Priamukhino's new masters, the Bakunins. Until the late seventeenth century, the Bakunin name was associated with a line of provincial military servitors and serf-holders in and around the central Russian province of Iaroslavl. In the eighteenth century, a branch of this family moved to St. Petersburg and became active members of its "well-born society"; they served in high places and owned one of the most distinguished houses in St. Petersburg—complete with a domestic theater. Even so, despite the Bakunins' power, privilege, and education, the private life and intimate reflections of this or any other branch of the Bakunin family remain undocumented until Liubov Petrovna's purchase of Priamukhino. The family's history has to be hunted in official records, service books, cemetery headstones, and the occasional outside memoirist, sources that tell us something about the Bakunins' status in society and service to the

---

[2] For a description of early-eighteenth-century estates in general, see Priscilla Roosevelt, *Life on the Russian Country Estate: A Social and Cultural History* (New Haven: Yale University Press, 1995), 2–74, 167–73; and Carsten Goehrke, *Russischer Alltag: Eine Geschichte in neun Zeitbildern*, vol. 2, *Auf dem Weg in die Moderne* (Zürich: Chronos, 2003), 113–17. On Priamukhino's construction, see V. I. Sysoev, *Bakuniny* (Tver: Sozvezdie, 2002), 62–65.

Liubov Petrovna Bakunina (1739–1814). From Vladimir Sysoev, *Bakuniny* (Tver: Sozvezdie, 2002). Courtesy: Tverskoi Gosudarstvennyi Ob"edinnënyi Muzei

state but only grudgingly give up other kinds of information.[3] In this, the Bakunins—despite their reputation—differ little from most of their fellow nobles before the Petrine era. "Virtually nothing can be derived about the emotional lives of the mass of provincial servitors," concludes one exhaustive history of the lives of the Muscovite gentry in the seventeenth century.[4]

It is only when the Bakunins and their new home come together in the late eighteenth century that documents begin to bring the intimate history of both into focus. Fragments from the family's correspondence in the 1790s are preserved (tellingly enough, these describe the family's struggle to hang on to their new home, having plunged, suddenly and deeply, into debt). A faded plan for a domestic celebration—a *Prologue for the New Year 1790*, written by one of the Bakunin daughters—gives us our first sustained look at her family's ambitions for life at Priamukhino; a collection of notebooks left behind by one of her brothers, who was hastily summoned home from the diplomatic corps, details his gradual conversion into a family man. Thereafter, what we can know about life at Priamukhino grows exponentially, in a wave of domestic documents that ends only with the revolution in 1917. The house abounds in letters, diaries, projects, notebooks—illuminating, from multiple angles, the family's ambitions and experiences in their new home. Historians of Russia's old regime—even more so than is true of early modern Europe in general—often have to rely on state archives for everything, even for our glimpses of everyday life.[5] At Priamukhino, by contrast, even the mundane was recorded. If—as happened once in the 1820s—a certain "Lisatovich was very funny," someone wrote it down.[6]

---

[3] There are three main repositories of Bakunin family papers in Russian archives today. All three contain little or no material before the end of the eighteenth century and large amounts from the century that followed. The so-called Priamukhino archive of the Bakunin family is held in the Manuscript Division of the Russian Academy of Sciences Institute of Russian Literature (Pushkin House), henceforth abbreviated IRLI, *fond* 16. I explore its history in detail in my essay, "On the Biography of the Bakunin Family Archive," in *Archive Stories: Facts, Fictions, and the Writing of History*, ed. Antoinette Burton (Durham, N.C.: Duke University Press, 2005), 209–31. *Fond* 825 of the State Archive of the Russian Federation (henceforth GARF) contains materials by both the Priamukhino Bakunins and their St. Petersburg and Moscow relatives, as well as a fair number of administrative records from their various estates. Last but still important is the collection of papers held in the State Archive of Tver *Oblast'* (henceforth GATO), *fond* 1407.

[4] Valerie A. Kivelson, *Autocracy in the Provinces: The Muscovite Gentry and Political Culture in the Seventeenth Century* (Stanford: Stanford University Press, 1996), 84.

[5] For recent reflections on this theme, see David Ransel, "The Diary of a Merchant: Insights Into Eighteenth-Century Plebeian Life," *Russian Review* 63, no. 4 (October 2004): 594–95.

[6] See V. A. Bakunina's *Memory Book* (*Pamiatnye zapiski*), IRLI f. 16, op. 6, no. 9, ll. 1–2 (July 1822).

Over time, this innovative domestic existence won the Bakunins considerable distinction. Yet what first drew them to Priamukhino? Perhaps more important, what explains the expressive and self-conscious character the Bakunins' home life suddenly acquired, when transported to an unexceptional estate hundreds of miles from the capital? Quite often, historians portray elite interest in estate life in eighteenth century Russia as a by-product of the Russian nobility's emancipation from state service.[7] Granted their "liberty" by an imperial manifesto published in 1762—the argument goes—rich nobles began to pursue their personal passions in the countryside, away from the hierarchies of court.[8] On occasion, scholars have even interpreted noble domesticity in the late eighteenth century as a demonstrative withdrawal from imperial life—a "protest from the right" meant to express the elite's estrangement from the empire's increasingly officious public world. Judged from this point of view, homes such as Priamukhino may appear to be fledgling "theaters of alienation"—the first institutions of an embryonic public opinion that was beginning to oppose imperial authority.[9]

There is, however, little in the Bakunin family's history that suggests such motives. Like many of their noble colleagues, the Bakunin men continued to serve long after 1762. It seems more likely that Liubov Petrovna's anticipated inheritance—rather than her husband's liberty—brought the Bakunins to Tver Province. Once there, however, the Bakunins soon found themselves at the epicenter of an experiment in Russian politics, then being conducted by

[7] I review some of the vast literature on Russian estates in my article "The Old Mansion: Revisiting the History of the Russian Country Estate," *Kritika* 1, no. 4 (2000): 729–49. For the broadest recent history, see Roosevelt, *Russian Country Estate.* On the attempts by some nobles to use their administrative skills to make estates more productive, see Michael Confino, *Domaines et seigneurs en Russie vers la fin du XVIII siècle: Étude de structures agraires et mentalités économiques* (Paris: Institut d'études slaves de l'Université de Paris, 1963); and also Edgar Melton, "Enlightened Seigniorialism and Its Dilemmas in Serf Russia, 1750–1830," *Journal of Modern History* 62 (December 1990): 675–708.

[8] On Peter III's manifesto, the controversial circumstances of its promulgation, and the equally live controversies surrounding its short- and long-term cultural impacts, see I. V. Faizova, *"Manifest o vol'nosti" i sluzhba dvorianstva v XVIII stoletii* (Moscow: Nauka, 1999), 3–18; Thomas Newlin, *The Voice in the Garden: Andrei Bolotov and the Anxieties of Russian Pastoral, 1738–1833* (Evanston: Northwestern University Press, 2001), 64–67; and Robert E. Jones, *The Emancipation of the Russian Nobility* (Princeton: Princeton University Press, 1973), 29–38, 275–87.

[9] I take the term "theater of alienation" from Roosevelt, *Russian Country Estate,* 153, 291–316, though she supports a broader view of the politics of private life in the late eighteenth century, as I discuss below. For an interpretation that sees estate ideals as a concerted "protest from the right," see G. A. Gukovskii, *Ocherki po istorii russkoi literatury XVIII veka. Dvorianskaia fronda 1750x–1760x godov* (Moscow-Leningrad: Izdatel'stvo Akademii nauk, 1936), 94–99. For a fuller discussion of the controversies surrounding Russian estate life, see Randolph, "The Old Mansion."

the imperial government. Seeking to use noble society to invigorate and discipline rural Russia, Catherine the Great and her advisers encouraged noble families to see their provincial private lives as an extension of the world of power and culture they had earlier known in the capitals. By engaging in exemplary self-conduct outside of formal service, the government suggested, Russia's noble families could advance the cause of imperial civilization in the provinces and win continued prominence for themselves. We can observe this new domestic theater of distinction in operation at Priamukhino by examining the script Liubov Petrovna's youngest daughter prepared for her family's New Year's celebration in 1790.

Before looking in on this celebration, however, it may be useful to recall in more detail how the Bakunins first came to their new home and the new politics of private life that they found there.

۞ﻌ۞

The Bakunin family name first appears in official records of the sixteenth century, when one Ivan Ivanovich Bakunin had both hereditary and service-grant lands near the central Russian town of Iaroslavl.[10] Many Russian elites—like their peers throughout Europe—claimed descent from foreign blood, and the Bakunins were no exception.[11] Family legend had it that the Bakunin name was brought from Transylvania by Zenislav Bakunin, who came with his two brothers to the court of Ivan the Great in 1492. He was, we are told, a member of the royal house of Bathory.[12] Whether or not that is true, the men who bore the Bakunin name in the sixteenth and seventeenth centuries were rank-and-file members of the Muscovite provincial gentry—militiamen and serf-lords in and around Iaroslavl. The first female descendants about whom anything is known held land and were alive in the

---

[10] The following description is based on the comprehensive genealogy of the Bakunin family compiled by I. S. Sidorov and given in Sysoev, *Bakuniny*, 420–33; as well as V. V. Rummel' and V. V. Golubtsov, *Rodoslovnyi sbornik russkikh dvorianskikh Familii*, vol. 1 (St. Petersburg: A. S. Suvorin, 1886), 100–105; A. Kornilov, *Molodye gody Mikhaila Bakunina: Iz istorii russkogo romantizma* (Moscow: M. and S. Sabashnikov, 1915), 1–6.

[11] On the cult of foreign origins in comparative context, see Richard Wortman, *Scenarios of Power: Myth and Ceremony in Russian Monarchy*, vol. 1, *From Peter the Great to Nicholas I* (Princeton: Princeton University Press, 1995), 13–41. See also Patrick J. Geary, *The Myth of Nations: The Medieval Origins of Europe* (Princeton: Princeton University Press, 2002).

[12] This version of events was accepted as accurate by the Tver nobility, as part of Aleksandr Mikhailovich's application to prove his family's noble status. See the results of the official inquiry, IRLI f. 16, op. 6, no. 13, ll. 2–4.

1620s. In good patriarchal fashion the two sisters are listed as *Mikhailovny* —that is, "Mikhail's daughters"—but their first names are not recorded.[13]

In the late seventeenth century, men and women bearing the Bakunin name step a little further into the light afforded by institutional archives, as they assume more important posts in Muscovite society. Nikifor Bogdanovich Bakunin served in Moscow's Chancellery of Crown Service and Appointments (*Razriadnyi prikaz*) and had a house there in the mid-seventeenth century. His daughter, Aksentia, was a nun at Moscow's famous Novodevichii Convent; she died sometime after 1680. Under Peter I (r. 1689–1725), Mikhail Ivanovich Bakunin—the direct, patrilineal ancestor of Priamukhino's Bakunins—became garrison commander in the frontier towns of Tsaritsyn and Astrakhan, hundreds of miles to the south and east of Moscow on the lower reaches of the Volga.

In the first two decades of the eighteenth century, Peter I moved to reform and resurrect his realm, mobilizing Muscovy's empire in pursuit of European power and culture. He built a new capital and administrative apparatus in St. Petersburg and compelled Russia's elite to join a new class of servitors, "wellborn" men and women who would not only serve Peter's new vision of Russian civilization but also illustrate it in their society, comportment, and dress.[14] The Bakunins soon staked their claim to be part of this new noble estate. A portrait survives of Mikhail Ivanovich's son Vasilii, in "German costume" and a wig—not that he spent much time in St. Petersburg. Perhaps employing knowledge gained at his father's side in the south, Vasilii Mikhailovich served as local expert and translator on military raids and diplomatic missions to Persia, the Caucasus, and the steppe, helping the new Russian empire expand ever farther. Along the way, he became the Bakunin family's first known author, writing official ethnographic descriptions of Kalmyk and Kabardinian peoples.[15]

---

[13] See I. S. Sidorov's genealogy the Bakunin family in Sysoev, *Bakuniny,* 421.

[14] On the social history of this process, see B. N. Mironov, *Sotsial'naia istoriia Rossii perioda imperii (XVIII–nachalo XX v.): Genezis lichnosti, demokraticheskoi sem'i, grazhdanskogo obshchestva, i pravovogo gosudarstva,* vol. 1 (St. Petersburg: Dmitrii Bulanin, 1999), 82–98; on its cultural implications and the nature of the new nobility's esprit de corps, see Marc Raeff, "La noblesse et le discours politique sous le règne de Pierre le Grand," in *Politique et culture en Russie: 18e–20e siècles* (Paris: École des hautes études en sciences sociales, 1996), 121–37; Raeff, *Origins of the Russian Intelligentsia: The Eighteenth-Century Nobility* (New York: Harcourt Brace Jovanovich, 1966), 53–59; Iurii M. Lotman, "The Poetics of Everyday Behavior in 18th Century Russian Culture," in *The Semiotics of Russian Cultural History,* ed. and trans. Alexander Nakhimovsky and Alice Stone Nakhimovsky (Ithaca: Cornell University Press, 1985), 67–77; Wortman, *Scenarios of Power,* 1:53–54. I will comment on this literature below.

[15] Kornilov, *Molodye gody,* 1–2; Vasilii Bakunin, "Opisanie kabardinskogo naroda," in *Kabar-*

Thereafter this branch of the Bakunin family line entered the uppermost circles of imperial officialdom, where it remained until the early nineteenth century. Two of Vasilii Mikhailovich's three sons—both named Petr—were among the leaders of the College of Foreign Affairs, deeply involved in imperial expansion and diplomacy as well as in the life of the court. The younger Petr Vasilievich, in particular, won fame as a master of official correspondence. His pen proved indispensable to a series of powerful patrons, beginning with Count Nikita Panin (the head of the College of Foreign Affairs) and continuing with Panin's rival and successor, Prince Aleksandr Bezborodko. Nor did Petr Vasilievich stand on the sidelines of the new, imperial culture. His house, on the palace side of the Neva River in St. Petersburg, hosted a domestic theater of some fame, and in 1786 he was elected a member of the Russian Academy of Sciences.[16]

By the mid-eighteenth century, the Bakunins had left their provincial roots and aligned themselves with the new imperial society coming into being in St. Petersburg.[17] There the family helped to create a new world of power, culture, and prestige, growing along with the empire. Even so, the brightest mementos of this new life still come from hands other than the Bakunins' own. The *St. Petersburg Bulletin* announces the Bakunins' regular progression up the official Table of Ranks; memoirists gossip about the men's participation in courtly intrigues; and there are portraits of the two Petr Vasilieviches in their ribbons and medals, painted by Dmitrii Levitsky (a famous artist and family friend).[18] But not even Petr Vasilievich the Younger —famous for his pen—seems to have recorded his own perspective on events for posterity. In context, this is not surprising. The practice of personal, as

dino-russkie otnosheniia v XVI–XVII Vv., comp. V. M. Bukalova, vol. 2 (Moscow: Izdatel'stvo Akademii nauk SSSR, 1957), 152–61; Sysoev, *Bakuniny*, 10.

[16] On the younger Petr Vasilievich, see *Russkii biograficheskii slovar'*, vol. 2 (St. Petersburg: Tipografiia Glavnoyo Upravleniia Udelov, 1900), 437–38; on his domestic theater, see K. Iu. Lappo-Danilevskii, "O literaturnom nasledii N. A. L'vova," in L'vov, *Izbrannye sochineniia*, ed. and comp. K. Iu. Lappo-Danilevskii (St. Petersburg: Acropol, 1994), 10; on the role of domestic theater in St. Petersburg life at the time, see Elise Kimerling Wirtschafter, *The Play of Ideas in Russian Enlightenment Theater* (DeKalb: Northern Illinois University Press, 2003), 20–21.

[17] There is, in their history, no more mention of lands in Iaroslavl.

[18] For Petr Vasilievich's career and involvement in the courtly politics surrounding his protector Nikita Panin, see E. N. Marasinova, *Psikhologiia elity rossiiskogo dvorianstva poslednei treti XVIII veka* (Moscow: Rosspen, 1999), 16; and David Ransel, *The Politics of Catherinean Russia: The Panin Party* (New Haven: Yale University Press, 1975), 254. The recently published indexes to *The Saint Petersburg Bulletin* (*Gazeta "Sanktpeterburgskie vedomosti": Ukazateli k soderzhaniiu*, ed. E. V. Anisimov [St. Petersburg: Biblioteka Rossiiskoi Akademii Nauk, 1992]), ongoing, show regular notices of the Bakunin men's advancement from the 1730s to the 1770s. Sysoev discusses their portraits in *Bakuniny*, 11–12.

opposed to official, correspondence, and of diaries as opposed to account books, was just beginning to blossom in Russia.[19] Like other prominent servitors of their time, the Petr Vasilieviches lived very active official lives, without engaging in experiments in written self-reflection; what there might have been was not socially relevant or durably preserved enough to come down to us.[20] About the rest of the family during this time — their sisters and wives — still less is known.

At first glance, their youngest brother, Mikhail Vasilievich (1730–1803), would seem even less likely to have had a memorable domestic existence. An anonymous portrait in wig survives. But Mikhail Vasilievich's descendants remembered him as a bullish *barin* — a giant man of "unbridled manner" — rather than a courtier. One family legend tells of how Mikhail Vasilievich seized a cheeky coachman and threw him into a river, taking the reins himself. Another anecdote has him beating off a pack of bandits with a post.[21] Like his brothers, but in less distinguished capacities, Mikhail Vasilievich served at court in St. Petersburg from 1754 to 1779. He achieved the fourth of the empire's fourteen civil-service ranks, that of Active State Councilor, laboring in the Revenue College. But then he retired and moved with his household to Priamukhino, nearly three hundred miles from the capital, in central Russia's Tver Province.

Just why he chose to do so is unclear. Certainly, after twenty-five years of service, Mikhail Vasilievich had both the right and the expectation of retirement.[22] And the estate was a traditional and logical place for a serviceman to

[19] Recent studies of intimate correspondence and memoiristic writing — all of which identify the late eighteenth century as a period when these genres were finally taking off in Russia — include Marasinova, *Psikhologiia elity*, esp. 46–47; A. G. Tartakovskii, *Russkaia memuaristika XVIII–pervoi poloviny XIX v.: Ot rukopisi do knigi* (Moscow: Nauka, 1991); Newlin, *Voice in the Garden*, esp. 21–24, 151–56; and Lina Bernstein, "The First Published Russian Letter-Writing Manual: *Priklady, Kako Pishutsia Komplimenty Raznye,*" *Slavic and East European Journal* 46, no. 1 (Spring 2002): 98–123.

[20] In this, courtly life in mid-eighteenth-century Russia echoed the relentlessly public character of courtly life in late-seventeenth-century France, on which it was modeled. See Nicole Castan, "The Public and the Private," in *Passions of the Renaissance*, ed. Roger Chartier, vol. 3 of *A History of Private Life*, ed. Phillipe Ariès and Georges Duby, trans. Arthur Goldhammer (Cambridge, Mass.: Belknap Press, 1989), 419–22; and Wortman, *Scenarios of Power*, 1:81–169.

[21] Kornilov, who heard them from the family in the early twentieth century, records these legends in Kornilov, *Molodye gody*, 3.

[22] Nobles since the 1730s had been allowed to retire after twenty-five years of service. See A. Romanovich-Slavatinskii, *Dvorianstvo v Rossii ot nachala XVIII veka do otmeny krepostnogo prava* (St. Petersburg: Tipografiia Ministerstva vnutrennikh del, 1870), 125–27; Mikhail Vasilievich's conformance with this older norm provides additional evidence that the Manifesto of 1762 affected the pattern of noble life only slowly and indirectly.

retire. But the Bakunin clan itself had no significant properties in Tver—indeed, the only property there that was ever held in Mikhail Vasilievich's name was a small wooden house in the district capital, Torzhok. The Bakunins' provincial properties—to the extent that they had any—were now not in Iaroslavl but near St. Petersburg itself.[23]

The simplest explanation for Mikhail Vasilievich's move has less to do with his own family's history than with his wife's. Liubov Petrovna (1739–1814) belonged to a princely family, the Myshetskys. Descended from the princes of Chernigov, the Myshetsky lineage was one of Russia's oldest, related to some of the empire's most renowned families, such as the Obolenskys, the Odoevskys, and the Riumins. That said, the Myshetskys were not prominent in the Muscovite court (never entering the boyar elite); and in the late seventeenth century an impoverished branch of the family formed the leadership of the so-called Vyg community, a group of Old Believers who denounced the Petrine state as the work of the Antichrist and withdrew to the far north to form their own countersociety.[24] The other Myshetskys about whom anything is known were all mid-level servitors of the Bakunins' rank or lower. Their daughters married into newly prominent noble families (such as the Diakovs). This suggests that the Myshetskys, like other Russian princely lines, held on to their titles but otherwise folded into the more general mass of the new Russian nobility.[25]

Unlike the Bakunins, however, the Myshetskys lived in and around

[23] See Sysoev, *Bakuniny,* 21–22.

[24] Andrei and Semen "Vtorushin" or "Denisov" were descended from the Myshetskys and aware of it: see Robert O. Crummey, *The Old Believers and the World of Antichrist: The Vyg Community and the Russian State, 1694–1855* (Madison: University of Wisconsin Press, 1970), 61–62, 71–100.

[25] On the Myshetskys, see *Kniazia,* vol. 1 of *Dvorianskie rody Rossiiskoi imperii* (St. Petersburg: IPK Vesti, 1993), 163–67; and for the Torzhok line, see M. Cherniavskii, *Genealogiia gospod dvorian, vnesennykh v rodoslovnuiu knigu Tverskoi gubernii, 1787–1869* (Tver: S.n., 1869), no. 786. Though the Myshetskys were not particularly prominent, their relationship to more famous princely lines was well known in the eighteenth century; see, e.g., *Rodoslovnaia kniga kniazei i dvorian rossiiskikh i vyezzhikh,* vol. 2 (Moscow: Universitetskaia tipografiia u N. Novikova, 1787), 292. Liubov' Petrovna's sister Avdot'ia Petrovna was married to Senator Aleksei Afanas'evich D'iakov. Still, this princely line makes no appearance in the lists of "duma men" who made up the Muscovite elite in the seventeenth century. See Marshall T. Poe, *The Consular and Ceremonial Ranks of the Russian "Sovereign's Court," 1613–1713,* vol. 1 of *The Russian Elite in the Seventeenth Century,* Annales Academiae Scientiarum Fennicae 322 (Vammala: Vammalan Kirjapaino Oy, 2004). The same, by the way, can be said of the Bakunins. Myshetskys do appear as fairly significant landowners in Moscow, Kaluga, and Novgorod regions in late-seventeenth-century-land registers—see O. A. Shvatchenko, *Svetskie feodal'nye votchiny Rossii v epokhu Petra I* (Moscow: RAN Institut istorii, 2002), 161—and occasionally in *mestnichestvo* (precedence) suits. See Iu. M. Eskin, *Mestnichestvo v Rossii, XVI–XVII vv: Khronologicheskii reestr* (Moscow: Arkheograficheskii tsentr, 1994), nos. 1445, 1464, 1482, 1596, 1645.

Torzhok from at least the seventeenth century. Several Myshetsky men were buried there.[26] More to the point, Liubov Petrovna was in line to inherit extensive holdings of land and serfs throughout Tver Province, including more than five hundred peasant "souls."[27] In eighteenth-century Russia, married noblewomen possessed broad property rights. They often managed their own properties and led economic lives that were independent of their husbands' fortunes.[28] The decision to move to Tver was undoubtedly influenced by Liubov Petrovna's future as the mistress of a large local inheritance.

Why Priamukhino in particular? Here again, Liubov Petrovna's family ties provide the most likely explanation. Priamukhino was purchased in Liubov Petrovna's name—along with some other, lesser properties—from the Myshetskys' relatives, the Shishkovs. It was the largest and most unified of these properties. Unlike many eighteenth-century estates, Priamukhino was not subject to "tenancy in common" (*obshchee vladenie*), whereby the land and its serfs were held jointly by several owners. According to the General Survey ordered by Catherine the Great in 1765, the only gaps in Liubov Petrovna's new dominion were the lands on which a small stone church stood and the plots of its priests. In addition, the general survey counted some 650 acres of plowland—alongside about half that much in pasture and over 4,000 acres of forest—as part of the estate. The soil was silty, the surveyor noted, but the harvests matched northern Russia's rather skinny average; and the Shishkovs and their serfs had made improvements. They dammed the Osuga River to power a flour mill, and they started a textile shop. There was a stable with carriage house and a cherry orchard.[29]

---

[26] See Grand Prince Nikolai Mikhailovich [Romanov], *Russkii provintsial'nyi nekropol'* (Moscow: Tipo-litografiia Tovarishchestva N. N. Kushnerov i Ko., 1914), 585. According to Cherniavskii, the earliest-known member of this branch was killed in the siege of Smolensk in 1634 (see Cherniavskii, *Genealogiia*, no. 786).

[27] For information on Liubov Petrovna's inheritance, see the settlement of her will, in GARF f. 825, op. 1, no. 4, ll. 1–10, which describes the acquisition of her various properties. A "soul" was an adult male peasant, as counted by periodic tax censuses. With Priamukhino and associated properties, the Bakunins would have 837 souls at the beginning of the nineteenth century: see Sysoev, *Bakuniny*, 71–72.

[28] On women's economic lives and active management of their inheritances, see Michelle Lamarche Marrese, *A Woman's Kingdom: Noblewomen and the Control of Property in Russia, 1700–1861* (Ithaca: Cornell University Press, 2002). Of course, the grim irony of having to arrange one's own life in anticipation of a relative's death was a great theme of Russian noble literature. In the famous opening scene of Pushkin's *Evgenii Onegin*, the hero attends upon a sick uncle, all the while hoping the devil will take him.

[29] This description was produced from the materials of the General Survey, which passed through Priamukhino in August of 1779: see RGADA f. 1355, d. 1472, microfilm roll number 4, l. 146 ob. for Officer Petelin's field notes on Priamukhino, and RGADA f. 1354, op. 502, d.

In sum, we may conjecture, Priamukhino represented a convenient base from which to begin an independent life as serf-lords in the countryside—for Mikhail Vasilievich to assume the role of *barin* that suited him so well and for Liubov Petrovna to begin living the life her inheritance destined for her. Perhaps this was the ambition the elder Bakunins brought to their new home. There is no evidence of any grander design on their part. Yet Catherine the Great and her advisers were drawing up their own, much more ambitious plans for rural Russia. The province to which the Bakunins retired in 1779 stood at the center of a new experiment in imperial life—the creation of a provincial civil society rooted in the serf-holding nobility. Regardless of the ambitions the elder Bakunins brought to Priamukhino, estate life in Tver Province was being reframed.

⊛⅍⅊⊛

Owing to its position on the roads and waterways that connected St. Petersburg to the rest of the empire, the ancient Russian principality of Tver took on new life in the eighteenth century, becoming a bustling center of transportation and trade. Some 2,500 boats passed through canals and locks at Vyshnii Volochek (a few dozen miles north of Priamukhino) each year, most of them barges hauled up the Volga for transfer to north-running rivers and thence to the capital. In addition, new construction was changing the face of Tver. When the town itself burned to the ground in the early 1760s, Catherine the Great took a close interest in its resurrection, supporting the efforts of successive governors to remake it as a model provincial city. Hundreds of new stone houses replaced Tver's historic center, which was repaved with widened streets and new bridges across the Volga. Greatly pleased, Catherine declared that "after St. Petersburg, Tver is the most beautiful city of the Empire." Similar reforms were ordered for smaller towns in the province— including Ostashkov and Torzhok, near Priamukhino.[30]

P211 (red check), l. 2331 for the map of Priamukhino the surveyors produced; see also Sysoev, *Bakuniny*, 62–65, where some of these materials are reproduced and more details added. Part of the surveyor's job was to ascertain whether estates were fragmented or held in *obshchee vladenie* (see, for example, excerpts from the survey of another of L. P. Bakunina's properties, Davydovo, which was held in common by several individuals: GATO f. 103, op. 1, d. 1401). On the complex claims that bedeviled the survey, and the problems of *obshchee vladenie*, see Robert D. Givens, "To Measure and to Encroach: The Nobility and the Land Survey," in *Russia and the World of the Eighteenth Century*, ed. R. P. Bartlett, A. G. Cross, and Karen Rasmussen (Columbus, Ohio: Slavica, 1988), 537–38.

[30] An incisive study of Tver's development in the late eighteenth century is Jones, *Provincial*

As Robert E. Jones has shown, Catherine the Great and her advisers lavished so much attention on Tver Province because they wanted to use it as a laboratory for imperial politics. Specifically, the government wanted to work out mechanisms whereby the state could enlighten the provinces—that is, mobilize them in pursuit of power, productivity, and increased prosperity. To that end, Catherine's experiments in Tver were not merely royal whims but calculated efforts to create a prosperous, vibrant, and patriotic civic realm. In the 1770s and 1780s, she and her close adviser Jakob Sievers imagined the Tver region as a testing ground for acts of civic legislation, such as the Statute on Provincial Administration of 1775 and the charters granted to Russia's nobility and townspeople in 1785.[31]

These efforts attempted to alter the relationship between government and society in the provinces. First, rural Russia was subdivided into smaller administrative units. Tver itself was carved out of an older and unwieldy territory the size of France and reorganized into a government split into districts with twenty thousand to thirty thousand male inhabitants each. Then the province was granted a new set of institutions: a remade provincial executive, new judiciary, reorganized police, and "bureaus of social welfare," charged with planning and constructing local schools, hospitals, and poorhouses. Members of local society—elected by social strata—were granted the right to participate in both the judiciary and the bureaus. This anticipated the more elaborate set of specific rights and privileges granted to townspeople and nobles alike in their charters of 1785. Not only did these institutions provide the basic administrative and legal infrastructure of Russian provincial life until the Great Reforms of the 1860s, but they also served to distinguish society from the state in the provinces.[32]

Development, 2, 57–81, 113–19, 120–57. The description just given is largely based on this work; Catherine the Great's approval of Tver is quoted on page 132. The plan for Tver's reconstruction, drafted by Catherine the Great's trusted adviser Ivan Betskoi, is reprinted in P. M. Maikov, *Ivan Ivanovich Betskoi: Opyt ego biografii* (St. Petersburg, 1904) as appendix 2. See also Isabel de Madariaga, *Russia in the Age of Catherine the Great* (London: Phoenix Press, 1990), 532–33; as well as G. K. Smirnov, exec. ed., *Svod pamiatnikov arkhitektury i monumental'nogo iskusstva Rossii. Tverskaia oblast'*, vol. 1 (Moscow: Nauka, 2002), 68–71. On Catherine's interest in architecture as a means of transforming the cultural landscape of her empire, see Dimitri Shvidkovsky, "Catherine the Great's Field of Dreams: Architecture and Landscape in the Russian Enlightenment," in *Architectures of Russian Identity 1500 to the Present*, ed. James Cracraft and Daniel Rowland (Ithaca: Cornell University Press, 2003), 51–66.

[31] See Jones, *Provincial Development*, 1–2, as well as throughout; see also Jones, *Emancipation*, 202–20.

[32] On the outlines of these reforms, see de Madariaga, *Russia*, 277–91, 296–305; Jones, *Emancipation*, 210–99. Much of the debate surrounding them since has focused on the extent to which

What did the transformation of Tver Province mean for noble families like the Bakunins, who moved to the very epicenter of the government's efforts? Most famously, the government's reforms granted the Russian nobility certain specific political privileges. These included the right to buy and sell villages and develop them as they saw fit; the right to keep genealogical records, testifying to each noble family's "well-born" pedigree; and the right to personal and domestic inviolability. Nobles were neither to be punished corporally nor to have troops quartered in their manor houses. Last, the 1785 charter confirmed the nobility's emancipation from the service obligations imposed by Peter the Great. The effect of all these privileges was to represent the nobility as the empire's first citizens — autonomous individuals who together represented Russian "society" — rather than simply its first servants. As Jones observes, the collective effect of noble liberty and the half century of provincial reform that followed was that the state began to look "upon the Russian nobleman as an estate owner who was expected to spend several years in service rather than as a servitor supported in part through ownership of an estate."[33] Not counterbalanced by similar charters defining the status and rights of serfs, Catherine's reforms furthered the nobility's ascendancy over the latter. As their masters assumed the roles of free citizens living private lives in the countryside, their dependents became more like slaves.

Why did Catherine's government grant these privileges? At various points, historians have hypothesized that noble pressure — a Russian "Fronde" — forced Catherine and her advisers to cede to the nobility's desires for more autonomy and liberty in the countryside.[34] As Catherine and her adviser

---

these new civic institutions were, in effect, stillborn, unable to survive traditions of personal and police rule. Among early works, see N. D. Chechulin, *Russkoe provintsial'noe obshchestvo vo vtoroi polovine XVIII veka.* (St. Petersburg: Tipografiia V. S. Balashev, 1889); S. A. Korf, *Dvorianstvo i ego soslovnoe upravlenie za stoletie 1762–1855 godov* (St. Petersburg: Tipografiia Trenke i Fiusno, 1906); and Vladimir Grigor'ev, *Reforma Mestnogo Upravleniia Pri Ekaterine II* (St. Petersburg: Russkaia skoropechatnia, 1910). Breaking with this paradigm, John Le Donne argues, in his *Absolutism and Ruling Class: The Formation of the Russian Political Order, 1700–1825* (New York: Oxford University Press, 1991), that the explicit aim and practical effect of government institution building across the eighteenth century was the "privatization of public power" in the hand of Russia's noble "ruling class," making it pointless to speak of a gap between state and society in eighteenth-century Russia (ix; 19–21). My point here, however, is not about power but about institutions and symbols. On the role of absolutist reform in distinguishing state and society in symbolic and institutional terms, a theory famously advanced by Jürgen Habermas and accepted into broader European historiography since, see James Van Horn Melton, *The Rise of the Public in Enlightenment Europe* (Cambridge: Cambridge University Press, 2001), 5.

[33] Jones, *Emancipation*, 283. De Madariaga contends this led to a similar change in some nobles' sense of themselves: see *Russia*, 89.

[34] See the literature cited in note 8, above; see also S. M. Troitskii, *Russkii absoliutizm i dvo-*

Sievers worked on their reforms of Tver, however, a much finer—and more modern—political calculus seems to have inspired them. Catherine the Great was initially suspicious about noble life in the provinces, regarding it as little more than an excuse for sloth. Through Sievers's nudging, however, the empress came to see how a civil society composed of ex-servitors could become an "instrument of order and progress" in the provinces.[35] Russia's monarchs had long struggled with the problem of how to get the most out of rural society. It was hard to build political mechanisms and metaphors expansive enough to mobilize their huge empire's provincial resources efficiently.[36]

Sievers planned to solve this problem by shifting governmental functions onto an enlightened citizenry, whose internal self-discipline would lead them to willingly align themselves with the Empire's interests, even when the government was not watching. Indeed, the manifesto granting liberty to the nobility in 1762 presented the patriotism, enlightenment, and self-awareness as the primary justification behind its emancipation. The nobility had matured: if, during Peter's reign, it had been necessary to teach nobles "how great are the advantages of enlightened states in human happiness over the countless peoples, still immersed in the depths of ignorance," by 1762 "noble thoughts have rooted an endless loyalty and love for Us in the hearts of all true patriots of Russia, as well as great zeal and remarkable diligence in Our service, and for that reason we no longer experience that need to compel service, which heretofore has been necessary."[37] The new provincial reforms called for the nobility to display this maturity and self-discipline. In 1775, the Statute on Provincial Administration provided for the nobility's election of local officials and judges; the Charter to the Nobility in 1785 both allowed and ordered the creation of local Noble Assemblies, to whom much responsibility for local civic development was given. In this way, the imperial government attempted to push its authority and ideas deeper into the provinces, using the private energies of its new noble citizens as a wedge. "We trust that every sensible person and every zealous son of the fatherland will diligently

rianstvo v XVIII v. Formirovanie biurokratii (Moscow: Nauka, 1974), 140–43; and John Le Donne, *Absolutism and Ruling Class: The Formation of the Russian Political Order, 1700–1825* (New York: Oxford University Press, 1991), 52–53.

[35] Jones, *Provincial Development*, 114.

[36] On Muscovy's successful but simple means of mobilizing the nation's resources, see Nancy Shields Kollmann, *By Honor Bound: State and Society in Early Modern Russia* (Ithaca: Cornell University Press, 1999).

[37] See the Manifesto "O darovanii vol'nosti i svobody vsemu Rossiiskomu dvorianstvu," 18 February 1762, *PSZ*, no. 11444, 912.

seek to conform to Our good intention," the Statute on Provincial Administration declares.[38]

Not all of this patriotic mobilization was aimed at men. In the early 1760s, Catherine the Great established the famous Smolnyi Institute for well-born girls. Modeled loosely on St. Cyr—Archbishop Fénelon's famous school for French noblewomen—Smolnyi Institute had as its goal the making of enlightened daughters, wives, and mothers of the sort who could inspire their families and raise the general morale of the provinces. In a letter to Voltaire, Empress Catherine indeed contrasted Smolnyi's social purpose to the religious vocations cultivated at St. Cyr: "We educate them [the noblewomen] with a view to making them the delight of their future families; we want them to be neither prudes, nor coquettes, but agreeable young ladies, capable of raising their own children and running their own homes."[39] In addition to a broad general program of education that included foreign languages, mathematics, and history, the *smolianki* were taught domestic skills and theatrical graces, doing handiwork and putting on plays. They were recruited young from their families, with the intention of returning them only after they had been molded into feminine agents of civilization. The result was a system that mimicked the early induction of young noblemen into service—as well as their later release into an appropriately fashioned and high-minded liberty.[40]

In sum, the new noble freedom and the provincial institutions that attended it were about more than governmental reform. They were about creating new social norms for the sphere of noble private life. By inventing public rituals such as noble assemblies—and by teaching noble girls to civilize their homes—the government provided new scripts to govern the nobility's use of its liberty. The effect was to try to mobilize noble society by

[38] From the introduction to the "Uchrezhdeniia dlia upravleniia Gubernii Vserossiiskiia Imperii," *PSZ*, no. 14392, 231. See also Jones, *Provincial Development in Russia*, 113–19.

[39] Robin Bisha et al., *Russian Women, 1698–1917: Experience and Expression* (Bloomington: Indiana University Press, 2002), 167–68.

[40] On the history of Smolnyi Institute and its role in Russian culture, see E. Likhacheva, *Materialy dlia istorii zhenskogo obrazovaniia v Rossii (1086–1796)* (St. Petersburg: Tipografiia M. M. Stasiulevicha, 1890), 137–236; and Catriona Kelly, *Refining Russia: Advice Literature, Polite Culture and Gender from Catherine to Yeltsin* (Oxford: Oxford University Press, 2001), 25–28. On its model St. Cyr—which Catherine the Great regarded as too religious and insufficiently civic and social—see Carolyn C. Lougee, "Noblesse, Domesticity, and Social Reform: The Education of Girls by Fénelon and Saint-Cyr," *History of Education Quarterly* 14, no. 1 (Spring 1974): 87–113. On the analogies between noblemen's administrative and military service and the emerging cultural service of noblewomen, see Barbara Alpern Engel, *Women in Russia, 1700–2000* (Cambridge: Cambridge University Press, 2004), 16–19, 38.

allowing it to view its private existence as a theater of distinction: a space where it could signal its loyalty to—and participation in—St. Petersburg's culture of power.

Such an approach built on well-established principles of Russian politics. As Richard Wortman has shown, Russian monarchy long relied on charismatic cultural scripts—"scenarios of power," involving ritual displays of authority and distinction—to enlist the sympathies and energies of the empire's most important subjects. Participation in this courtly culture offered advantages to ruler and ruled alike. It galvanized elite support for the throne while providing a means for the nobility's continued cultural and political elevation above the mass of Russian society and the empire's many subject peoples. If the most public scenarios of Peter's reign drew their power from such traditional values as service, patriarchy, and the divine right of kings, by the mid-eighteenth century, Russian monarchs were exploring more intimate and sentimental registers. Catherine, as Wortman establishes, made elaborate displays of her love and affection for the nobility a central emblem of her rule. The empress also occasionally appeared in public life in private and semiprivate roles, as when she participated (through transparent incognito) in literary disputes or played cards or chess with her courtiers at balls. Catherine made it clear that she expected her nobility to respond to her expressions of "love" with mutual expressions of their own, conducted from the platform of their new, private existence.[41]

Intimacy, of course, was a very old element of elite political culture. The court of Moscow's grand princes was steeped in affection (boyars usually being the princes' literal kin). Peter the Great was notoriously familiar with his most elite servitors, shaving their beards, pulling their teeth, and otherwise violating their notions of propriety in his efforts to draw them into his revolutionary camaraderie. What distinguished the intimate appeals of the Catherinean era, as Wortman observes, was the fact that the theater for the enactment of this scenario was the new civic realm then being built—not the court—and that the play was expected to go on without Catherine's immediate direction or participation. The nobility was encouraged to "go beyond choral participation and to stage their own ceremonies of fealty"—as in the Bakunins' new home province of Tver in 1776, when a Te Deum, a banquet, and a ball cel-

---

[41] On Catherine's ruling style, see Wortman, *Scenarios of Power*, 1:110–35, esp. 131–32. On Muscovite courtly ritual, see also Michael S. Flier, "Breaking the Code: The Image of the Tsar in the Muscovite Palm Sunday Ritual," in *Medieval Russian Culture*, ed. Michael S. Flier and Daniel Rowland, vol. 2 (Berkeley: University of California Press, 1994), 213–42.

ebrated the first elections to the institutions created by the Provincial Statute of 1775. (Catherine applauded the event from afar.)[42]

Much was at stake in this attempt to sculpt a new pattern of social existence for the nobility. Catherine and her advisers desired much more glory (in political, cultural, and economic terms) than the effective but cautious patriarchal political order of old Muscovy—or even Peter's revolutionary but authoritarian methods—could muster. By the mid-eighteenth century, the imperial government wished to project its vision of civilization far out from the two capitals, St. Petersburg and Moscow; and to do so, it needed to enlist its elite subjects' resources and zeal, even when they were outside the range of the court and its charismatic, disciplining scenarios. It should also be said that this appeal to noble civilization and self-discipline rested on a reasonable assessment of who noble families such as the Bakunins really were—or could be—at midcentury. Though constitutionally disinclined to oppose themselves to the monarchy, Russia's elite servitors were nonetheless acquiring new ambitions for themselves, ambitions only partially at home in the hierarchies that governed their lives in the capitals. Among these were desires for independence, self-invention, and societies and intimacies of their own making.[43]

Given all these considerations, it is not hard to see how Catherine, Sievers, and the other architects of elite liberty might have believed that noble pleasure and imperial utility could readily be combined in the provinces. A new noble culture of private life—supported by serfdom and disciplined by patriotism and civic institutions—could mobilize the private resources of Russia's elite. It also built on normative assumptions about the nobility's culture, self-discipline, and loyalty that laced imperial proclamations of the second half of the eighteenth century. At the same time, it did not threaten the

---

[42] Wortman, *Scenarios of Power,* 1:130–31. Here Wortman builds on the work of Jones, *Emancipation,* 247–50. On the elaborate, intimate, and profane rituals Peter the Great created to mobilize and inspire his closest servants, see Ernest A. Zitser, *The Transfigured Kingdom: Sacred Parody and Charismatic Authority at the Court of Peter the Great* (Ithaca: Cornell University Press, 2004). On the intimacy of the Muscovite court, see Nancy Shields Kollmann, *Kinship and Politics: The Making of the Muscovite Political System, 1345–1547* (Stanford: Stanford University Press, 1987). Wirtschafter provides a thoughtful discussion of imperial attempts to inspire civic consciousness is her study *Play of Ideas in Russian Enlightenment Theater,* 3–29.

[43] Here see Marc Raeff, "La noblesse et le discours politique sous le règne de Pierre le Grand," *Cahiers Du Monde Russe et Soviétique* 34, no. 1–2 (1993): 38–41; Kollmann, *By Honor Bound,* 213–15; Marasinova, *Psikhologiia elity,* 158–203, 238–39; Newlin, *Voice in the Garden,* 17–33; Douglas Smith, "Freemasonry and the Public in Eighteenth-Century Russia," in *Imperial Russia: New Histories for the Empire,* ed. Jane Burbank and David L. Ransel (Bloomington: Indiana University Press, 1998), 281–304; Roosevelt, *Russian Country Estate,* 291–92.

government's administrative apparatus, still supported by the temptations of wealth and power and the presumption that dedicated service remained a necessary part of the properly lived noble life. In this sense, noble liberty was indeed framed as much as a new responsibility as a release from an old burden. "The desire of all honest men in society is, or will be, to see their entire Fatherland raised to the highest degree of prosperity, glory, bliss, and tranquility," Catherine declared in 1767, mixing present and future tenses in an imposing manner.[44]

How successful—indeed, how sincere—were the empress and her advisers in their efforts to create a sphere of civic liberty in Russian life? Historians have generally been skeptical about the provincial public realm created in the second half of the eighteenth century. Squeezed to perform public functions without public power, we are told, nobles failed to embrace the new provincial institutions, seeing them as pointless, corrupt, and ultimately more of a burden than a privilege. This noble apathy, it seems, was only encouraged by the contradictory mix of suasion and compulsion that characterized Russian politics in the second half of the eighteenth century. Though Catherine was tempted at times to think about politics in a philosophical vein, both she and her government relied on heavy-handed police methods for day-to-day rule and administration.[45]

Yet the public sphere was not the alpha and omega of the new noble liberty. It also had a private life component. And here we have much more consistent evidence of real noble initiative and investment. Scores of new neoclassical manor houses were built in Tver Province in the second half of the eighteenth century, as well as an impressive number of mansions in the provincial capital itself.[46] With their stately façades and elaborate parks, gar-

[44] I quote here from Catherine's preface to her 1767 *Grand Instruction,* in many ways her most detailed account of what an ideal future civic realm should look like in Russia. See N. D. Chechulin, ed., *Nakaz Imperatritsy Ekateriny II, dannyi Kommissii o sochinenii proekta novogo ulozheniia* (St. Petersburg: Imperatorskaia Akademiia nauk, 1907), 1. The burdens of being a respected member of society are also a theme of the original manifesto, granting liberty to the nobility of 1762, which speaks of the elimination of "crudity of those who are negligent about the common good" (*PSZ,* no. 11444, 912). On the Russian government's persistent projection of future scenarios as a way of attempting to fashion social norms, see Stephen Lessing Baehr, *The Paradise Myth in Eighteenth Century Russia: Utopian Patterns in Early Secular Russian Literature and Culture* (Stanford: Stanford University Press, 1991), 112–24.

[45] See the works by Chechulin, Korf, and Grigor'ev cited above, as well as Jones, *Provincial Development,* 156. Laura Engelstein provides a colorful rumination on the tension between philosophy and brutality in Catherine's Russia in Laura Engelstein, "Revolution and the Theater of Public Life in Imperial Russia," in *Revolution and the Meanings of Freedom in the Nineteenth Century,* ed. Isser Woloch (Stanford: Stanford University Press, 1996), 317–20.

[46] The best catalogs of these houses are Smirnov, *Svod Pamiatnikov,* 7–156; M. V. Budylina,

dens, and trompe l'oeils, these houses make it plain that their masters intended to do much more than exploit their estates. They wanted to transform
them, inside and out, remaking their manors according to their new understanding of science and civilization. Root cellars were adorned with fanciful
entrances in the shape of pyramids; domestic chapels opened to the sky in imitation of the Pantheon. Mill ponds sprouted islands of tranquility, complete
with grottoes for contemplation; and rare was the new home that failed to
have wings or a Palladian portico.[47]

Scholars have sometimes interpreted this ornate domesticity as a demonstrative withdrawal from imperial life into a self-centered and even seditious
private existence. The main problem with such interpretations, however, is
that they ignore the extent to which the neoclassical idiom most nobles used
in pursuing their new home life was an officially approved style in Catherinean Russia. As one expert notes, imperial mansions built in the Palladian
style—such as Pavlovsk near St. Petersburg—"were the stylistic models for
the majority of private ones."[48] For this reason, Patricia Roosevelt is undoubtedly right to argue that noble investment in country homes primarily
served as a marker of distinction, rather than an act of estrangement.[49] By
mounting a Palladian entrance on their homes, nobles could present their estates as outposts of the imperial sphere of power that Russia's monarchs had
so assiduously created at court. This reinforced their attachment to the capital's reserves of wealth and status and hedged against the prospect that residence in the countryside could erode their symbolic elevation above the rest
of Russian society.

A new politics of private life was thus emerging in Tver Province by the
time the Bakunins moved there in the early 1780s and began to make a new
home for themselves in Priamukhino's old-style mansion. Like the rapidly
expanding exteriors and interiors of noble and bourgeois Europe, Russia's
country houses were becoming the centerpieces of newfound forms of dis-

O. I. Braitseva, and A. M. Kharlamova, *Arkhitektor N. A. L'vov* (Moscow: Gosudarstvennoe izdatel'stvo po stroitel'stvu, arkhitekture, i stroitel'nym materialam, 1961), 53–91; and Roosevelt,
Russian Country Estate, passim.

[47] I take most of these examples from the work of Nikolai L'vov, a prominent estate architect
and friend of the Bakunins, discussed in more detail in chapter 2. For pictures of these designs,
see Budylina, Braitseva, and Kharlamova, *Arkhitektor N. A. L'vov*, 64–67.

[48] Dimitri Shvidkovsky, "Catherine the Great's Field of Dreams," 56.

[49] See Priscilla Roosevelt, "Russian Estate Architecture and Noble Identity," in *Architectures
of Russian Identity 1500 to the Present*, ed. James Cracraft and Daniel Rowland (Ithaca: Cornell
University Press, 2003), 67.

tinction, maintained through lavish consumption and refined sociability.[50] In Russia, this phenomenon was recognized and even encouraged by the imperial government. The emperors and empresses of the mid-eighteenth century—and in particular, Catherine the Great and her advisers—overcame their traditional suspiciousness of idle nobility to try to take advantage of the platform rural towns and estates offered for expanding the reach of imperial culture and its scenarios of power. The luxury and theatricality for which Russian noble life of this period is famous should not be interpreted solely as the product of changing cultural fashions, or of a decadent, disaffected mindset created by a combination of education and idleness. They are best understood, rather, as a "privatization" of modes of distinction heretofore associated primarily with the throne.[51]

Despite bearing the imprimatur of official sanction, this privatization of imperial distinction allowed for important, qualitative shifts in the way this theater of power worked. First and perhaps most important, the production of distinction and elevation ceased being the sole prerogative of the court. Instead, it became something entrusted to—and stage-managed by—noble families themselves, albeit with heavy imperial guidance. This opened the way for the nobility to create its own forms of distinction, eventually including acts of opposition. (In the eighteenth century, of course, the range and power of such private scenarios of power—as yet unpublicized by literature, scholarship, and journalism—paled before those of the court.)[52] Second, the valorization

---

[50] For stimulating discussions of the cultural and political ambit of home life in the late eighteenth and early nineteenth centuries, see Catherine Hall, "The Sweet Delights of Home," in *From the Fires of the Revolution to the Great War*, ed. Michelle Perrot, vol. 4 of *A History of Private Life*, ed. Philippe Ariès and Georges Duby, trans. Arthur Goldhammer (Cambridge, Mass.: Harvard University Press, 1990), 47–93; Leonore Davidoff and Catherine Hall, *Family Fortunes: Men and Women of the English Middle Class, 1780–1850* (Chicago: University of Chicago Press, 1987); Amanda Vickery, *The Gentleman's Daughter: Women's Lives in Georgian England* (New Haven: Yale University Press, 1998); Peter Mandler, *The Fall and Rise of the Stately Home* (New Haven: Yale University Press, 1997).

[51] The "theatricality" of Russian noble culture was famously thematized by Iurii Lotman in works such as "The Poetics of Everyday Behavior in 18th Century Russian Culture," in *The Semiotics of Russian Cultural History*, ed. and trans. Alexander Nakhimovsky and Alice Stone Nakhimovsky (Ithaca: Cornell University Press, 1985), 70–73; see also Roosevelt, *Russian Country Estate*, 130–53.

[52] Over time, however, such intimate dramas could have wide impact when mediated by literature and other civic institutions. For a discussion of this theme, see John Randolph, "'That Historical Family': The Bakunin Archive and the Intimate Theater of History in Imperial Russia, 1780–1925," *Russian Review* 63 (October 2004): 574–93, as well as below. For a comparative context on the publication of documents produced in private life, see Dena Goodman, *The*

of private life encouraged the emergence of noble youth as important social actors and not merely as subordinate members of their patriarchal clans.[53] Such was certainly the ethos at Smolnyi, where the elder Bakunin daughters were educated to enlighten their home. Such also was the broad romance of noble emancipation itself, in which liberty was presented as a reward for culture and self-discipline: for maturity, in a word, rather than mere seniority.

The transformation just described was nearing full swing when Mikhail Vasilievich and Liubov Petrovna uprooted themselves and their children and moved to Tver Province in 1779. What did they think of it? To what extent did the Bakunins see their new home life as an opportunity for new kinds of roles in imperial society and with them new kinds of distinction?

☯☯☯

Nothing in the written record shows that Mikhail Vasilievich or Liubov Petrovna devoted much thought to the grander cultural and political vistas opening up before home life in the late eighteenth century. More than likely they were somewhat reserved in their attitude toward them. Mikhail Vasilievich grew ill and infirm in his retirement, and he seems to have relied on his wife to conduct most of his family's business. He appears in the family papers mostly in the form of short postscripts added to letters drawn up by his wife.[54] As for Liubov Petrovna, when not managing her husband's illness she was busy managing her estates. Her sole recorded foray into cultural activity was her determined lobbying for permission to build a new family chapel next to Priamukhino's manor house. In 1796, she asked Irinei, Bishop of Tver, to permit her to displace a graveyard and build a new, two-story stone structure next to her family's wooden home in order to house a domestic chapel. Permission was granted, and the first of what was to be several additions to the Bakunin home was built.[55] The fact that Liubov Petrovna's

---

Republic of Letters: A Cultural History of the French Enlightenment (Ithaca: Cornell University Press, 1994); Karen Chase and Michael Levenson, *The Spectacle of Intimacy: A Public Life for the Victorian Family* (Princeton: Princeton University Press, 2000).

[53] For a telling analysis of the role of the state in fostering ideas of individuality over clan loyalties, see Marc Raeff, "La noblesse et le discours politique sous le règne de Pierre le Grand," in *Politique et culture en Russie: 18e–20e siècles* (Paris: École des hautes études en sciences sociales, 1996), 121–24, 136–37.

[54] See, e.g., a letter of 1 September 1792, written by Liubov Petrovna to her son Mikhail Mikhailovich, with a brief greeting by Mikhail Vasilievich: GATO f. 1407, op. 1, d. 2, ll. 1–2.

[55] Irinei's letter granting permission is IRLI f. 16, op. 6, no. 3. See also Sysoev, *Bakuniny,* 75–77.

piety drove the Bakunins' first efforts to expand their manor house is important. Yet her hopes for what this chapel might accomplish remain unclear.
Was it primarily her family's own salvation Liubov Petrovna sought from her
church, or something more expansive?

From the winter of 1789–1790, however, there survives a tattered notebook written by the Bakunins' youngest daughter, Praskovia. This notebook
contains a short rustic melodrama—a *Prologue for the New Year 1790*—that
Praskovia evidently hoped would be performed as a part of her family's New
Year's Eve celebration that year.[56] Whether or not the *Prologue* actually was
performed is, of course, impossible to say. Still, the job of any prologue is to
provide a frame for the dramatic action to follow. Since Praskovia's *Prologue*
provides our first sustained glimpse of home life at Priamukhino in the late
eighteenth century, it makes sense to consider this script and its author in
more detail. What ambitions did Praskovia have for her family as it entered
the new year?

Praskovia Mikhailovna was the youngest of the Bakunins' eight children.
She was born in 1775, having been preceded in birth by her siblings Pelageia
(1761), Mikhail (1764), Ivan (1766?), Aleksandr (1765 or 1768), Anna
(1767), Varvara (ca. 1770), and Tatiana (not later than 1774).[57] Praskovia's
siblings, by and large, grew up in the capital. Her brothers matured and entered service before the family purchased their new home: Mikhail and Ivan
became military officers, while Aleksandr was enrolled in the College of Foreign Affairs. Pelageia and Anna, meanwhile, stayed behind in St. Petersburg
when the family moved. They completed their studies at Smolnyi, rejoining
their family in the countryside only in the mid-1780s. Praskovia herself, however, was only four years old when her father retired. It seems likely she had
few memories of St. Petersburg. Priamukhino was her world until 1790; and
yet as her *Prologue* shows, she imagined its drawing room could hold a microcosm of Russian society.

The *Prologue* tells a simple story of common life, set in the nameless Everywhere of the Russian countryside. ("The action," Praskovia writes simply at
the top of the script, "takes place in the village" [*Deistvie—v derevne*].) The play
begins with the appearance of a peasant named Vlas Artemiev, played (as a
list of the dramatis personae tells us) by Praskovia's brother Mikhail. In fiction as in real life, the New Year is approaching, and Vlas is seen sweeping
out the courtyard in front of his house to prepare his home for guests. Happy,

---

[56] The *Prologue* is GARF f. 825, op. 1, no. 1061, ll. 1–11 ob.
[57] Sidorov in Sysoev, *Bakuniny*, 424–25, gives this birth order.

hardworking, deferential, and prosperous, Vlas explains that he has only one worry in life: his brother Fedot, a soldier, is away fighting the Swedes. He has not been heard from in a while, and Vlas fears the worst.

Suddenly, exciting news arrives: a wagon train bearing the *molodoi barin* —the young master—has arrived from the war. With him come servants and soldiers. Do they have news about Fedot? Vlas sends his wife Katerina (played by Praskovia's sister Anna) to investigate. Katerina fetches one of the master's footmen (played by brother Ivan) and presses him for information. After a series of comic misunderstandings, it is revealed that this footman is none other than Vlas's long-lost brother Fedot himself. (Since he is much changed by his absence, Katerina does not recognize him at first.) A celebration ensues. Katerina invites Fedot inside their home to rest and relax, while Vlas continues cleaning in anticipation of his guests, who soon will be arriving.

Suddenly, however, the wind begins to blow, and the sky flickers with lightning. A mysterious supernatural being—the oracle Sibyl (played by Pelageia)—appears on the stage, descending from the heavens to choral and musical accompaniment provided by the rest of the Bakunin sisters (who for the moment are still offstage). Frightened, Vlas crosses himself fervently and prepares for the worst. Yet Sibyl reassures him that she is not some "unholy power." Rather, she has come to reward him for his exemplary life: "You live in harmony with your wife, take care of your children, honor your lords, and therefore in your station are a virtuous man!" Since he is such an upstanding fellow, Sibyl continues, Vlas deserves all possible blessings in the coming New Year. This, indeed, is the reason she has come: "I am commanded to bring Peace, Love, and Health to all those whose lives are an example to others!"

At Sibyl's command, Peace, Love, and Health now arrive from on high (played by Varvara, Praskovia, and Tatiana, respectively). They bless Vlas and his kin, who return to the stage. A piano is mystically summoned, at which point the peasants turn to the audience (presumably, the Bakunin parents and their real-life New Year's guests). Katerina predicts that their peasants will multiply and cover the fields with happy workers. Fedot promises that sadness and boredom will flee them, as the Turks flee Russia's armies. Last, Vlas wishes everyone a sound, healthy sleep—something (we are told) that enervated city dwellers will never know.

After this last bit of rustic theater, the *Prologue* then enters its finale on a personal and intimate note. The Bakunin children drop their guises and turn as themselves to sing a song of filial devotion to their parents.

> We know life through you:
> You put this blood in our veins.
> We are happy, because of you:
> Oh, sweetest love!

With this chorus of "sweetest love," the play ends.

A theatrical medley dreamed up for a family holiday, Praskovia's *Prologue for the New Year 1790* is easy to dismiss as domestic ephemera. The script makes no claim to originality. On the contrary, everything about it seems forgettably stereotypical: its idyllic setting, its sentimental plot, its closing crescendo of filial devotion. The purpose of a prologue, however, is not to serve as an independent dramatic action but rather to introduce one. Praskovia's goal, clearly, was to please her family while laying out a vision of where they lived, who they were, and what it was they were doing in their home in the countryside on a cold New Year's Eve. What's important about her *Prologue* is not its originality but the frame it seeks to place on Bakunin family life—a frame, we may presume, Praskovia hoped would meet with her parents' approval.

The first thing to note is Praskovia's choice of location: an idyllic Everywhere identified only as "the village" or "the countryside" (the Russian word *derevnia* means both). There are many possible explanations for her choice. Sentimental visions of idyllic contentment in the countryside so dominated Russian literature and culture in the second half of the eighteenth century that one scholar has called it a "pastoral revolution."[58] Idyll was the quintessential genre of private life, providing a location and occasion for countless cultivations and explorations of individual sensibility. In particular, idyll was a popular genre for imagining family life: its unchanging natural world embodies, as the critic Mikhail Bakhtin observes, the "age-old rootedness of the life of generations."[59] As well, some have explained idyll's popularity in Russia at this time by pointing to its use as an ideal form of escapist fantasy for Russia's privileged nobility. Idyll provides a comforting vision of an innate social order, Grigorii Gukovsky notes, one that exists separately from politics or oppression. "Here natural institutions/Govern common customs," the poet Aleksandr Sumarokov declared at midcentury—either delusorily or

---

[58] Newlin, *The Voice in the Garden*, 27–32; see also Joachim Klein, *Die Schäferdichtung des russischen Klassizismus* (Berlin: Otto Harrossowitz, 1988); and Gitta Hammarberg, *From the Idyll to the Novel: Karamzin's Sentimentalist Prose* (Cambridge: Cambridge University Press, 1991), 1–93.

[59] See M. M. Bakhtin, "Forms of Time and of the Chronotope in the Novel," in *The Dialogical Imagination: Four Essays*, ed. Michael Holquist (Austin: University of Texas Press, 1981), 224–36, esp. 229; and Newlin, *Voice in the Garden*, 146–48.

willfully oblivious to the scale of coercion required to maintain rural Russia's serf order.[60]

Whatever Praskovia's literary inspirations or personal motivations, however, we should not forget the political dimensions of her choice. The fact of the matter is that idyll was integral to the landscape of Russia's Enlightenment, as imagined by Catherine the Great. The empress, when she described the future of her realm, pictured its gradual transformation into a *Gartenreich* — a "garden kingdom" cultivated by the plans of wise rulers and the energies of virtuous subjects. Voltaire was in this respect telling the empress what she wanted to hear in the early 1760s, when he claimed to be dying of desire to see "two thousand leagues of countryside, civilised by heroines."[61] To a large extent, the project of noble liberty depended on convincing noble families to see the countryside through arcadian lenses — to live, as it were, in the garden kingdom of the future rather than in the existing village of the present. (This involved a rather impressive process of unlearning, given the deep associations Russia's imperial political culture had established between village life, ignobility, and backwardness.)[62]

Far from being an exercise in epicureanism, then, there was something public-spirited, and indeed almost patriotic, about Praskovia's decision to set her family's celebration against the backdrop of an arcadian rural world. This conclusion is reinforced by Praskovia's choice of plot: a soldier's homecoming. Soldiers' stories — and in particular stories about happy homecomings — were a staple of imperial theater in the eighteenth century. They attracted large urban audiences and won official support. In the process, as Elise Kimerling Wirtschafter has shown, they helped Imperial Russian theaters find an idiom for speaking of the joys and sorrows of imperial society as a whole. The reasons for these plays' popularity and social resonance are not hard to find.[63] Their plots offered an ideal resolution to a fundamental ten-

[60] Quoted in G. A. Gukovskii, *Ocherki po istorii russkoi literatury XVIII veka. Dvorianskaia fronda 1750x–1760x godov* (Moscow-Leningrad: Izdatel'stvo Akademii nauk, 1936), 96.

[61] See W. F. Reddaway, ed., *Documents of Catherine the Great: The Correspondence with Voltaire and the Instruction of 1767 in the English Translation of 1768* (New York: Russell & Russell, 1971), 9; see also Shvidkovsky, "Catherine the Great's Field of Dreams," 54–55, 65; Baehr, *Paradise Myth,* 71–84; and Wortman, *Scenarios of Power,* 1:138–41.

[62] On "foreignness" as an essential element of political elevation in Russia, see Wortman, *Scenarios of Power,* 1:4–7, 42–80; on eighteenth-century notions of peasant "backwardness" and the politics of reform, see Esther Kingston-Mann, *In Search of the True West: Culture, Economics, and Problems of Russian Development* (Princeton: Princeton University Press, 1999), 9–60.

[63] Elise Kimmerling Wirtschafter, "The Common Soldier in Eighteenth-Century Russian Drama," *Reflections on Russia in the Eighteenth Century,* ed. Joachim Klein, Simon Dixon, and

sion that affected the majority of Russian subjects: the conflict between duty and desire. How could one be a good servant—as almost everyone in the empire was expected to be—and still find happiness? Homecomings like Fedot's implied—somewhat improbably, in a world where military service was for life—that in the end, Russians could find time for both.

Not shirking his duty, Fedot goes out into the world; but in the end he is rewarded by seeing his family again. He becomes a stranger in the process—and is not recognized by Katerina—but his home is there for him all the same in the end, waiting with open arms. That is because those who remained behind attended conscientiously to their own role: laboring in the domestic economy, honoring social and gender conventions, and otherwise maintaining the normality against which the sacrifices of service can be seen as but a moment in time. In this sense, the oracle Sibyl descends on the Artemiev home not simply because it is a rustic utopia and they are Everymen but because the Artemievs illustrate how to balance the burdens of Russian life. As Sibyl observes, they deserve to be rewarded because they are an "example to others."

What, then, of the real-life Bakunins? What sort of role in Russia's New Year 1790 does the *Prologue* imagine for them? There seems little doubt that although Praskovia and her siblings put on peasant garb to enact this little moral drama, its audience would have understood that it was the Bakunins themselves who deserved applause for being a good "example to others." Through the lens of Praskovia's *Prologue*, we see this former clan of Petersburg servitors transformed into a theatrically "representative" Russian family—"representative" not in the sense that they themselves were in any way average, but in the sense that the domestic norms the Bakunin children performed at Priamukhino were conventions that might someday animate and order Russian society as a whole, from the humble Artemievs on up. Catherine the Great's provincial reforms—and the politics of private life they stimulated—helped to create this private theater of civic distinction, in the hopes of inspiring provincial patriotism. Had the empress herself been invited to Priamukhino on December 31, 1789, she might even have been proud of the way in which the Bakunins had taken it upon themselves to use their domestic celebration to represent virtuous social norms. By the same token, she and her advisers had taken a calculated risk. If, as seems to be the case, the

---

Maarten Fraanje (Köln: Böhlau Verlag, 2001), 367–76; and Wirtschafter, *Play of Ideas in Russian Enlightenment Theater*, 53–83.

domestic enlightenment for which the Bakunin family became so famous found its first inspiration in the civic idealism of the Catherinean era, there was certainly no guarantee that the moral dramas the family produced would conform to official expectations, or present roles that fit so comfortably within the empire's existing social and political order. Having helped illuminate the sphere of private life at Priamukhino with some of its own distinction, even the court could not be certain of the direction this exemplary life would take.

☻☙☙❀

Liberty posed uncomfortable dilemmas for the Bakunin family as well.[64] Some of these were social; some were political; still others, metaphysical. While she labored on the script, Praskovia considered the big question: just who or what was the ultimate guarantor of the idyllic world she imagined? At first, Praskovia imagined that Sibyl delivered her rewards "by command of the Almighty." The oracle introduces herself to Vlas as "one of His attendants." But this loose, deistic frame—surrounding the activities of a pagan muse—eventually dissatisfied Praskovia, and she crossed it out. In the final script, Sibyl simply appears, without explanation as to whom or what she represents. The metaphysical status of the Bakunins' new home life—its relationship to either divine or earthly sanction—would remain a long-term problem.

More prosaically, noble liberty was supported by serfdom, a coercive and endemically violent institution. From time to time this violence could (and did) rebound on the manor in the form of murder, arson, and revolt. Even without such breakdowns, the provincial home life the Bakunins desired rested on shaky social and economic ground. In their first decade at Priamukhino, the Bakunin family ran up incredible debts, so much so that they decided they had to withdraw their youngest son, Aleksandr, from service. In late 1789—even as Praskovia was writing her *Prologue*—Liubov Petrovna sent a series of desperate appeals to one of the family's last connections in St. Petersburg, a high-ranking official with the Imperial College of Foreign Affairs. (Count Arkadii Ivanovich Markov was a former colleague of the now-dead Petr Vasilievich Bakunin, the Younger.) Liubov Petrovna begged

---

[64] As a group, the "anxieties" of the "Russian pastoral" are superbly described in Newlin, *Voice in the Garden.*

Count Markov to release Aleksandr from his post as a translator for the Russian imperial diplomatic mission in Sardinia.

Markov's reply testifies to the Russian government's attention to—and invocation of—domestic virtues in its relations with the nobility. Aleksandr was not easy to replace, Markov informed Liubov Petrovna. And yet he could not find it in his heart to refuse a mother's request. If the Bakunins would pay Aleksandr's travel expenses, he would be sent home immediately. "I hope that you will do me justice," Markov concluded, "and see that not one of the feelings common to humanity is unknown to me, and that in particular I am able to appreciate parents' ardor for their children."[65] Soon Liubov Petrovna had her son back.

Before long, however, Aleksandr so despaired of clearing his family's debts that he feared for his own sanity. Fleeing to the nearby district capital, Aleksandr sent a desperate message to his friend and protector, the courtier Nikolai Lvov. "Can it be that an Evil Fate will have no mercy on us—must we finally default—must I lose my mind?"[66] As Aleksandr had discovered, playing an ideal family in the countryside was one thing; finding any real role for himself there was quite another.

[65] See A. I. Markov to L. P. Bakunina, letter of 6 November 1789, IRLI f. 16, op. 9, no. 206, ll. 1–1 ob.

[66] See A. M. Bakunin to N. A. Lvov, letter of 1 March 1792, IRLI f. 16, op. 4, no. 37/2, ll. 1–2 ob.

CHAPTER TWO

Aleksandr's Idyll

Bleeding himself freely from his left arm, to "reduce the pain in my chest" and thin blood "congealed by worry," Aleksandr considered the possibilities. Without Lvov's prompt intervention, he explained to his friend, the Bakunins would lose Priamukhino. Mikhail Vasilievich and Liubov Petrovna would finish their lives in disgrace, while Aleksandr watched helplessly. If Lvov rescued them, however, Aleksandr promised to resurrect his new home. "In a Confederation hat, old sheepskin coat, a spyglass in my hands and skis on my feet, I am surveying the locale." He surmised that the "simplest of measures and reforms" would right his family's finances. And then he could make Priamukhino bloom. He would plant an alley of trees along the road leading to town; use careful landscaping to build the village's lumber mill back into the surrounding countryside; and convert the estate's last scrap of wasteland into a verdant lawn, "on which sheep will be pastured in the English manner" —"for fertilization of the soil." This corner of rural Russia would turn into a productive, harmonious idyll, complete with a flock. "But let all this remain between us for now," Aleksandr concluded, returning to reality: "A project conceived and published is a project abandoned."[1]

The appeal worked. Just what Lvov did—whether he used his connections to cancel the Bakunins' debts or just provided money—is unclear. But the immediate crisis passed and the Bakunins held on to Priamukhino, which

[1] See A. M. Bakunin to N. A. L'vov, letter of 1 March 1792, IRLI f. 16 op. 4, no. 37/2, ll. 1–4.

Aleksandr Mikhailovich Bakunin (1765[8?]–1854). From Vladimir Sysoev, *Bakuniny* (Tver: Sozvezdie, 2002). Courtesy: Tverskoi Gosudarstvennyi Ob"edinnënyi Muzei

then remained their home until 1917.[2] Aleksandr Bakunin inherited his family's estate and proceeded to build his idyll, planting elaborate botanical gardens around its perimeter and adding neoclassical wings to the old manor house. Quitting service permanently, he became known throughout Tver as a committed country family man, a loving husband and father who fostered a freethinking atmosphere within his home. Aleksandr's children, his contemporaries, and historians all credit him with being the founder of a new, enlightened tradition of family life on the Bakunin estate.[3]

Some of this reputation seems misplaced. Priamukhino's enlightenment was not entirely of Aleksandr's making. The manor's potential new role in society and culture had already been sketched by Catherine the Great's provincial reforms and his sister Praskovia's pen. Yet it is also true that Aleksandr became passionately committed to this ideal of domestic enlightenment and invested his considerable education and authority into its development. This commitment to home life is all the more remarkable when we remember that this was not the life for which Aleksandr was raised. Very likely he had never seen Priamukhino, or Tver Province, before 1790. He was educated in Italy as a diplomat destined for long service, only to be abruptly summoned home by his father's illness. If his letter to Lvov is to be believed, his first months at Priamukhino were enough to make him open his wrists. What inspired his subsequent transformation into a family man and made him pursue his idyllic "project" long after the euphoria surrounding his family's salvation passed?

Most portraits of Aleksandr Bakunin employ vague and often contradictory generalizations about his politics and cultural tastes. He is variously de-

[2] On Priamukhino's seizure by peasants and nationalization during 1917, see Vladimir Sysoev, *Bakuniny* (Tver: Sozvezdie, 2002), 272–74.

[3] For his children's admiring if bittersweet recollections of their father's efforts to enlighten their home, see IRLI f. 16, op. 2, no. 62, ll. 1–2 (an abortive family history by daughter Tatyana), and the memoirs of Mikhail Bakunin, *Sobranie*, I:25–27; for modern historical accounts of Aleksandr Bakunin's role as the creator of the "Priamukhino idyll," see A. Kornilov, *Molodye gody Mikhaila Bakunina: Iz istorii russkogo romantizma* (Moscow: M. and S. Sabashnikov, 1915), 29–41, esp. 29–30; V. P. Stepanov, "Aleksandr Mikhailovich Bakunin," in *Russkie pisateli, 1800–1917*, vol. 1, ed. P. A. Nikolaev (Moscow: Sovetskaia entsiklopedia, 1989), 141; Sysoev, *Bakuniny*, 57–97; Priscilla Roosevelt, *Life on the Russian Country Estate: A Social and Cultural History* (New Haven: Yale University Press, 1995), 292, 297–98; Lydia Ginzburg, *On Psychological Prose*, trans. and ed. Judson Rosengrant (Princeton: Princeton University Press, 1991), 35–36; N. Pirumova and B. Nosik, "Premukhino Bakuninykh," *Nashe Nasledie* 3, no. 15 (1990): 143–58; L. G. Agamalyan, "Russkii sad Aleksandra Bakunina (K voprosu ob avtorstve Priamukhina)," in *Genii vkusa: Materialy nauchnoi konferentsii, posviashchennoi tvorchestvu N. A. L'vova*, ed. M. V. Stroganov (Tver: Tverskoi gosudarstvennyi universitet, 2001), 236–52.

scribed as a "liberal," an "enlightened conservative," and a reactionary *kre-
postnik* (or serf-lord) — a moderate man of reason who was also an "admirer
of Rousseau."[4] None of these historical epithets, however, does much to explain his commitment to his home. Yet that, in the end, was the central ambition of his life. Fortunately, Aleksandr himself left an abundant record of
his engagement with home life in his first two decades at Priamukhino, in the
form of numerous letters, projects, and poems that have only recently begun
to be published.[5] These documents allow us to see that Aleksandr's reinvention of himself as a family man took place in the context of a larger debate
about the true meaning of private experience for Russia's Enlightenment.
Were country houses such as Priamukhino merely stages, on which nobles
should enact a culture brought from elsewhere, or were they dispersed forums for private reason that could reform Russian society and culture from
the ground up? More to the point for young Aleksandr, what sort of role
could he himself expect to play in this process, as a cultured man suddenly
transplanted to the provinces?

Aleksandr's long-unpublished projects show that his unusual commitment
to Priamukhino rested on the conviction that noble home life in the provinces
could become a laboratory for the creation — and not merely the representation — of virtuous social norms. Under Lvov's mentorship, Aleksandr came
to believe that the home offered a perfect forum for enlightenment, because
it could be counted on to discipline and domesticate human rationality, curb-
ing its excesses and preventing its alienation from the whole of human nature.
Repudiating the arbitrary patriarchal authority which was their birthright,
these noblemen sought to replace it with a paternalistic domesticity, the le-

---

[4] On disagreements over Bakunin's politics, see V. M. Bokova, "A. M. Bakunin i ego traktat
'Usloviia pomeshchika s krest'ianami,'" *Vestnik Moskovskogo Universiteta*, Seriia 8: *Istoriia*, no. 5
(1992): 53–54. Aileen Kelly, *Mikhail Bakunin: A Study in the Psychology and Politics of Utopianism*
(New Haven: Yale University Press, 1987), 22, and E. H. Carr, *Michael Bakunin* (London:
Macmillan, 1937), 9, inherit the idea of Bakunin's Rousseauianism from Kornilov, *Molodye gody*,
36. See also Ginzburg, *Psychological Prose*, 35, for a broader characterization of Bakunin as a sentimentalist.

[5] See N. D. Kochetkova, exec. ed., *Russkaia literatura: Vek XVIII*, vol. 1, *Lirika* (Moscow: Khudozhestvennaia literatura, 1990), 532–36; K. Iu. Lappo-Danilevskii, "Iz literaturnogo naslediia
A. M. Bakunina," in *Literaturnyi arkhiv: Materialy po istorii russkoi literatury i obshchestvennoi mysli*,
ed. K. N. Grigorian (St. Petersburg: Nauka, 1994), 94–117; Agamalian, "Russkii sad Aleksandra Bakunina," 236–53; Agamalian, "Istoriia Rossii v izlozhenii A. M. Bakunina," *Novyi Zhurnal*
2 (1997): 164–80; Agamalian, "A. M. Bakunin i ego proekt 'Uslovie pomeshchika s krest'ianinom,'"
in *Pamiatniki kul'tury. Novye otkrytiia* (St. Petersburg: Nauka, 1999), 52–73. A. M. Bakunin, *Sobranie stikhotvorenii*, ed. M. V. Stroganov (Tver: Zolotaia bukva, 2001). The following analysis is
based for the most part on the archival originals, and therefore my reference will generally be
to them.

gitimacy of which rested on its purported rationality and social utility. In this way, Aleksandr began to see himself neither as a servitor nor as an aspiring serf-lord, but rather as a provincial family man, whose opinions deserved respect because they were rooted in domestic experience. The more Aleksandr studied Priamukhino, the more he hoped the life his family was building there could serve as a model for Russia's future.

⊛ℛ⊛

Admittedly, this interpretation contradicts much of what has heretofore been known about Aleksandr Bakunin and his idyll. Most scholars judge the man and his ideals on the basis of a lengthy ode that Aleksandr wrote in the late 1820s. (It is titled "Osuga," after the name of the river that ran past his family's estate.) Sentimental but cantankerous in tone, full of antirevolutionary rhetoric and scorn for serfdom's critics, "Osuga" combines loving scenes of family life at Priamukhino with a stiff defense of autocratic, unemancipated Russia.[6] In the end, however, "Osuga" is better read as a response to the heated political environment of the late 1820s—when the hair-raising failure of the Decembrist Revolt of 1825 placed noble families like the Bakunins under great suspicion—than as a statement of the man Aleksandr wished to be in 1792. What follows looks forward in time, not backward.[7]

Aleksandr Bakunin was born in the late 1760s, most likely in 1768.[8] At a very young age—perhaps as early as nine—Aleksandr was sent to Italy for education and eventual enrollment in the College of Foreign Affairs. By 1783, he was assigned to Turin, where he served as part of the imperial mission to the Kingdom of Sardinia. His climb up the imperial government's famous Table of Ranks began. By 1784, he was a College Assessor (the eighth of the fourteen ranks). Aleksandr pursued the study of natural philosophy along-

---

[6] Until recently, "Osuga" was known only through excerpts published by Kornilov, *Molodye gody,* esp. chapters 1–6. In the mid-1990s, "Osuga" was edited and published in full by Dmitrii Oleinikov, "Aleksandr Bakunin i ego poema 'Osuga,'" *Nashe nasledie* 29–30 (1994): 51–63. I will analyze "Osuga" itself in chapter 4.

[7] Most of Aleksandr Bakunin's manuscripts are preserved at the Institute of Russian Literature, where they are IRLI f. 16, op. 2.

[8] The basic biographical accounts of Aleksandr Bakunin's life are Kornilov, *Molodye gody,* 7–28; and Stepanov, "Aleksandr Mikhailovich Bakunin." Stepanov lists Aleksandr's birth date as 1768 or 1763(?); Sidorov's geneaology lists it as 1765 or 1768(?): see Sysoev, *Bakuniny,* 424. Most of the biographical information about Aleksandr's early years of service come from the testimony provided by his family's application to be registered in the genealogical books of the Tver nobility: see IRLI f. 16, op. 6, no. 13, ll. 2–5.

side his official duties, receiving a diploma of membership from the Turin Academy in recognition of his dissertation—written in Latin—on intestinal worms. In the spring of 1790, however, his summons home arrived, and Aleksandr took a leave of absence from imperial service in June of that year. As of March 31, 1791, he was officially retired at the rank of Collegiate Councillor, the sixth rank. Full despair at the future that family life offered him came little more than a year later, by the first of March 1792.

Aleksandr's first resolution, after Lvov saved his family's fortune, was never again to allow himself to be beaten down by circumstances. Imagining himself relaxing with Lvov on the "island of tranquility" that decorated Lvov's estate Nikolskoe-Cherenchitsy, Aleksandr anticipated a better day when

> I shall with satisfaction remember those hours when my senses were blinded to all the charms of family life by temporary misfortune; I shall remember that you began by helping, and then explained that he who can be crushed by misfortune is unworthy of the well-being granted to those who earn it in the sweat of their brow.

This led to his second resolution. Like a settler in the newly won lands of Siberia or America, Aleksandr promised, he would now set off for a life of productive liberty. Not only would he transform his family's estate into the idyll he had sketched in his "project," but he would learn to live life on his own terms and according to the dictates of his own reason, "acting, rather than working (people work only against their will)."[9]

This ambition to convert his sudden liberty into a more meaningful freedom immediately encountered an obstacle, however. Neither society nor his family yet had a meaningful or free role for Aleksandr to play at Priamukhino. His return home was quite obviously forced by necessity, not choice. From this point of view, the late-eighteenth-century valorization of private life placed youngest sons like him in a dilemma. For his was a liberty of the wrong kind. The most positive vision of noble private life in Russia at the time—the Catherinean ideal—was in essence a life of retirement after years of diligent service, not instead of it. The more basic noble norm (extending back to Peter's time and indeed before) was a life where distinction and power were earned by dedication to the emperors and their vision of the "common good," not by immersion at a

---

[9] "... [D]eistvuiua, a ne rabotaia (rabotaiut tol'ko po nevole)." See A. M. Bakunin to N. A. L'vov, letter of 27 March 1792, IRLI f. 16, op. 4, no. 37/2, ll. 5–6.

young age in the details of estate life.[10] Nor had Aleksandr's family sent him to the Kingdom of Sardinia to learn how to manage a serf estate.

Indeed, his new life at home threw Aleksandr deep into the shadow of his older and more successful brothers, whose careers continued to advance. Liubov Petrovna was thrilled when her eldest son, Mikhail, married the daughter of one of St. Petersburg's leading families, Varvara Ivanovna Golenishcheva-Kutuzova, in 1792.[11] As she was no doubt aware, this brilliant pairing meant a promising service career. (In time, Mikhail Mikhailovich became civil governor of St. Petersburg and a member of the Imperial Senate.)[12] Aleksandr's brother Ivan, meanwhile, died gloriously during the Persian campaign, in the Caucausus Mountains. "Our late brother was wounded in the arm, but bravely, coldly continued to command," Mikhail informed his parents from the battlefield. "Everyone compares him to Leonidas."[13] In an age when noblemen contested for such neoclassical titles, no one would ever liken Aleksandr to a fallen Spartan king.

Though it was better, of course, to be alive, Ivan's death and Mikhail's upward momentum tightened Priamukhino's grip on Aleksandr. The expenses of setting up a household in St. Petersburg (and living up to rising social prospects) meant that there was little chance Mikhail could help save the family estate. "Please send money in the future when you can," Aleksandr wrote to his brother in the summer of 1793, "but always remember that you must found a fortune for your wife and children"—a fortune quite separate from their parents' home.[14] Though two of Aleksandr's sisters (the youngest

---

[10] Richard Wortman, *Scenarios of Power: Myth and Ceremony in Russian Monarchy*, vol. 1, *From Peter the Great to Nicholas I* (Princeton: Princeton University Press, 1995), 128–35; see also Marc Raeff, "La noblesse et le discours politique sous le règne de Pierre le Grand," *Cahiers du monde russe et soviétique* 34, no. 1–2 (1993): 38–41; Raeff, *Origins of the Russian Intelligentsia: The Eighteenth-Century Nobility* (New York: Harcourt Brace Jovanovich, 1966), 34–38.

[11] Varvara Ivanovna was the sister of Pavel Ivanovich Golenishchev-Kutuzov, one of Nikolai Karamzin's earliest enemies in the literary conflicts of the 1790s. She was herself the author of a memoir of the Persian campaign of 1796, as well as diaries of Petersburg during the War of 1812. See M. K. Evseeva, "Varvara Ivanovna Bakunina," in Nikolaev, *Russkie pisateli, 1800–1917*, 1:144; and V. E. Vatsuro, *Zapiski kommentatora* (St. Petersburg: Gumanitarnoe agenstvo "Akademicheskii proekt," 1994), 71–75. Liubov Petrovna, overjoyed at the engagement, wrote a letter immediately to her future daughter-in-law, see GATO, f. 1407, op. 1, d. 1, l. 2.

[12] On Mikhail Mikhailovich's career (which eventually ended in charges of corruption) see Sysoev, *Bakuniny*, 39–42; Kornilov, *Molodye gody*, 4–5.

[13] Undated letter of 1796 by M. M. Bakunin to his brother and parents, IRLI, f. 16, op. 7, no. 1, l. 1. "Leoniudist [Leonidas]," as Mikhail calls his brother, was a Spartan king whose heroic stand against a Persian army was immortalized by Herodotus.

[14] See Aleksandr's note to his brother, in a letter by their parents and dated June 27, 1793, GATO, f. 1407, op. 1, d. 3, ll. 9–10.

two, Tatiana and Praskovia) married well, three (including the Smolnyi graduates, Pelageia and Anna) did not marry at all, meaning that they would bring no further wealth into the family.[15] (Praskovia, the author of the happy *Prologue for the New Year 1790*, became the wife of a highly placed civil servant, Petr Andreevich Nilov, and lived in St. Petersburg and Kiev, founding a school for well-born girls in the latter city.) For all these reasons, Aleksandr's virtuous but not fortunate function within family life was to be the obedient and self-sacrificing son—to "not abandon the old folks, not for anything in the world," as he put it to Mikhail in 1801. And in this same letter, written a full decade after his return to Priamukhino, he warned his brother to stay far away from the countryside. "Your children are growing up, can you undertake to educate them in the village, and thus as bumpkins?" Aleksandr wrote to Mikhail. It was much better to live modestly (*en bourgeois*) in the city and give up on rustic fantasies, which too often ended in illness and oblivion.[16]

Aleksandr's father died in 1803; his mother, who then became head of household, lived until 1814. Thus some twenty years passed between Aleksandr's summons home in 1790 and the day he was able to set up his own household. By that time, he was at least forty-six years old.

All along he was free, of course, to try to carve out some smaller space for himself alongside his obligations as dutiful son. One possibility was to embrace ironic detachment: to sit outside his own life and judge it independently, as it were, from afar. It would be another thirty years before the poet Aleksandr Pushkin would stamp the lives of such detached, "superfluous men" deep into the imperial social imagination, in his novel *Evgenii Onegin*. But Aleksandr seems to have begun verse experiments along these lines in the mid-1790s. He sent a mocking, multipart epistle, "On Envy, Boredom, Imagination, and Idleness," to Nikolai Lvov in 1795 or early 1796. Lvov was among the supporting subscribers of a sentimental almanac titled *The Muse*. Had *The Muse* published Aleksandr's poems, Aleksandr might be known today (or more likely forgotten) as one of Onegin's cultural ancestors.[17]

Lvov, however, had other plans. He used his Aleksandr's epistle as an oc-

---

[15] See Sysoev, *Bakuniny*, 38. I discuss the fates of the sisters who remained near Priamukhino in chapter 3.

[16] See A. M. Bakunin to M. M. Bakunin, letter of 4 April 1801, GATO f. 103, op. 1, no. 1396, ll. 41–42. See also A. M. Bakunin to M. M. Bakunin, undated letter, GATO f. 1407, op. 1, no. 24, ll. 15–16.

[17] On *The Muse*, see A. V. Dement'ev, A. V. Zapadov, and M. S. Cherepakhov, eds., *Russkaia periodicheskaia pechat' (1702–1894): Spravochnik* (Moscow: Gosudarstvennoe izdatel'stvo politicheskoi literatury, 1959), 94–95.

casion to publish a stirring reply ("A Fragment from a Letter to A. M. B.,
who from the Countryside Sent to the Author Some Verses on Envy, Boredom, Fantasy, and Idleness"), in which he laid out the virtues of country living. Ostensibly a "Fragment" from their personal correspondence, Lvov's
poem lets the world know that his friend "A. M. B." finds country life idle
and constraining. Yet this, Lvov argues, is a misreading of the situation. Yes,
the Russian countryside remains locked in winter. Yes, its potential has not
yet been unleashed. But if one only listens, one will find that nature itself
speaks with a voice "as intelligible to the mind as to the heart." And in the
song of a nightingale, one hears the moral:

> O, mortal, do not be afflicted!
> Love, work, play:
> This whole world is a throne for bliss.

The ideal around which his friend should orient his life is that of the "golden
mean," praised by pastoral poets from antiquity to modern times—from Horace to Gessner. If he but surrendered himself to the gentle, natural rhythms
of love, work, and play, Aleksandr would see another, happier side to the
world. Yet in what sense was this humdrum private calling a life fit for a Russian nobleman, raised on visions of service to the empire and the "common
good"? If a man like Aleksandr wedded his sentiments and talents to a life in
the actual Russian countryside, would the result be anything other than a
dreary idleness?

The short answer to these questions is that Lvov believed that it was precisely by falling in love with the countryside—by surrendering his heart to
its eternal, natural rhythms—that a Russian nobleman like A. M. B. could
learn how to unleash Russia's true potential and prosperity. From this moment on, Lvov became Aleksandr's definitive mentor in the ways of home life.
But understanding just what they hoped to achieve on their estates requires
stepping back for a moment to consider Lvov's broader social vision and its
place in the controversies surrounding the meaning of noble liberty for Imperial Russian life.

❁⚜❁

Born in 1751, in a village not far from Priamukhino, Nikolai Aleksandrovich
Lvov had established himself, by the mid-1790s, as Russia's leading architect

of estate life.[18] Like Aleksandr, he was a member of the hereditary nobility, but in most other respects the two men's lives were quite different. Born in the provinces, Lvov gained access to St. Petersburg and its civilization by enrolling in the prestigious Preobrazhensky Regiment in the 1770s. He then worked his way into elite society by serving under a series of powerful protectors, among them Aleksandr Bakunin's uncle, Petr Vasilievich the Younger. (Lvov met his wife, Maria Diakova, during rehearsals for a play in Petr Vasilievich's domestic theater.)[19] Lvov's architectural skills, apparently largely self-taught, drew the attention of Catherine the Great in 1780. She chose his project as the best design for a cathedral to commemorate her meeting with Joseph II at Moghilev. This success raised Lvov's fortunes considerably. As a reward, Catherine sent Lvov on a trip to Italy to learn what he could of the arts there. He returned with a diary full of ideas and sketches, which would fuel a remarkable burst of cultural activity across the next two decades.[20]

In the 1780s and 1790s, Lvov made his mark in areas as diverse as diplomacy, civil service, mineralogy, engineering, dramaturgy, literature, geology, and aesthetics. In 1790, he published one of the earliest collections of Russian folk songs. He carried this folk lexicon over into his poetry, which gradually evolved from epicurean salon performances into autobiographical epistles and narrative poems. As an inventor, Lvov designed novel plans for peat-fired stoves and the making of brick. As a result of these many endeavors, Lvov has entered Russian cultural history under a variety of hats. He has been called a "sentimentalist," a "pre-Romantic," a "Rousseauan," a "protonationalist," or, most simply and commonly, a "Renaissance man."[21] Yet none

[18] For L'vov's biography, see A. Glumov, *N. A. L'vov* (Moscow: Iskusstvo, 1980); K. Iu. Lappo-Danilevskii, "O literaturnom nasledii N. A. L'vova," in L'vov, *Izbrannye sochineniia*, ed. and comp. K. Iu. Lappo-Danilevskii (Petersburg: Acropol, 1994), 7–22. The best guides to his architectural activities are M. V. Budylina, O. I. Braitseva, and A. M. Kharlamova, *Arkhitektor N. A. L'vov* (Moscow: Gosudarstvennoe izdatel'stvo po stroitel'stvu, arkhitekture, i stroitel'nym materialam, 1961) and A. V. Tatarinov, "Arkhitekturnye raboty N. A. L'vova," in L'vov, *Izbrannye sochineniia*, 371–93. See also Lindsey Hughes, "N. A. L'vov and the Russian Country House," in *Russia and the World of the Eighteenth Century*, ed. R. P. Bartlett, A. G. Cross, and Karen Rasmussen (Columbus, Ohio: Slavica, 1988), 289–300, and Roosevelt, *Russian Country Estate*, 291–94.

[19] By this marriage, he became the Bakunins' distant relative: Maria Diakova was Liubov Petrovna's second cousin.

[20] See K. Iu. Lappo-Danilevskii, "Ital'ianskii dnevnik N. A. L'vova," *Europa Orientalis* 14 (1995): 57–93.

[21] For discussions of L'vov and his place in history, see G. A. Gukovskii, *Russkaia literatura XVIII veka* (Moscow: Aspekt Press, 1998), 266–67; Hans Rogger, *National Consciousness in Eigh-*

of these broad characterizations really explores or explains Lvov's most famous passion: his love of country homes.

Architecture, as one contemporary noted, was the "most beloved subject of his [Lvov's] studies."[22] In it he concentrated above all on creating a new, enlightened idiom for noble home life on the estate. A list of his architectural works, composed by A. V. Tatarinov, includes over eighty-seven entries, including dozens of houses and estates, many of them built for Lvov's own family, friends, and neighbors.[23] Though capable of working in many different styles, Lvov for most of his career espoused the virtues of Palladian architecture — helping to make it the style most associated with the new noble "liberty." Indeed, in 1798 he translated Andrea Palladio's seminal work *The Four Books on Architecture* (1570) into Russian, using a rare and expensive copy he himself had brought back from his Italian voyage a decade earlier. (In his introduction to this work, Lvov called Palladio "the common architect of all enlightened peoples.")[24] Had he contented himself with simply designing homes in Palladio's style, we might be justified in thinking that Lvov was just following Catherine's lead. (The empress made Palladianism her style of choice in the 1780s.)[25] But Lvov clearly took pride in his status as the publisher of "a Russian Palladio," and his translation and publication of *The Four Books on Architecture* helped secure Palladianism's position as the essential norm for gentry home construction until the 1860s.[26]

---

teenth-Century Russia (Cambridge, Mass.: Harvard University Press, 1960), 269–71; William Edward Brown, *A History of Eighteenth-Century Russian Literature* (Ann Arbor: Ardis, 1984), 416–27; Lappo-Danilevskii, "O literaturnom nasledii" For an in-depth discussion of L'vov's interest in folk music and its place in late-eighteenth-century culture, see chapter 1 of Richard Taruskin, *Defining Russia Musically: Historical and Hermeneutical Essays* (Princeton: Princeton University Press, 1997). L'vov's collection of folk songs has been translated and published as Nikolai Lvov and Ivan Prach, *A Collection of Russian Folk Songs*, ed. Malcolm Hamrick Brown (Ann Arbor: UMI Research Press, 1987).

[22] See M. N. Murav'ev, "Kratkoe svedenie o zhizni g. tainogo sovetnika L'vova," in L'vov, *Izbrannye sochineniia*, 361.

[23] On L'vov's numerous architectural works in Tver Province, and devotion to country houses, see Budylina, Braitseva, and Kharlamova, *Arkhitektor N. A. L'vov*, 53–91; Tatarinov, "Arkhitekturnye raboty N. A. L'vova"; Hughes, "N. A. L'vov"; and Roosevelt, *Russian Country Estate*, esp. 293–95.

[24] N. L'vov, "Ot izdatelia russkogo Palladiia," in *Chetyre knigi palladievoi arkhitektury, v koikh po kratkom opisanii piati Ordenov, govoritsia o tom chto znat' dolzhno pri stroenii chastnykh domov, dorog, mostov, ploshchadei, ristalishch, i khramov*, ed. and trans. N. L'vov (St. Petersburg: I. K. Shnor, 1798), 1.

[25] Dimitri Shvidkovsky, "Catherine the Great's Field of Dreams: Architecture and Landscape in the Russian Enlightenment," in *Architectures of Russian Identity 1500 to the Present*, ed. James Cracraft and Daniel Rowland (Ithaca: Cornell University Press, 2003), 61–63.

[26] On the predominance of Palladianism in estate architecture, see William Craft Brumfeld,

The first conceit on which Lvov's vision of home life rested was that the home is the original structure from which human society emerged. This view finds expression in the opening chapters of *The Four Books of Architecture,* which present the home as a norm for all kinds of architecture—and indeed for all kinds of society as well. According to Palladio, any account of architecture (or indeed of history) must begin with domestic spaces, since "buildings built by private persons were the foundation for public buildings." Palladio reasons as follows (in Lvov's translation):

> Private man [*chastnyi chelovek*] built first for himself; but later seeing the need for help from others to obtain a fuller happiness (if such happiness indeed is our lot here) he quite naturally fell in love with the society of his peers; from many houses villages were made, from villages—cities, and in these last public buildings [*publichnye zdaniia*] were erected.

Palladio thus imagined that homes precede the social contract itself and set the shape for the public world to follow. First "private man"[27] builds the original shelter he needs, based on his own independent desires and requirements. Later, society forms as the union of such structures, eventually being crowned by public buildings erected in cities. On the basis of this logic, Palladio concluded that homes were a kind of basic model, or norm, that should be a foundational part of every man's education: "No part of architecture is so necessary for a man [*chelovek*] to know, nor indeed so frequently used by him, as the building of private houses."[28]

Lvov's reconstruction of his own home—Cherenchitsy—may serve as a good example of this. Like Priamukhino's mansion, the house at Cherenchitsy entered the 1780s as a rustic wooden structure. Lvov decided to raze it, erecting in its place a series of stone structures with regular geometrical shapes. He built a new master's house in the shape of a cube and capped with a cupola. He added a food cellar whose entrance was a pyramid made of un-

---

A History of Russian Architecture (Cambridge: Cambridge University Press, 1993), 388–89; E. G. Nikulina, "Razvitie poniatiia o gorodskoi usad'be," *Russkaia Usad'ba* 3 (19) (1997): 16. For L'vov's translation of Palladio's *Four Books,* see *Chetyre knigi palladievoi arkhitektury, v koikh po kratkom opisanii piati Ordenov, govoritsia o tom chto znat' dolzhno pri stroenii chastnykh domov, dorog, mostov, ploshchadei, ristalishch, i khramov,* ed. and trans. N. L'vov (St. Petersburg: I. K. Shnor, 1798). For the best recent English translation, see Andrea Palladio, *The Four Books on Architecture,* trans. Robert Tavenor and Richard Schofield (Cambridge, Mass.: MIT Press, 1997).

[27] More literally "private person" in Russian, but it seems hard to believe that L'vov imagined women as the founders of homes, given the paternalism that informs his work as a whole.

[28] Palladio, *Chetyre knigi,* 4.

cut boulders, and he built a circular family chapel, double-domed so that extra light could be let in through a porous and Pantheon-like outer cupola. The church was circled by a columned pavilion; underneath was a mausoleum. To this day shafts of light descend through specially cut portals to meet in the middle of this final resting place for Lvov and his family. Above, in the chapel, Lvov conducted elaborate family ceremonies, carefully staged and lit. One such (performed in a church Lvov built on his uncle's nearby estate) consisted of a choir of family members, gathered in the dead of night but surrounded by decorated lamps, burning incense, and a "palm forest," which Lvov contrived to grow inside. Describing such domestic celebrations in his letters, Lvov asked his friends, "Tell me, is this an everyday phenomenon? An indifferent spectacle?" No, he answered: anyone who looked in on the family life he made must involuntarily admit, "How blessed are they!"[29]

What inspired Lvov's passion for estates? Most commentators have seen his commitment to domestic life as a sentimental rejection of the court in favor of "life in the bosom of nature." According to this line of interpretation, the country house represented a withdrawal from the world inward into intimacy, finding there a "refuge from the hurly-burly of public life."[30] Yet the elaborate care with which Lvov arranged his domestic "spectacles" suggests that they played a more public function than a "refuge" would imply. Clearly, Lvov took some pride from the fact that his home life was not an "everyday phenomenon" but rather a sign of his family's inventiveness and unusual happiness. For this reason, Lvov's homes are best interpreted as scripts for that theater of imperial distinction, which was then forming on provincial noble estates. The elaborate sets and "spectacles" Lvov designed for provincial life testify to his passion to participate in this new forum. More important, Lvov's critical writings show him attempting to address the thorniest question surrounding noble liberty: should it become a creator of public values, or merely their reflection?

By the 1790s this question had become one of the most sharply contested and culturally productive issues in elite life. Though the manifesto of 1762

[29] For descriptions of Cherenchitsy, see Budylina, Braitseva, and Kharlamova, *Arkhitektor N. A. L'vov*, 14–17, and Hughes, "N. A. L'vov," 294–95. L'vov praises his handiwork in a 1791 letter to P. L. Vel'iaminov and a 1797 epistle to A. M. Bakunin. See L'vov, *Izbrannye sochineniia*, 339–40, 71.

[30] See Budylina, Braitseva, and Kharlamova, *Arkhitektor N. A. L'vov*, 16; Hughes, "N. A. L'vov," 295; and Roosevelt, *Russian Country Estate*, 294–98. Likewise, both Gukovskii and Brown read L'vov's literary efforts as part of a late eighteenth-century turn inward, away from public life and reason and toward emotion: Gukovskii, *Russkaia literatura*, 266–67; Brown, *18th Century Russian Literature*, 425.

laid out a series of broad norms for noble liberty—that it should be disciplined, cultured, and informed by a continuing passion for service—these
guidelines were hardly exhaustive or definitive. Nor did they specify exactly
how the nobility's private activities should inform its civic life as servitors and
citizens of the empire. Yet noble liberty produced the potential for different
kinds of roles in society: to live *en bourgeois* in St. Petersburg was not the same
thing as to be a Russian traveler in Paris, a mason in a Moscow lodge, or a
family man in the provinces.[31] At the same time, the optimistic assumptions
that provided the conceptual core of Catherinean political discourse began
to fracture as doubts began to emerge about reason's essential unity and sta-
bility in the late eighteenth century. In the wake of the twin assaults of the
French Revolution and philosophical skepticism, few were as certain by 1790
that private reasoning would line up naturally with the cultural and political
priorities set by rulers on their thrones. Perhaps the most famous expression
of this fear in the Russian context was Catherine the Great's gradual withdrawal of support from institutions of civic life of which she had been so
proud. In the wake of the proclamation of the French Republic in 1792,
Catherine clamped down on literature and dampened the fires of unofficial
society. (Just a few months before her death, censorship brought Lvov's own
journal, *The Muse*, to a hasty end.)[32]

All these developments made the question of the proper relationship between private and public life in Russia all the more pressing and all the more
politically loaded. The governing Catherinean norm was one in which priorities were set by Russia's enlightened government. According to this vision,
Russia's patriotic citizens should align the whole of their lives—at court,

---

[31] See Iurii Lotman's famous typology of social roles in "The Poetics of Everyday Behavior in
18th Century Russian Culture," in *The Semiotics of Russian Cultural History*, ed. and trans. Alexander Nakhimovsky and Alice Stone Nakhimovsky (Ithaca: Cornell University Press, 1985), 67–
94. As Lotman notes throughout his oeuvre, the creation of new social roles for the nobility—as
well as new "human types" (*chelovecheskie tipy*) for Russian culture—was one of the most productive and provocative cultural trends of the late eighteenth century. See, for example, Iu. M.
Lotman, "Poeziia 1790–1810–x godov," in *Poety 1790–1810–x godov*, comp. Iu. M. Lotman, prepared by M. G. Al'tshuller (Leningrad: "Sovetskii pisatel'," 1971), 8–11; as well as G. P. Makogonenko, "Anakreontika Derzhavina i ee mesto v poezii nachala XIX v," in *Anakreonticheskie
pesni*, by G. R. Derzhavin, prepared by G. P. Makogonenko, G. N. Ionin, and E. N. Petrova
(Moscow: Nauka, 1987), 263–65.

[32] On Catherine's growing suspicion of civil society—about which she had long been ambivalent—see Isabel de Madariaga, *Russia in the Age of Catherine the Great* (London: Phoenix
Press, 1990), 341–48; Douglas Smith, *Working the Rough Stone: Freemasonry and Society in Eighteenth-Century Russia* (DeKalb: Northern Illinois University Press, 1999), 173–75; on the fate of
The Muse, see Dementev, Zapadov, and Cherepakhov, *Russkaia pechat'*, 94.

in society, and at home—to priorities established by the "Minerva on the throne."[33] By the 1790s, however, other ways of imagining the relationship between public and private life existed as well. For example, Russia's freemasons claimed the right to conduct ornate rites of self-improvement, to which they denied outsiders access. They insisted that these rites, based on rules of their own making, made them better sons, subjects, and citizens. As Douglas Smith has shown, however, neither Catherine nor the noble elite tolerated this murky fraternity, which made everyone aware of its intimate activities but kept all but a select few men at arm's length from them. The masonic system, in which a stridently private set of rituals prepared men for social activity, was subsequently suppressed by official bans and unofficial opprobrium.[34]

Much more successful—although in some ways more duplicitous—were writer Nikolai Karamzin's attempts to create an acceptable relationship between personal life and public identity. A one-time protégé of the masons, Karamzin was a man who cultivated an endless number of civilized public personae for himself. Over the course of his life, he appeared before his readers under a variety of guises: the earnest Russian traveler, the salon dandy, the soberly methodical historian. Yet as Iurii Lotman has shown, Karamzin saw all these roles as theatrical "self-creations." They were opposed, in the writer's mind, to an inner, intimate, authentic self that Karamzin carefully cultivated but also kept so hidden from others that they did not even know of its existence.[35]

The 1780s and 1790s, then, were a time when new kinds of norms were being created, all of which sought to model the relationship between private reason and the broader development of imperial social discourse. Lvov's efforts to establish a new enlightened idiom for Russian noble life on the estate are best understood as a variation on this theme. Specifically, Lvov's bottom-up, Palladian vision held that home life's proper role was to generate useful truths and norms that could guide Russia's future social and political development. By embracing home life, Lvov believed, he and his friends could transform themselves into the virtuous paternal leaders of this process and

[33] Wortman, *Scenarios of Power*, 1:110–47.

[34] See Douglas Smith, "Freemasonry and the Public in Eighteenth-Century Russia," in *Imperial Russia: New Histories for the Empire*, ed. Jane Burbank and David L. Ransel (Bloomington : Indiana University Press, 1998), 292–94; and Smith, *Rough Stone*, 160–75, 178–79.

[35] Iu. M. Lotman, *Sotvorenie Karamzina* (Moscow: Kniga, 1987), 16–29, 316–17. See also Iu. M. Lotman and B. A. Uspenskii, "'Pis'ma russkogo puteshestvennika' Karamzina i ikh mesto v razvitii russkoi kul'tury," in *Pis'ma russkogo puteshestvennika*, prepared by Iu. M. Lotman, N. A. Marchenko, and B. A. Uspenskii (Leningrad: Nauka, 1987), 525–606.

agents of a truly Russian Enlightenment. Lvov's literary works of the 1790s —along with the visions of home life contained in poetry by his friends—allow us to explore the assumptions underlying these ambitions in more detail.

❀❧❀

If Palladio directed Lvov to see the home as the fundamental unit from which civilization was built, Lvov found a model for the social meaning of private life more generally in poetry attributed to the ancient Greek poet Anacreon of Theos (born ca. 570 BCE). In 1794, Lvov published a translation of Anacreon's works, using his introduction to defend the man's reputation and to underscore why he felt Anacreon's legacy was valuable. Before Lvov's book, Anacreon was widely derided in eighteenth-century Russian culture as a hedonistic poet of wine, women, and song, utterly lacking in civic virtues.[36] Not so, Lvov declares in his introduction. For Anacreon's supposed hedonism is actually a form of private experimentation, allowing the poet to offer his public only the most tested of fruits. Ancient authors such as Anacreon should serve as models, Lvov believed, because they "communicated to the world only those things, of which they themselves had been convinced by experience." Unlike the "false brilliance of French lyricists"—whose work was rooted in the artifice of salon talk—Anacreon's poems provided tested principles. "I can often use his verses as guides, to my own benefit," Lvov writes, "rather than merely showing off, by repeating them in conversation."[37] Summarizing his vision of the proper relationship between private and public life into a neat, Rousseauian formula, Lvov concluded: "It is desirable that the opinions published in a book should always be the real rules of the author's private life."[38]

Lvov thus presented Anacreon's poetry as a model for a publicly useful but intimate form of reason, one that was more productive than the abstract

---

[36] On the controversy surrounding Anacreon in Russia, see G. N. Ionin, "Tvorcheskaia istoriia sbornika 'Anakreonticheskie pesni,'" in Derzhavin, *Anakreonticheskie pesni*, 300–303.

[37] From L'vov's "Zhizn' Anakreona Tiiskogo," in L'vov, *Izbrannye sochineniia*, 108.

[38] For L'vov's analysis of Anacreon, see L'vov, *Izbrannye sochineniia*, 107–10. Lappo-Danilevskii describes these concerns as programmatic in his editorial introduction, "O literaturnom nasledii," 21. Though Lvov does not credit Rousseau's influence here—and perhaps could not, given the political climate of the time—his formula echoes Rousseau's plea in his "First Discourse": "How delightful it would be for those who live among us if our external appearance were always a true mirror of our hearts, if good manners were also virtue, if the maxims we spout were truly the rules of our conduct." See Jean-Jacques Rousseau, "The First Discourse: 'Discourse on the Sciences and Arts,'" in *The Social Contract and the First and Second Discourses*, ed. Susan Dunn (New Haven: Yale University Press, 2002), 49.

productions of the salon because it was rooted in actual experience. When combined with Palladio's vision of the country house as the fundamental atom of society this Anacreontic logic framed the domestic existence of "private men" as the root of a real enlightenment. Not dependent on salons—or their feminine mistresses or artful heroes, such as the notoriously elegant Karamzin—Lvov and his friends hoped to work out their own norms in the countryside. They expected that this experience would transform them into paternal stewards of Russian society, emerging from their private experiences to create beneficial norms and truths for society. Their distinction would be the kind achieved by self-legislation: by the generation of their own domestic scenarios rather than through the performance of plays written by others.

As Lvov's contemptuous reference to French artifice and the feminized realm of salon talk make plain, a certain anxiety about the direction of Europe's enlightenment and their own status within it as men laced these ambitions. On the one hand, these were self-consciously "enlightened" noblemen, committed to using reason to advance the cause of civilization and to win distinction for themselves in the process. On the other hand, they were quite aware that Europe's version of enlightenment seemed to be overturning the social, political, and even philosophical order. The French Revolution did not cause these anxieties—many critiques of abstract reason, including Jean-Jacques Rousseau's and Immanuel Kant's, predate it—but of course France in the 1790s became a symbol for them.[39] As a result, the question of how to harness reason so that it would reform rather than destroy the existing social order became a central concern for liberal and conservative opinion alike.

Perhaps the most popular solution to this dilemma—one widely embraced as a foundation of the post-revolutionary order—was to imagine the "natural" norms of family life as a logical limit to critical reason's scope.[40] Such

---

[39] On the critique of reason before the revolution, see Frederick Beiser's superb work *The Fate of Reason: German Philosophy from Kant to Fichte* (Cambridge, Mass.: Harvard University Press, 1987).

[40] On the domestic compromise, see Michelle Perrot, "The Family Triumphant," in *From the Fires of Revolution to the Great War,* ed. Michelle Perrot, vol. 4 of *A History of Private Life,* ed. Philippe Ariès and Georges Duby, trans. Arthur Goldhammer (Cambridge, Mass.: Belknap Press, 1990), 100–111; Margaret H. Darrow, "French Noblewomen and the New Domesticity, 1750–1850," *Feminist Studies* 5, no. 1 (1979): 41–65; Leonore Davidoff and Catherine Hall, *Family Fortunes: Men and Women of the English Middle Class, 1780–1850* (Chicago: University of Chicago Press, 1987), 18–19, 74–75. On the attempts by *Aufklärer* such as Kant and Fichte to reassert the rationality of the domestic order—while excluding critical reason from it—see Hull, *Sexuality,* and Anthony J. La Vopa, *Fichte: The Self and the Calling of Philosophy, 1762–1799* (Cambridge: Cam-

an approach had advantages, from the point of view of many vested interests. At a time when patriarchal authority seemed too arbitrary to be suffered any longer, it offered a rationale for continuing male leadership in society and the maintenance of strictly defined gender roles. (By the same token, its paternal logic reinforced the authority of the old over the young.)[41] The cult of family values also rationalized the exclusion of women from public institutions by imagining them as a domestic sex.[42] If mid-eighteenth-century culture often presented itself as the product of private salons hosted by refined women, many paternal apologists for reason now emphasized the importance of intellectual spaces outside the home—clubs, journalism, universities—where men could think for and by themselves.[43]

The domestic vision proposed by Lvov deserves to be understood in this context for several reasons. First, it is clear that he and his friends saw themselves as participating in this pan-European controversy and, indeed, hoped to distinguish themselves by resolving it. Expressing masculine antipathy to salons, they busied themselves imagining another forum for enlightenment. Unlike some ideologues of civil society in the West, however, Lvov and his friends chose not to build their domestic idyll as a natural counterweight to the world of critical reason.

Instead, they chose to imagine the home itself as reason's proper forum. Such an approach offered several advantages for them. On the one hand, reasoning through the home seemed to them to resolve many of the crises faced by Europe's Enlightenment at the end of the eighteenth century. To those

---

bridge University Press, 2001), 348–67. Hull and La Vopa disagree about the source of this paternalism (the mores of the time or the Enlightenment itself), reflecting the broader disagreement about the "masculinist" nature of eighteenth-century public reason. See Margaret C. Jacob, "The Mental Landscape of the Public Sphere: A European Perspective," *Eighteenth Century Studies* 28, no. 1 (Autumn 1994): 98; Dena Goodman, "Public Sphere and Private Life: Toward a Synthesis of Current Historiographical Approaches to the Old Regime," *History and Theory* 31, no. 1 (1992): 15–20.

[41] On domesticity as a response to the political and philosophical anxieties of the late eighteenth century, see Lynn Hunt, "The Unstable Boundaries of the French Revolution," in Perrot, *From the Fires of Revolution*, 13–45; Hunt, *The Family Romance of the French Revolution* (Berkeley: University of California Press, 1992).

[42] On the ways in which the Enlightenment and paternalism intertwined in eighteenth-century Europe both before and after the revolution, see Isabel V. Hull, *Sexuality, State, and Civil Society in Germany 1700–1815* (Ithaca: Cornell University Press, 1996).

[43] On the controversies surrounding the salons—and their relationship to desires for masculine self-legislation in the late eighteenth century—see Dena Goodman, *The Republic of Letters: A Cultural History of the French Enlightenment* (Ithaca: Cornell University Press, 1994), 90–136, 233–80.

who argued that reason was too untested, Lvov and his friends presented the home as a microcosm that could illustrate the results of reform in advance. To those who argued that critical thinking was too abstract, they could reply that home life stabilized reason by bringing the whole of human rationality (including its imaginative and even erotic components) into play. Frederick Beiser has shown that early German Romanticism sought to broaden reason beyond disembodied calculation to create the sort of thinking that could save the Enlightenment from itself.[44] Without recourse to grand philosophical systems, working through the home offered Lvov and his friends a chance to engage in a similar project.

Finally, imagining home life as a forum for reason suited the social and political context in which these noblemen lived. Many of Russia's civic institutions were still relatively embryonic in the late 1790s. Noble home life on the estate, meanwhile, offered tremendous resources and was being valorized by imperial political discourse at that very time. From this point of view, Lvov and his friends could hope that their enlightened manor houses could provide a definitive new norm for Russian private life while at the same time offering a solution to the crisis of reason affecting Europe at large. To see evidence of these ideals in action, one need only examine the domestic projects produced by Aleksandr in the late 1790s, as under Lvov's mentorship he sought to reimagine himself as an enlightened family man.

❀⁓❀

At the end of his first decade at Priamukhino, Aleksandr Bakunin was at once the least and most provincial man within his circle of friends. Unlike Lvov and Derzhavin, Aleksandr had not been born in the countryside. Yet his family's circumstances withdrew him much earlier from service. Lvov recruited Aleksandr to come to Emperor Paul I's court in Gatchina in 1797, where Lvov was building a Gothic-style residence (the Priorat) for the Order of the Knights of Malta. But the experiment ended after a few months, at Liubov Petrovna's insistence. Aleksandr returned to Priamukhino to stay.[45] He oversaw Priamukhino's expansion and reconstruction along Palladian lines and

---

[44] See Frederick C. Beiser, *The Romantic Imperative: The Concept of Early German Romanticism* (Cambridge, Mass.: Harvard University Press, 2003), esp. 59–63, 88–90.

[45] Aleksandr served in Gatchina from January 12, 1797, until November 14 of that same year (see the record of his service prepared for the Tver nobility, IRLI f. 16, op. 6, no. 13, l. 3). On L'vov's work on the Priorat, see Budylina, Braitseva, and Kharlamova, *Arkhitektor N. A. L'vov,* 159–61.

added a botanical garden.[46] In addition, he created his first present for Lvov, a cycle of six poems in the style of Anacreon.

Aleksandr's poems tell the story of his repatriation and moral rebirth in the countryside; it also draws a picture of the effect he hoped his life there would have.[47] The collection opens with a dedication, "To My Friend Nikolai Aleksandrovich," which also begins the tale of Aleksandr's rebirth.

> Near a stream, a wasteland, in sorrow
> Lay fruitless as wastelands do;
> Flowers did not shade him
> And weeds grew across him,
> Until a stream, with living current
> Turned him over, to the good,
> And brought forth a first blossom.
> As it has grown in rural freedom,
> So this flower is now brought to you:
> Take it—you are nature's friend:
> And this flower was by nature born.[48]

The key to understanding the biographical subtext of this poem is to work back from its final image, which presents the notebook itself as the first fruit of a wasteland revived and made productive by the life-giving waters of a stream. Aleksandr, of course, is the notebook's author; he himself, then, is the wasteland suddenly brought into production by the stream. Obvious here by context, this image of his youthful self as a wasteland evidently pleased Aleksandr, who returned to it in poetry written nearly two decades later.[49]

Who or what is this "stream" that brings idle Aleksandr to life and initiates his labors? The notebook's third poem, titled "The Stream," answers this question. "The Stream" depicts a rural estate animated and invigorated by life-giving waters. At one point, the poem explains, this landscape was mired in a deadly, fetid bog. Treacherous pathways—carved by unnamed vil-

---

[46] Aleksandr's physical transformation of Priamukhino during these years is best described in Sysoev, *Bakuniny*, 65–95.

[47] For the notebook itself, see IRLI f. 16, op. 2, no. 1. In what follows, I give references to recent, published versions of these texts, in Kochetkova, *Russkaia literatura*, 532–36; and Lappo-Danilevskii, "Iz literaturnogo naslediia."

[48] See Kochetkova, *Russkaia literatura*, 532.

[49] See Oleinikov, "Aleksandr Bakunin i ego poema 'Osuga,'" 59, where Bakunin writes of his youth: "*Ne ia li byl pustyr' bezvodnyi . . .*" ("Was I myself not a waterless wasteland?").

lains—led the unwary to their destruction. Now, however, a new channel has dissolved the bog, draining its fetid pools and opening up a verdant lawn, on which nightingales now sing and villagers dance. Outshining all are two beautiful, ecstatic serf girls. As they dance, they sing a song of thanks to the stream and to the mistress of the estate:

> Flow, stream, o nature's beauty,
> Show us the path to happiness!
> Increase your clear waters
> To our mistress's pleasure!

Not leaving the interpretation of this biographical allegory to his readers' discretion, Aleksandr at this point introduces a series of footnotes into the text. The estate, the notes explain, is Lvov's Cherenchitsy. At one time, it had indeed been mired by a bog. But then Lvov built a canal to drain it. On one level, the stream is thus Lvov himself, or rather his practical reason, intervening to engineer a solution to the countryside's problems. Thanks to Lvov's drainage system, the footnote claims, real birds sing and real flowers bloom at Cherenchitsy. The footnotes also identify the dancing serf girls as Liza and Dasha, the real-life servants of Lvov's wife Maria Alekseevna.

Here, however, Aleksandr introduces a wrinkle. Just when we think we understand who the stream is and what it has done, the poet adds:

> No, that's not a stream, that's mighty *Lel'*,
> Who has hidden his image in these waters,
> And life's genius, flowing in them
> Has made this dead valley come to life.

It is not abstract reason but rather *Lel'*—the Slavic Eros, the life-producing genius of love—that has caused all this to happen.[50] On the autobiographical level, this means that it is Lvov's love for his wife—Maria Alekseevna—that inspired his endeavors. On the philosophical level, this means that the "genius" at work in the nobleman's country life is not pale calculation but rather an embodied, emotional force, working out of passion as well as pru-

---

[50] L'vov and his friends systematically substituted a putatively Russian folk mythology for ancient Greek figures. Thus the key figure Cupid-Eros—the sexual figure that drew man's attention to his helpmate—was called by a Slavic name, *Lel'*. See Ionin, "Tvorcheskaia istoriia," 358–72.

dence. The Slavicization of Eros as *Lel'* here serves to underscore that Lvov acts not as a foreign agent but rather as a rational Russian man attracted to the countryside by the whole of his being.

Water was routinely used by Lvov and also by his good friend the poet Gavrila Derzhavin as a symbol of holistic reason, encompassing not only calculation but also intuition and inspiration. Lvov insisted on life-giving waterworks in all of his landscape designs; as his biographer Glumov writes, water was a symbol for Lvov of the "eternal movement of thought."[51] Water and its symbolic status as enlightenment likewise links the various parts of Derzhavin's oeuvre together. It defines and connects the broad imperial spaces that were this proudly provincial man's home; and more generally speaking it stands, in Derzhavin's work, as a symbol of the connection between the physical and metaphysical worlds—the tangible and the true.[52]

How does the reason embodied in the stream work, within Aleksandr's notebook? Holistically, as a broadened notion of reason should. First, it acts by direct, physical intervention: the wise draining of the bog. Yet it also works in less mechanical ways—by reflection and inspiration. The clear waters of the stream provide a mirror in which the two serf girls admire themselves (*liubuiusia soboi*—literally, "love themselves"). Awakened, they begin to dance and urge Lvov on to still greater endeavors for his mistress. This dance, in turn, summons another actor onto the stage: Aleksandr Bakunin himself, drawn in by the happy spectacle. In the cycle's next poem, "The Harvest," Aleksandr imagines taking the lovely Dasha by the hand and claiming her as his partner in life. The stream, then, not only has beautified the country and transformed—in Pygmalion style—its female denizens, but has also inspired another like-minded man to begin building his own rural idyll.

Here again there was a biographical subtext: the two real-life serf girls "Lizynka and Dashinka" were the subjects of an elaborate, eroticized cult among Lvov and his friends. Derzhavin celebrated these "Russian girls" and their dances in verse; the painter Vladimir Borovikovsky painted them dressed as society maidens, in jewelry and fashionable, raised-waist dresses.[53] Signing his letters to Lvov, Aleksandr Bakunin rakishly enjoined Lvov to kiss Dasha on his behalf.[54] "The Harvest" tells the story of the final consumma-

[51] Glumov, *N. A. L'vov*, 183.

[52] Alexandre Levitsky, "La symbolique de l'eau chez Derjavine," in *Derjavine: Un poète russe dans l'Europe des Lumières*, ed. Anita Davidenkoff (Paris: Institut d'études slaves, 1994), 65–66.

[53] See G. R. Derzhavin, *Anakreonticheskie pesni*, 55; Liudmila Markina, *Vladimir Borovikovskii* (Moscow: Belyi gorod, 2001), 16–17.

[54] See Bakunin's letter to L'vov of 1 March 1792, IRLI f. 16, op. 4, no. 37/2, l. 4.

tion of this desire, imagined as the final act of Aleksandr's moral awakening in the countryside.[55]

The poem begins with the poet's lyrical invitation to Dasha:

> Bind up your flowing braids,
> Put on a light dress,
> Take a sickle, give me a scythe
> And we'll meet the day in the fields.

Never tiring because they never work to excess, providing for themselves and their neighbors by prudent labor, relaxing from time to time on a bed of moss under a nearby tree, this (noble) man and his (peasant) woman secure for themselves the good life:

> We know how to work and love,
> How could we not be happy?

The poet's vision then broadens to show an entire countryside of such happy households:

> Do you hear, Dasha, into sonorous songs
> The villagers are pouring their souls
> Look — how prosperously
> They harvest and dance and sing
>
> . . . .
>
> See how they work
> Among their families
> How they forget their exhaustion
> When they look at their children.

By the ripple effects of rational, modest labors, the countryside is converted into paradise — such a paradise, Aleksandr remarks in closing, that if Death

---

[55] The text of "The Harvest" (*Zhatva*) edited by Lappo-Danilevskii and published in Kochetkova, *Russkaia literatura*, 534–36, is a later variant, completed after 1799. The most favored of Bakunin's poems (see below) "The Harvest" went through several versions. The version in the L'vov notebook, analyzed here, was published by B. I. Koplan in the late 1920s. See B. I. Koplan, "Iz literaturnykh izyskanii kontsa XVIII–nachala XIX v. (A. M. Bakunin i V. V. Kapnist)," *Materialy Obshchestva Izucheniia Tverskogo Kraia* 6 (1928): 15–16. In the text of the poem, the serf girl to whom the invitation is directed is specifically identified as Dasha.

himself were to come, he would leave these happy couples alone, "saying: 'They are still too young!'"

Though Aleksandr's notebook to Lvov contains three other poems—two are short, epigrammatic meditations on the golden mean and one is a wedding song for Lvov's uncle Fedor—"The Harvest" is the collection's thematic climax. In "To My Friend Nikolai Aleksandrovich," we were introduced to Aleksandr as an undeveloped, barren field—a rather ironic nickname for a man educated at the University of Padua. But the point is that his abilities were going to waste. This disguise also allows Aleksandr to write himself back into the Russian landscape by imagining his rebirth out of it. Awakened (as if for the first time) by Lvov's inspiration, this new man is drawn in by the model of Cherenchitsy and its beautiful denizen Dasha. Some of this idyll's appeal is narrowly rational—it is thriving, productive, and happy. Yet much of it is also erotic. Aleksandr's union with Dasha—a Marianne-like representative of village and nation but also a fetish—plays a crucial role in re-uniting Aleksandr's alienated ego with the countryside. A sort of erotic social exchange is imagined: even as she binds up her hair for him, he accepts a scythe from her, becoming her partner even as he remains her master.

As it completes the story of Aleksandr's repatriation into rural life, this evocative image accomplishes something else as well. It provides a vision of a happy, paternal social order—led by masculine reason but inspired by feminine beauty—that the author clearly hopes others will adopt as a guiding norm for their own private lives. In this sense, Aleksandr's notebook for Lvov sounds a proudly ideological note. Having argued that reason could be best domesticated on the estate—where its energies could be inspired and contained by love—Aleksandr is only too happy to present the "first fruits" of his own experience as a model for others to emulate. This civic ambition indeed lies at the heart of the distinction Aleksandr wanted to win for himself as an aspiring family man.

⊗﷯⊗

Aleksandr's poetry was widely respected by his friends but did not reach a wider public. This is not to say that it was written solely for a restricted, intimate audience. No less an authority than the poet Derzhavin recommended "The Harvest" to students of literature as a model idyll.[56] Under the right cir-

---

[56] See V. I. Panaev, "Vospominaniia o Derzhavine," in *Bratchina*, pt. 1 (St. Petersburg, 1859), 112–15.

cumstances—had Lvov, for example, not suffered a series of reversals in the late 1790s and early 1800s before his death in 1803—Aleksandr's lyrics might have seen print.[57] More important, the model of publicity under which these noblemen labored did not assume that literature was the primary or even best method of spreading their version of enlightenment. Even the greatest literary talent in the group—Derzhavin—did not make literature his central concern until after his final fall from official favor in the early 1800s. (At that point, he published his own *Anacreontic Songs*, though because of his age and reputation they were received less as innovations than as works of an old master.)[58] Instead, in keeping with their notion of acting through example and inspiration, Lvov, Aleksandr, and their friends focused on living their enlightenment, refining and perfecting their domestic vision while promoting it through more traditional—if not necessarily less powerful—forums than Russia's developing print culture.[59]

One such channel led directly to the court of the new emperor, Aleksandr I (r. 1801–1825). Though Lvov was by now often ill, Derzhavin became minister of justice under the new emperor. Perhaps more important for Aleksandr Bakunin, another friend and distant relative—Aleksei Nikolaevich Olenin—became a highly placed official in the Ministry of Internal Affairs.[60] There Olenin was involved in discussions over whether and how to reform the institution at the heart of estate life: serfdom.

In 1802, Aleksandr I and his advisers began to quietly solicit opinions about the "peasant question," looking for models for reforming serfdom, up to and including ideas for its eventual repeal. By March 1803, these discussions resulted in the so-called Statute on Free Cultivators, allowing landlords

---

[57] In the late 1790s, L'vov's great patron Prince Bezborodko died, his scheme to mine coal in Tver province failed, and he suffered a series of illnesses.

[58] Appointed minister of justice in 1802 by Emperor Aleksandr I, Derzhavin lost a political battle at court and retired in 1803. He dedicated himself to theater (a notorious failure) and to promoting his Anacreontic works (with somewhat more success). On Derzhavin's honored but somewhat awkward place in the literary world, see Gukovskii, *Russkaia literatura*, 342–43; and Makogonenko, "Anakreontika Derzhavina," 251–53.

[59] I take the phrase "living the Enlightenment" from Margaret C. Jacob, *Living the Enlightenment: Freemasonry and Politics in Eighteenth-Century Europe* (New York: Oxford University Press, 1991).

[60] Olenin was related to Bakunin by marriage. His wife, Elizaveta Markovna, née Poltoratskaia, was the sister of Tatiana Bakunina's husband, A. M. Poltoratskii. The Olenins' home just outside St. Petersburg—Priiutino—was another famous example of enlightened domesticity, very much in the spirit of Aleksandr's idyll, though different by virtue of being a suburban *dacha* rather than an estate. On Olenin and Priiutino, see L. V. Timofeev, *V krugu druzei i muz: Dom A. N. Olenina* (Leningrad: Lenizdat, 1983), 12–64; Stephen Lovell, *Summerfolk: A History of the Dacha, 1710–2000* (Ithaca: Cornell University Press, 2003), 22–23.

to emancipate their serfs and sell them land according to mutually negotiated contracts.[61] Aleksandr Bakunin's friendship with Olenin made him aware of these discussions and also opened up a channel for him to participate in them. Seizing upon this opportunity, Aleksandr prepared a series of prose tracts on estate life, exploring the character of serfdom and imagining how it might be changed.

First, he wrote a twenty-one-point model social contract for a serf village, titled an *Agreement between Landlord and Peasant.* Aleksandr completed this work in late 1802 and immediately sent it to Olenin, intending him to forward it to a third, unnamed but evidently highly placed official. Then he created a series of philosophical *Letters on Gardening to My Friend N. A. L.* in 1803, codifying the philosophical and political beliefs he had acquired in his decade in the countryside.[62] Both documents had their predecessors and analogues within Russian culture. Landlords had long prepared model codes—"instructions"—for the running of their estates, some of which they attempted to publish.[63] Gardening and philosophical treatises on it were also popular

---

[61] "Ukaz ob otpuske pomeshchikami svoikh krestian na voliu po zakliuchenii uslovii, na oboiudnom soglasii osnovannykh," in *Rossiiskoe zakonodatel'stvo X–XX vv.,* vol. 6, *Zakonodatel'stvo pervoi poloviny XIX veka,* ed. O. I. Chistiakov (Moscow: Iuridicheskaia literatura, 1988), 32–34.

[62] The *Agreements between Landlord and Peasant* exists in a manuscript copy in Olenin's archives: RNB f. 582, d. 506. Most of it has been published, albeit broken into two pieces, by L. G. Agamalian: Bakunin's historical preface to his social contract is Agamalian, "Istoriia Russii," while the main body of the contract is Agamalian, "A. M. Bakunin i ego prockt." Agamalian speculates—quite plausibly—that Aleksandr intended his *Agreement* to serve as a model for the discussions leading to the promulgation of the 1803 statute. Olenin's archive includes a draft letter of introduction, addressing Aleksandr's project to an unnamed but evidently quite highly placed official. Even so, the exact circumstances surrounding the *Agreement*'s composition—as well as the nature of its intended audience—remain unclear. See Larisa Georgievna Agamalian, "Prosvetitel'skie idei v tvorchestve A. M. Bakunina v kontekste russkoi kul'tury vtoroi poloviny XVIII–pervoi poloviny XIX veka" (avtoreferat dissertatsii, Sankt-Peterburgskaia gosudarstvennaia Akademiia kul'tury, 1998), 16–17; and also Olenin's letter, from the opening pages of the *Agreement,* RNB f. 542, d. 76, ll. 1–2). The *Letters on Gardening* exist in drafts dedicated to N. A. L'vov (IRLI f. 16, op. 2, no. 6) and Olenin (RNB f. 542, d. 168). See L. G. Agamalian, "Pis'ma A. M. Bakunina k N. A. L'vovu," *Ezhegodnik Rukopisnogo otdela Pushkinskogo Doma na 1997* (1997): 43–95.

[63] On the instructions, ranging from simple orders to bailiffs to complex domestic legislations, see Michael Confino, *Domaines et seigneurs en Russie vers la fin du XVIII siècle: Étude de structures agraires et mentalités économiques* (Paris: Institut d'études slaves de l'Université de Paris, 1963); E. B. Smilianskaia, *Dvorianskoe gnezdo serediny XVIII veka: Timofei Tekut'ev i ego "Instruktsiia o domashnikh poriadkakh"* (Moscow: Nauka, 1998). In the breadth and ideological nature of its vision, Bakunin's project is closest to the instructions of "enlightened seigneurs" described by Edgar Melton in "Enlightened Seigniorialism and Its Dilemmas in Serf Russia, 1750–1830," *Journal of Modern History* 62 (December 1990): 675–708. Bakunin's seems distinguished from these latter mainly by its patriotic and domestic frames. On the one hand, it is situated in a na-

occupations for the late-eighteenth-century nobility.[64] What distinguished Aleksandr's projects, however, was the breadth of historical, social, and ideological vision he brought to these plans. Suddenly finding himself in possession of a chance to speak directly to the throne, Aleksandr used this opportunity to argue that the government should install a new domestic order in rural Russia's peasant communities.

This argument finds systematic expression in the model social contract Aleksandr sent to St. Petersburg, his *Agreement between Landlord and Peasant*. In it, Aleksandr argued that Russia's reformers should use their power to convert Russia's peasant communes into collections of productive, autonomous, and happy homes, to be guided by paternal reason rather than patriarchal tradition. Structured properly, he hoped, a village made of such homes might invigorate and unify rural society.

The *Agreement between Landlord and Peasant* begins with a denunciation of serfdom as a historical perversion: "It is not hard to show from the acts of the Russian people, that slavery together with ignorance was brought to Russia by foreigners, grew through disasters, took root through coercion."[65] In a lengthy historical preface, Aleksandr described ancient Russia as a paternal, constitutional monarchy in which "power was given by the people to the prince, as to their father, who respected the people as his family."[66] Aleksandr believed that ancient Russians had descended from the Greeks, with their strong civic traditions. After the Mongol invasion, however, Russia's ancient civic order was lost. "The enslaved princes enslaved the people, and slavery began in Russia."[67] This dealt a wound to the body politic that foreign wars and internal troubles had never allowed to heal. On the contrary, Russia's rulers had deepened the bondage of Russia's common people (the *poseliane*, or "villagers," as Aleksandr called the serfs). The equalization of

---

tional context, with its acceptance as a model by the government being imagined as the beginning of a new and important chapter in Russian history. On the other hand, its concern with the peasant's "moral order" (Melton's phrase) extends more deeply into the home. Whereas most landlords, like most serf owners, were content to deal with patriarchs, Bakunin wanted to deal with loving fathers. On the link between serfdom and patriarchy, see Steven L. Hoch, *Serfdom and Social Control in Russia: Petrovskoe, a Village in Tambov* (Chicago: University of Chicago Press, 1986).

[64] D. S. Likhachev, *Poeziia Sadov: K Semantike Sadovo-Parkovykh Stilei (Sad Kak Tekst)* (St. Petersburg: Nauka, 1991); Iu.M. Lotman, "'Sady' Delilia v perevode Voeikova i ikh mesto v russkoi kul'ture," in *Izbrannye stat'i v trekh tomakh*, vol. 2 (Tallinn: Aleksandra, 1993), 265–81.

[65] See RNB, f. 542, d. 506, l. 2.

[66] Agamalian, "Istoriia Rossii," 168.

[67] Ibid., 171.

serfdom and slavery under Peter the Great was the "final blow to the people's liberty."[68]

Why had Russia's rulers allowed Russia to descend ever deeper into such a humiliating condition? Like many contemporaries, Aleksandr blamed war and also the rulers' own obsessions with imperial conquest. But Aleksandr also regarded slavery as a cultural evil whose effects were not easily reversed and which caused even enlightened rulers like Peter the Great to reach their wits' end. Though ending slavery, Aleksandr argued, would have brought Russia more good than the Northern War did, Emperor Peter "saw with despair that it was impossible to remove the reins from a people brutalized by having worn them for so long."[69] Thus, for Aleksandr, as for reformers from Catherine the Great to Aleksandr II, ending serfdom was as much a cultural and social problem as a political one. Serfdom, he believed, had left a legacy of ignorance, barbarity, and lassitude that was not easily undone. To underscore this fact, Aleksandr appended to the *Agreement* a vocabulary of expressions that he believed could be eliminated from Russian life if the project he was advocating were carried out. They included such notions as "begging," "fugitives," "as you wish," "infanticide," "arson," "slavery," "seize him!," "bowing to the ground," "how would I know [*znat' ne znaiu*]," and, interestingly enough, "wasteland."[70]

What were the keys to this moral regeneration from Aleksandr's domestic perspective? First, the serfs had to be granted a well-defined legal stake in society, a patrimony (*otechestvo*) with a set of rights that were hereditarily and inalienably theirs and could not be violated by the landlords.[71] Second, the peasants' new legal existence had to be arranged by reformers with the precision of a well-made clock—with attention to its internal as well as external operations—so that the civic life it created was not endangered by the degradations left over from serfdom. In keeping with his domestic vision, Aleksandr settled on the individual household, headed by peasant fathers, as the basic unit of this new rural order.

Aleksandr's intention to reconstruct rural society through the home is built

---

[68] Ibid., 173.

[69] Ibid.

[70] Ibid., 175.

[71] Of course, *otechestvo*, or *patrie*, more normally means Fatherland with a capital F, in the sense of the state. That this is not what Bakunin had in mind, however, is clear from the opening lines of the *Agreement*, where he praises Aleksandr I for having decided to "allow the nobility to give an *otechestvo* to their villagers." Agamalian, "Istoriia Rossii," 175. From this, two things follow: the end of serfdom is to be accomplished by noble, rather than imperial, fiat; and Bakunin by *otechestvo* has in mind something smaller than the fatherland, and more like a patrimony of one's own.

into the very form of the *Agreement,* which is a contract signed between two fathers: the paternal nobleman Ivan Dobrokhotov, or "Ivan Well-Wisher," and a folksy peasant father named Miron Artemiev.[72] As Steven Hoch has demonstrated, serfdom in fact depended on constant cooperation between seigneurial authority and patriarchy within peasant life.[73] But the *Agreement*'s first act was to take this principle of Russian life and make it the subject of a legal, binding contract. Meeting before the gathered community for a sacred, public vow, Dobrokhotov and Artemiev swear, on behalf of themselves and their descendants, to honor the agreement "in all points." By this last exercise of patriarchal power, then, Russia's fathers agree to put rational restrictions on their own authority.

The contract then specifies the rights of Miron and his household. Aleksandr began with property rights: "Without hereditary tenure there is no property, without property—no citizenship, and if a farmer is not a citizen, then he is a prisoner," Aleksandr argues.[74] Miron and his family were to be granted an allotment of fifteen *desiatiny* (roughly forty acres) of farmland, of which two-thirds had to be suitable for plowing. This property was to pass from Miron to his wife and then, after her, to their eldest son—without ever being subject to reduction or communal redivision. Forced corvée labor was to be eliminated in favor of hereditary rents to the landlord set at one-third of production. The contract also specified that the peasants had the right to engage in "outside enterprise," such as craftwork or industrial wage labor. But the intent of the contract was not to open a door toward the peasants' proletarianization; rather, it sought to convert former serfs into an estate of independent farmers living under carefully specified conditions.

The most basic of these conditions was that every peasant household should consist only of parents and children. Miron's sons, as they reached maturity, were enjoined to strike out on their own, receiving an allotment of land equal to that of their fathers to start their own household. (His daughters, rather than inheriting land, would have to marry into it to leave their parents' household.) At the same time, the nobleman Dobrokhotov was specifically forbidden to force marriages or break up households. Military recruitment was also taken out of his hands and placed completely under control of the peasant community. In the end, the nobility had to renounce "all

[72] Like "Ivan Well-Wisher/Ivan Dobrokhotov," Bakunin's name for the peasant partner in his contract permits decoding. Miron could be falsely derived from *mir,* making it mean "man of the commune," whereas Artemev could derive from Artemas, "gift of Artemis"—that is, son of nature.

[73] Hoch, *Serfdom and Social Control.*

[74] See "Usloviia," RNB f. 542, d. 506, ll. 17–19.

coercive rights," from the right to sell villagers to the right to take them as servants. The serf order as such was to be eliminated entirely and replaced by a society of households arranged on a single legal basis.

Like Palladio, Aleksandr clearly believed that the family home was the natural, normal foundation of all other human societies. In his agreement, he refers to his domesticated village as a world where "all private wills will agree."[75] Yet he also believed that the legacies of serfdom and Russia's traditions of arbitrary, unreasoned authority might prevent his reforms from taking root. In fact, Aleksandr wrote, one could see serfdom's harsh effects written on the faces of the least protected members of the village community: village girls.

> Eight- or nine-year-old peasant girls already work; in the winter, the girl knits, in the summer she harrows, helps with the gathering of straw, takes horses to drink, sometimes spends the night tending sheep; from the age of fourteen she begins to harvest, at sixteen or seventeen they marry her off, and she tends to cattle, and to the hut, chops wood, plows and attends to other difficult jobs, and above and beyond all this gives birth to and feeds children. It is this excessive labor which makes a girl who at fifteen seemed beautiful by age forty an ugly old woman, and this untimely old age greatly abets the population scarcity of Russia.[76]

To her parents, loathing the prospect of paying a dowry, she was a burden to be gotten rid of. For this reason, as part of the countryside's new constitution, regulations needed to be enacted to correct and contain the peasants' "hard morals" so that patriarchy would not destroy beauty in the countryside.

Aleksandr also hoped that enlightened landscaping might soften peasant morals. As a condition of the contract, villagers were required to plant fruit-bearing trees, keep bees, and drain bogs. Agricultural innovations such as the potato—an insurance against hunger, in Aleksandr's view—were also required. He also argued that peasant houses themselves must also be rebuilt. Whereas many of the present villages were dilapidated (making Aleksandr suspect that their "first architects" were Tatars and Lithuanian invaders), the new village would have widened, fire-safe streets and new sanitary building techniques (including chimneys, brick construction, etc.). With a little cultivation, Aleksandr thought, the village could cultivate the villagers: "Natural blessings will soften even the hardest morals."[77]

[75] RNB, f. 542, d. 506, ll. 43–44.
[76] RNB, f. 542, d. 506, l. 63 ob.–64.
[77] See RNB, f. 542, d. 506, l. 26.

Even these improvements, Aleksandr feared, might not work fast enough to alter the dynamics inside peasant homes. In particular, Aleksandr was afraid that Miron Artemiev, his peasant Everyman, would remain a brutal patriarch rather than become a loving and rational paterfamilias. The nobleman's last act in his contract, before finally renouncing his "coercive rights," was to try to install limits against patriarchal tyranny in the peasant household. If Artemiev attempted to force one of his daughters to marry before age sixteen, Dobrokhotov retained the right to intervene and prevent the marriage. She could also appeal at a later time to the landlord:

> If the bride announces to me that she is being married against her will, or wishes to marry another, then I, announcing this to the priest and the commune in church on Sunday, have the right to forbid the marriage (in the first case) or allow it (in the second).

In effect, then, Aleksandr reserved for his well-wishing landlord the right to act as a loving father if the girl's real father did not. As Ivan Dobrokhotov ceased to be the master of his estate, he became its paternal father, acting only in the name of "the sweet duty of defending suffering humanity." Ceasing to be a *pomeshchik*, the nobleman became the father of a community of families.[78]

In his *Letters on Gardening*, Aleksandr Bakunin finally turned to systematizing the domestication of reason he and his friends had been working on for some time. The key to progress, he argued, was not the adoption of just any learning but "clean seeds"—carefully cultivated strands that would be free of weeds and defective fruits. The problem with Russia's civilization so far—and with civilization in general—was that it tended to take its inspiration from a single, foreign source:

> Will our people be happy when it learns that Russians have their soul in their backs (Montesquieu), that Peter the Great was merely a talented carpenter (Frederick II), that neither good nor evil exists in the world (La Mettrie), that everything that feels good is good, and everything that doesn't is bad (Bentham), that a father's worst enemies are his children (Helvétius), that faith is nothing more than hocus-pocus (Voltaire), that all sovereigns are thieves (J.-J. Rousseau), that slaves have the incontrovertible right to strangle their masters, and so on . . .

[78] RNB, f. 542. d. 506, l. 28.

Couched in sarcastic and, indeed, xenophobic terms, this assault on the major names of the European Enlightenment might lead one to believe Aleksandr was a simple reactionary. But it was the slavish imitation of foreign principles, rather than the principles themselves, that was his true target. When it came to laying out the substance of his plans for "our enlightenment," Aleksandr expressed them in a six-point plan in which every suggestion was an almost textbook restatement of eighteenth-century reform. The judicial system must be "revived"; the clergy "cleansed" of superstition; property must be secured by law, with rights being everywhere protected from tyranny.[79]

In the end, Aleksandr was a proponent of reform but on Russia's own domestic terms. How could one graft "fruitful branches" onto the nation's "healthy and deep-set roots," replacing the corruptions of recent Russian history? The key to this process, Aleksandr argued in his projects, was home building. Russia's rulers, and its serf-lords, must grant the population a private existence of its own, delineating clearly the "mutual rights and responsibilities of governors and governed, of the rulers and the rules." Well-wishing noblemen like him should lead peasantry away from patriarchy, encouraging the establishment of neat, separated, nuclear households, supported by more scientific forms of agriculture. If they did this, they would delineate a space in which a new, rational generation of Russians would grow. (Likening this act to the creation story in Genesis, Aleksandr claimed that his reforms would "create man" [*sotvorit' cheloveka*]).[80] The home would both root their affections and repatriate them in Russia, and in so doing it would create the basis for a safe, self-sustaining Enlightenment, based on a full-bodied reason contained and channeled by domestic norms. Placed on this footing, the village would indeed prosper as a free world in which "all private wills will agree." The blandishments of Europe's ethereal Enlightenment would be replaced by a light emanating from the Russian countryside.

❀❧❀

In this way, Aleksandr's decade-long interest in reimagining his family's estate reached its culmination in his notebooks of the early 1800s. Having reimagined himself as a family man in his lyrics to Lvov, Aleksandr set out to create a model set of domestic norms that—he hoped—might transform the most unenlightened and unfree part of Russia, the serf community, replacing

---

[79] RNB, f. 542, d. 168, ll. 7–10 ob.
[80] Ibid., l. 10.

obligation and patriarchy with self-governance under the guidance of paternal reason. Yet it is unlikely that either his *Agreement* or his *Letters on Gardening* ever exerted much influence in Russian official circles. They exist today
only in manuscript form, with little indication of who might have read them.
Nor is it altogether clear whether Aleksandr himself ever sought to implement the village social contract he had imagined. His family later claimed that
he had indeed tried to install a "constitution" (the *Agreement,* evidently) at Priamukhino, but that the peasants had rejected it as a dangerous and unwanted
innovation. Such a version of events seems somewhat mythical and improbable, however. Nothing in the *Agreement* itself seems designed for Priamukhino in particular; and indeed, the text as written depends on a number of
new institutions and innovations not specifically provided by the 1803
statute. (For example, Aleksandr imagined that the local guarantor of his village's new social contract would be a new kind of estate court composed of
the village's male heads of household. The statute creates no such institution
and instead orders that the contracts be reviewed by the Ministry of Internal Affairs.)[81] Aleksandr clearly hoped that the government would build
some of the domestic values contained in his *Agreement* into its anticipated
peasant reforms. The 1803 statute itself, however, makes no recommendations as to what sort of contract the landlords and peasants should create between themselves, and it certainly does not hint at anything as complicated
as the privately negotiated paternal order imagined by Aleksandr's sample
social contract.

Even setting aside the question of its broader political sanction, Aleksandr
believed that he himself could never implement his plans, at least not in the
world that existed as of 1805. "Having read this," Aleksandr declares at the
end of yet another notebook on estate management, "some will consider me
crazy, others—a mere project-maker, and so on and so on." "A wiser man
would ask," he continues, "why don't you begin to execute all this?" Answering this rhetorical question, Aleksandr lists the main obstacles he perceived to the immediate realizations of his plans. First, it was harder to begin
a new order than to continue an old one. His family also had no capital for
immediate innovations, however beneficial they might be in the long run. The
peasants, accustomed to exploitation, did not believe in work; Russia's
provincial nobility—hardly more energetic—demanded that a proper manor
house be larded with servants. Finally, there was a simple fact: "I am not the

---

[81] For Aleksandr's proposed court system, see RNB, f. 16, d. 506, ll. 46–60; for the statute's
provisions, see "Ukaz ob otpuske," 33.

master." He could not bring his plans to fruition because he was not, in the end, really in charge. Though his father, Mikhail Vasilievich, had died in 1803, his mother, Liubov Petrovna, remained Priamukhino's mistress for another ten years.[82]

In the end, perhaps the most important transformation wrought by Aleksandr's plans and projects was in his own attitude toward his home. Lvov's Palladian vision of enlightenment through private life resolved the most immediate dilemma Aleksandr faced as he stared out at Priamukhino in the 1790s: how to imagine his sudden, forced repatriation into the countryside as anything but a stroke of bad luck. Under Lvov's mentorship, Aleksandr ceased thinking of himself as a failed servitor and determined to become a distinguished family man—a paternal voice of reason, emerging from the countryside to help show Russia a way to prosperity and happiness. Not satisfied with simply living "exemplary" lives, these men wished to use their houses to become the creators of new social norms. In the process, they became spokesmen for the virtues of provincial domesticity, a role that Aleksandr tried to play in society after his mother's death.

This task was made more complicated by the fact that his was not the only ambition animating home life at Priamukhino during these years.

[82] From a set of notebooks titled "Various Notes on Estate Management," (ca. 1805), IRLI f. 16, op. 2, no. 7, l. 19 ob.

CHAPTER THREE

La Vie Intérieure

Liubov Petrovna died in early October 1814. Aleksandr, now in his forties, became the most senior member of his family in Tver Province. By provision of his mother's will, he also inherited Priamukhino. Some four years earlier he had married, and he and his wife by now had three children. For all these reasons, the second decade of the nineteenth century marked a transition to maturity and authority for Aleksandr. No longer simply the youngest son, he was now the master of a distinguished estate, father of a growing family, and chief representative of a proud noble line now resident in the countryside. In a lengthy "Instruction to Myself" he wrote at this time, Aleksandr set out to decide just how he would try to use all this authority.[1]

Thinking back on Priamukhino's life during his mother's final years, he concluded that their home had become a "house of boredom and captivity, not only for strangers but also for ourselves." He blamed this general unhappiness on Liubov Petrovna's increasingly dogmatic embrace of religion and on her impatience with any disobedience. "Leaning especially heavily on her faith after father's death," Aleksandr reasoned to himself, "she demanded that we find the same consolation, the same need for lengthy prayers and attendance at all church services." "The slightest contradiction or disagreement with her opinions drove her to despair," he continued, "and as a result all sin-

---

[1] Aleksandr's ruminations on his mother's death have been reprinted in A. Kornilov, *Molodye gody Mikhaila Bakunina: Iz istorii russkogo romantizma* (Moscow: M. and S. Sabashnikov, 1915), 36n1; they are in the Priamukhino archive as IRLI f. 16, op. 4, no. 39.

House at Priamukhino, front lawn (1860s). Album of N. S. Korsakova-Bakunina (IRLI f. 16, op. 6, no. 64).

Road across Osuga, toward Priamukhino's Church (1860s). Album of N. S. Korsakova-Bakunina (IRLI f. 16, op. 6, no. 64).

House at Priamukhino, rear (1860s). Album of N. S. Korsakova-Bakunina (IRLI f. 16, op. 6, no. 64).

cerity disappeared among us." Aleksandr proceeded to contrast this pious, pensive, pessimistic existence with his own hopes for his family's future. He vowed that from here on out, life at Priamukhino would be characterized by moderation, rationality, and transparency. If his wife or children ever disagreed with his judgments, he would seek "to convince them of the truth by advice, examples, reason, and not patriarchal authority." He would encourage them to form social connections outside the family—for these "will be the guarantee of their future and continued happiness after I am dead"—and he would never require them to be religious "regardless of their own beliefs." His only goal would be to encourage them "to never be idle and to live joyfully and pleasantly, within our means."[2]

There seems little reason to doubt that Aleksandr felt these goals were modest and unexceptional and that he fully intended to pursue them without excessive reliance on his new seniority and "patriarchal authority." Even so, getting all of his family's "private wills" to agree with his ambitions for their home proved more difficult than he imagined. His sisters wished to live lives centered on religious devotion, not pleasant sociability. His new wife—the

[2] Ibid.

House at Priamukhino, entrance (1860s). Album of N. S. Korsakova-Bakunina (IRLI f. 16, op. 6, no. 64).

woman he invited to play the role of the happy, fecund Dasha in his idyll —came to her husband's home trained to see life through Romantic, melancholy lenses. As a result, Aleksandr's ideals were far from the only source of inspiration at Priamukhino in the first quarter of the nineteenth century. The family's intellectual life expanded greatly during these years. But it also became increasingly complex, as Aleksandr attempted—with varying degrees of success—to convince his own family to live according to the "rational" domestic norms he hoped life at Priamukhino would exemplify.

Though Liubov Petrovna's death allowed Aleksandr to emerge from his parents' shadow and become his own man, it also initiated a fragmentation of the Bakunin family's fortune, with important consequences for the family's cultural life. By 1814, Liubov Petrovna had acquired—mostly through her inheritance—a vast estate in Tver Province, including at least ten peasant villages and some 837 "souls." The Bakunin family also had some properties in Tula and a village in Kazan Province. Yet while peasant-rich, the family remained money-poor. Of their 837 souls, some 685 were still mortgaged to the various banks the Russian government had helped establish in the late eighteenth century to capitalize the gentry's new investment in estate life.[3] In addition, according to an old tradition of Russian noble life, Liubov Petrovna's will subdivided and distributed her vast holdings among her children after her death. Aleksandr's married and unmarried sisters received villages in Tver as well as the village in Kazan. Aleksandr inherited Priamukhino—the largest and most impressive of the family's Tver estates—and his brother Mikhail took the Bakunins' Tula properties. But by a provision of Liubov Petrovna's will, the brothers also assumed the burden of paying the family's debts. (Their joint financial responsibility would gradually sour relations between them. In the end, Mikhail Mikhailovich's career as an official would collapse in financial scandal in the second decade of the nineteenth century, when he was accused of misusing official funds.)[4]

This fragmentation of the Bakunin family's considerable resources meant that although Aleksandr became master of Priamukhino, the resources at his disposal were not as great as those that had been in his mother's hands. In addition, he felt obliged to fulfill many of his mother's ambitions, at least one of which survived her by some twenty years. As was noted earlier, Liubov Petrovna began the physical expansion of Priamukhino's manor house in 1796, when she added a domestic chapel. In 1808, she conceived an even grander project: a large stone church on a spot some seventy feet from the manor house. An enormously expensive project that taxed the family's resources for much of Aleksandr's life, this chapel was not completed until nearly thirty years later. In this sense, Liubov Petrovna's religious aspirations for her family were in operation long after her death.[5]

Though Aleksandr honored his mother's considerable financial commitments, in his admonitions to himself about fatherhood he specifically singled out inordinate piety as the antithesis of the open, reasoned family life he himself desired. In his own religious convictions, Aleksandr seems to have been moderately deist in the eighteenth-century mode, willing to go through the motions of Orthodox ritual but primarily interested in God as a providential

---

[3] The Bakunins' properties and financial situation in the early nineteenth century are best described by three separate documents: Liubov Petrovna's draft will of 1806 (IRLI f. 16, op. 6, no. 4); Aleksandr's letter to his brother Mikhail of 26 June 1804 (GATO f. 103, op. 1, d. 1395, ll. 157–60); and the settlement of Liubov Petrovna's will in 1814 (GARF f. 825, op. 1, d. 4, ll. 1–9).

[4] On Mikhail Mikhailovich, see Vladimir Sysoev, *Bakuniny* (Tver: Sozvezdie, 2002), 40–41.

[5] On the construction of the church, see Sysoev, *Bakuniny*, 79–81.

guarantee of the triumph of reason in this world and of immortality in the next. Some of his siblings—his brother Mikhail and his sisters Tatiana and Praskovia, who married early and left home—may have felt the same way.[6]

Aleksandr's eldest sisters—Pelageia, Anna, and Varvara—were devoutly religious and built their own lives around their spiritual ambitions. Though Pelageia and Anna, it will be remembered, had won stars at Smolnyi for their civilization and social graces, they joined Varvara in dedicating themselves to a life of prayer and seclusion on the estates that they had inherited from their mother. They set up housekeeping at Kozytsino—one of Liubov Petrovna's larger estates in Tver Province—which soon became known in family correspondence as a monastery of sorts. "About our everyday life," Varvara writes once to Aleksandr, "I'll say that we live as usual in our little Kozytsino hermitage [*kozytsinskaia pustyn'ka*], in hopes for God's mercy." Their days were spent on the management of their inheritance, on charity work, and on trips to local shrines and monasteries throughout Tver Province. Varvara's letter captures the mood and substance of their routine: "If the Lord helps, sister Anna Mikhailovna wants to go first to pray to our holy miracle workers, and then in your direction to see you all and to check in on her estate at Zaikovo."[7]

Endowed, in effect, by Liubov Petrovna's will, the pious "Kozytsino hermitage" helped sponsor new spiritual currents—and with them, alternative visions of what home life was for—within the Bakunin family. To be sure, a life of prayer and estate management was in some sense traditional for Russian noblewomen in the provinces. Anna Labzina, a memoirist of the late eighteenth century, recalled her own widowed mother living such a life.[8] Yet the spirituality cultivated at Kozytsino seems to have drawn on a broad variety of modern spiritual authors. This included the teachings of such French-

[6] Tatiana married a local landlord and litterateur named Aleksandr Poltoratsky, while Praskovia became the wife of Petr Nilov, governor of Tambov and Kazan; she also founded a school for girls in Kiev. Sysoev, *Bakuniny*, 38. On Aleksandr's religious convictions, see Kornilov, *Molodye gody*, 69–71.

[7] See V. M. Bakunina to A. M. Bakunin, letter of 7 September 1829, IRLI f. 16 op. 7, no. 22, l. 46. See l. 47 and l. 49 ob. for more examples of the phrase "Kozytsino hermitage." It is unlikely this term, though cute, was meant as a simple joke. Varvara's letters abound with pious phrases such as "with God's help," "thanks be to God," "may God have mercy," and "God be with you and with us," which occur in almost every other sentence.

[8] See Rachel May and Gary Marker, trans. and eds., *Days of a Russian Noblewoman: The Memories of Anna Labzina, 1758–1821* (DeKalb: Northern Illinois University Press, 2001), 1–15; see also Barbara Alpern Engel, *Women in Russia, 1700–2000* (Cambridge: Cambridge University Press, 2004), 35–40.

Catholic prophets of personal devotion as St. Francis de Sales (1567–1622) and Jeanne-Marie Bouvier de la Mothe-Guyon (1648–1717), more commonly known as Madame Guyon. Just how this "French school of spirituality" (as it was famously called by Henri Brémond) entered the Bakunin family's life is not clear.[9] From around 1800 into the 1820s, the officially sponsored Russian Bible Society brought a broad range of spiritual writers—including Madame Guyon—to Russian audiences. The society sheltered these works from the attacks of the more traditional wings of the Orthodox Church and temporarily lent them the stamp of official approval.[10] Yet it is also possible that these texts, which circulated among Russia's Freemasons, came to Priamukhino earlier.[11] Family legend in the nineteenth century held that Aleksandr's brother Ivan—killed in the Caucasus—was a "mystic and a Jansenist" and had imparted his beliefs to his Kozytsino sisters before he died in 1796.[12] Madame Guyon's spiritual teachings, meanwhile, were revered and defended at St. Cyr, the school on which Smolnyi Institute was modeled. It is entirely possible that some of this reverence passed into the education Pelageia and Anna brought with them from the capital.[13]

However they arrived, St. Francis de Sales's *Introduction to the Devout Life* and Madame Guyon's *Christian and Spiritual Letters on Various Subjects Which*

---

[9] See Henri Bremond, *Histoire littéraire du sentiment religieux en France depuis la fin des guerres de religion jusqu'à nos jours*, 8 vols. (Paris: Bloud et Gay, 1916–28).

[10] A. N. Pypin, *Religioznye dvizheniia pri Aleksandre I* (Petrograd: Ogni, 1916), 111, passim. In time, Pypin argues, the Bible Society became a hypocritical fad driven by a desire to get into official good graces.

[11] On Madame Guyon among the Masons, see Ia. Barskov, "Perepiska moskovskikh masonov 18–go veka" (Petrograd, 1915), 102–3, 301. I thank Douglas Smith for this reference. On the greater circulation of mystical religious writings among the Masons, see Zdenek V. David, "The Influence of Jacob Boehme on Russian Religious Thought," *Slavic Review* 21, no. 1 (March 1962): 43–64.

[12] Kornilov, *Molodye gody*, 6.

[13] It is true that Madame Guyon's writings were eventually repudiated by the school's founder, Madame de Maintenon. Even so, their informal influence was felt thereafter, and Archbishop Fénelon (who helped design the school's curriculum) was a supporter of Madame Guyon. See Marie-Florine Bruneau, *Women Mystics Confront the Modern World: Marie de L'Incarnation (1599– 1672) and Madame Guyon (1648–1717)* (Albany: State University of New York Press, 1998), 128. Catherine opposed the "constant caterwauling in church" characteristic of Fénelon's school—see her 1772 letter to Voltaire, Robin Bisha et al., *Russian Women, 1698–1917: Experience and Expression* (Bloomington: Indiana University Press, 2002), 167—but it should not be forgotten that Smolnyi itself was a monastery. According to the regulations governing the young women's education, catechism was taught as the "first foundation of everything," and failure to attend church services was punished by shaming and isolation. See E. Likhacheva, *Materialy dlia istorii zhenskogo obrazovaniia v Rossii (1086–1796)* (St. Petersburg: Tipografiia M. M. Stasiulevicha, 1890), 127.

Concern Inner Life joined other French-language spiritual titles to form the core of the theology section of the Bakunin family library.[14] Evidence of the family's engagement with this literature is indirect but broad. In the late 1810s, Varvara Mikhailovna recopied—by hand—a hundred-page French-language *Anthology of Mystical Theology* and kept it for her family's use.[15] In the 1830s, Aleksandr's children remembered having been required to read St. Francis de Sales (alongside more traditional Orthodox reading such as the lives of the saints) during their youth and adolescence.[16] The exalted French idiom of these works—full of themes of abandon and abnegation before the mysteries of God's will—exerted a profound influence on family correspondence, itself conducted in a French. Contemporaries remarked upon the "half-philosophical, half-mystical" atmosphere that reigned at Priamukhino, noting how the home seemed to oscillate between an intense engagement in this world and a passionate anticipation of the next.[17]

Such a dualism, in fact, suited the worldview cultivated by these Christian writers, whose works above all strove to carve out a space for spiritual contemplation and spiritual activity within the framework of modern social life.[18] "Wherever we may be, we can and should aspire to a perfect life," St. Francis de Sales proclaims in *Introduction to the Devout Life* (first published in 1609), aiming his work specifically at a woman who, though not free to become a nun, wishes to integrate continual devotion and private spiritual prac-

[14] See IRLI f. 16, op. 6, no. 36, ll. 19–20. Although this is the foreign-language section of the library catalog, there are relatively few Russian-language titles that touch upon religious matters. Authors listed include Madame Guyon, St. Francis de Sales, St. J.-B. La Salle, J.-B. Massillon, and Emanuel Swedenborg. There is also a *Life* of St. Francis of Sales. The catalog is from the 1840s; however, as I show in what follows, it is clear that at least some of these titles were in circulation in family life well before then. The most notable Orthodox writings include a collection of sermons by Feofan Prokopovich (1681–1736) and Metropolitan Platon (1737–1812), formerly Archbishop of Tver. Platon's Pietist leanings may have fed in to the modern mystical current in the Bakunin family's life. See David, "Influence of Jacob Boehme," 49, 57; as well as Pypin, *Religioznye dvizheniia*, 167, 170.

[15] See IRLI, f. 16, op. 10, no. 60, "Abregé de la theologie mystique."

[16] See, e.g., letter to A. A. Beyer, 6 April 1836 (Bakunin, *Sobranie*, I:258; cf. *Oeuvres [CD-ROM]*, 8); also V. A. D'iakova to N. A. D'iakov, letter of 18 January [1838?], IRLI f. 16, op. 4, no. 492, l. 6; this letter is reprinted in full in Kornilov, *Molodye gody*, 331–35, esp. 335.

[17] See I. I. Panaev, *Literaturnye vospominaniia* (Moscow: Izdatel'stvo Pravda, 1988), 179–80; P. V. Annenkov, *Nikolai Vladimirovich Stankevich: Perepiska ego i biografiia* (Moscow: Tipografiia Kat'kova, 1857), 155 and 159.

[18] In this context, a good description of the tension in modern Christian culture is Franois Lebrun, "The Two Reformations: Communal Devotion and Personal Piety," in *Passions of the Renaissance*, ed. Roger Chartier, vol. 3 of *A History of Private Life*, ed. Phillipe Ariès and and Georges Duby, trans. Arthur Goldhammer (Cambridge, Mass.: Belknap Press, 1989), 69–109.

tice into her life.[19] The exercises St. Francis de Sales recommends rest on a sharp reassertion of Christianity's traditional philosophical dualism. He believed, as did Madame Guyon, that the physical, exterior world is a "captious" and profoundly deceptive place, and therefore Christians not only can but must seek salvation along their own "interior path."[20] St. Francis de Sales urges his pupil, "Philothea," to fulfill all her external duties faithfully but also "to retire at various times into the solitude of your own heart even while outwardly engaged in discussions or transactions with others."[21] God works, according to this school of thought, through our intimate selves, which should be continuously developed and distinguished from the outside world through reading, writing, prayer, and spiritual exercises.[22]

To this end, St. Francis de Sales recommended regular and purifying spiritual exercises—contemplation of one's sins, confession, and acts of penance—preferably under the advice of a spiritual director. Madame Guyon advised her followers to go still further in the purification of self, advocating a nondiscursive mode of prayer known as "orison." Through this practice, believers would seek to lose all cognition and memory and attain a "pure love" of God, indifferent even to their own salvation. Only full abnegation of one's earthly sense could prepare one for full unity with God: "Let us follow God, without seeking the route / And content ourselves with walking in his steps."[23] This state of orison, Varvara Mikhailovna's *Anthology* informs us, "is a gift from God."[24]

On a practical level, the Christian ideal of an individual inner life helped to clear space for the Bakunin women's self-expression within the increasingly defined routines of family life. Whether through reading, prayer, con-

[19] See Francis de Sales, *Introduction to the Devout Life*, trans. John K. Ryan (New York: Doubleday, 1972), 45. Guyon likewise imagined her teachings as destined for a person who intended to give himself or herself "entirely to God" within the constraints of a nonmonastic life. See Jeanne Marie Bouvier de la Motte Guyon, *Lettres chrétiennes et spirituelles sur divers sujets qui regardent la vie intérieure, ou l'esprit du vrai christianisme. Nouvelle edition, enrichie de la correspondance secrète de Mr. de Fénelon avec l'auteur,* vol. 1 (London [i.e. Paris], 1767–68), 1–2; on the role of the French school in moving piety outside the monasteries and into private homes, see Lebrun, "The Two Reformations," 99.

[20] See de Sales, *Introduction to the Devout Life*, 35; and also Madame Guyon, as quoted by Bruneau, *Women Mystics*, 142.

[21] De Sales, *Introduction to the Devout Life*, 97.

[22] On the interconnection between French spiritual writing and the development of internalized, personal piety, see Lebrun, "The Two Reformations," 99–100, passim.

[23] From the spiritual poetry of Madame Guyon, quoted in Benjamin Sahler, ed., *Madame Guyon et Fénelon: La correspondance secrète, avec un choix de poésies spirituelles* (Paris: Dervy-Livres, 1982), 312; on "orison," see Bruneau, *Women Mystics*, 143.

[24] See IRLI f. 16, op. 10, no. 60, l. 2.

fessional conversation among themselves, or writing—as Varvara Mikhail-ovna's laborious recopying of her *Anthology* makes clear—spiritual practice allowed the Bakunin sisters to pursue self-perfection on terms of their own choosing, rather than merely performing the role of muse laid out for them in early-nineteenth-century culture. In the case of Varvara and Pelageia, the scale of this reinvention was striking. In the 1790s, they lived briefly at Derzhavin's house in St. Petersburg and were celebrated in his Anacreontic songs as talented domestic muses and erotic "Russian girls":

> How beautiful you are, Variusha!
>
> . . . .
>
> In your sky-blue turban
> You sit, letting your hair fall
> On your forehead for loveliness,
> Captivating everyone in an instant
> With your charming smile.

In their adult lives at the Kozytsino hermitage, however, the Bakunin sisters shed these talents for an independent life of provincial seclusion and piety on their own estate.[25]

Philosophically, the mystical theology Varvara and her sisters preferred fostered extreme skepticism about the limits of human reason and discourse. It called for acts of faith and a search for a less subjective and more divine purpose in life. This does not mean, of course, that such theology was some-how more behind the times than their brother's brand of rational meta-physics. On the contrary, such religious currents contributed to the skeptical critique of abstract reason that broke through in the last decades of the eigh-teenth century to become a major source of inspiration for Romantic litera-ture and philosophy.[26]

Projected into the Bakunin family's life deep in the Russian countryside, these currents infused it with a not-so-subtle intellectual tension. Aleksandr's paternal desire to lay out the whole of the Bakunins' home life on a more pro-

[25] See the poems "Portret Variushi," "Na razluku," "Arfa," and "Variusha," as well as their commentaries, in G. R. Derzhavin, *Anakreonticheskie pesni*, prepared by G. P. Makogonenko, G. N. Ionin, and E. N. Petrova (Moscow: Nauka, 1987), 51, 56–58, 426, 430–31. This excerpt is from "Variusha," ibid., 56, a poem begun in 1799.

[26] On this point, see Frederick C. Beiser, *The Sovereignty of Reason: The Defense of Rationality in the Early English Enlightenment* (Princeton: Princeton University Press, 1996), 213–19; Isaiah Berlin, "Herder and the Enlightenment," in *The Proper Study of Mankind*, ed. Henry Hardy and Roger Hausheer (New York: Farrar, Straus, and Giroux, 1997), 381–82.

ductive and prosperous plan ran up against his sisters' desires to see the home as a space for personal spiritual struggle and self-development. The ambitions, ideals, and even languages of the two visions of what domestic space was for constantly provoked and tested one another over the coming decades, vying for expression within Bakunin family life. Aleksandr's own daughter Varvara later remembered that, as a child, she had experienced spiritual longings that her father could neither sympathize with nor understand; but she always found comfort in the presence of her aunt Varvara Mikhailovna, quietly kissing the hem of her dress as one might adore the clothing of a saint. "I saw light, whenever I looked at her": and it was this Christian form of private enlightenment that the Bakunin aunts sponsored and inspired from their hermitage at Kozytsino.[27]

❀⚜❀

At Priamukhino itself, Aleksandr could—and, it seems, did—insist that such spiritual ecstasies remain subordinate to the more reasoned and earthly vision of home life he preferred. Nonetheless, the idyll Aleksandr planned so carefully depended on feminine inspiration. It was Dasha's presence, after all, that attracted masculine reason to the countryside in Aleksandr's idyll. More specifically, Aleksandr required a wife. Though he never seems to have seriously thought about marrying a peasant woman, the question of just whom he might marry grew more pointed as he grew older. By 1810, his friends teasingly called him an "old lady-killer" who would never dare settle down.[28] But in their franker moments they described him as a kind fellow going to seed in the country. He was "short-sighted, ill at ease, not terribly neat" and had "black hair and grown-together eyebrows," according to an acquaintance who saw him in Torzhok about this time.[29]

Suddenly, in 1810, Aleksandr married. Taken aback by the rush, his friend Vasilii Kapnist sent him a hastily composed wedding song, in which he imagined Aleksandr's bride sight unseen.

[27] See V. A. Bakunina to M. A. Bakunin, undated letter [1837 or 1838?], IRLI f. 16, op. 4, no. 661, ll. 51–52. The only copy of this letter that survives is one made for Aleksandr Kornilov, who reprints part of it in *Molodye gody*, 66–68.

[28] See V. V. Kapnist to A. M. Bakunin, letter of 9 December 1810, in B. I. Koplan, "Iz literaturnykh iskanii kontsa XVIII–nachala XIX v. (A. M. Bakunin and V. V. Kapnist)," *Materialy obshchestva izucheniia Tverskogo kraia* 6 (Tver: Obhshchestvo izucheniia Tverskogo kraia, 1928), 3–4.

[29] As cited in Sysoev, *Bakuniny*, 100.

Varvara Aleksandrovna (Muravieva) Bakunina (1791–1864). From Vladimir Sysoev, *Bakuniny* (Tver: Sozvezdie, 2002). Courtesy: Tverskoi Gosudarstvennyi Ob"edinnënyi Muzei.

> It seems to me her face
> Must be round and white, like an egg;
> Her hair — a long black braid,
> Longer than a shaft of rye.[30]

He imagined Aleksandr's new wife, in short, as pastoral Dasha, a homespun girl of few pretensions. Nothing, however, could have been further from the truth. Aleksandr's actual bride, Varvara Muravieva, was a society maiden raised according to the latest Romantic principles. Though by some accounts she was a playful and vivacious young woman, the tone society expected her to strike was decidedly more pensive, personal, and elegiac. To woo and win "sweet Varinka" (as he called her), Aleksandr had to define for her the nature of their future family life in very explicit and contractual terms, bringing her into his idyll but also leaving space for her own personal enthusiasms.

It is not clear when the two met. She was born in 1791, and her father, Aleksandr Fedorovich Muraviev, died shortly thereafter. Her mother, a member of the Mordvinov family, soon remarried, to Pavel Markovich Poltoratsky. By birth, Varvara was thus related to some of the more ambitious and accomplished families in the tightly knit noble elite of the early nineteenth century. The Mordvinovs, Poltoratskys, and Muravievs all left their mark in imperial administration, society, and politics. All these families were also the Bakunins' relatives — though not close enough to prevent a pairing. Aleksandr's sister Tatiana was married to Pavel Poltoratsky's brother Aleksandr. By marriage, then, his new bride was a relative — though no one seems to have paid much attention to that.

More meaningful was the difference in their ages. By 1810, Aleksandr was into his forties; Varvara was nineteen. Varvara was also very much a child of the postrevolutionary era. Her mentor and best friend, as a child, was a French émigré named Louise Titot. Living with Titot on the Poltoratsky estate, Varvara seems to have breathed in the air of exile, so to speak, so much so that Louise later scolded her. "You have too much affect, you seem to take pleasure in penetrating yourself with sorrow. . . . Is it possible, that young, attractive as you are, and in a rank, which thank God places you beyond all need, you can truly say to me that you have no other consolation?" In her letters, she pleaded with Varvara to remember the moral maxim: "L'esprit qu'on

---

[30] Quoted from Koplan, "Iz literaturnykh iskanii," 3–4.

veut avoir gâte celui qu'on a" ("The spirit one wants to have impairs the spirit one has").[31]

The problem, however, was that the melancholy spirit young Varvara affected was a product not simply of her desires but of societal expectations. It is instructive, in this regard, to consider the contents of her poetry album, a souvenir begun before her marriage that has come down to us. A well-maintained poetry album was a semipublic document in the noble culture of the day. In part, it was her calling card, a demonstration of her personal taste and cultural acumen. Just as important, it offered her friends and relatives a chance to inspect and comment on her education, adding their own advice along the way.[32]

Varvara's album is a rectangle of roughly five by eight inches, covered with leather and embossed with gold trim.[33] Its opening biblical inscription — undoubtedly from the time of its presentation — already conveys a warning not to trust to earthly reasoning: "The fear of the Lord is the beginning of all wisdom." Other entries in various hands convey softer but still cautionary messages about the world the girl will face. In German: "A pearl sparkles brightly — but virtue brighter still!" In Russian: "Let a divine and pure joy live in your soul." A distinctly more gothic tone is struck by a rather frightening figure drawn in the center of the album. It shows a demon, dancing on a tightrope, over a deep crevasse labeled "the Abyss." The French inscription reads: "Here is the Devil's portrait. I do not know if he tempts you, but I know that you tempt the Devil." In still another poem, inscribed by a "cousin M. P.," a young woman yields to her lover's demands, passing a day indolently in his embraces: "Love makes time pass." She is taken sharply aback, however, when her suitor, having sated himself with her charms, abandons her for another. She realizes to her horror: "Time makes love pass."[34]

The majority of the album's inscriptions are in a single hand, Varvara's own. Most are elegies by now-forgotten French poets, made popular in Rus-

---

[31] See, respectively, Louise Titot to V. A. Muravieva, letter of 23 April 1806, IRLI f. 16, op. 9, no. 478, l. 4; letter of February 1806, ibid., l. 25; and letter of 20 April 1807, ibid. l. 16.

[32] On poetry albums, and Varvara Muravieva's album in particular, see V. E. Vatsuro, "Literaturnye al'bomy v sobranii Pushkinskogo doma," *Ezhegodnik Rukopisnogo otdela Pushkinskogo Doma na 1977 god* (1979): 10; and Gitta Hammarberg, "Flirting with Words: Domestic Albums, 1770–1840," in *Russia. Women. Culture,* ed. Helena Goscilo and Beth Holmgren (Bloomington: Indiana University Press, 1996), 297–319.

[33] It is IRLI f. 16, op. 6, no. 55.

[34] See IRLI f. 16, op. 6, no. 55, l. 49 (the first two inscriptions); l. 32 (Devil); l. 5 (love's passage).

sia by the exiles.[35] Their titles convey their sad content well: "The Hour Advances When I Must Die"; "A Resolution in Vain"; "Romance, Far from You"; "Absence"; "Nothing"; "The Sad Dream of Life." If there is a central theme to this oeuvre, it is the constant tension between duty and desire in human life. These poems are full of unrequited love, more or less stoically faced. Most take the form of secret confessions to paper, detailing an intimate struggle whose only external expression is a certain distant and chaste melancholy.

Take, for example, the drama of "A Sleepless Wife." She tosses and turns in her bed, lying between her spouse and her child:

> I am awake and burn in the night
> Like the solitary lamp
> Which pains me with its feeble light.

She cannot expel from her mind the image of the man she loves — the image of a man who is not her husband:

> O you, who come to trouble my life,
> You, whose name must be kept in secret
> Spare me, at least, I beg of you,
> What little remains of my reason.

Then she reflects on the crux of her dilemma:

> Duty, love, you fickle pair,
> Happy he, who can reunite you,
> Happy he too, who can separate you,
> And be able to obey only one or the other.
> But how can one not be the victim
> Of the torment one feels
> When one cannot love without crime
> Nor cease to love, without dying?

Incapable of being inconstant to either duty or desire, the sleepless wife spends the night locked in the agony of these reflections. Finally, her child

---

[35] Vatsuro describes the inscriptions of Varvara's album as being from the school of Antoine de Bertin and Évariste de Parny (see more about Parny below). See Vatsuro, "Literaturnye al'bomy," 10. Parny's style and themes greatly influenced the Russian poets Batiushkov and Pushkin.

awakes with the dawn, forcing her to lock away her own troubles: "Ah, we must hide the pain from him . . ."[36]

Such gloomy elegies dominated the periodicals published for women in the early nineteenth century, including the influential *Journal des dames*, whose editor, Évariste de Parny, was among the most popular poets of this school. Various explanations have been advanced for their popularity. Some cynical critics later scoffed them off as mere fashion, a new form of coquetry deployed by "young girls looking to marry." (Teasing their beaux with the "white veil of melancholy," it was said, these new women captivated men all the more rapidly.) Modern literary historians point to the turbulence of the opening decades of the nineteenth century and to the colonial roots of men like Parny (born off Africa on what is now Reunion Island). As an atmosphere of exile and displacement settled over Europe, it is argued, these poets naturally became its lyrical heroes.[37] Finally, the demonstrative sorrows of French noblewomen—the sorrows of Varvara's friend Louise Titot—have been read as a political response to the revolution. By bearing themselves as if in mourning and cultivating a chastened but deepened air, noblewomen sought to atone for the sins of the Old Regime (and stake a moral claim for continued influence in the new world of the nineteenth century).[38]

What Varvara herself took from these pensive poems—a mode of thinking, or merely a *mode*—is hard to say. But these elegies dramatized the difficulties inherent in a role that young Russian noblewomen were increasingly being urged to play in the opening decades of the nineteenth century. If in the eighteenth century Russian girls were eroticized and celebrated for their graces and external civilization, in the nineteenth century they were expected to be the embodiment of a more internal ideal: that of pure, untainted, and uncompromised morality. The icon of the new age was no longer the witty salon mistress but the self-sacrificing mother with a child on her breast, the empress in mourning for her lost husband, or (somewhat later) Pushkin's Tatiana, staring out the window of her provincial home.[39] The flip side of this

[36] IRLI f. 16, op. 6, no. 55, ll. 12 ob.–13.

[37] See Henri Potez, *L'Elégie en France avant le Romantisme (de Parny à Lamartine), 1778–1820* (Geneva: Slatkin Reprints, 1970), 290–307, esp. 295–96; and Henri Stavan, "L'amour dans la poésie personelle de quelques auteurs de la fin du XVIII siècle," *Studi Francesi* 47–48 (1972): 357–62. On themes of displacement in general after the revolution, see Peter Fritzsche, *Stranded in the Present: Modern Time and the Melancholy of History* (Cambridge, Mass.: Harvard University Press, 2004), 55–91.

[38] See Margaret H. Darrow, "French Noblewomen and the New Domesticity, 1750–1850," *Feminist Studies* 5, no. 1 (1979): 41–65.

[39] See Iu. M. Lotman's analysis of the position of women in the early nineteenth century in

phenomenon is also worth noting: the burdening of women's private lives with the need to embody an increasingly defined set of social ideals.[40]

Rephrasing Louise Titot's critique of Varvara's character somewhat, we may say that the pensive and pessimistic spirit others wanted her to have impinged on the spirit she might have had. Varvara's solution to this di-lemma—evidently a common one—was to embrace wholeheartedly the gloomy role given to her. Demonstrably "penetrated by sorrows" (to again cite Titot), she presented visitors to her poetry album with a steady diet of "the sad dream of life." Her favorite play—she confessed to a friend—was Racine's *Iphigénie* (a drama of cruel sacrifice, in which the daughter of the mighty King Agamemnon casts herself into the sea to break a curse that hov-ers over her father's fleet).[41] Her favorite place was the tomb of Rousseau, where "nature's friend," a sensitive and "pure soul," at long last ended his un-happy life.[42] In this way, perhaps, young Varvara managed that most deli-cious of feats—being obedient and disobedient at the same time.

Aleksandr had known Varvara since she was a child, but in the summer of 1810 his intentions toward her changed. He began to court her, with her parents' approval and consent. According to family legend, this first phase of their courtship had an ending worthy of a sentimental novel. Aleksandr, de-spairing of winning any favor at all from sweet Varinka, announced himself utterly lost and threatened to shoot himself. His sister Tatiana, terrified that he might finally lose his mind and actually do it, rushed to the Poltoratsky es-tate and pleaded with Varvara to consider his proposal. Whether or not this actually happened, on June 3, 1810, Aleksandr and Varvara were engaged.[43]

---

his *Besedy o russkoi kul'ture. Byt i traditsii russkogo dvorianstva (XVIII–nachalo XIX veka)* (St. Pe-tersburg: Isskustvo, 1994), 57–63. See Richard Wortman, *Scenarios of Power: Myth and Ceremony in Russian Monarchy*, vol. 1, *From Peter the Great to Nicholas I* (Princeton: Princeton University Press, 1995), 247–54 (on the Empress Maria Fedorovna, mourning for Pavel I); and Olga Pe-ters Hasty's analysis of Tatiana's struggles in *Pushkin's Tatiana* (Madison: University of Wiscon-sin Press, 1999).

[40] On Romantic woman as the "realization of society's ideal," see Lotman, *Besedy*, 57–63. For a controversial analysis of the shadow this cast over women throughout the nineteenth century, see Barbara Heldt, *Terrible Perfection: Women and Russian Literature* (Bloomington: Indiana Uni-versity Press, 1987).

[41] See E. Muravieva to V. A. Bakunina (the elder), letter of [*1812*], IRLI f. 16, op. 9, no. 249, ll. 57–58, in which Muravieva declares herself won over to Racine by Varvara's enthusiasm. As we shall see, Varvara Aleksandrovna would be shocked to see her own family life taking on echoes of this play in the early 1830s.

[42] See the elaborate meditation on Rousseau's grave in her album, IRLI f. 16, op. 6, no. 55, l. 27.

[43] See Sysoev, *Bakuniny*, 98–101, for a biographical outline of their courtship.

Given the difference between their ages—and the shocking, novelettish de-
nouement of the first phase of their courtship—rumors soon flew that the
match was forced. Even close relatives assumed, Aleksandr discovered to his
dismay, "that *maman* [Varvara's mother] had all sorts of pains to make you
consent to promise me your hand" and that "in other words I showed very
little consideration in desiring you to marry me in spite of yourself." Varvara
fervently denied this was the case—"if you knew how much your doubts af-
flict me," she responded—but Aleksandr still felt compelled to borrow her
poetry album for several days and lay out a contract, of sorts, to govern their
new life at Priamukhino.[44]

After a string of opening compliments (he had never met a woman who so
successfully combined "softness with gaiety, vivacity with virtue, amiability
with innocence, and grace with modesty"), Aleksandr addressed what he assumed to be the heart of the matter. Varvara, quite naturally, was afraid that
she would be unhappy outside her parents' home. She was unsure if she
wanted, or could fulfill, the burdens that came with married life at Priamukhino. Here, he assured her, she was making two big mistakes. First, she
was underestimating herself and her ability to take a more active and reasoned role in her own life. Second, she underestimated the scope for personal
fulfillment Priamukhino would offer her and how fulfilling its duties would
harmonize with her desires. Like Louise Titot, Aleksandr judged Varvara's
melancholy to be all pose: "Despite your pretense of disaffection, I perceived
instantly that you were what I have been looking for so long." She was not
gloomy and distracted at all, but "lively and gay"—and eminently level-
headed: "[Y]ou are and will always be reasonable whenever you so desire."

The question was now to find an environment where this happy, rational
character, instilled by her parents, could be developed. Here he offered his
hand in a number of roles: "I will be, in turn, your love, your husband, your
friend, your brother. But this will only be if you yourself wish it." He would,
in sum, be her partner rather than her overlord, and if any unforeseen squab-
bles separated them, he pledged to allow her parents to be the ultimate "tri-
bunal." Theirs would be a frank and open-minded marriage, founded on
mutual interest and strengthened by family ties.

At first glance, he admitted, Priamukhino might seem an unlikely home
for such a union. His was a "sad house": Liubov Petrovna, increasingly aged

[44] See A. M. Bakunin to V. A. Muravieva, [Summer 1810?], IRLI f. 16, op. 4, no. 5, ll. 5–5
ob.; V. A. Bakunina, letter of 23 July 1810, IRLI f. 16, op. 4, no. 63, ll. 1–1 ob.; Aleksandr's entry, which is in the final pages of Varvara's album, is IRLI f. 16, op. 6, no. 55, ll. 100–107.

and temperamental, was subject to fits of sorrow over her deceased husband and fallen son. Yet he promised Varvara there would be space at Priamukhino for her to practice all manner of individual "occupations": drawing, music, reading, promenades on horseback or by foot through the garden, alone or in the society of their friends and relatives. Far from disapproving of these personal "occupations," Aleksandr underscored that "occupation is absolutely necessary for you," as a guard against ennui, dissatisfaction, and despair. As for her duties at Priamukhino, they would be structured so as to be entirely in accord with her own nature and desires.

The conflict between duty and desire that inspired her melancholy was more apparent than real, Aleksandr assured her, and would cease altogether within the happy home. Aleksandr used the prospect of children—and before them, sex—to symbolize this unity. He imagined Varvara would blush at the topic but insisted that one "need blush only if one marries as if undertaking a pleasant amusement, without having carefully reflected first." Thought through, their marriage would not be an "illusion of the senses," and therefore they should dare to think of passion. "The feelings you have for me are still weak, but let yourself follow them—and do not repress them—do not be ashamed—they can do no harm." Virtue could and should be rewarded with a harmonious and satisfying life: at Priamukhino, "Varinka will be as happy as she deserves to be."

Aleksandr and Varvara were married on October 16, 1810. As the final entry in his wife's poetry album, Aleksandr wrote a poem of his own invention, a wedding song titled (logically enough) "For the 16th of October." It imagined the couple as two Arcadians, retiring home to reap the fruits of their virtuous labors.

> Our happiness is in our power,
> Varia, dear, believe,
> We have worked our day in the fields,
> Now let's go and have our rest.
>
> . . . .
>
> A heavenly flame will be kindled
> As divinity fills our breasts,
> And innocence will consent
> To sleep in the arms of tenderness.[45]

---

[45] See K. Iu. Lappo-Danilevskii, "Iz literaturnogo naslediia A. M. Bakunina," in *Literaturnyi arkhiv: Materialy po istorii russkoi literatury i obshchestvennoi mysli*, ed. K. N. Grigor'ian (St. Peters-

Closing out Varvara's romantic and melancholy album, this assertion of the right to seize happiness provides something of an odd and fairy-tale ending. Tearing off the "white veil of melancholy," Aleksandr brought his bride into his idyll. The process was more direct than Varvara herself probably realized. As it turns out, "For the 16th of October" was cribbed, more or less whole, from an earlier cycle of poems Aleksandr had aimed at one of his peasant mistresses. Recopying it into the final pages of his wife's album, Aleksandr simply removed Dasha's name and put in Varia's.[46]

Yet as the reasoned contract that preceded this wedding song shows, recruiting Varvara Muravieva to be his wife was not as simple as all that. To get sweet Varinka to accept his invitation, Aleksandr had to make certain subtle concessions to the romantic longings of his young bride. He promised that she would be able to regard her educational and artistic attainments as her own personal "occupations" within the home, to be pursued for her own satisfaction. As taught at Smolnyi and practiced heretofore at Priamukhino, such *jolis talents* as sewing, singing, and child raising were seen as eminently social pursuits — part of the civilization of Russian social life in the provinces. Aleksandr's contract with Varvara contained a much more private vision of what these feminine attainments were about, however. Varvara needed her occupations, above all, to ward off melancholy and skepticism. Having her own personal sphere of activity would allow her to tame the wild spirit of the century within her and to find her individual home within the domestic realm, protected and cultivated by her loving, companionate husband. In this way, the notion of a personal feminine vocation at Priamukhino — of and for Varvara herself, separate from, but not contradictory to, the greater life of the home — was written into Aleksandr's idyll as part of his search for a woman who would play the role of Dasha. In the process, Aleksandr also acknowledged that sweet Varinka had the right to an inner life that was quite different from his own.

⊛⁂⊛

Aleksandr's marriage and the formation of a new family at Priamukhino mark a turning point, of sorts, within the Bakunins' life. From the late eighteenth century until about 1920, what we know of family life at Priamukhino con-

---

burg: Nauka, 1994), 105, for the text, which, as discussed below, was actually part of a longer poem. See Varvara's album, PD, f. 16, op. 6, no. 55, l. 107, for the original.

[46] This substitution is observed by Lappo-Danilevskii, "Iz literaturnogo naslediia," 117n9.

sists mostly of documents written in the future tense: prologues, lyrics, and projects imagining what a happy family life might look like. Most of these come from the pen of Aleksandr himself; the activities and ambitions of the rest of the household are much more dimly illuminated. With the birth of children at Priamukhino, however, the family's archive—and with it the realm of domestic activities open to historical interpretation—expands dramatically. First educational materials for the next generation, then letters in the children's own hands begin a wave of family correspondence, much of it centering around life at Priamukhino. The domestic enlightenment posited by Catherinean reform—and worked out in great detail by Aleksandr himself—now began to be lived, and through its documents the family's present begins to be illuminated.

The ideal at the heart of everything, of course, was still posterity.[47] When the young Aleksandr imagined his future family life in "The Harvest," he spied a vast field of children, partners in his work and prosperity. Varvara, who was plagued by morning sickness and complained of a "crainte de devenir grosse" after having her first child, seems to have been more ambivalent about the matter.[48] Nevertheless, tradition, law, sentiment, and a steady supply of serf wet nurses were on her husband's side, and the Bakunins soon had a veritable nation of children. Daughters Liubov (born in 1811) and Varvara (1812) were followed by nine more siblings, including three sisters and six brothers, with rarely more than a year separating births: firstborn son Mikhail (in 1814); two more daughters, Tatiana (1815) and Aleksandra (1816); then five sons in a row, Nikolai (1818), Ilia (1819), Pavel (1820), Aleksandr (1821), Aleksei (1823); and finally a daughter, Sofiia (1824). While infant mortality among nineteenth-century Russian peasants was high, the Bakunins enjoyed much higher standards of health and care. Only Sofiia died in infancy, in 1826; the rest survived to adulthood.

Contemporaries who visited this bustling home in the first half of the nineteenth century and witnessed the active family life there were constantly struck by the freethinking atmosphere that seemed to reign at Priamukhino. They credited this intellectual activity and openness to Aleksandr's benevolent reign as head of household. "Not a single free speech was ever interrupted by his arrival," recalled Lazhechnikov, who visited Priamukhino in

---

[47] On posterity's role in Enlightenment thought and culture, see Carl L. Becker, *The Heavenly City of Eighteenth-Century Philosophers* (New Haven: Yale University Press, 1932), 119–68.

[48] "Crainte de devenir grosse" means "fear of becoming pregnant." See E. N. Muravieva to V. A. Bakunina, letter of 3 January 1812 (IRLI f. 16, op. 9, no. 249, ll. 45–46), where Muravieva discusses her friend's fears and tries to refute them.

the 1830s and 1840s.[49] And indeed, as he began his life as a father in earnest in 1811, Aleksandr reaffirmed his commitment to seeing reason and rational communication as the guiding principles of his family's new life. This repudiation of patriarchy and Orthodoxy as principles for home life did not, of course, limit Aleksandr's authority within his own household in any binding sense. By law and custom, Aleksandr possessed broad patriarchal control over his family; the decision to rule with a rational, paternal hand was his alone. What's more, looking at family life through an enlightened lens (as opposed to the purely patriarchal one), seemed to legitimize, in Aleksandr's eyes, a certain diminution of his wife Varvara's status in the family. "My Varinka is so young," he reasoned in his 1814 admonition to himself on fatherhood, "that I may consider her one of the children. She, as the eldest daughter, should run the household."[50]

Nonetheless, the liberal ethos Aleksandr chose to install at Priamukhino helped enshrine communication and education, its enabling condition, as central practices of family life. From their earliest years, the Bakunin children were schooled in expression. Aleksandr later bragged that no fewer than five languages were spoken at night in the living room. These were, in rough order of fluency, Russian, French, German, Italian, and English. To teach all these languages—and the social graces that went along with them—the Bakunins retained a governess named Julie Nindel and a German language and music instructor, Peregrin Feigerl.[51] Inevitably, the children's education bore the stamp of their parents' own preferences as well. Varvara Aleksandrovna herself created a *Petite dictionaire pour les enfants* [*A Small Dictionary for the Children*]. An evocative fragment of the letter "A" survives:

> *Abaissement, abaisser, abandon, abandonnement, abandonner, abattement, abattre, abbaye, abbé, abbesse, abhorrer, abjection, abject, abjuration, abnégation. . . .*[52]

[49] See I. I. Lazhechnikov, "Zametki dlia biografii Belinskogo," in *Polnoe sobranie sochinenii,* vol. 12 (St. Petersburg: Tovarishchestvo M. O. Vol'f, 1900), 257.

[50] On the broad legal authority of husbands in Russian law in the early nineteenth century, see William G. Wagner, *Marriage, Property, and the Law in Late Imperial Russia* (Oxford: Clarendon Press, 1994), chap. 1. Kornilov, *Molodye gody,* 36n1.

[51] For the correspondence surrounding their hire, see IRLI f. 16, op. 9, no. 332 (Nindel), and IRLI f. 16, op. 9, no. 522 (Feigerl). Aleksandr brags about the many languages spoken in his home in his poem "Osuga," discussed in chapter 4, below. See Dmitrii Oleinikov, "Aleksandr Bakunin i ego poema 'Osuga,'" *Nashe Nasledie* 29–30 (1994): 58.

[52] See IRLI, f. 16, op. 4, no. 82, ll. 50–52, for the fragment of this little vocabulary. The words cited translate: "abatement, to abate, abandon, with abandon, to abandon, exhaustion, to beat, abbey, abbott, abbess, abhor, abjection, abject, abjuration, abnegation."

Skipping more prosaic words like *abajoue* (cheek-pouch), *abaque* (abacus), *ab-batis* (giblets), and *abeille* (bee), this Romantic vocabulary prepared the Ba-kunin children to read, speak, write, and think in the elegiac idiom Varvara Aleksandrovna preferred. The most important point was that they should develop their verbal capacities as quickly and fluently as possible. "If Liubasha loved her mother," Varvara Aleksandrovna wrote in her eldest daughter's album when the girl was nine, "she would have listened to her and would already speak both French and German."[53]

Language was not the only focal point of the Bakunin children's home education, in which the parents took an active part. To teach her children geography, Varvara Aleksandrovna calculated the number of square versts in Europe ("9,065,000").[54] Though Aleksandr did not expect his sons and daughters to believe in church dogma blindly, he did retain a parish priest to teach them catechism. Under the influence of their aunts, meanwhile, the four Bakunin daughters were given a rigorous religious instruction. Liberal and reverent readings from the lives of the saints as well as practices from St. Francis de Sales's *Introduction to the Devout Life* encouraged the Bakunin sisters to develop an active sense of their own spiritual vocation and *vie intérieure*.[55] Aleksandr wrote long history textbooks for his children — one runs to over two hundred pages — and took them on long botanical walks through Priamukhino's gardens.[56] Family life was peppered with the arts as well. In addition to retaining a music instructor for their children, the elder Bakunins saw to it that theatrical productions were staged in Priamukhino's parlor on a regular basis. In 1822 (according to family diaries), the Bakunins mounted *The Tragedy of Dmitrii Donskoi* in their home, and in 1828 they presented Prince A. A. Shakhovskoi's phenomenally popular comic satire of Karamzinian sentimentalism, *The New Sterne*.[57]

[53] The entry itself was made in French, indicating little Liubin'ka could at least read, if not speak, the language of Parny; see PD, f. 16, op. 6, no. 56, l. 2 for the album and inscription.

[54] See PD, f. 16, op. 4, no. 82, l. 52 ob.

[55] See Kornilov, *Molodye gody*, 64–66, for a discussion of aunt Varvara Mikhailovna's religous zeal and the daughters' religious education. The children's recollections of this experience will be discussed in more detail in chapter 5 below.

[56] See IRLI, f. 16, op. 2, nos. 17 and 20, for these history notebooks. Relying largely on "Os-uga" and on later testimonies drawn from letters and memoirs, Kornilov provides an interesting description of the Bakunin children's education in his *Molodye gody*, 39–41.

[57] See V. A. Bakunina's *Memory Books* (*Pamiatnye zapiski*) (whose genesis is described in more chapter 4 below) IRLI f. 16, op. 6, no. 9, under the dates July 1822 and November 1828. For the *New Sterne*, see James von Geldern and Louise McReynolds, eds., *Entertaining Tsarist Russia: Tales, Songs, Plays, Movies, Jokes, Ads, and Images from Russian Urban Life, 1779–1917* (Bloomington:

A long-awaited second phase of this educational era in Bakunin family life began in the 1820s, when the children began to speak and write for themselves. From a very early age, the Bakunin parents urged their children to participate in family occasions by writing. For her father's birthday in 1823, eleven-year-old Varvara prepared a special birthday card in French, calling it "the first fruits of composition by your tender and respectful daughter." In 1824, young "Michel" (as Mikhail was known in the family), then just ten, made a similar present to his mother. His older sisters, he wrote, were preparing needlework this year, "but I, who know not how to do such things, will instead write you a letter as best I can." Two years later he wrote a birthday greeting in German, in studied block letters that suggest supervised dictation.[58] In this way, correspondence soon began to illuminate family life, even when the family was all still in one place.

⊗⁄-⁙⊛

The evidence provided by these educational efforts begins to give us a new and qualitatively different vantage point on Bakunin family life. The world of Aleksandr's idyll is hypothetical and largely univocal. It exists in the realm of maybe and reflects a stable, paternal point of view. As the Bakunin children learned to speak, however, the distinction hitherto reserved for domestic celebrations and projects for the future began to devolve on everyday life, turning it into a running story of development: a romance. Suddenly, every expression—and not just carefully scripted ones—acquired a meaning derived from its place in Priamukhino's ongoing history and its ability to provide some commentary on the ideals the house represented.

Nor was participation in this domestic romance reserved for the Bakunins themselves. Aleksandr's determination to have an open, sociable house meant that Priamukhino saw a never-ending stream of visitors. From the beginning, Priamukhino's fascination stemmed from its ability to suggest a happy and well-ordered domesticity. "Never did a family live more harmoniously," Lazhechnikov writes, expressing an opinion often repeated in the 1830s and 1840s.[59] Yet the reality is that the Bakunins' expressive home life was always

---

Indiana University Press, 1998), 31–41. Which *Tragedy of Dmitrii Donskoi* is meant here is not entirely clear.

[58] See IRLI f. 16, op. 3, no. 51, ll. 1–5.

[59] I. I. Lazhechnikov, "Zametki dlia biografii Belinskogo," in *Polnoe sobranie sochinenii*, vol. 12 (St. Petersburg: Tovarishchestvo M. O. Vol'f, 1900), 256.

animated by contrasting and often conflicting ambitions. Aleksandr—who often set the tone for conversations about Priamukhino—liked to present his home as a world so structured by reason that "all private wills will agree." But his wife and sisters spoke in a Romantic and religious idiom laced with suspicion about existing forms of society and reason. They sought some measure of spiritual independence from both and in the process helped to form a still more intimate, skeptical, and personal tradition in family life. From this point of view, notions of Priamukhino's innate harmony were something of a paternal myth, fostered by early-nineteenth-century domestic discourse.

As the Bakunin children grew older, conflicts within the family would begin to challenge this myth, in both the Bakunins' eyes and in the eyes of outsiders. When they did, the Bakunin family's distinguished life—meant to exemplify enlightened domesticity—would instead launch a bitter controversy over why these norms failed function in Russia and why Priamukhino's supposed "harmony" collapsed. During the first years of childhood, however, the Bakunins struggled with a different problem: how to define and defend Priamukhino's very existence within historical currents that threatened to push it to the margins of nineteenth-century life.

CHAPTER FOUR

Keeping Time

When Varvara and Aleksandr married in October 1810, Liubov Petrovna fixed the date of the ceremony in a small printed almanac:

> On the sixteenth day of this month the wedding of my children Aleksandr Mikhailovich and Varvara Aleksandrovna was celebrated. I pray to God that they be healthy and prosperous, and live until the deepest of old age.

In the years that followed, this little book became a register for births, deaths, and weddings at Priamukhino, as the new family grew and developed a habit for keeping track of time. Some entries are in Aleksandr Mikhailovich's hand; some are in his wife's; still other hands continue the book after their deaths, well into the late nineteenth century. (The last entries in this little book dating from 1810 were made in the 1880s.) Throughout, dates are grandly written out in words and interlaced with events on the Orthodox religious calendar. Thus Varvara Aleksandrovna records:

> In the year one thousand eight hundred and fourteen on the eighteenth of May, the Feast of the Holy Spirit, at five thirty in the afternoon our Misha was born. He was baptized by *matushka* Liubov Petrovna and Pavel Markovich . . .
>
> March 25 — in the first hour of the morning in the year one thousand

eight hundred twenty-three, on the very day of the Annunciation God
gave us a son Aleksei.

In this way, Liubov Petrovna's almanac became the spine of the first running
chronicle of life at Priamukhino, establishing a sacred and circular frame that
united generations. Here it was forever 1810, and every member of the family found a home amidst the same printed set of religious holidays and imperial birthdays.[1]

Though it provided the first and longest-running Bakunin family chronicle, Liubov Petrovna's almanac was hardly the only expression of the Bakunins' increasing interest in keeping time. From 1810 to 1813, her son
Aleksandr kept a diary describing the first three years of his married life. Not
satisfied with the journal of events recorded in the family's almanac, his wife
Varvara kept her own *Memory Books* beginning in 1822, noting the comings
and goings of family life month by month, year by year. Her children continued this *Memory Books* after her death in 1864. They also produced family
histories of their own, even as they archived the family's ever-increasing collection of private communications.[2] In this way, the Bakunin family developed practices of recording and conceptualizing their relationship to history
that defied the traditional silence that had enveloped the intimate lives of their
ancestors. "It is strange and disconcerting to see just how little the traces of
intellectual life have been valued in Russia," their contemporary Prince Petr
Viazemsky complained in the 1840s. "With what infantile disregard those
very things are given to oblivion and decay, which should be carefully and
reverently preserved in family archives!"[3] The same, however, could never
be said of the Bakunin family papers.

What was it, then, that stimulated the Bakunin family's new interest in
keeping time? We might, of course, be tempted to see these historical habits
as merely a function of the historical times in which the Bakunins lived. The
family's first efforts to plot out their place in time are indeed framed by two

---

[1] The almanac, titled *Mesiatsoslov na leto ot rozhdestva khristova 1810, kotoroe est' prostoe,
soderzhashchee v sebe 365 dnei, sochinennyi na znatneishie mesta Rossiiskoi imperii,* can now be found in
GATO f. 1407, op. 1, d. 72; see l. 28 for Liubov Petrovna's inscription; l. 18 and l. 10 for the boys'
birthdays.

[2] For a full description of the Bakunin family's historical activities in the second half of the
nineteenth century, see John Randolph, "'That Historical Family': The Bakunin Archive and
the Intimate Theater of History in Imperial Russia, 1780–1925," *Russian Review* 63 (October
2004): 583–91.

[3] P. Viazemskii, *Fon-Vizin* (St. Petersburg: Tipografiia Departamenta Vneshnei torgovli,
1848), 68.

of the most definitive events in the life of Imperial Russia's nobility: the "Patriotic War" against Napoleon on the one hand and the so-called Decembrist Revolt of 1825 on the other. Yet Bakunins of the seventeenth and early eighteenth centuries met equally historical upheavals—the great Russian civil war of the early seventeenth century, for example, and the reign of Peter the Great—without, as far as we can tell, documenting a subjective peep. Perhaps they repressed the historical impulses these events induced in them or could not express them—or perhaps they did not have such impulses at all. We will likely never know.

As the Bakunins' early efforts to record their family's history show, however, what mattered most to them during this period was their right to establish Priamukhino's own domestic version of history. At stake in this effort was the family's continued claim to liberty and the influence and distinction it afforded in a political climate that began to regard homes like the Bakunins' with deep suspicion. And here is where we run into an odd but important paradox. From one point of view the Bakunins—newcomers to the provinces with a proudly self-inventive tradition of home life—were the least historical feature in the Russian countryside. Yet their education and privilege allowed them to open their lives to the new historical self-consciousness coursing through Russian society at this time as few other actors could. Throughout the early 1800s, the Bakunins sought various ways of historicizing their carefully cultivated home life. And while many of these schemes would subsequently be repudiated by more powerful historical conceptions, the timekeeping habits of the period helped to create an intimate theater of history at Priamukhino—a stage where scenarios of historical self-creation and distinction could be performed not only by the Bakunins themselves but also by the various societies that began to gather around the Bakunin home.

Through this process, perhaps unnoticed by the Bakunins themselves, the family began to trade its traditional social distinction as a noble family for a more complex, but no less distinguished, historical identity. Having been drawn to the provinces by the hope of exemplifying certain social norms, the Bakunins gradually embraced the role of being an example of their time. Though this historical self-consciousness was in many ways bittersweet, it was not entirely a product of events beyond the family's control. Rather, it may be better read as a response to the opportunity their life at Priamukhino offered to "domesticate history."[4] By writing larger historical narratives into

---

[4] I take the term "domestication of history" from Thomas Newlin's provocative analysis of Andrei Bolotov's attempts to incorporate time into his estate idyll. See Newlin, *The Voice in the Gar-*

their own developing domestic romance, they could at least hope to become historical on their own terms.[5]

⊛⅍⊰⅞⊛

Two small notebooks from 1813 mark the beginning of the Bakunin family's new habit of keeping time. They contain Aleksandr Bakunin's memoirs of his family's life during 1811 and 1812—during the approach and outbreak of Russia's war with Napoleonic France. Aleksandr was certainly not the only one to reconstruct his personal vision of these tumultuous years. According to A. G. Tartakovsky's calculations, the Patriotic War (as the Russian government styled it) transformed memoir writing in Russia, taking it from the preserve of a few men and women of letters and turning it into one of the most widely practiced and popular literary genres. Between 1812 and 1916, no fewer than 509 memoirs about this period were published, with uncounted numbers more remaining in manuscript. This collectively produced memorial of 1812, Tartakovsky observes, became a cultural landmark, fixing one end of nineteenth-century Russians' perception of their place in history.[6]

An odd fact about Aleksandr's memoirs, however, underscores the degree to which his participation in this project was governed by a desire to take history on his own terms. It turns out that Aleksandr's memoirs—a self-contained narrative some sixty pages long, produced (as Aleksandr tells us) over the course of four days of writing in February 1813—started as part of an ongoing diary. A family quarrel, however, induced Aleksandr to burn his notebooks for 1811 and 1812. "Getting angry for nothing," he writes at the top of his memoirs, "a few days ago I burned my whole journal from Ilya's Day 1811 on." Regretting this decision later, he decided to "replace this loss from memory," reconstituting his lost diaries in memoir form. Thus Aleksandr's memoirs represent a memory once destroyed and then rewritten. Ironically, they are the only part of his diary project to survive today.

Why did Aleksandr bother to resurrect his memories of 1811 and 1812? He himself tells us that that he wanted to "preserve the names of those who

---

den: Andrei Bolotov and the Anxieties of Russian Pastoral, 1738–1833 (Evanston: Northwestern University Press, 2001), 168–78. Newlin establishes many themes that guide my thinking in this chapter, though I place less stress on anxiety and more on opportunity than he does.

[5] See Peter Fritzsche, *Stranded in the Present: Modern Time and the Melancholy of History* (Cambridge, Mass.: Harvard University Press, 2004), 1–54, 160–200.

[6] See A. G. Tartakovskii, *1812 god i russkaia memuaristika* (Moscow: Nauka, 1980), 259–63, 300 (table 1).

performed some service to us during this time or became our friends."[7] Yet Aleksandr's diaries quickly reveal to us a man more eager to reflect on this historical impact of his experiences than this practical explanation suggests. Dividing his tale into two dramatic episodes—the one a tale of courtly politics, the other the story of how war came to Priamukhino—Aleksandr shows how his historical experience confirmed his commitment to home life even as it transformed his understanding of its social and historical context. The resulting memoir, in other words, is a developmental romance, returning Aleksandr to his home a changed but deepened domestic man when peace resumes after two years of war.

Aleksandr's rewritten diaries begin in early 1811. Immediately after his marriage to Varvara, we are told, Aleksandr realized that he would have to leave Priamukhino for the provincial capital, Tver. Though Varvara was already expecting a child, Aleksandr judged that she was too young to begin her married life in isolation from society. One assumes (as Aleksandr himself later admits) that his own desire to get out from what was still his mother's house and to try to present his views in society also played a role. After a lengthy and strained good-bye, during which Liubov Petrovna complained bitterly that Aleksandr and Varvara were neglecting their duties to her, the young couple left on the road to Tver. (Their possessions followed them on a raft.) Once they reached the provincial capital, the civil governor helped them acquire a piano and a birthing chair, though an apartment was much slower in coming.[8] At this point, Aleksandr's return to court gave him a chance to reprise a role that he and his friends had long imagined, without ever playing it successfully: that of a seasoned landlord and family man, lending his experienced hand to public affairs.

In the 1790s and early 1800s, the court occupied an ambiguous position in Aleksandr's worldview. On the one hand, he and his mentors denounced the court in their idylls, portraying it as a servile and inauthentic world that was the exact opposite of the freedom and self-expression they thought characterized home life. The court was a deceptively "high" place laced with illusion and danger, whereas "lowness is a shield against storms," as Aleksandr observes happily in "The Harvest."[9] This sentimental critique never led them to abandon the idea of participating in government, however. Most of Alek-

[7] The "diaries" (actually, memoirs) are IRLI f. 16, op. 2, no. 12. See l. 2 for the passages just cited.

[8] IRLI f. 16, op. 2, no. 12, ll. 2–4.

[9] N. D. Kochetkova, exec. ed., *Russkaia literatura: Vek XVIII*, vol. 1, *Lirika* (Moscow: Khudozhestvennaia literatura, 1990), 533.

sandr's friends held high office. Through his brief sojourn in Gatchina and his model "constitution" for serf estates, Aleksandr tried to participate in imperial politics to the extent that his family responsibilities allowed. Though neither of these attempts met with much success, his new life in Tver provided him with his best opportunity yet.

Tver in 1811, as Aleksandr explains, was the scene of an unprecedented— indeed, self-consciously historical—political ferment. The Grand Duchess Ekaterina Pavlovna and her husband Prince Georg of Oldenburg, upon settling in Tver in 1809, rapidly converted their royal residence into a new kind of court. Though their palace was hardly free of the pretensions that Aleksandr resented—"I had to dress in uniform, curl my hair, and so on, which all seemed very silly"—the royal couple made a systematic attempt to draw in the support and sympathy of the provincial nobility. Within a few days of his arrival, Aleksandr had an audience with Prince Georg, Tver's governor general. The prince, Aleksandr claims, asked him what it would take to encourage provincial noblemen to add their voices to the court's conversations. "I answered," Aleksandr writes in his memoirs, "that it would depend on Her Majesty to attract them, by earning their love."[10] In the meantime, however, Aleksandr became a regular at court, presenting himself (and being received by others) as an educated voice of the provinces.

This voice was all the more valued, it seemed at first, because the debates held at the grand duchess's court in Tver involved wide-ranging discussions of Russia's nature and political future. More specifically, Ekaterina Pavlovna's court was one of the first forums for the development of a Russian brand of modern political conservatism. In Tver, prominent aristocrats and servitors were encouraged to speculate aloud about the ties that linked Russia's autocratic order to its particular history, traditions, and society. Without arguing for any legal limits on imperial authority—indeed, the nobles who gathered at the grand duchess's court were against constitutional charters—these new Russian conservatives believed that the autocracy must limit itself by respecting certain historic principles that undergirded (in their view) the Russian polity. The most important of these were serfdom and the privileged status of the nobility. Serfdom, according to this reasoning, reflected the able but as yet undisciplined character of the mass of the Russian people, who needed a stern hand to govern them. A privileged nobility, meanwhile, was equally necessary because only its patriotism and civilization could create a ruling class capable of responding to the empire's changing needs. "Not

[10] IRLI f. 16, op. 2, no. 12, ll. 4–5.

forms, but men are important," the most famous of Ekaterina Pavlovna's guests, the court historian Nikolai Karamzin, argued pithily. Bureaucratic procedures such as the ministries favored by Aleksandr's liberal friends could never master a land as large and protean as Russia; only a properly formed and human nobility could.[11]

In his memoirs, Aleksandr describes himself as both fascinated and re-pelled by political debates he observed at court. On the one hand, he shared the concern (voiced in the new conservative circles) that the gradual pro-fessionalization of Russia's civil service was marginalizing the provincial nobility.

> I dared remark to Her Highness that the military schools were insuffi-cient for the education of all noble children, that the seminarians had in any case wormed their way into all the openings, that clerks, from an early age accustomed to paperwork, move smoothly into official ranks, whereas poor nobles, growing up in ignorance, without any for-tune, and retiring quickly upon reaching officer, remain burdens to themselves and to their Fatherland and, by virtue of their number, may even with time become dangerous.[12]

What Aleksandr was objecting to was, in effect, the onset of an era when the sort of man he wished to be—an autonomous, provincial man, schooled by his private experience as a landlord—would no longer be recognized as valuable or useful by the Russian government. Aleksandr remembers being pleased to see that this point of view seemed to find favor with the grand duchess, the prince, and other important figures at court. There were even rumors, he records in his memoirs, that "I would pop up into the elite."[13]

Yet the new conservative politics had many more prominent ideologues and spokesmen. Among them was the empire's official historiographer, Karamzin, whose vision Aleksandr soon decided represented the antithesis of his own. Throughout the winter of 1811, as Aleksandr and his wife in-stalled themselves in Tver, Karamzin conducted a series of strategic visits to

[11] See in particular Alexander M. Martin, *Romantics, Reformers, Reactionaries: Russian Conser-vative Thought and Politics in the Reign of Alexander I* (Dekalb: Northern Illinois University Press, 1997), 91–108. For Karamzin's critique of Aleksandr's advisers' "excessive love for state re-forms" and bureaucratic structures, see Richard Pipes, *A Memoir on Ancient and Modern Russia: The Russian Text* (Cambridge, Mass.: Harvard University Press, 1959), 52–63; Karamzin argues for the need of men rather than forms on pages 109–14.

[12] IRLI f. 16, op. 2, no. 12, l. 18.

[13] On this episode, see more generally IRLI f. 16, op. 2, no. 12, ll. 17–19.

the grand duchess's court, where he presented his conservative manifesto, a *Memoir on Ancient and Modern Russia*.[14] Aleksandr's immediate hostility to Karamzin at first glance seems quite surprising. As Russia's most renowned writer of sentimental fiction, Karamzin built a cult around personal experience in the 1790s and early 1800s. Karamzin's conservative theories indeed placed such cultivated individuals—incorporated as a nobility—at the center of the nation's hopes for progress.[15] This sentimental, humanistic conservatism might seem to accord well with Aleksandr's own views. What bothered Bakunin, however, was that Karamzin's vision of personal and social progress had little to do with respect for the provincial nobility, with its "roots into the ground." Where Aleksandr and his friends saw home life on the estate as a laboratory for enlightenment, Karamzin emphasized the civilizing role of literature and salon society.[16] As a result, Karamzin's political vision and even his carefully cultivated personality seemed impossibly airy and elitist to Aleksandr.

For example, Karamzin embraced the so-called Norman theory of the genesis of the Russian state, according to which Russian monarchy had been founded by Scandinavian warlords, not native Slavic people.[17] This implied, Aleksandr observed to the grand duchess, that the Russian nation was incapable of generating a state out of its own inner resources.

> Karamzin said that ancient Romans had ruled the earth and now it was the turn of the Germans—I observed that remnants of Tatar rule and so on were preserved in Russia to this very day, but there were no traces of German rule whatsoever. The Grand Duchess, smiling, moved away from us.

Above and beyond such historical differences, Karamzin struck Aleksandr as a hopeless aristocrat and a snob: "He talked down to me intolerably, and his wife was worse."[18]

---

[14] On Karamzin's *Memoir*, see Martin, *Romantics*, 92–99.

[15] See the passages cited from Karamzin's *Memoir*, in note 11; see also Iu. M. Lotman, *Sotvorenie Karamzina* (Moscow: Kniga, 1987).

[16] On Karamzinian cultural politics, see William Mills Todd III, *Fiction and Society in the Age of Pushkin: Ideology, Institutions, and Narrative* (Cambridge, Mass.: Harvard University Press, 1986).

[17] In his *Memoir*, Karamzin imagined that Russia's first Scandinavian rulers were part of a historic moment when German rulers replaced old Roman institutions with a new "system," of which Russia was an integral part. (See Pipes, *Memoir*, 1–2). For Aleksandr's description of his response, see IRLI f. 16, op. 2, no. 12, l. 29.

[18] See IRLI f. 16, op. 2, no. 12, l. 29.

While at times the grand duchess seemed to sympathize with his objections, Aleksandr tells us, in the end he was outmaneuvered in the new realm of conservative politics. His voice and experience as a real-life provincial nobleman were no match for Karamzin's slick cultural vision of nobility, and Karamzin's *Memoir* predominated at the Tver court as a model for gentry conservatism. Increasingly, Alexsandr was "annoyed, remorseful, and silent."[19] In the meantime, Aleksandr fell victim to an old-fashioned sort of court intrigue, all the more damning (in his eyes) because it violated the sanctity of his life with Varvara.

Throughout Aleksandr's 1811 memoirs, the story of his married life runs parallel to the story of his participation in courtly politics. The two worlds at first stay quite separate; and if courtly life made Aleksandr morose, his description of life with Varvara is filled with affection. Most of the time, he tells us, the two stayed to themselves. Not needing to supervise field labor, Aleksandr rose late every morning and had coffee with his wife. He would then go to his study while "Varinka studied the bass violin." At two o'clock the couple would go for a stroll along a recently constructed promenade on the banks of the Volga River. Aleksandr writes, "In the evenings we occupied ourselves with music, drawing, and reading"—all the while waiting, expectantly, for the arrival of their first child.[20]

In the end, however, it did not prove possible to keep his new family life and courtly life separate, and the Bakunins soon found themselves ensnared in what Aleksandr ruefully calls a "scene from Molière." The scene, which Aleksandr describes in intimate and graphic detail, began on September 9, 1811. That evening, with Varvara's pregnancy very near term, the couple retired straight to bed after dinner.

> Varinka was very bothered by some sort of rash—she wasn't so much scratching as scraping her legs, making them bleed—afraid of bad consequences, I asked her to leave it alone, but she didn't listen, I grew annoyed and turned away from her—and she cried, and went to *maminka's* room. Having been there for a little while, she came back, lay down, and fell soundly asleep. But then at one in the morning all of a sudden she jerked and jumped from the bed as if struck by something—she shook with a strong fever—I woke up *maminka*, sent Osip for the midwife and Kirezha for Dr. Bakh—the midwife came and announced that Varinka was giving birth.

[19] See ibid., l. 8.
[20] Ibid., ll. 7–8.

The household sprang into action: the "colossal" Matrena Andreevna (the midwife) tied Varvara into the birthing chair, Dr. Bakh sat down at her head, and two serf maids helped hold her down while Aleksandr held her hand. *"Maminka"*—Aleksandr's mother-in-law, Varvara Mikhailovna—fainted after fervent prayer. Aleksandr himself grew queasy: "To my great distress it seemed that the midwife wasn't very skilled and Bakh no accoucheur." Fortunately, after several hours of labor, "as the bells rang for morning services and it began to grow light, Varinka successfully gave birth." The newborn daughter was named after Aleksandr's own mother, Liubov.[21]

Under the supervision of Bakh, a doctor highly recommended by the grand duke, Varvara decided to breast-feed little Liuba herself (practicing by feeding the children of serf wet nurses brought from the village). Both Aleksandr and Varvara's close friend Ekaterina Muravieva were against the idea. Aleksandr cited Varvara's weak physical condition, while Ekaterina protested on the basis of her own bad experiences with breast-feeding, adding : "On peut être bonne mère sans celà."[22] All the same, Liubov stayed at her mother's breast for the first few weeks. One evening, however, Varvara grew pale and fainted as she fed her daughter. Bakunin called in another physician, Dr. Gari, for a second opinion, and the child was given, despite her mother's protests, to a wet nurse. Dr. Bakh was insulted. He was later offended again when it came time to vaccinate Liubov against smallpox. Dr. Bakh being unavailable, the family turned to Dr. Gari once more.

As trivial as the family's choice of doctor might have seemed, it triggered the downfall of Aleksandr's position at court (or so he explains in his memoirs). Dr. Bakh, feeling slighted, complained to his patron, Prince Georg. The prince's affection for the Bakunins cooled notably. This, Aleksandr claims, was the real reason the rumored post at court was not given him: "I noticed it then, but was not a bit sorry."[23] After living in Tver a little while longer (on loans) in anticipation of a possible appointment, the Bakunins returned to Priamukhino. The absurd Molièrean comedy of their life at court—full of modern politics but tripped up by the machinations of palace factions—drew to a close at that point and with it the first chapter of Aleksandr's memoirs.

By identifying a comic structure in his recent experiences while rewriting

---

[21] Ibid., ll. 11–13.

[22] "One can be a good mother without that." Ekaterina Muravieva wrote several long letters to Varvara about motherhood: see IRLI f. 16, op. 9, no. 249, ll. 25–26, for exhortations on breast-feeding. Aleksandr describes the controversy about breast-feeding in their home in his memoirs, IRLI f. 16, op. 2, no. 12, ll. 13–14.

[23] Ibid., ll. 13–15; ll. 22–23.

his diary of 1811 as a memoir, Aleksandr strove to take some of the sting out of a historic lesson. Their return home to Priamukhino was a joyful one, and all was well that ended well. Even so, Aleksandr's bitingly comic depiction of the "arrogant" poseur Karamzin and the fumbling Dr. Bakh cannot hide the fact that the drama he describes ends with the final collapse of one of his most enduring ambitions: his desire to exert influence on Russian politics and society on his own domestic terms from his self-invented position as a family man and provincial landlord. Not even the new cultural world of conservative politics — at first glance receptive to this provincial voice — was immune to the petty politicking that haunted all courtly life. Yet there was no other public that Aleksandr ever imagined engaging. In the end, then, he returned to his home with part of his sentimental vision comically confirmed and part of it permanently dispelled. The court was indeed a dangerous and artificial realm, but there was no immediate hope of that realm's ever being transformed by common sense from the provinces. That much, at least, Aleksandr had now learned definitively — a lesson from experience that his reconstituted diary now archived for his family.

The second chapter of Aleksandr's memoirs begins with the new family happily ensconced in their idyll, seemingly for good this time. Trading visits with Varvara's parents at Bakhovkino throughout the winter and spring of 1812, Aleksandr reports, "we lived idly and not so idly."[24] Aleksandr set his hand to the plow and worked in the fields, clearing a new meadow. His wife dug several flowerbeds in the garden, around which her husband planted the violets he had discovered while clearing the front lawn. At the end of each day, he would ascend a cliff overlooking the Osuga to play with little Liuba. The two invented a game: whenever Liuba thrust her hand forward, her father would throw a rock down the ravine and into the river's swiftly flowing waters.[25]

Remembering these days with great tenderness, Aleksandr the memoirist also uses them to set up a dramatic turn that both he and the reader know is coming: the Patriotic War. "Our repose was suddenly shattered by the Sovereign's rescript announcing the French invasion across our borders."[26] If Aleksandr plots his brief abandonment of Priamukhino for Tver in 1811 as a comedy in which the Bakunins more or less voluntarily enrolled, the Patriotic War is presented as a national drama that threatens his family with per-

[24] Ibid., l. 45.
[25] Ibid., ll. 43–45.
[26] Ibid., l. 45.

manent exile into history. As before, Aleksandr's reconstituted diary provides a means by which he can take the Patriotic War on his own terms and see it as an educative experience that deepened his attachment to his home.

When war broke out, Aleksandr explains, he expected to play an active role in the countryside's mobilization. Serfs remained the backbone of the Russian army, and rumors circulated that the government was considering an extraordinary levy. Indeed, Aleksandr reports, the provincial nobility was summoned to Tver to hear announcements by Ekaterina Pavlovna amidst rumors of decisive victories and catastrophic defeats. Upon his arrival, however, Aleksandr was shocked and horrified by the lack of patriotism most of his fellow nobles displayed. Courtiers, he says, greeted the news of the court's imminent evacuation to Iaroslavl with a lascivious joy, contemplating the prospect of endless fields of virgin serf girls. A scandal also accompanied debates over how many recruits landowners should offer for enlistment. At first, the nobility—rather stingily, in Aleksandr's opinion—voted one recruit per forty souls. The grand duchess, insulted, crafted for her spokesman an elaborate and histrionic speech, pleading for further patriotic sacrifice. Although the tactic almost backfired—the nobility's rank and file was insulted by what it viewed as demagoguery—a levy of one soul per twenty-five souls was then voted.[27]

Aleksandr portrays his disillusionment with his fellow nobles as being accompanied by a sudden awareness that everything would depend on the actions and sympathies of his serfs. When he returned to Priamukhino, the painful process of giving away recruits (conscripted serfs) into the army accelerated the dissolution of his previous understanding of life on his estate. In his memoirs, Aleksandr remembers waking one morning to hear the screams of soldiers' families, as men from the village marched to war:

> How sad the procession of these people departing for the city—they were sent away very early—but we couldn't sleep, of course—we rather listened, as the howls of the relatives seeing them off came first closer, growing strongest near the church, and then gradually falling silent as they grew more distant.[28]

[27] Ibid., ll. 51–53.

[28] Ibid., l. 54. Aleksandr Bakunin mentions in his journal that he tried to get household servants to volunteer, promising them freedom upon their return. His mother owed twenty-eight recruits from Torzhok *uezd*, and to "take them all from the peasantry would be to bankrupt oneself voluntarily." In the end, twenty-one peasants went, accompanied by six men Aleksandr identified as "drunks and villains," including two shoemakers and a cook.

In his plans and projects, Aleksandr regarded Russia's serfs (and by extension his own) as innocent but uncultured folk, requiring careful paternal instruction from their landlords. But now, when the landlords had shown themselves hopelessly incapable of discipline, he struggled with anxiety over what the peasants might do as they were pushed to fight. This anxiety doubled, Aleksandr tells us, on August 12, when the news arrived that the French had taken Smolensk and the borders were now undefended. The family made plans to flee for the city: "Afraid of disturbances among the serfs, I announced to Varinka over supper that in the morning we must go to Torzhok — Varinka listened to the news of the approaching danger steadfastly."[29]

At that point, however, family life forced the Bakunins to remain at home. "That morning," Aleksandr writes,

> Varinka complained that she had a little stomachache. I went into the other room and began to write, when suddenly maminka came running in and informed me that in Evva Ivanovna's opinion, Varinka was giving birth. Stunned, I went to her — she was already in labor. *Maminka,* Uliana, Nastasia, and I hurried to set up the settee — rushed — Varinka suffered and walked around — she lay down on the settee — grandmother sat down — I held Variuta by the hand and kissed her — *maminka* ran around the garden, the courtyard — Varinka patiently bore her sufferings — almost never screamed, and when she cried out, Ulianushka scolded her. Her sufferings lasted about an hour and a half, and then Varinka successfully gave birth to Varinka, whom she had already decided to feed herself . . . but I was very worried: what will become of her if the enemy approaches, what if the peasants revolt?[30]

And so, instead of fleeing Priamukhino for the estate near Kazan, the Bakunins remained at home. As a nobleman-turned-family man who had never served in the military, Aleksandr was forced to organize the peasants, whose discipline he had always distrusted, into an army.

The experience, Aleksandr explains, transformed his life in a number of

[29] IRLI f. 16, op. 2, no. 12, l. 56.

[30] Ibid. Though it is not possible to identify all the characters mentioned here with certainty, Uliana and Nastasia were likely serfs and serving women, while Evva Ivanovna was likely a midwife. (Uliana may have been Uliana Andreevna, identified as the serf nanny who had raised Varvara herself as a child. See Dmitrii Oleinikov, "Aleksandr Bakunin i ego poema 'Osuga,'" *Nashe Nasledie* 29–30 [1994]: 58). "Variuta," like Varinka, is an affectionate form of Varvara, while Ulianushka is short for Uliana. The "Varinka" to whom Varvara gives birth is the couple's daughter Varvara.

ways. His brother, Mikhail Mikhailovich, then a high-ranking official in St. Petersburg, all but ordered Aleksandr to evacuate their aging mother, Liubov Petrovna. But when *matushka* refused to be moved, Aleksandr found himself the target of his brother's wrath. (Aleksandr's anger over this incident, we are told, is what later motivated him to burn his original diary in an attempt to expunge this painful memory from the record.)[31] Meanwhile, Aleksandr was stunned by what he and his serf army accomplished:

> I bought powder, lead, and distributed to the people thirty rifles and sixty sabers, and several hundred pikes—I armed the Tepterevo peasants as well with pikes, and ordered the Rzhevsk peasants armed— Pavel Markovich armed his people—everywhere night watches were instituted—all night, the sentries called to each other.[32]

When the French finally approached, the local peasants mounted fierce resistance and turned them back. Aleksandr found himself in debt to a rural world he had previously seen solely as the target of reform. "We are very, very obliged to the peasants of Sychevka," he records in his memoir, naming the partisans whose stand against the French helped save Tver.[33]

Viewed in retrospect, Varvara's birth, by preventing the family's evacuation, forged the final tie between the Bakunins and their estate. French forces fell back from Moscow in mid-October, and the late fall of 1812 became a period of celebration and commemoration at Priamukhino. Present when the newly appointed commander-in-chief Kutuzov visited Tver in the gloomiest days of the campaign, Aleksandr "planted in the latter's honor a grove of seven linden trees in Varinka's garden on the banks of the Osuga." On a hill earlier intended for a neoclassical pavilion in memory of his good friend Nikolai Lvov, Aleksandr constructed a monument to Kutuzov instead. This consisted of a large white quartz stone on the hill's crest, as if to mark a spot where the general sat and planned Napoleon's defeat. Last, he and his wife planted a grove of lilacs and poplars to root the time ever deeper into the estate's landscape. "This planting should be preserved—it will remind us of this horrible epoch."[34]

---

[31] IRLI, f. 16, op. 2, no. 12, l. 60.

[32] Ibid., ll. 58–59. Tepterevo and Rzhevsk are the names of two local communities. Pavel Markovich was Aleksandr Bakunin's father-in-law, Pavel Markovich Poltoratsky.

[33] Ibid.

[34] See IRLI, f. 16, op. 2, no. 12, ll. 62–68, for a description of this victory garden. On Kutuzov Hill, see also Vladimir Sysoev, *Bakuniny* (Tver: Sozvezdie, 2002), 87.

Like "Kutuzov Hill," the Bakunins' various victory gardens were monuments to the family's victory over historical currents that threatened to wash
them away. These monuments both recalled the Patriotic War and attempted
to put it safely behind. The same thing, in the end, may be said of Aleksandr's
memoirs. Though it took him only four days to write his sixty-page account
of the family's life in 1811 and 1812, the patient journalistic task of sustain-
ing his diary seems to have had little appeal thereafter. Finishing his memoir
on February 13, he added entries for the next four days. Then the diary ends,
though there were many pages left in his notebook. Aleksandr withdrew from
courtly life, left history on his own terms, and focused on developing the reasoned, paternal home life he had planned for his family at Priamukhino. In
an odd way, the war of 1812 saved Aleksandr Bakunin from the collapse of
his faith in Russia's public realm by underscoring the reality and historicity
of the more immediate manorial world in which he lived. Priamukhino had
been revealed not merely as a wasteland subject to his cultivation but as an
organic community with its own life and logic, sturdy enough to stand up pa-
triotically against Napoleon's army. After his mother died in 1814, Aleksandr
Bakunin settled for good into his long-imagined role as a benevolent paterfamilias, leaving the capricious world outside to its own devices.

In 1822, Aleksandr's wife began a chronicle devoted to an entirely internal
family time — a series of *Memory Books* (*Pamiatnye zapiski*), as she called them.
Like the family's almanac, these books proved a surprisingly durable frame
for the family's timekeeping habits. They were maintained by Varvara until
the late 1850s and were later carried forward by a daughter-in-law into at
least the 1870s.[35] Yet if the almanac places a circular, sacred frame on the
family's life — registering every birth and death in the midst of an eternal
1810 — the *Memory Books* take a chronological approach. Family history is
composed of a calendar of social and domestic events, recorded faithfully one
after the other. Take, for example, the notebook's opening year, 1822:

[35] The original *Pamiatnye zapiski* are IRLI f. 16, op. 6, no. 9. In the early twentieth century, the
historian A. A. Kornilov and his wife, E. Kornilova, prepared a collation of the Bakunin family
chronicle, based on a running notebook kept by Varvara Bakunina's daughter-in-law N. S. (Kor-
sakova) Bakunina. This copy is preserved as IRLI f. 16, op. 2, no. 70. I have not been able to
find N. S. Bakunina's original notebook, but the copy prepared by the Kornilovs shows clearly
that it was based on the *Pamiatnye zapiski.*

January. Annette is with us—the Vulfs haven't been for a long time. Iakov Pavlovich Gladkov and Sergei Ivanovich (who hasn't been to see us since 1820) came with them.

March. Lent. The first week we all went to the Veliashevs and to Bernovo.

April. Konstantin Osipovich came from Petersburg. He spent the sacred holiday with us.

June. We were in Torzhok with Konstantin Osipovich. We came back from Torzhok on a splendid evening. The Feast of St. Peter—at the Veliashevs'. Charades at the Vulfs'. Gredenko. I fell ill. Katinka Gladkova came for a visit, to Priamukhino.

July. All the Vulfs came for a visit. Battle on the water. Anna Nikolaevna won. Theater. Imberg came with his wife. Lisatovich was very funny.

Read in isolation, the chronicle communicates the sense of a self-sufficient world, where time takes on rhythms set by the family's own activities. Dramatis personae enter and exit this chronicle, leaving their names, like calling cards, behind. If some months are filled with enigmatic "battles on the water," others pass by without leaving a trace. "I don't remember," Varvara Aleksandrovna writes, under the heading September 1822.[36] (Such comments seem to indicate that the *Memory Books*, like Aleksandr's war diaries, were often composed retrospectively, on occasion after several months had passed.)

The focal point of Varvara's *Memory Books*—well illustrated by this opening excerpt—is the Bakunin family's intimate social calendar: the whirlwind of years spent visiting with relatives and friends. Because the Bakunins' relatives were among the most politically and culturally active members of the Imperial Russian elite—and kept careful biographical records of their own—it is almost always possible to identify these people and places. For example, Bernovo (which the Bakunins visited in March 1822) was an estate in Tver Province belonging to the Vulf family, who were close relatives.[37] The

---

[36] The *Memory Book* is IRLI f. 16, op. 6, no. 9; see ll. 1–2 for the entry listed above.

[37] In the nineteenth century, the Bakunins and Vul'fs were bound by a variety of ties. Most worth mentioning here is the fact that Pavel Markovich Poltoratsky—Varvara Bakunina's stepfather—was the brother of Petr Markovich Poltoratsky. Petr Markovich, in turn, was married to Ekaterina Ivanovna Vul'f, whose father owned Bernovo. In visiting Bernovo, the Bakunins were thus visiting relatives. Petr Markovich and Ekaterina Ivanovna, in turn, were the parents of Anna Petrovna Poltoratskaia, better known to history as Anna Petrovna Kern/Markova-Vinogradskaia. See below for discussion of Kern.

"Annette" mentioned in Varvara's chronicle — Anna Nikolaevna Vulf — occupies an awkward juncture in the poet Pushkin's carefully documented biography. She was briefly courted by Pushkin for two weeks in 1826, shortly after his still more famous affair with her cousin, Anna Petrovna Kern. (Pushkin's attraction to Kern resulted in his most famous love lyric, "I recollect a wondrous moment" [*Ia pomniu chudnoe mgnoven'ie*].)[38]

In a letter written in 1852, Kern herself left the following recollection of the Bakunins at Bernovo, captivating in its intimate depiction of these years:

> Tell the honorable Aleksandr Mikhailovich, that I remember him from after his marriage, when he came to Bernovo, and we fell in love with his children, his ability to live and to love his wife. She was a young, joyous, playful girl; he — a serious, steady man, yet even so it was pleasant to watch them. I remember them sitting next to each other amicably, and how he enveloped her into his long arms, and from the expression of her face it was evident, how happy she was with this love and protection. From time to time she would put him on the floor and jump across him like a playful kitten. His position then was neither funny nor strange. And yet what conquering power and kindness, what ideal kindness, manifested itself with love! I remember as well a ball one evening; they came into the common room we shared with mother; he lay on her bed, she lay next to him in a light white dress, and he — jokingly — tried to convince her that the ring on his finger could no longer be removed, that it was growing into him. And she got worried, removed it, and ordered that water be brought, and soap, and he smiled and finally reassured her that it was all a jest. And in everything there was the same love — even in trifles![39]

This memoir of the early years of the Bakunins' marriage acquires a certain extra poignancy when contrasted with Kern's own story. Like Varvara, Anna Kern was married at an early age to a man many years her senior. But in Kern's case the pairing proved a horribly unhappy one, with Kern straining to live with her elderly husband for ten years before leaving him. Her life as a woman in flight from her marriage brought her to her historical encounter

---

[38] On these moments in Pushkin's life, see T. J. Binjon, *Pushkin: A Biography* (New York: Knopf, 2003), 202–7.

[39] A. P. Kern (Markova-Vinogradskaia) to E. V. Bakunina, letter of 1 May 1852, in A. P. Kern (Markova-Vinogradskaia), *Vospominaniia. Dnevniki. Perepiska*, comp. A. M. Gordin (Moscow: Izdatel'stvo Pravda, 1989), 320.

with Pushkin (a paradigmatic milestone, of sorts, in the history of romantic love in Russia, of which Kern herself, through her diaries and memoirs, was an important author). But it also left her open to poverty and social scorn, which indeed dogged her for the rest of her life. (Fortunately she seems to have eventually found a kindred soul of sorts in her second husband, Aleksandr Vasilievich Markov-Vinogradsky.)[40]

By enabling such private historical intersections and social cross-referencing, Varvara's *Memory Books* were part and parcel of the creation of new forms of Russian history in the early nineteenth century, in which private actors operating outside the state—families and homes, in addition to poets and thinkers—are the main protagonists. Even as prominent writers like Prince Viazemsky bemoaned the absence of well-organized family archives, the noble society in which the Bakunins lived began to create a space of private historical distinction, where living itself became something that had a weight and meaning worth recording.[41] In this sense, far from being an exercise in idyllic isolation, the Bakunin family chronicle can be read as part of an attempt to create a private chronology for modern Russia, one that kept time according to the rhythms of noble sociability. In the case of the Bakunins, however, broader national narratives soon began to stake a claim on this sphere of intimate historical distinction. In particular, the Bakunin family chronicle's detachment from high politics could not be maintained amidst the aftershocks of a radical coup mounted by some of their closest relatives: the Decembrist Revolt of 1825.

⊛⚮⊛

September. Pavel Nicholaevich is courting cousin Liza. Papa is very sick.
November. Sovereign Aleksandr I died. An oath to Nicholas Pavlovich. Iakov Petrovich Liubovnikov and Girsh are here with us.

---

[40] On Kern's historical life and poverty, see A. M. Gordin, "Anna Petrovna Kern i ee literaturnoe nasledie," in Gordin, *Vospominaniia*, 5–24, esp. 11–14.

[41] In Russia, untangling the dense biographical legacy of the early nineteenth century remains a vital ongoing enterprise, carried out in massive scholarly commentaries. See, e.g., the works of the late great V. E. Vatsuro, collected in *Zapiski kommentatora* (St. Petersburg: Gumanitarnoe agenstvo Akademicheskii proekt, 1994). Within this collection, the essay "Bunina ili Bakunina?" (71–75) provides another example of an intersection between Bakunin family history and literary history. The anxiety over the degree to which the public record reflects the full sweep of Russian history has deep roots in Russian intellectual culture: I discuss nineteenth-century precedents in Randolph, "'That Historical Family,'" 577–80.

December 14. A Revolt in Petersburg. Miloradovich died. What will
happen to the Muravievs?
—From the *Memory Books* of V. A. Bakunina, under the year 1825

On November 19, 1825, Emperor Alexander I died unexpectedly. Everyone anticipated that his eldest brother, Grand Duke Constantine, would be
the next tsar. But by a secret agreement signed some two years before, Constantine had renounced the throne in favor of the youngest brother, Grand
Duke Nicholas (without, however, informing society of this fact). For nearly
a month, confusion reigned. Explanations flew between St. Petersburg and
Warsaw, where Constantine lived. Finally, on December 14, the government
ordered military units stationed in St. Petersburg to swear a definitive oath
to Grand Duke Nicholas.

At this point, however, events took a shocking turn. A secret patriotic society composed of elite veterans of the Napoleonic Wars launched a coup
against the Romanov Dynasty. In a hastily improvised plan, the rebel officers
urged their troops to refuse the new loyalty oath and prepared to install one
of their own, Prince Sergei Trubetskoi, as Russia's temporary "dictator." (He,
in turn, was charged with giving the empire a constitution, according to draft
projects the society had prepared.) But Trubetskoi lost his nerve; a lengthy
standoff developed that played into the government's hands, and in the end
the rebellion collapsed in a bloody massacre. A conspirator shot and killed
the loyalist General Mikhail Miloradovich, a war hero popular with the army.
This steeled the government to order cannons fired at the demonstrators. After two or three salvos of canister shot, seventy or eighty lay dead, and the
rebel officers were arrested. Despite a second, equally disorganized coup attempt in Ukraine, Emperor Nicholas I was securely on his throne by the second week of January.

The Decembrist Revolt neither engaged nor affected most of the empire.
Yet it set in motion a grand moment of reckoning in imperial life and politics
by helping to frame the existential anxieties and ambitions of the nineteenth
century as Imperial Russian problems. During the French Revolution and
Napoleonic Wars, Russia's ambiguous relationship to Europe had allowed
Russian elites to imagine that the empire need not fully embrace the restless
spirit of the age. It could be stared down or defeated by force of arms. But
the odd, awkward, and ultimately tragic way the Decembrist Revolt played
out showed that neither the government nor its opponents were entirely at
home in the nineteenth century. "Russia is, unhappily, as easy to agitate as all
other countries in our time," observed the conservative Austrian minister

Prince Klemens Metternich, not without a touch of schadenfreude. Equally characteristic was the embarassment that leading Decembrists were said to have felt at the moment of their execution. Though they often doubted their coup would succeed, the conspirators had counted on an unequivocal martyrdom: "We shall die, oh, how gloriously we shall die!" enthused A. I. Odoevsky before the revolt. Yet when the scaffold failed to function at his execution, the thwarted revolutionary hero Sergei Muraviev-Apostol was left to cry out in frustration, "Poor Russia! We cannot even hang properly!"[42]

The newly crowned Nicholas I and his advisers, as they planned their own response to the revolt, quickly decided that its root causes lay in "an idleness of the mind more dangerous than idleness of the flesh." Emancipated by privilege and yet lacking "firm knowledge" and moral principles, they declared, a "handful of monsters" had given in to willful revolutionary fantasies of their own concoction, betraying their faith, their tsar, and their fatherland in the process. The government's first and most visceral reaction to the events of December 1824 was to launch a sweeping purge of the intricate networks of patronage and kinship that bound the empire's *grand monde* together. Anyone who had ties to the secret societies—no matter how old—was considered complicit in the coup. More than 120 men from this small social world were sentenced to exile and hard labor, while hundreds of others suffered the harrowing experience of official investigation. The government encouraged the exiles' wives to renounce them and smoothed the path to divorce for those who chose to do so. Some women did; others abandoned their homes and families instead and joined their husbands in Siberia. Houses went dark and the salons of the capitals emptied out.[43]

An imperial manifesto of July 1826 laid out the broad outlines of the government's longer-term response. The recent revolt, the manifesto declared, was the result of an evil "infection" that had penetrated deeply into the imperial social body. Fortunately, "by the unanimous union of all faithful sons of the fatherland," this revolutionary infection had been defeated. Yet the cri-

---

[42] The sentiment was plausibly general: other authors attributed this bit of gallows humor to other men. See Patrick O'Meara, *K. F. Ryleev: A Political Biography of the Decembrist Poet* (Princeton: Princeton University Press, 1984), 305–6. Odoevsky is quoted in John L. H. Keep, *Soldiers of the Tsar: Army and Society in Russia, 1462–1874* (Oxford: Clarendon Press, 1985), 267–68. For Metternich's observation, see Anatole G. Mazour, *The First Russian Revolution, 1825: The Decembrist Movement* (Stanford: Stanford University Press, 1961), 203.

[43] The standard work on the Decembrist Revolt in English is Mazour, *First Russian Revolution;* see also Keep, *Soldiers,* 250–72. On the fate of the Decembrist wives in particular, see Barbara Alpern Engel, *Women in Russia, 1700–2000* (Cambridge: Cambridge University Press, 2004), 43–47.

sis had revealed a moral weakness in the imperial social fabric. Specifically, the revolt showed that parents must double and triple the attention they paid to the education of their children. Otherwise, Russians risked wandering off down destructive routes, traveling "into dreamy extremes, of which the beginning is moral decay and the end—destruction." Though the government would do its part to provide such "firm knowledge," families must cooperate as well. "All the government's efforts, all of its sacrifices will be in vain, if home education will not prepare morals and assist with the government's aims."[44]

Nicholas's manifesto showed in no uncertain terms that the tsar expected Russian home life to fall in line with priorities set by the government. This applied especially to noble families, who, it declared, should be an "example to all other estates."[45] As the tsar was well aware, some of the most culturally ambitious and developed noble families were also at the source of the revolt. Their houses had served as the meeting places of secret societies; their networks of marriage and kinship had fostered the societies' expansion and development. For all these reasons, Nicholas's message to noble homes was plain. "Let parents turn their attention to the moral education of their children"—and let no one allow their family life to wander off in a freethinking direction again.[46]

How was this message received at Priamukhino? In memoirs written toward the end of his life Mikhail Bakunin presented 1825 as a decisive turning point in his family's life. "After the fatal outcome of the December conspiracy (1825) my father, scared by this rout of liberalism, changed our educational system." Mikhail continued: "From this point on he decided to make us loyal subjects of the Tsar. To this end, I was sent to St. Petersburg at the age of fourteen for enrollment into Artillery School." The idyllic age of childhood at Priamukhino—with its liberal life "outside reality"—was exchanged for a much more regimented existence, both at home and (in Mikhail's case) in the barracks.[47]

Was this true? Was Aleksandr so panicked by the outcome of the Decembrist Revolt that he betrayed his earlier convictions and adopted a new, conservative politics at home? At first glance, Mikhail's statement might be taken as a bit of revolutionary mythmaking. Using 1825 to infuse his memoirs with historic tension, we might think, the old radical built a clash between progress and reaction into the story of his childhood. The one event

---

[44] "Vnutrennie izvestiia," *Severnaia pchela*, no. 85 (17 July 1826).

[45] Nicholas's manifesto repeats this classic formulation. Ibid.

[46] Ibid.

[47] Bakunin, "Istoriia moei zhizni," *Sobranie*, I:27–28.

Mikhail marshals to support his claim—his dispatch into military service at the age of fourteen—would likely have happened with or without the Decembrist Revolt. Many of his relatives were military men; his own father had been sent into service at age eleven, and in any case the Bakunin family was too large to remain on the estate forever. With the subdivision of the Bakunins' heavily mortgaged properties through dowry and inheritance looming on the horizon, the only way the family could renew its wealth was through officialdom and St. Petersburg.

Yet recognizing that there may be an element of radical mythology in Mikhail Bakunin's memoirs does not eliminate the questions they raise. It is a fact that the conspiracy and its aftermath affected the Bakunins quite intimately. Just before visiting Priamukhino in June 1816, Varvara's cousin and childhood friend Aleksandr Nikolaevich Muraviev had helped found the first of the secret patriotic societies, from which the conspiracy sprang. Of the five initial members of the group, three were also Varvara's cousins: Nikita Muraviev and Matvei and Sergei Muraviev-Apostol. Though Aleksandr Muraviev seems to have withdrawn from the plot in the early 1820s, long before the coup itself, he was arrested and exiled to Siberia in early 1826. Nikita Muraviev—author of the Northern Society's draft constitution—likewise received Siberian exile, while Sergei Muraviev-Apostol was hanged. (His brother Ippolit, believing Sergei had been killed during the insurrection, shot himself.)[48] In addition, another member of the Muraviev family later contended that Aleksandr Bakunin himself had been included in some of the secret societies' discussions. There he was supposed to have played a moderating and conservative role, arguing in favor of the monarchy and against all conspiratorial schemes; but even so, participation alone was enough to provoke official suspicion and arrest of many others.[49]

[48] On the Muraviev-Apostols, see Elmo E. Roach, "Murav'ev-Apostol, Matvei Ivanovich (1793–1886) and Murav'ev-Apostol, Sergei Ivanovich (1796–1826)," in Joseph L. Wieczynski,ed. *The Modern Encyclopedia of Russian and Soviet History*, vol. 23 (N.p.: Academic International Press, 1981), 198–202. See also the entries under A. M. Muraviev, A. N. Muraviev, A. Z. Muraviev, M. N. Muraviev, N. M. Muraviev, and V. M. Bakunin in M. V. Nechkina, ed., *Dekabristy: Biograficheskii spravochnik* (Moscow: Nauka, 1988). On the other hand, Ivan Modestovich Bakunin, still another cousin, was awarded the Order of St. Vladimir for his enthusiastic participation in the suppression of the revolt. (Ivan Modestovich commanded a cannon battery on Senate Square on December 14; when his men hesitated over whether to shoot the demonstrators, he screamed furiously at them until they fired.) On I. M. Bakunin, see Sysoev, *Bakuniny*, 17–19.

[49] Unfortunately, it has not been possible to either corroborate or disprove this account, related by Sergei Nikolaevich Muraviev to the historian D. A. Kropotov. See D. A. Kropotov, *Zhizn' Grafa M. N. Murav'eva, v sviazi s sobytiiami ego vremeni i do naznacheniia ego Gubernatorom v*

Beyond the immediate concern for their cousins the Muravievs—regis-tered in Varvara's *Memory Books*—the Bakunins undoubtedly worried about what the aftermath of the revolt might mean for Priamukhino. Indeed, the family's papers show that Varvara Bakunina contacted (through relatives) the government's new minister of public enlightenment, Admiral Aleksandr Shishkov, and submitted her various plans for her children's education for his consideration and approval. Her sister-in-law, Varvara Mikhailovna, re-ported that Shishkov listened to these "projects" carefully and made several approving suggestions.[50] Unfortunately, no further information survives about this consultation. Yet the mere fact that Varvara sought out such ad-vice from the highest levels of the imperial government—and from a man well known in Russian society for his conservative cultural tastes—testifies to a desire to begin to bring her children's education in line with official designs.

There also exists a final and strangely paradoxical product of Aleksandr Bakunin's devotion to Priamukhino, an awkward ode to family life, written in the late 1820s. As was mentioned earlier, historians have often relied on "Osuga" as a portrait of family life at at Priamukhino, but the poem is in fact something more openly ideological.[51] It attempts to provide an apology for Russian estate life, by presenting homes like the Bakunins' as the products of history rather than reform.

❀❖❀

In the years immediately following his marriage, Aleksandr had largely given up on poetry, so closely linked to his hopes and dreams as a young man. For a long time he failed to express himself in a genre that was captivating his closest poetic mentors: the domestic ode. In 1807, for example, Gavrila Der-

---

Grodno (St. Petersburg, 1874), 207–11; A. Kornilov, *Molodye gody Mikhaila Bakunina: Iz istorii russkogo romantizma* (Moscow: M. and S. Sabashnikov, 1915), 22–26.

[50] See Varvara Mikhailovna's letter of [1826], IRLI f. 16, op. 7, no. 20, l. 5.

[51] "Osuga" exists in several variants in the Bakunin archive. The very first seems to be IRLI, f. 16, op. 2, no. 39. The following analysis will use the published version prepared by Dmitrii Oleinikov, "'Osuga,'" which seems to reflect the final, finished version. Oleinikov dates the gen-esis of the poem to the late 1820s (54), though the poem itself, as will be explained in a moment, continued to be written for at least a decade thereafter. As was mentioned in chapter 2, Kornilov published extensive excerpts from "Osuga" in his family history of the early 1900s (*Molodye gody*, esp. chapters 1–6). For a long time historians had to depend on "Osuga" for a vision of family life at Priamukhino (see, e.g., Priscilla Roosevelt, *Life on the Russian Country Estate: A Social and Cultural History* [New Haven: Yale University Press, 1995], 298), but could not appreciate its significant departures from Aleksandr's earlier poetic and political visions, or indeed, its some-what grotesque character.

zhavin sought to immortalize his life in the countryside, in his famous "To Evgenii: Life at Zvanka." Vasilii Kapnist, another close friend, sang of his home in "Obukhovka," published in 1818. Elegant achievements in verse, both poems may be regarded as the completion of their authors' efforts to create distinguished provincial lives. "At peace with my neighbors," Kapnist writes,

> In harmony with my conscience,
> In my love for my lovely family,
> Here I measure in joys alone
> The flow of gentle days.[52]

As is traditional in such odes to estate life—whose history goes back to Horace's odes and Virgil's *Georgics*—a note of nostalgia and sadness informs these efforts. Both poets acknowledge that they are no longer building their homes but merely living in them in anticipation of their inevitable demise. With stoic sangfroid, Derzhavin stares at his own apocalypse:

> This house will fall down, the forest and garden wither,
> Even the name of Zvanka will nowhere be remembered.

Yet, in both cases, these sad reveries are interrupted by the hope of finding immortality in their reputations as patriots and poets—as good, honest men. These houses may fall, but the lives lived there will survive them, as their verses are meant to ensure. (In the unlikely event that this doesn't happen, Derzhavin instructs Bishop Evgenii Bolkhovitinov, the church historian to whom his poem was dedicated, to awaken "posterity from its sleep with your pen" and remind them that "'here lived the poet of God and Felitsa.'" "God" and "Felitsa" were the titles of Derzhavin's most famous works.)[53]

At first glance, "Osuga" would seem to be Aleksandr's effort to place his own home in this venerable tradition, recently invented for Russia by his friends. An odic meditation on home life in the countryside—complete with a sad prophecy of the poet's death—lies at "Osuga's" base. But the ode's wild expansion beyond this foundation betrays a radically different purpose and indeed eventually makes "Osuga" a radically different kind of poem. At 250

[52] V. V. Kapnist, "Obukhovka," in *Sobranie sochinenii*, ed. D. S. Babkin, vol. 1 (Moscow-Leningrad: Izdatel'stvo Akademii Nauk SSSR, 1960), 250–54, esp. 250.

[53] G. R. Derzhavin, "Evgeniiu. Zhizn' Zvanskaia," in *Anakreonticheskie pesni*, ed. G. P. Makogonenko, G. N. Ionin, and E. N. Petrova (Moscow: Nauka, 1987), 127–33, esp. 132.

lines, Derzhavin's stately "Life at Zvanka" remains a study in style and precision. Kapnist's "Obukhovka" ends its graceful journey after 145 lines. "Osuga," by contrast, comes to a rather arbitrary halt after more than 1,000 lines. Aleksandr constructs for his monument to estate life an ever-expanding structure, built around simple, four-line stanzas. The result is an open-ended, almost journalistic kind of verse, into which themes and events far outside the idyll's normal repertoire could fit. By the poem's end, Aleksandr has commented on an oddly encyclopedic range of contemporary themes, including recent literary disputes, the revolution in France, his favorite dog, the recommendations of Adam Smith, and the perils of venereal disease. Such an ungainly structure could hardly be accidental. Though Aleksandr was nowhere near the poetic equal of either Derzhavin or Kapnist, his earlier poems testify that he could certainly produce fine (and concise) verse. (Derzhavin, it will be remembered, recommended Aleksandr's "The Harvest" as an ideal idyll.)

In the end, it seems, Aleksandr came to "Osuga" with a determination to do more than celebrate his family's life or ensure its poetic immortality. He wished to situate his home more explicitly within the cultural and political landscape of his day while simultaneously offering a historical justification for his family's existence. Traditionally, themes of independence and distinction surrounded the mythology of estate life. "Life at Zvanka," for example, begins with an invocation of rural freedom ("Happy he, who depends less on people.") It then turns, with an almost fetishistic relish, to the specific details of life on the Derzhavin estate. "Osuga," by contrast, opens with an image of distance and dependence, a salutation to the river that flows past Priamukhino and links it to the rest of the world:

> Flourish, gentle Osuga,
> Soul of Priamukhino's fields
> And too my faithful friend,
> And wet nurse of my children.[54]

Tellingly, the Bakunin home is, as yet, nowhere to be seen. Using a folky couplet—"And too my faithful friend / and wet nurse of my children" [I vernaia moia podruga / kormilitsa moikh detei]—Aleksandr indicates his family's close, almost kindred relations with the countryside. The river is their benefactress and nourisher, but it is its own force as well. It is a soul that under-

---

[54] Oleinikov, "'Osuga,'" 55.

lies the countryside—and originates deep in the provinces, well before Priamukhino itself.

In this sense, "Osuga" marks a radically new treatment of water, a symbol
much beloved by Aleksandr and his friends in the 1790s. In "The Stream,"
water had served as a symbol of the whole of human reason. It stood for the
restorative and reformative genius his friend Lvov was bringing to the dark
and dangerous Russian countryside. "Osuga," by contrast, is a much more
independent spirit, driven by forces that extend well beyond any personal inspiration. After his brief invocation of his family's dependence on this river,
Aleksandr spends the next two hundred lines—the length of his friends' entire odes—depicting the Osuga's emergence from and unification of provincial Russia's landscape. He describes in great detail how the river descends
from the upper-Volga watershed, crisscrossing fields, marshes, and "the native children of Russia's flora: cherry blossoms and forest roses." He explains,
with the assurance of a local folklorist and historian, that the Osuga passes
through an ancient battle site.

> There is preserved a distant memory
> That here we fought Lithuania:
>
> Their corpses were thrown in Deep Lake,
> While ours were properly buried—
> And that is why memory has named this place
> With the title "Burial Ground."

He also notes that "in oldentimes" (*v starinu*) there had been an ancient shrine
on this spot, a healing spring that could resurrect the dead. "Yet nowadays
everything has changed," Aleksandr comments bitterly: young men are sent
to the Caucasus to recover from their love adventures and "Philosopher's disease."[55]

This sudden, sarcastic, and invidious transition from "oldentimes" (*sta-
rina*) to "nowadays" (*nynche*) reminds us that the Osuga, as it flows across
Russia's geography, history, and custom, is also a river of time. Derzhavin
himself came to this ancient image toward the end of his life. According to an
anecdote reported in the journal *Notes of the Fatherland*, on July 6, 1816—three
days before his death—Derzhavin glanced up from his desk to inspect a popular historical wall chart, *Time's River, or An Emblematic Representation of Global*

---

[55] Ibid.

History, assembled by a German scholar named Strass. Seized by inspiration, Derzhavin dashed off the first four lines of a never-completed poem.

> Time's river in its coursing
> Carries off all that people do,
> And drowns in oblivion's chasm
> Nations, kingdoms, and kings.[56]

Unlike the river of time in Derzhavin's famous poem, however, Aleksandr's Osuga is a constructive, preservative force rather than an apocalyptic and destructive one. It works to sustain Russia's ecological and historical continuity, even when these time-honored norms are ignored by contemporary reason and fashion. As a result, the awareness of time and change that shoots through the poem goes hand in hand with an increasingly cantankerous and conservative social vision. In "Osuga," Aleksandr works hard to present his home and the village economy that supports it as expressions of history's spirit rather than just his own.

Perhaps the most bracing challenge to his earlier reformist vision of family life is contained in the poem's sudden and shocking apology for serfdom. Passing out of the Russian landscape toward its first glimpse of human community, the Osuga arrives at a peasant hamlet:

> I see a peaceful village
> of industrious villagers.
>
> I don't know why our know-it-alls
> Call them slaves —
> By feasible daily labor
> They pay their regular rents
>
> And having their own plot in exchange,
> Fields, meadows, livestock, a house,
> They are — as are their masters —
> The masters of their daily lives.[57]

---

[56] G. R. Derzhavin, *Stikhotvoreniia,* 2nd ed., ed. D. D. Blagoi (Leningrad: Sovetskii pisatel', 1957), 360. See also V. A. Zapadov's commentary to the poem, Derzhavin, *Stikhotvoreniia,* 452.
[57] Oleinikov, "'Osuga,'" 55.

If we knew nothing about Aleksandr's earlier projects, we might simply assume he was a traditional landowner, unthinking in his embrace of the servile order on which the life of his class depended. But as he first imagined his idyll some twenty years before, Aleksandr stridently and frequently called serfdom "slavery." In his *Agreement between Landlord and Peasant*, discussed in chapter 2, he had imagined that the only way to fix this historic evil—introduced into Russia by foreign invasion, he claimed at the time—was the institution of a new legal order, superseding traditional ways of life. In "Osuga," however, Aleksandr paints a picture of an order that is at once historical, humane, and reasoned, without such contractual trappings. Implicitly rejecting his earlier self as a know-it-all, Aleksandr claims to see a historical logic at work in existing village relations.

In a direct political aside quite alien to the idyllic tradition, Aleksandr declares that it is precisely this traditional, estate-based order that makes his homeland freer than the political, contractual liberty of the revolutionary West:

> I do not desire that freedom,
> Which, like an evil boa,
> Draws people to their doom
> Entrancing them with a malicious gaze,
>
> But that freedom which gives
> To every estate its own way of life
> And ties people together with utility
> And does not whirl them around on a rope.

This defense of serfdom is not only expressly political; it is aimed against real-life antagonists. For example, in the third chapter of *Evgenii Onegin*, Pushkin provides a scathing commentary on the cruel delusions of the serf order. He portrays a chorus of serf girls singing sweetly as they gather berries—only to reveal that they are being forced to do so by their greedy masters:

> And they sang in a choir, as instructed
> (An instruction given so that
> The master's fruit in secret
> Could not be eaten by wicked lips,
> Now occupied by singing . . .)

Here, what seems national and natural is revealed as invented, exploitative, and forced. In "Osuga," however, Bakunin counters this charge with an explanation of his own:

> . . . In the summer beautiful maidens
> Sing in the dense raspberry bushes,
>
> And the sovereign of the forest hurries
> To flee into the bush:
> A bear does not fear a rifle
> So much as the buzz of women's voices.

Thus peasant work song becomes once again a natural reflex, a cultural tradition inspired by Russia's flora and fauna, rather than by serf exploitation.[58] This is a community that has grown over time rather than one that has been planted by human intention, ideological or otherwise. It reflects the natural evolution of Russian life, not the ambitions of any one class.

It is only after winding through this mature historical environment that Aleksandr finally turns to the central subject of his poem, a description of his family's estate. Following the Osuga through the countryside, Aleksandr suddenly finds his home:

> In a garden, on the steep crest
> Of Osuga's hilly banks,
> A master house now
> Groans under the weight of years.[59]

In fact, of course, much of his home was quite new. Aleksandr himself had painstakingly reconstructed it along Palladian lines in the 1790s and early 1800s. But it is the marks left by time that "Osuga" chooses to valorize. The poet portrays his home as a proud and venerable seigniorial residence, groaning "under the weight of years."[60]

---

[58] See Oleinikov, "'Osuga,'" 55. For Pushkin's text, see his *PSS*, VI:71. Kornilov observes a tension as well between Pushkin's famous 1819 poem, "The Countryside" (*Derevnia*) and "Osuga," *Molodye gody*, 11n1.

[59] Oleinikov, "'Osuga,'" 56.

[60] "Osuga" exists in several manuscripts, some obviously working drafts, others copies made by later generations. The very first version seems to be the one quoted in this instance, IRLI, f. 16, op. 2, no. 39, ll. 5 ob.–6.

Entering this house in the garden, we see that it has a spare interior, large but unadorned, without carpets, fine china, elaborate furniture, or even card tables. The family has no need of such props for its contented domestic existence:

> But we without boredom, cards, or smoke
> Pass away the winter nights. . . .[61]

Instead, the house is decorated with sentimental objects, the accumulated traces of the family's past. In the dining room stands an antiquated clock — "as old as I am," the poet muses. A portrait of Catherine the Great dominates the guest room, next to an old divan and an armchair, kept covered except for special occasions. A few caged birds sing pleasantly in another room.

The secret of the family's happiness lies not in consumption but in the spirit of unity that reigns in the home. To explain this almost instinctive accord, and the degree of harmony and balance the family has achieved, Aleksandr compares his home to a beehive.

> When, in the evening-time
> The whole family draws together,
> Like a swarm of bees,
> Then I am happier than the Tsar.[62]

Here, as throughout "Osuga," Aleksandr's vision relies on a figure drawn from nature to provide a model of a beneficial social order. Previously his visions of his home were based on human reason responding to nature, often in self-conscious and contractual terms. In "The Harvest," for example, Aleksandr appeals to his Dasha to take his hand voluntarily; in his parental admonition to himself from 1814, he made it a rule to reason with his children. Here, such rational notes are submerged in a more impersonal naturalism, in which family life is something that is not made by merging reason and nature but simply by following nature's dictates.

Indeed, throughout "Osuga" we can see Aleksandr striving to give his family's life a more national and conservative cast — creating, in effect, a historical apology for his home as part of an evolving natural order. Is this what Mikhail later had in mind when he said that the Decembrist Revolt had made

---

[61] Oleinikov, "'Osuga,'" 56.
[62] Ibid.

his father change the system of home life at Priamukhino? Perhaps. Yet it also seems unjust to conclude that "Osuga" was simply an attempt to appease official suspicions about the idleness and restlessness of noble private life. By the late 1820s, Aleksandr was in his sixties. It seems equally probable that his political views grew more conservative with age. Already in his war diaries of 1812, we can see him beginning to appreciate the autonomy and historicity of an order that fought off Napoleon.

In this respect, perhaps the most important context for understanding "Osuga" is provided by the Bakunin family's new habits of timekeeping, developed during the period from 1810 into the 1820s. Collectively, they demonstrate a desire to become historical on terms of the family's own choosing—to create new kinds of relationships toward time rather than have these relationships created for them. Like contemporaries ranging from the Decembrists on the scaffold to Emperor Nicholas himself, Aleksandr sought to earn a place in the nineteenth century by aligning himself and his home with history. In very short order, however, the conservative historical myth Aleksandr spun out in "Osuga" was itself out of date and supplanted at Priamukhino by more dynamic visions of the relationship between reason, self, and history. In this sense, what was important about "Osuga" was not that it represented a new and reactionary system but that it continued the process by which a historical culture developed in family life.

❀❧❀

Aleksandr started writing "Osuga" in the late 1820s and worked on it for well over a decade, constantly trying to integrate his idyllic vision of family life into the river of time. Even as he did so, however, his personal letters to his wife began to frame story of life at Priamukhino in very different terms: as an uncertain romance about his own children's maturation. In 1828, Varvara took Liubov to a ball in Moscow and reported that her social debut there was a success. "It pleases me greatly that they have greeted her warmly, *qu'on la trouve charmante*," Aleksandr replied, "but I admit I am afraid of the consequences—what if now she will be sad and bored at Priamukhino?"[63]

"The circuitous journey back home," as M. H. Abrams observes in *Natural Supernaturalism*, is perhaps the central metaphor of Romanticism, literarily and philosophically. Romantic writers and philosophers couched their

---

[63] "That they find her charming." From A. M. Bakunin to V. A. Bakunina, letter of February 6, 1829, IRLI, f. 16, op. 4, no. 6, ll. 16–17.

stories of development as pilgrimages that led through the world and back again: "Philosophy is actually homesickness," the German poet Novalis once remarked, "the drive above all to be at home."[64] As Aleksandr quietly considered his family's life as such a narrative in the late 1820s, he had several reasons to be optimistic it would end happily. He himself certainly believed his family's life was rational and happy enough. The Nicholaevan government championed the virtues of domesticity with a passion equal to his own and indeed offered young women like his daughters few other options. Last but not least, as his children made friends outside of Priamukhino, the company they chose for themselves were not head-spinning aristocrats, but rather a mild group of university students. These students also saw the home as a normative touchstone and indeed soon flocked to Priamukhino, hoping to catch a glimpse of this ideal family.

As it happened, however, the domestic romance that played out at Priamukhino took a radically different turn. Fierce intergenerational conflict broke out at Priamukhino; the Bakunins won for themselves a reputation of being an oddly philosophical rather than a normal family; and in the process the Bakunins' home life fostered a new and radical tradition in Russian social thought: the romance of Russian Idealism.

---

[64] M. H. Abrams, *Natural Supernaturalism: Tradition and Revolution in Romantic Literature* (New York: W. W. Norton, 1971), 169–95, esp. 191, 195.

Romance

A Prologue for the New Year 1830

The Bakunin children entered a social world quite different from the one their father and mother had exited some twenty years before. As the family had developed its own idyll, the surrounding landscape of state-society relations changed. The Catherinean conception of noble liberty rested on a set of optimistic assumptions. In conceding a private sphere of noble initiative, the government trusted that the ambitions developed there would be in harmony with its own. After the Decembrist Revolt, however, this supposition lay in tatters. Nicholas I's reign began on a much more suspicious note. The new emperor and his advisers aggressively reasserted the role of the government itself in the direction of elite society.

The first and most active part of this new Nicholaevan system lay in the control of public life through police measures. The arrests and trials that ripped through noble society in the late 1820s were accompanied by the creation of a new political police force, the Third Section of His Majesty's Personal Chancery. The relatively liberal censorship policies established in the early 1800s were replaced by a much stricter system whose aim was to establish the government's ideological control over what Russia read. Plans for greater social initiative in policymaking—long a leitmotif of Russian political reform—were shelved indefinitely in favor of an emphasis on closed, bureaucratic solutions. The new-style officials, often old Karamzinians, were those who could keep their private sentiments and public roles divorced. The emperor thought of himself as a military man and thrilled to the spectacle of soldiers on parade.[1]

Not all of the new government's political initiatives were repressive, however. Nicholas himself, and still more his chief advisers, believed that the reign needed a positive ideology as well—a "system," in the famous expression of the education minister Sergei Uvarov (1786–1855). The most famous expression of this new Nicholaevan system was the formula "Orthodoxy, Autocracy, and Nationality," which Uvarov developed as a summary of official values. But there were other, equally important ideological choices made at this time. First, the new government embraced a dynastic vision of Romanov rule developed by Nicholas I's mother, Empress Maria Fedorovna. Alongside the parade ground, the sentimental, paternal family was raised as an emblem of Nicholaevan values, with Nicholas as the empire's loving father. This was not so much the public triumph of private values as an imperious attempt to co-opt them and to present the royal family (recostumed in sentimental fashion) as the "epitomes of the nation."[2] For this reason, we might call Nicholas I's the reign of "Official Domesticity," alongside Uvarov's "Official Nationality."

Second, the Nicholaevan government launched an ambitious plan of educational reform, meant to take the sentimental young men provided by educated families and convert them into loyal, effective servitors. The chief staging ground for this new ideological effort was the university system. In the immediate aftermath of the revolt, it is true, the universities were policed tightly and the number of student enrollees reduced. Members of lower classes were squeezed out in favor of noblemen, whose development was a central ambition of the policy. Yet the government remained committed to education and to the universities in particular. Eager to have enlightened bureaucrats and still more eager to have loyal ones, it saw higher education as

[1] See P. S. Squire, *The Third Department: The Establishment and Practices of the Political Police in the Russian of Nicholas I* (Cambridge: Cambridge University Press, 1968); Charles A. Ruud, *Fighting Words: Imperial Censorship and the Russian Press, 1804–1906* (Toronto: University of Toronto Press, 1982), 53–96; Richard S. Wortman, *The Development of a Russian Legal Consciousness* (Chicago: University of Chicago Press, 1976), 121–66; W. Bruce Lincoln, *Nicholas I: Emperor and Autocrat of All the Russias* (Bloomington: Indiana University Press, 1978), 17–196.

[2] See Richard Wortman, *Scenarios of Power: Myth and Ceremony in Russian Monarchy*, vol. 1, *From Peter the Great to Nicholas I* (Princeton: Princeton University Press, 1995), 247–378, esp. 296–332; Rebecca Friedman, *Masculinity, Autocracy, and the Russian University, 1804–1863* (New York: Palgrave Macmillan, 2005), 99–124; Barbara Alpern Engel, *Women in Russia, 1700–2000* (Cambridge: Cambridge University Press, 2004), 20–26; Richard Stites, *The Women's Liberation Movement in Russia: Feminism, Nihilism, and Bolshevism, 1860–1930* (Princeton: Princeton University Press, 1978), 15–17.

an instrument to transform the raw, sentimental youths provided by elite families into knowledgeable young men who would willingly align themselves with the "administrative ideal" advanced by the government.[3]

This educational initiative had several important effects. Most generally, it lent legitimacy and prestige to Russia's developing student subculture. It also helped usher in an era when German Idealism—then at the apogee of its reputation as the queen of modern knowledge—dominated Russian intellectual life. Uvarov and his advisers gave preference to Idealist methods for a number of reasons. On the one hand, this was not French learning, then in disrepute for its freethinking ways. On the other hand, the man at the center of the Idealist tradition was a man very much like the one the government wanted to recruit: a conscious, disciplined man, whose thought and conduct were governed by an internalized system of values and who was neither a skeptic nor an enthusiast. (Among the Idealists' chief glories, and the one that found them a home in Russian seminaries, was that their systems not only allowed for but claimed to defend religious belief.) Above all, Uvarov strove to create a new breed of men with an eye for the place their existences played in a whole, men of firm principles who were self-conscious actors guided by a consistent worldview. He hoped his students could be educated to see themselves as part of a historic development—Russia—and align their agency with that of the state.[4]

For much of the nineteenth and twentieth centuries, historians tended to regard these various political and educational initiatives as having failed to heal a growing breach between the government and elite society. More recent scholars, however, have advanced the opinion that Nicholas and his advisers achieved much of what they wanted with their educational plans. They reared a generation of outstanding officials and built a modern bureaucracy that held on to political power in Russia throughout the nineteenth century

---

[3] I take the phrase "administrative ideal" from Rebecca Friedman's *Masculinity*, 14.

[4] On education, student subculture, and Idealism under Nicholas I, see Patrick L. Alston, *Education and the State in Tsarist Russia* (Stanford: Stanford University Press, 1969), 30–41; Cynthia H. Whittaker, *The Origins of Modern Russian Education: An Intellectual Biography of Count Sergei Uvarov, 1786–1855* (DeKalb: Northern Illinois University Press, 1984), 86–127, 152–88; Alexander Vucinich, *Science in Russian Culture: A History to 1860* (Stanford: Stanford University Press, 1963), 280–86, 293–363; Wortman, *Development*, 197–234; P. N. Sakulin, *Iz istorii russkago idealizma: Kniaz' V. F. Odoevskii, myslitel,' pisatel,'* Tom pervyi, chast' pervaia (Moscow: Izdanie M. i S. Sabashnikovykh, 1913), 99–112; Alain Besançon, *Éducation et société en Russie dans le second tiers du XIXe siècle* (Paris: Mouton, 1974), 8–12; N. V. Riasanovsky, *Nicholas I and Official Nationality in Russia, 1825–1855* (Berkeley: University of California Press, 1959), 168–78; Friedman, *Masculinity*. On the agenda of Kantian and post-Kantian thought more generally, see the introduction, as well as the chapters that follow.

and indeed survived the revolutions of the early twentieth.[5] Yet it also remains true that the culture of academic Idealism yielded more than servitors and statists. It also produced students who took the Idealist aspirations they learned in the classroom quite seriously—but who sought to practice them in their own lives and on their own terms, outside the institutions and roles provided by officialdom. Perhaps most important, they began to align themselves not with the Russian state but with larger, more abstract entities: society, humanity, and progress. To do so, they began to create new social roles and practices for themselves, traditions that in time would become part and parcel of radical politics and culture in Imperial Russia and indeed beyond. One such set of narratives concerns the life and activities of the so-called Stankevich circle, a group of Moscow University students gathered around the charismatic personality of a young man named Nikolai Stankevich (1813–1840).

There are many myths about this circle, but perhaps the most famous are the stories of the intensity of its alienation from the society and values of Nicholaevan Russia. In his influential memoir, *Past and Thoughts* (written in the 1850s and 1860s), Aleksandr Herzen presented the Stankevich circle as one of two student groups—the other being his own—whose isolated, internal development contained within it the seeds of a new, progressive social consciousness:

> Thirty years ago the Russia of the future existed exclusively among a few boys, hardly more than children, so insignificant that there was room for them between the soles of the great boots of the autocracy and the ground—and in them was the heritage of the 14th of December, the heritage of a purely national Russia, as well as of the learning of all humanity. This new life sprouted like the grass that tries to grow on the lip of a still smouldering crater.[6]

[5] For narratives of alienation, see, e.g., Isaiah Berlin, "A Remarkable Decade," in *Russian Thinkers*, ed. Henry Hardy and Aileen Kelly (London: Penguin, 1994), 114–209; Martin Malia, *Alexander Herzen and the Birth of Russian Socialism* (New York: Grosset & Dunlap, 1965); Andrzej Walicki, *The Slavophile Controversy: History of a Conservative Utopia in Nineteenth-Century Russian Thought*, trans. Hilda Andrews-Rusiecka (Notre Dame: University of Notre Dame Press, 1975); for histories that emphasize the ability of Nicholaevan educational institutions to produce statesmen and servitors, see Wortman, *Development*; W. Bruce Lincoln, *In the Vanguard of Reform: Russia's Enlightened Bureaucrats, 1825–1861* (DeKalb: Northern Illinois University Press, 1982). Other examples of both could be produced.

[6] Alexander Herzen, *My Past and Thoughts*, ed. Dwight Macdonald, trans. Constance Garnett, intro. by Isaiah Berlin (Berkeley: University of California Press, 1973), 245.

And indeed, this group of students produced many celebrated personalities — the most famous of whom chose something other than officialdom for
their careers: Vissarion Belinsky (1811–1848), the critical journalist and
voice of Russian realism; Timofei Granovsky (1813–1844), historian and inspirational instructor; Stankevich himself, dead in 1840 at age twenty-seven
from tuberculosis but memorialized by his comrades as the ideal man of his
age. It is also common to include in their number the young Mikhail Bakunin (1814–1876), future anarchist revolutionary, then among the most elo-
quent exponents of Idealist philosophy.

Mikhail's case, however, reminds us of a certain analytical untidiness
along the edges of Stankevich's circle, which it should be the job of a cultural
history of Russian social thought to investigate. For Mikhail was never a
Moscow University student; he came to Moscow's students because they
came to his family in pursuit of visions of domestic happiness and ideal femininity that were far from unofficial in Nicholaevan Russia. Herzen, in fact,
was too close to the cultural values and practices of his day — and too far from
the scene, when these events actually took place — to appreciate the extent to
which the ambitions, practices, and historical myths invented by the Stankevich circle depended for their advancement on the developing culture of enlightened private life that Priamukhino represented. Far from growing on the
"lip of a still smouldering crater," Stankevich and his friends associated themselves with seats of great privilege and distinction — noble homes. They made
use of this domestic world's distinction, dramas, and documentary practices
to enact their most prized Idealist ambitions: self-knowledge, moral autonomy, and participation in history. If we are to catch this circle in its full social and cultural context — for neither these personalities nor their legends
were entirely internal developments, and their charisma comes not just from
their brilliance but from where they stood — we must investigate them as actors on the stage of private life and at Priamukhino in particular.

Understanding how they found their way onto this stage, in turn, means
understanding more about the lives, ambitions, and activities of the women
whose presence drew them there: the Bakunin sisters.

CHAPTER FIVE

Charades and Devotions

Throughout the early 1830s, Liubov and Varvara traveled frequently to Moscow on a schedule set by the nobility's social calendar and by their parents' desire to find them husbands. While in the ancient capital, they often visited with two young friends from Tver, Natalia and Aleksandra Beyer. The Beyers, like the Bakunins, were young noblewomen from a provincial family. They were roughly the Bakunin sisters' age (Natalia was born in 1809, Aleksandra in 1810), and the Beyer family had an estate not far from Priamukhino.[1] The four girls grew up together as neighbors and friends, with Tatiana and Aleksandra, the younger Bakunin sisters, toddling along behind. In the late 1820s, however, the Beyers began to live in Moscow. Their widowed mother had a house there, and she kept it open to attract suitors for her daughters. She also had a son, Aleksei, who was a student at Moscow University. Many of the family's frequent guests were his friends and fellow students. (The coming and going of this *petit monde* of potential suitors, Aleksandra noted, made her anxious mother happier — "plus gaie.")[2] The Bakunin sisters came to know this busy salon in person and through it entered

---

[1] Unfortunately, we have very little biographical information about the Beyers. The birth dates given above are listed in the reference catalog of the manuscript division at Pushkin House (the so-called *kartoteka Modzalevskogo*, card number 778). For additional information on the Beyers, see A. Kornilov, *Molodye gody Mikhaila Bakunina: Iz istorii russkogo romantizma* (Moscow: M. and S. Sabashnikov, 1915), 73–74. See also M. Aronson and S. Reiser, *Literaturnye kruzhki i salony*, ed. B. M. Eikhenbaum (Moscow: Agraf, 2001), 134–35.

[2] See A. A. Beyer to L. A. Bakunina, letter of 1831, IRLI f. 16, op. 8, no. 40, l. 2.

Liubov Aleksandrovna Bakunina
(1811–1838). From Vladimir Sysoev,
Bakuniny (Tver: Sozvezdie, 2002). Courtesy:
Tverskoi Gosudarstvennyi Ob"edinnënyi
Muzei.

into the new, Idealist student culture fostered by the university. A small group
of students, meanwhile, soon found themselves fascinated by the Bakunin
daughters and by rumors of their happy country home, Priamukhino.

By birth and sex, the four Bakunin sisters formed a distinct cohort among
the Bakunin children. They were older than most of their brothers (Mikhail
being the exception). They matured faster and assumed adult responsibilities
within the household more quickly; they educated their siblings and ventured
into "well-born" society first. As a result, Liubov, Varvara, Tatiana, and Aleksandra formed the initial face of Priamukhino's younger generation, both inside and outside the home. Their occupations, their entrance into the world,
the attachments they made, and the impressions they left defined Priamukhino throughout the 1830s. When their parents grew anxious, when the
neighbors tut-tutted, when idealistic young students swooned and recovered,
it was first and foremost the life and image of the Bakunin daughters they
had in mind. "When I saw you for the first time," Vissarion Belinsky recalled
to Mikhail in 1838, "I trembled with confusion as I shook your hand, because
it was the hand *of their brother.*"[3] "You are my *Muse,*" the young Ivan Turgenev

[3] Belinskii, *PSS,* XI:329 (letter of [12–24 October] 1838 to M. A. Bakunin). Emphasis in the
original.

Varvara Aleksandrovna Bakunina (1812–1866). From Vladimir Sysoev, *Bakuniny* (Tver: Sozvezdie, 2002). Courtesy: Tverskoi Gosudarstvennyi Ob"edinnënyi Muzei.

declared romantically to Tatiana in 1842, repeating the ritual praise of the Bakunin sisters that had begun in the early 1830s, "and everything that I think and invent is miraculously tied to you."[4]

The Bakunin sisters, in short, stood at the center of the discussions that enveloped the Bakunin home in the 1830s. Their fates caused the most bitter of Priamukhino's intergenerational conflicts; the creative mysteries of Idealist philosophy and literature, so their student devotees claimed, depended on the young women's presence. Yet the truth is we know very little about the Bakunin sisters' own ambitions and activities. Their letters have lain, mostly unread, in the family archive for more than a century. As a result, it is hard to say what the sisters' role was in the controversies that surrounded them. Many observers regard them primarily as the victims of others' schemes: the patriarchal determinations of their father on the one hand or the metaphysical projects of Idealist philosophy on the other. The respected literature scholar Lydia Ginzburg has gone so far as to label the Bakunin sisters an ex-

---

[4] As quoted in N. L. Brodskii, "'Premukhinskii roman' v zhizni i tvorchestve Turgeneva," in *I. S. Turgenev* (Moscow, 1923), 110.

ample of "romantic female parasitism," arguing that they merely basked in the aura of a romantic adulation that developed quite independently of "their personal qualities and gifts."[5]

There is no question that as young provincial noblewomen coming of age in the 1830s, the Bakunin daughters experienced an odd mixture of subordination and adoration. Theirs was a privileged life encased in restrictions and expectations. Though their father promised to respect their opinions, patriarchal authority was far from dead, either at Priamukhino or throughout Russian society. Neither the Russian state nor the Russian Church sought to restrain the authority of fathers and husbands during this period; on the contrary, they zealously supported male privilege, codifying women's subordination within the family and all but eliminating divorce. It was true that if the Bakunin daughters never got married at all, they could hope for an independent (if often disparaged) existence like those of their aging, "maiden" aunts, the mistresses of Kozytsino.[6] But this would mean investing themselves in estate management and indeed in serfdom itself, and neither institution seems to have had much appeal for them. The 1830s was also a decade when women were imagined to have a high moral calling in society. Numerous voices warned that civilization could not do without a constant supply of supportive wives, self-sacrificing mothers, and "household Penates." Russia also had its Hannah Mores—women who embraced the new conventions about their sex and became the public voices of domesticity, maternity, and femininity. Yet the Bakunin sisters showed little enthusiasm for becoming one of their

[5] See Lydia Ginzburg, *On Psychological Prose*, trans. and ed. Judson Rosengrant (Princeton: Princeton University Press, 1991), 43–44; Richard Stites summarizes an important strand of liberal thought about the women of the 1830s when he describes them as victims of the Idealists' "metaphysical pogroms" in *The Women's Liberation Movement in Russia: Feminism, Nihilism, and Bolshevism, 1860–1930* (Princeton: Princeton University Press, 1978), 15–19. Similar formulations abound in the works of Mikhail Bakunin's biographers—including E. H. Carr, Aileen Kelly, and Arthur Mendel—in a line of interpretation that extends back to Vissarion Belinsky's scathing critiques of the Bakunins from the late 1830s (discussed in chapter 9). The Bakunin family's own biographer, Aleksandr Kornilov, *Molodye gody*, 29–30, 79–82, saw a lingering "patriarchy"—a symptom of the serf system that underlay the Bakunin family's life—as the root of family conflict in the 1830s. In a similar vein, see Marshall S. Shatz, "Mikhail Bakunin and the Priamukhino Circle: Love and Liberation in the Russian Intelligentsia of the 1830s," *Canadian-American Slavic Studies* 33, no. 1 (Spring 1999): 1–29, which comes closest to the interpretation advanced below, albeit without the archival evidence I adduce.

[6] They could not be sure of such an inheritance: given the number of children in the Bakunin family, there were not that many estates to go around, and in the end the married Bakunin sisters lived on their husbands' estates, while Tatiana, who never married, lived out her life at Priamukhino.

number; indeed, only awkwardly and with evident struggle did they enter into private lives as wives, mothers, and estate mistresses.[7]

Why? How indeed was it that, rather than simply becoming the sorts of women everyone expected they should become, the Bakunin sisters soon found themselves in situations and conversations that violated the sexual conventions of their time? What ambitions halted their marriages and helped make them the idols of Russian Idealism, a technical philosophical movement sponsored by an academic institution — Moscow University — to which they, as women, were denied access? Reading the Bakunin sisters' letters from this period gives us a chance to explore these questions in detail. It also shows how wrong it is to imagine the Bakunin daughters primarily as the playthings of other peoples' ideals. To be sure, their letters show marks of subordination, exaltation, and self-absorption. Yet they also show that the daughters themselves were painfully aware of these debilities and wished to find a way to combat them. Adopting the mystical religious tradition embraced by their aunts, they sought to build a better and more autonomous "inner life" for themselves, freed from the subjective delusions that they believed surrounded them.

It was precisely the Bakunin sisters' desire to be the makers of their own moral lives that created the social and intellectual space at Priamukhino for the practice of Idealist philosophy in the 1830s. In defiance of their parents' judgment, they refused to retire quickly into the marriages that were arranged for them. This extended their rotation through Moscow society and allowed them to form ties with other, similarly minded youth. Though the Bakunin sisters lacked formal philosophical training, their desire for moral self-determination helped them forge a common language with Moscow's students. This prepared a means for Idealism's exit from its strictly academic confines and entrance into the distinguished sphere of noble home life. Perhaps most important of all, the Bakunin sisters' determined embrace of their own "religion" sparked a fierce intergenerational conflict at Priamukhino that

[7] See Robin Bisha et al., *Russian Women, 1698–1917: Experience and Expression* (Bloomington: Indiana University Press, 2002), 26–32; Barbara Alpern Engel, *Women in Russia, 1700–2000* (Cambridge: Cambridge University Press, 2004), 22–38; Richard Wortman, *Scenarios of Power: Myth and Ceremony in Russian Monarchy*, vol. 1, *From Peter the Great to Nicholas I* (Princeton: Princeton University Press, 1995), 322–32. See also Natalia Pushkareva, *Women in Russian History from the Tenth to the Twentieth Century*, trans. Eve Levin (Gloucestershire: Sutton Publishing, 1997), 187–201; and Catriona Kelly, *Refining Russia: Advice Literature, Polite Culture, and Gender from Catherine to Yeltsin* (Oxford: Oxford University Press, 2001); for a provocative rumination on this theme, see Barbara Heldt, *Terrible Perfection: Women and Russian Literature* (Bloomington: Indiana University Press, 1987).

lasted for most of the following decade and inevitably raised the question of how this, seemingly the happiest and most harmonious of Russian homes, could have become so sad and divided. Though the Bakunin sisters struggled to become the heroes of the moral drama that engulfed their family, they helped set the stage for its performance and exerted considerable influence over its plot.

❀❧❀

Long before the Bakunin sisters became muses of the Idealist imagination, they were raised by their parents as the angels of their own home. Their education was reasonably broad: they learned history, literature, and foreign languages, as well as to dance, draw, act, and sing. But the use proposed for their education was relatively narrow. A woman needs such "talents," Aleksandr Mikhailovich mused in "Osuga,"

> [S]o that she can root them in the home,
> And pass leisure time, relaxing
> Without cards or ennui.[8]

Just like their aunts (the Smolnyi Institute graduates), the Bakunin daughters were thus raised to enlighten and enliven domestic society. Since Priamukhino was already enlightened by the early 1830s, this domestic mission was no longer the avant-garde affair it had been during their grandparents' time, when Catherine the Great still sat on the throne. The roles the Bakunin daughters were expected to assume had been premiered by others and reduced to a set number of tasks.

First, the daughters were charged with educating their younger brothers and preparing them to assume much more respected positions in society. The daughters' letters from this period are full of references to these tutoring responsibilities.[9] Second, they were expected to use their musical and theatrical talents to combat "ennui" (*skuka*), a disease of modern private life that plagued the provincial Russian nobility (and, one suspects, noblemen in particular, as women had plenty to do). Such campaigns involved staging cha-

---

[8] Dmitrii Oleinikov, "Aleksandr Bakunin i ego poema 'Osuga,'" *Nashe nasledie* 29–30 (1994): 57.

[9] See, e.g., L. A. Bakunina to the Beyer sisters, letter of 4–5 December [1832?], IRLI f. 16, op. 4, no. 526, l. 1. Aleksandr Mikhailovich celebrates his daughters' mentorship of the boys in "Osuga," Oleinikov, "'Osuga,'" 57.

rades and concerts to mark important occasions or even simply to change the household's mood.[10] Last, but ultimately most important, the Bakunin daughters were expected to marry off and form their own enlightened households. "For woman: home life," Aleksandr Mikhailovich reasons in "Osuga," "Like an angel she preserves it / Beneath the cover of her wings."[11] (In more prosaic moments, the Bakunin father also complained that—given his family's size and debts—his daughters would have to marry into good homes, or have none.)

As a group, Liubov, Varvara, Tatiana, and Aleksandra were intelligent, active young women, who seized upon the education provided them. From their earliest days, however, the guise of sentimental muse and dutiful wife did not fit them very well. None of the daughters was beautiful by classical or sentimental standards. With dark, wavy hair, "broad features and heavy lips" (as E. H. Carr once observed from portraits), they looked more oracular than ornamental.[12] Nor did the daughters manage to repress this side of themselves to chase after provincial society's somewhat outdated sense of *la mode.* In ways that shocked their parents, the daughters embraced the outlandish. In 1830, Varvara Aleksandrovna's *Memory Books* record, Liubov ran out into a storm and failed to come back. Varvara later found her daughter on a hilltop, oblivious to the "lightning, and the clouds as black as night. I almost carried her home."[13]

Such ecstatic moments betrayed a sense of self and a desire for self-expression that were not very easily reconciled to the preestablished order of the sentimental household. Though they were expected to live up to the same ideal, the Bakunin daughters had strong individual characters. Liubov, by all accounts, was the warmest and gentlest of the sisters, the most eager to "be rational," and to please. Whenever asked to perform for friends and neighbors, however, she was gripped by anxiety and withdrew, to the embarrassment of her parents. "I cannot overcome myself, despite all my desire to do

[10] It will be remembered that Praskovia Mikhailovna's *Prologue* for 1790 ended by banishing melancholy and insomnia from the home (see chapter 1). For an insightful description of Andrei Bolotov's many attempts to fight off debilitating ennui, see Thomas Newlin, *The Voice in the Garden: Andrei Bolotov and the Anxieties of Russian Pastoral, 1738–1833* (Evanston: Northwestern University Press, 2001).

[11] Oleinikov, "'Osuga,'" 57.

[12] As E. H. Carr perceptively observes, the heavy features that made the Bakunin daughters seem "ungraceful" were read as strong and prophetic in their brothers. See Carr, *Michael Bakunin* (London: Macmillan, 1937), 35.

[13] See IRLI f. 16, op. 6, no. 9, l. 9 (entry for July 27, 1830).

so," she wrote, recalling one such collapse.[14] Varvara, by contrast, was a confident and talented singer who wrote and played her own compositions. But they were often melancholy romances ("Varinka's song pierces the soul," Tatiana wrote after hearing one) and expressed spiritual longings that made her moderate father uncomfortable.[15] Tatiana preferred studying, translating, and writing in her family's office to sitting around the table in the evening. Her letters provide a constant stream of candid commentary on family life, which she contrived to observe from the sidelines.[16] Aleksandra, the youngest Bakunin sister, was also the least self-reflective. By the same token, she was the least like a muse, preferring (by her father's own admission) a good game of Boston to the more cultured occupations the home offered.[17]

Where did this willfulness come from? No doubt in part from her personality. But the Bakunin daughters' characters were also shaped by family traditions that extended beyond their father's domestic idyll. Their mother, for example, may well have recognized something of herself in her daughters' willful episodes. Their theatrical behavior and melancholy language strongly recalls the "triste rêve de la vie" of Varvara Aleksandrovna's own youth, infused by liberal helpings of her favorite elegies and tragedies by Racine. (Had Louise Titot still been around, she might well have scolded the daughters for having too much affect, as she had scolded their mother years before.) In addition, the Bakunin sisters admired their Kozytsino aunts, whom they visited often and respected for their integrity, warmth, and faith.[18]

Indeed, if there was a single passion in particular that separated the Bakunin daughters from the rationalized routines of their studiously enlightened home, it was religion. Yet much of what we can surmise today about the young women's religious education and beliefs derives from later recollec-

[14] Characteristically, Liubov analyzes this fear and the pain it causes her parents in her letter: see L. A. Bakunina to N. A. Beyer, letter of 6 March [1833?], IRLI f. 16, op. 4, no. 521, ll. 1–3.

[15] See IRLI f. 16, op. 4, no. 582, l. 50. On Varvara's religious longings and conflicts with her father, see Kornilov, *Molodye gody*, 67–71.

[16] See, for example, her portrait of life at Priamukhino in the fall of 1834, written to her brother Mikhail (IRLI, f. 16, op. 4, no. 582, ll. 2–3). Her commentaries are of great use in working out events in the Bakunin home and are cited extensively below. Later on, Tatiana turned her pen to translation and transcription and family history: see her manuscript translations of Bettina von Arnim, IRLI f. 16, op. 2, no. 61, and her abortive chronicle of life at Priamukhino, ibid., no. 62.

[17] See Oleinikov, "'Osuga,'" 57; see also Sysoev's extended portraits of the Bakunin sisters in Vladimir Sysoev, *Bakuniny* (Tver: Sozvezdie, 2002), 232–54; and Kornilov, *Molodye gody*, 63–73.

[18] See V. A. Bakunina to M. A. Bakunin, undated letter [1837 or 1838?], IRLI f. 16, op. 4, no. 661, ll. 51–52. The only copy of this letter that survives is one made for Aleksandr Kornilov, who reprints part of it in *Molodye gody*, 66–68.

tions. This is unfortunate, as the memoirs the Bakunins and their friends wrote in the late 1830s tend to interpret their youth through elaborate (and polemical) philosophical frames.[19] Nonetheless, a few generalizations about the daughters' spiritual aspirations can and should be made here because it is impossible to understand the conflicts in the Bakunin home at the beginning of the 1830s without them.

First, it is clear that the Bakunin sisters—and Varvara in particular—began to see themselves and their lives through a religious prism very early on. "La religion fait ma vie, elle n'a jamais cessé d'être tout pour moi," Varvara wrote in the late 1830s, recalling her life since early childhood.[20] Theirs, however, was not the Orthodox catechism they learned from their rural priest, Ivan Alekseevich; nor was it their father's liberal piety, in which observance of Orthodox ritual concealed essentially deistic beliefs. Instead, the Bakunin daughters fashioned their own spiritual system out of the wide variety of inspirational literature available at Priamukhino or Kozytsino. The sisters' letters from the early 1830s mention a raft of Romantic and religious writings, including Young's *Night Thoughts*, the life of St. Mary of Egypt, accounts of pilgrimages and voyages to Jerusalem, French prayer books, and recent Russian poets, especially the repentant ones.[21] Out of all this reading, the Ba-

---

[19] Mikhail, for example, describes his sisters' early spiritual lives in a long letter to his father, completed around December 15, 1837 (see M. A. Bakunin to A. M. Bakunin, letter of 15 December 1837, *Oeuvres [CD-ROM]*, 27–30). But this letter puts Varvara's spiritual history in a Hegelian frame — as a movement from unconscious faith through alienation to her final spiritual resurrection under Mikhail's tutelage. It is also very disparaging about the sources of the sisters' early religious convictions, in particular St. Francis of Sales, which Mikhail makes out to be the enemy of his own Idealist convictions.

[20] "Religion is my life, it has never ceased to be everything for me." See V. A. Bakunina to N. N. Diakov, letter of 18 January [1837?], IRLI f. 16, op. 4, no. 492, l. 4. This letter, written in French, is excerpted in translation by Kornilov, *Molodye gody*, 331–35. Use of "religion" (French, *la religion;* Russian, *religiia*) in this broad, noninstitutional sense runs like a red thread throughout the sisters' correspondence of the 1830s. There are many examples of it in the following text. On the passionate development of the Bakunin sisters' sense of religion and Aleksandr Mikhailovich's inability to respond to it see Kornilov, *Molodye gody*, 62–71.

[21] For discussions of literature, see, e.g., A. A. Beyer to L. A. Bakunina, letter of [March 1833?], IRLI f. 16, op. 8, no. 40, ll. 6 ob.–7 (Young); A. A. Beyer to L. A. Bakunina, letter of [1831?], IRLI f. 16, op. 8, no. 40, ll. 1–2 (Mary of Egypt and prayer manuals); A. A. Beyer to L. A. Bakunina, letter of 12 October [1833?], IRLI f. 16, op. 8, no. 66, l. 2 ob. (pilgrimages). Liubov's poetry album, whose earliest entries date from the late 1820s, contains works on Christian themes by such European and Russian authors as Chateaubriand, Madame de Staël, Iazykov, Venevitinov, and Shevyrev, as well as notes on Bossuet's conception of providence. This notebook is IRLI f. 16, op. 6, no. 57. For an idea of the variety of theological and inspirational titles available to the Bakunins in the first part of the nineteenth century, see the catalogs of their library: IRLI f. 16, op. 6, no. 36, esp. ll. 18–22.

kunin daughters gradually developed their own view of Christianity — "la religion," as they call it simply in their letters — and made it the centerpiece of their self-conception and private practices. "I remember how they gave me a life of the Savior for the first time, when I was ten," Varvara claims in one letter, "I remember the sweet tremor that passed through me, as I kissed the picture on which the crucified Christ was drawn."[22]

Second, the form of religion the Bakunin sisters pursued was an intensely personal one that called for a direct relationship with God — and at the same time placed the focus on the believer. On the one hand, the sisters saw their faith as a personal interaction with God and expected it to suffuse and guide their everyday lives. "You should feel fortified, encouraged in all your good resolutions, after the good fortune you have had in being reunited with your God, a God of beauty and mercy," Liubov wrote to a friend in early 1833, congratulating her on having passed through a spiritual crisis. "Why does religion exist, if not to console us, to show us an all-powerful Being up above," Varvara similarly declared, "a Father whose love for his children, his ungrateful, rebellious children, is beyond anything that the human heart can experience, that our feeble human spirit can conceive?"[23]

Yet as these same statements show, the sisters also pictured their religion as a kind of personal spiritual struggle against skepticism and willfulness. You could lose "your" God and need to find Him again; worse, you could rebel. Varvara remembered herself as gripped by passionate extremes throughout her childhood, experiencing a range of emotions from a warm certainty of God's love to a sudden conviction that "there is no God! There is no God!"[24]

Personal in conception, *la religion* was also practiced by the sisters in private, separate from the household's sentimental routines at Priamukhino. Individual occupations were, of course, an expected part of family life. As angels of the home, the daughters were supposed to work on themselves, perfecting their various attainments. Yet they soon learned that their parents regarded their religious passions as a dangerous, distracting symptom of youth.

[22] See V. A. Bakunina to M. A. Bakunin, undated letter [1836–1838?], IRLI f. 16, op. 4, no. 460, ll. 44–45.

[23] See L. A. Bakunina to N. A. Beyer, letter of 20 February [1833?], IRLI f. 16, op. 4, no. 524, l. 5; see also V. A. Bakunina to N. A. Beyer, undated letter [of the early 1830s?], IRLI f. 16, op. 4, no. 487, l. 1 ob.

[24] See Varvara's memories, as expressed in her letter to Mikhail, undated but attributed by Kornilov to 1837, IRLI f. 16, op. 4, no. 661, ll. 51–52 (reprinted in Kornilov, *Molodye gody*, 66–68); and to her husband, N. N. Diakov, 18 January [1837?], IRLI f. 16, op. 4, no. 492, ll. 3–6 (Kornilov, *Molodye gody*, 331–35).

For example, when Varvara—then in her teens—undertook to perform some of the spiritual exercises recommended by St. Francis de Sales, Aleksandr Mikhailovich attacked such pursuits as a useless enthusiasm. This encouraged Varvara to fast and pray in private.[25] Of her encounter with a book about Christ when she was ten, Varvara writes, "It's likely no one thought it would make such a strange impression on me, or they wouldn't have given it to me."[26] Nor did the sisters, seemingly, confide their spiritual longings to their Kozytsino relatives. In her later recollections of this period, Varvara presents her aunt Varvara Mikhailovna in nostalgic terms, as a loving, holy, but simple woman who neither knew nor understood such doubts as she herself was having. Indeed, Varvara later claimed that she had at first believed that even her younger sisters would not understand her religious leanings. Eventually, however, they, along with Liubov, joined Varvara in her interest in "la religion," which the sisters discussed and practiced among themselves and in letters to friends.[27]

⊛⊱⊰⊛

The Bakunin sisters' spiritual ambitions and activities pressed Priamukhino's governing assumptions from an uncomfortable angle, namely, from within. The Bakunin parents fully expected that their children would have minds of their own and disagree with their parents' convictions. Aleksandr Mikhailovich nervously imagined his daughters' entry into the world as a sentimental moment of reckoning, after which they would either embrace their family home or long forever more for "the world."[28] For their part, the daughters claimed to be all too happy to leave *le monde* behind. "I quit Tver and its pleasures without a single regret," Liubov wrote after the noble social season in 1833. "[N]ow I am completely happy to return to Priamukhino, and my peaceful occupations."[29] What finally did estrange the Bakunin daughters

[25] This from Mikhail's later memoirs, contained in a letter to his father of 15 December 1837 (Bakunin, *Sobranie*, II:111–12).

[26] See V. A. Bakunina to M. A. Bakunin, undated letter [1836–1838?], IRLI f. 16, op. 4, no. 460, l. 45.

[27] See V. A. Bakunina to M. A. Bakunin, undated letter [of winter 1836?], ibid., ll. 44–45. For a portrait of the conflicts over religion in the Bakunin home that comes to similar conclusions, see Kornilov, *Molodye gody*, 63–74.

[28] A. M. Bakunin to V. A. Bakunina, letter of 6 February 1829, IRLI f. 16, op. 4, no. 6, ll. 16–17.

[29] See L. A. Bakunina to N. A. Beyer, letter of 6 March 1833, IRLI f. 16, op. 4, no. 521, l. 2. For a similar declaration, see V. A. Bakunina to the Beyer sisters, letter of 1832, IRLI f. 16, op. 4, no. 481, l. 1.

from their family's expectations, however, was their determination to develop themselves privately, on their own terms. When he imagined his future family relations at Priamukhino, Aleksandr Mikhailovich thought they would be open and friendly and organized by shared, "rational" assumptions of the good and happy life. To quote the language of his 1803 *Agreement between Landlord and Serf,* the ideal community was a world "where all private wills will agree."[30]

Yet whether because of their father's suspicion of their interest in religion — or more simply because the parents possessed the last word in familial debates — the Bakunin daughters tended to pursue their introspection outside the common life of the house. For them, it seems, Priamukhino's routines acquired the air of rituals or charades, performed with an increasingly thick layer of hidden emotion. To imagine their everyday lives on moral and religious terms of their own choosing, the Bakunin sisters turned to correspondence with their two Moscow friends, Natalia and Aleksandra Beyer.[31]

In the beginning, discussions of the young women's cultivated occupations dominate their correspondence. From one point of view, letter writing was itself a form of occupation, a chance to practice the social and linguistic skills their parents, governors, and governesses sought to develop in them. The correspondence starts in a dutiful, polite, and somewhat artificial French, reminiscent of the language of letter-writing handbooks. "Avec quel plaisir je m'empresse de répondre à toutes les questions que vous faites," Liubov begins to the Beyers in 1831.[32] Inevitably, however, discussion of their domestic occupations gave the women an opportunity to express their own personal tastes. The friends exchanged piano primers and favorite compositions, adding suggestions on what and how to play and sing. (Natalia preferred to practice, in Romantic fashion, "by the mysterious light of a blue lamp.")[33] The young women also discussed literature, preferring the introspective and the spiritual. In 1831, Natalia sent her friends a prophetic poem by Nikolai Iazykov, a master of album verse who was striving to undergo moral rebirth

[30] See the discussions of the *Agreement* in chapter 2 and also Aleksandr's "Instruction to Myself," above.

[31] The main collections of these letters are in Pushkin House, IRLI f. 16. For the years 1829–1835, covered by this chapter, the most important folders are op. 4, nos. 519, 520, 521, 524, 527 (by L. A. Bakunina); op. 4, no. 487 (by V. A. Bakunina); op. 8, nos. 66, 89 (by N. A. Beyer); and op. 8, no. 40 (by A. A. Beyer). Altogether, this is some two hundred pages of correspondence.

[32] "With what pleasure I hasten to respond to all of the questions, which you have asked of me." L. A. Bakunina to N. A. Beyer, letter of 24 January [1831?], IRLI f. 16, op. 4, no. 520, l. 1.

[33] For discussions of music see L. A. Bakunina to N. A. Beyer, ibid., ll. 1–1 ob; and L. A. Bakunina to N. A. Beyer, letter of 4–5 December [1832?], IRLI f. 16, op. 4, no. 524, l. 3 ob.

and exit the confines of salon culture.[34] Not content with French, the young women pursued English and German, not used much in the polite conversation of their day.[35] (Though the Beyers had a German surname, they were not native German speakers and indeed were somewhat behind the Bakunins in this respect.)

As developing but dependent individuals, the Bakunins and the Beyers shared a common experience: the tension between their duties to their family and their desire to pursue their self-development on their own terms. The more seriously they regarded their occupations as a kind of vocation, the less eagerly they served as muses. In one letter, Alexandra Beyer describes sitting down for a long-anticipated piano practice session only to be interrupted by the arrival of her brother's university friends: "Stankevich came, and a few others, and once again it was impossible to practice. There goes another day, and every day passes in the same way, that's Moscow life!"[36] Both Liubov and her father enjoyed reading history, but their tastes were quite different. Aleksandr Mikhailovich, as he gradually went blind, asked that his daughters spend long evenings reading to him from Thucydides. "Quelle barbarie!" Liubov exclaimed to the Beyers, as she plunged again through the bloodshed of the Peloponnesian War.[37] For her part, Liubov preferred modern authors and modern histories, such as Schiller's *History of the Revolt of the Netherlands*, which she read in German "with great satisfaction."[38]

Unable to control their daily schedule—and also unable to express themselves fully in the society of their own households—the young women soon took to discussing their day-to-day lives more intimately among themselves. They strove to hold their conduct and emotions to their own standards and judged each other's performances. In December 1832, for example, the Beyers sent the Bakunins a letter, recounting a visit by Ianuarii Neverov, a student and possible suitor. Repeating what she read, Liubov praised the Beyers' conduct during the young man's visit.

[34] The poem, "To the Poet," is IRLI f. 16, op. 8, no. 89, ll. 1–2 ob. They also read poetry by Khomiakov and Shevyrev. See N. A. Beyer to L. A. Bakunina, letter of 26 March [1833?], ibid., l. 44 ob.

[35] See Liubov's exhortations to Natalya to study these out-of-the way languages: L. A. Bakunina to N. A. Beyer, letter of 24 January [1831?], IRLI f. 16, op. 4, no. 520, l. 2 (English); L. A. Bakunina to N. A. Beyer, letter of 18 December [1832?], IRLI f. 16, op. 4, no. 524, l. 2; N. A. Beyer to L. A. Bakunina, letter of 18 January [1833?], IRLI f. 16, op. 8, no. 89, l. 8 (German).

[36] See A. A. Beyer to L. A. Bakunina, letter of [1831?], IRLI f. 16, op. 8, no. 40, l. 2.

[37] "What barbarity!" See L. A. Bakunina to N. A. Beyer, letter of 24 January [1831?], IRLI f. 16, op. 4, no. 520, l. 2.

[38] See L. A. Bakunina to N. A. Beyer, letter of 18 December [1832?], IRLI f. 16, op. 4, no. 524, l. 2.

I believe I can see Monsieur Neverov entering, addressing you with compliments and I share in the pure sentiment of amour propre that floods through your heart, my dear Natalie. Then, with you, I repent it. I admire next the courage and firmness of my dear Alexandrine. With what pleasure I would have embraced you at the moment when reason, duty triumphed over the passions. I see you participating in the conversation with tranquility and self-contentment. What I would have given to be in your place, what is there more delicious than a pure conscience?[39]

Liubov's analysis places an obvious premium on self-consciousness and self-control. She imagines her friends experiencing sudden rushes of flattery and passions. But she is pleased to see that they recognize and control these emotions and carry out the dictates of reason and duty. The "pure conscience" Liubov praises is the result of having understood the forces at work in one's own psyche and having found the correct path to take among its various crosscurrents.

Where did these habits of self-reflection and self-analysis come from? These letters have an obvious, artificial quality, as if the young women were enacting a script from a pious novel or moral guidebook. Mikhail once accused his sister Varvara of chaining her life to "all those petty formulas for virtue à la Madame de Genlis."[40] We might also be tempted to explain them as products of socially induced narcissism. Martin Malia—discussing the letters of Natalia Zakharina, Aleksandr Herzen's wife and the Bakunin sisters' contemporary—calls her extreme piety and self-reflection an example of the "sentimental compensations for a cramped and frustrated existence so common to her generation."[41] Most generally, the self-consciousness of educated

[39] See L. A. Bakunina to the Beyer sisters, letter of 4–5 [December 1832?], ibid., l. 3 ob.

[40] M. A. Bakunin to V. A. D'iakova, letter of 9 March 1836, Bakunin, *Oeuvres [CD-ROM]*, 4. Stéphanie-Félicité, comtesse de Genlis (1746–1830), was an author of novels both widely praised and mocked for the moral principles and self-reflection they tried to instill in women. Pushkin presents Tatiana as one of her readers in *Evgenii Onegin;* Catriona Kelly presents her as a prophet of maternalism and femininity in *Refining Russia: Advice Literature, Polite Culture and Gender from Catherine to Yeltsin* (Oxford: Oxford University Press, 2001), 29–32.

[41] See Martin Malia, *Alexander Herzen and the Birth of Russian Socialism* (New York: Grosset & Dunlap, 1965), 157. For an attempt to read Zakharina's life and ambitions in more individual terms, see Judith E. Zimmerman, "Natalie Herzen and the Early Intelligentsia," *Russian Review* 41, no. 3 (July 1982): 249–72. It should also be noted that the sometimes morbid notes that sound in women's writings from this period are not unique to Russia (and its patriarchal, autocratic order). Amanda Vickery explains them as a product of the anxieties of childbirth and child rearing in an age of high mortality. See Vickery, *The Gentleman's Daughter: Women's Lives in Georgian England* (New Haven: Yale University Press, 1998), 86–125.

noblewomen surely reflects the self-consciousness expected of the "well-born" nobility as a whole, charged with the empowering and yet essentially estranging role of being exemplars of imperial civilization. Such tensions likely acted with special force on Russian noblewomen in the 1830s. Exhorted on all sides to become the empire's most virtuous subjects, they were often bothered, no doubt, by an awareness that their lives and souls fell short of these ideals. According to Oleg Kharkhordin, such pressures manifested themselves in an introspective, self-analytical gentry culture, rooted in the Masonic practice of public self-confession.[42]

Yet however we choose to explain the origins of these habits—whether in cultural, sociopsychological, or political terms—it is important to remember that the self-reflection practiced by the Beyers and Bakunin sisters was not, itself, un–self-reflective. To put it another way, these young women anticipate our attempts to psychologize them because they themselves understood their lives to be filled with psychological challenges. They believed that they were surrounded by deceptive temptations and unrealistic expectations, and they turned to correspondence and discussions of religion for guidance on how to achieve self-awareness and moral self-determination amid these pressures. Though often guilty of extravagant decisions, these women studiously tried to make all their choices fully their own. In particular, they imagined themselves as steering between the selfish temptations and blind enthusiasms that tugged at their lives: between the extremes of "egoism," as they called it, and "exaltation."

In February 1833, for example, Natalia Beyer notes that Moscow life has given her an extensive "occasion to study my character." "I see," she continues with chagrin, "that it is founded on the coldest egoism." She "babbled" with men who pleased her—messieurs Stankevich and Neverov—testing how thoroughly she could engage them. Partly against her wishes and partly with guilty pleasure, she aroused an amorous adoration on the part of the Bakunins' cousin Petr Poltoratsky. On reflection, she decided that she was giving in too easily to temptation:

[42] On the pressure on Russian noblewomen to become exemplars of pure, untainted, uncompromised morality, see Iu. M. Lotman, *Besedy o russkoi kul'ture. Byt i traditsii russkogo dvorianstva (XVIII–nachalo XIX veka)* (St. Petersburg: Isskustvo, 1994), 57–63; as well as Stites, *Women's Liberation*, 15–18. On the "subjectifying practices" of the Russian nobility, see Oleg Kharkhordin, *The Collective and the Individual in Russia: A Study of Practices* (Berkeley: University of California Press, 1999), 264–67. Nor, despite a healthy historical tradition to the contrary, should we see the European nobility in general as an unreflective class, as Jonathan Dewald argues in *Aristocratic Experience and the Origins of Modern Culture* (Berkeley: University of California Press, 1993).

I am in a terrible state right now — my conscience tells me that I am not on the right path, that I am only acting according to egotistical sentiments, that my amour propre is so strong that I do not have the courage to examine the depths of all the evil that is in me, and even less courage to unveil it, to speak of it. Oh, my dear friends, what I would give to fly to be near you, to consult you, to vivify myself (so to speak), to take in your pure and serene spirits the calm which is ravaged in mine.

The only remedy for such egoism, Natalia concludes, is self-reform, inspired by God but accomplished through self-study and self-determination.

No, I see that Providence now delivers me to myself, forces me to reenter myself, to re-create myself. It is well past time to destroy the false sheen of good qualities, of which I have only the appearance, and to attempt on my own to acquire true ones.[43]

Later, building on this theme of a need for moral rebirth, Natalia writes: "I ask of Heaven's grace only that it purify my soul of all unworthy egoism, that it nullify this powerful 'I,' that reigns there as a tyrant."[44]

"Exaltation" was the other extreme the sisters sought to avoid — the Scylla opposite the Charybdis of egoism. If egoism was the temptation to give in to selfish desires, exaltation was enslavement to an ecstatic inspiration or ideal: an altruistic wish, a romantic infatuation, an impossible vision of duty. In the summer of 1833, for example, Aleksandra Beyer confessed to her friends — and indeed to the man himself — that she had fallen in love with her family's piano instructor. For three years, the man had come and been little more than polite during their lessons; but now, she could not restrain herself from confronting him, despite the possible consequences: a loss of his respect, the disturbance it might cause in her family, disgrace in *le monde*. "You will tell me once again that I am only an *exaltée*," Aleksandra writes to Liubov. "And why? Because I love without hope." Ignoring her friends' pleas, she talked to the teacher, only to see him refuse her entreaties and withdraw with embarrassment.[45] When their lessons resumed after several months, Alek-

---

[43] Letter by N. A. Beyer to the Bakunin sisters, 14 February [1833?], IRLI f. 16, op. 8, no. 89, l. 11 ob.

[44] See N. A. Beyer to L. A. Bakunina, letter of 23 [September?] 1833, IRLI f. 16, op. 8, no. 89, ll. 27–28.

[45] See A. A. Beyer to the Bakunin sisters, letter of 12 June [1833?], IRLI f. 16, op. 8, no. 40, ll. 14 ob.–15.

sandra analyzed her feelings and decided that her friends had been right all along. She had allowed herself to become hypnotized by music as much as by the man, and she had quite taken leave of her senses:

> My delight in music in the end merged with the being who provided it to me and I·fell in love with him so fierily and unaccountably that I was prepared to sacrifice everything; and so it was that a brief, pure delight gave way to lengthy suffering which—thanks to God's mercy, the prayers of my friends, and my own constant tireless efforts—now may finally end, and reason triumph.

Retiring to her room to read the Psalms, Aleksandra hoped now to cure herself of her fantastic passion. "A thousand sentiments agitate my spirit, I will try all the same to analyze them all for you."[46]

As they analyzed their spirits, the Bakunins and Beyers treated egoism and exaltation as opposing conditions. Egoism, in the romantic cliché of the day, was "cold" like calculation; exaltation, by contrast, was "hot" like passion. Yet egoism and exaltation—as mental states—had much in common as well. Both were forms of delusion, in the sense that they led away from self-awareness. Natalia's "coldest egoism," she felt, prevented her from exploring her own faults, while Aleksandra the *exaltée* decided that her love had been for music, not the man. Both egoism and exaltation were also debilitating, in the sense that neither the egotistical nor the exalted will could ever be fulfilled. Egoism, in Natalie's expression, is a "tyrant" self, an "I" who reigns unchallenged and unsatisfied—much like the unaccountable exaltation that Aleksandra decided drove her toward self-sacrifice and disguised her true feelings. In the end, egoism and exaltation had to be fought because they frustrated self-awareness and self-realization, instilling delusion and subordination.

Today it is quite difficult to say exactly what inspired the young women to frame their introspection in this particular way. As fighting words and objects of condemnation, both exaltation and egoism played a fundamental role in the development of modern European culture. They served as mainstays in the debates over the relationship between faith and reason that broke out in the early seventeenth century and continued to rage in the early nineteenth.[47] In that sense, these young women could have been exposed to the

---

[46] A. A. Beyer to L. A. Bakunin, letter of 12 October 1833, IRLI f. 16, op. 8, no. 66, l. 2.

[47] On exaltation and its cognate enthusiasm as the "anti-self of the Enlightenment," see

dangers of both emotions by reading almost any book of their day. Yet there is a local, likely, and in retrospect quite ironic source for this framework for self-analysis as it entered these young women's lives: early-nineteenth-century theories about feminine nature and the educational steps needed to control it.

The proper formation of feminine reason was a leitmotif of the French-language pedagogical works that circulated in the Bakunin home. That women should be raised to think and make independent (though not blasphemous) moral choices was a given. "There are no grounds to rob them of the privilege of obeying the divine law reason reveals," argues the Comtesse de Rémusat, whose *Essai sur l'éducation des femmes* was in the Bakunin family library. But because of women's particular natures and destiny, Rémusat continues, this reason must be carefully fashioned. Feminine wiles and "coquetry"—already identified as a fearsome source of social power by Rousseau in the mid-eighteenth century—give scope to women's vices; while "the majority of our virtues are not exercised without some amount of exaltation," such enthusiasms could prove all too reckless if women themselves were in charge of political life. In sum, Rémusat contends, the rationality women need in order to play their part in modern civilization must be structured to place feminine ego and emotionalism in check. "Holding women to their true station is truly in the interest of men," Rémusat concludes. "To raise and contain their nature by morality—that is what should be the goal of their education."[48]

Madame de Genlis (whose pedagogical novels Mikhail later blamed for

---

Stephen Haliczer, *Between Exaltation and Infamy: Female Mystics in the Golden Age of Spain* (Oxford: Oxford University Press, 2002), 4; Michael Heyd, *"Be Sober and Reasonable": The Critique of Enthusiasm in the Seventeenth and Eighteenth Centuries* (Leiden: E. J. Brill, 1995); and J. G. A. Pocock, "Enthusiasm: The Antiself of Enlightenment," in *Enthusiasm and Enlightenment in Europe, 1650–1850*, ed. Lawrence E. Klein and Anthony J. La Vopa (San Marino, Calif.: Huntington Library, 1998), 7–28. On charges of voluntarism and naked egoism that were often aimed at the new reason, see Frederick C. Beiser, *The Sovereignty of Reason: The Defense of Rationality in the Early English Enlightenment* (Princeton: Princeton University Press, 1996), 41–45; Frederick C. Beiser, *The Fate of Reason: German Philosophy from Kant to Fichte* (Cambridge, Mass.: Harvard University Press, 1987), 46–91, esp. 82–83; and, of course, Jean-Jacques Rousseau's "Discourse on the Origin and Foundations of Inequality Among Mankind," which dates man's fall from his natural state at the point where there was "egoism involved; reason rendered active": "The Second Discourse: 'Discourse on the Origins and Foundations of Inequality Among Mankind,'" in *The Social Contract and the First and Second Discourses*, ed. Susan Dunn (New Haven: Yale University Press, 2002), 122–38.

[48] Claire Elisabeth Jeanne Gravier de Vergennes comtesse de Rémusat, *Essai sur l'Éducation Des Femmes* (Paris: Chez L'Advocat, 1824), 8–13, esp. 13. This work is entered in the Bakunin family library catalog, at IRLI f. 16, op. 6, no. 36, l. 29.

his sister Varvara's moral obsessions) describes the feminine mind and the goals of women's education in very similar terms. Genlis, like Rémusat, argues that women by nature are vexed by extremes of emotion and ego: "Love leads them astray. Ambition teaches them to intrigue." It follows, she contends, that one should never praise any qualities in a woman "but those of the mind and understanding," in the hopes that "she will be good through system and inclination." Genlis concludes that "a just way of reasoning" should be the foundation of feminine education, that women may possess "great moderation in their inclinations, and no passions."[49] And indeed, the forms of egoism and exaltation Natalia and Aleksandra Beyer wrestle with in their letters are those of flirtation and coquetry on the one hand and romantic infatuation on the other — precisely the characteristic feminine weaknesses that Rémusat, Genlis, and many other early-nineteenth-century advocates of women's education decried.

Whether or not these theories of education held any currency in the Bakunin or Beyer households, the young women's close monitoring of their tendencies to egoism and exaltation reflects the sort of skepticism about feminine nature — and the need to discipline feminine reason — the theories advocate. If such educational treatises really did help inspire the particular forms of self-analysis and self-discipline these young Russian noblewomen practiced, this process had at least two deep ironies. The first is that while a profound belief in feminine weakness suffuses the work of Rémusat and Genlis, it is combined with an equally fundamental insistence that women are autonomous moral beings. "Woman is, on the earth, the companion of man, but she exists for her own account as well," Madame de Rémusat writes. "She is inferior, but not subordinate."[50]

"I am eighteen, the future still belongs to me," the heroine of one of Madame de Genlis's novels reflects. "I too can compose it myself, like the holy virgins, make it certain, know it in advance."[51] Such visions of feminine au-

---

[49] See Stéphanie-Félicité comtesse de Genlis, *Adelaïde and Theodore: Or, Letters on Education* (London: C. Bathurst and T. Caddell, 1783), 29.

[50] Rémusat, *Essai sur l'éducation des femmes*, 3.

[51] Stéphanie-Félicité comtesse de Genlis, *La duchesse de la Vallière* (Paris: Chez Maradan, 1813), 35–36. This is a speculative example, meant merely to show parallels between Genlis's language and the Beyer-Bakunin correspondence, conducted in a French that could well have been modeled after Genlis's. It should be said, however, that the image of Madame de la Vallière — portrayed in tragic terms by Genlis as a woman doomed "by the disastrous influence of guilty passion" — was familiar to the Bakunins. Among the numerous anonymous lyrics in V. A. Bakunina the elder's poetry album is an apocryphal epistle by Madame de la Vallière to Louis XIV, begging him to release her heart. See IRLI f. 16, op. 6, no. 55, l. 62. The novel *La duchesse de la*

tonomy and self-creation should make us skeptical of the idea (expressed by Mikhail) that the most women could take from these writings was petty "little formulas for virtue." In the end, the carefully argued (if purposefully constraining) moral system Rémusat and Genlis advocated came packaged with something more profound: the ideal of feminine self-determination through self-analysis. Being raised according to these principles would have encouraged these young women to "to reenter myself, to re-create myself"—as Natalia Beyer puts it—with no guarantee that the particular moral and sexual assumptions that these educational treatises made would survive the process.

Perhaps the most basic assumption these works made was that the home was the ideal space for feminine self-development. The home, they contended, discouraged such presumed weaknesses as feminine coquetry and egoism while providing a properly limited framework for feminine enthusiasm. It is pleasing to submit to parental authority, a character from one of Madame de Genlis's novels remarks: "Who could revolt against reason and sentiment combined?"[52] This brings us, however, to a second deep irony surrounding the role played by moral literature and educational theory in the framing of these women's ambitions for self-development. As the Bakunin daughters practiced self-analysis in their correspondence with the Beyers, they soon began to believe that reason and sentiment were far from united at Priamukhino. Their home was not the idyll their contemporaries believed it to be; rather, it was filled with hidden desires, demands, and exaltations. These conflicts reinforced the daughters' desires to create their own system of beliefs and, indeed, their own roles in the life they had been given. We can observe this process by tracing the first rifts in Priamukhino's reputation as an idyllic and happy home, as they find expression in the Bakunin-Beyer correspondence.

⊛⁄≈⊗

As the Bakunin daughters passed through Moscow in the early 1830s, those familiar with the Beyer salon came to picture the Bakunins as the most enlightened and contented of families. Ianuarii Neverov, one of the Beyers' student friends, called Priamukhino a "temple of happiness," despite having

---

Vallière is one of two works by Madame de Genlis listed in the catalog of the Bakunin family library, compiled in the 1830s and 1840s: see IRLI f. 16, op. 6, no. 36, l. 32. (The other listed work is *Les Chevaliers du Cygne ou la cour de Charlemagne*, IRLI f. 16, op. 6, no. 37, l. 20.)

[52] Genlis, *Duchesse*, 24.

never seen it. Letters of the time draw a stark opposition between the Beyers' hectic houselife in Moscow and Priamukhino's contentment and ease. "We are deprived of the means to do wrong," Liubov wrote wistfully to the Beyers in November 1832, commenting on the rational and harmonious construction of her family's life. "Yes, my good friends, you have much more merit than we in following the path of virtue."[53] (In this respect, Aleksandr Mikhailovich's fear that his daughter would grow bored at Priamukhino was starting to come true.) Just about this time, however, a conflict developed that both belied Priamukhino's pretensions and saw the daughters rethink the relationship between family life and their own moral and religious aspirations. The conflict centered on Liubov's marriage to a husband of her father's choosing.

By late 1832, Liubov Bakunina was twenty-one years old. Though certainly not an old maid, she was no longer young by country standards, and she vexed her parents by rejecting various suitors they found for her.[54] In December 1832, Aleksandr Mikhailovich came to believe that one of Liubov's uncles, Aleksei Pavlovich Poltoratsky, had fallen in love with her. Worse, he believed that Liubov was not entirely indifferent to her uncle's affections. Liubov herself wrote to the Beyers that although she felt a "brotherly love" for her uncle, this affection was misunderstood by everyone involved (including, it seems, Aleksei Pavlovich).[55] Aleksandr Mikhailovich was, in any event, in no mood to take chances. The Bakunins lived in a world where ecstatic visions of feminine virtue went hand in hand with great anxiety about its destruction. Liubov herself, in a letter from 1831, recalls being pulled aside by a wise old woman at a ball. Pointing out a lady whose reputation had been stained by an unwise affair, the old woman whispered: "Les plus belles choses ont un pire destin" — "The most beautiful things have the direst of fates."[56]

[53] See L. A. Bakunina to the Beyer sisters, letter of 25 November 1832, IRLI f. 16, op. 4; no. 520, ll. 3–4; Natalia reports Neverov's praise of Priamukhino in her letter of 25 September 1833 (IRLI f. 16, op. 8, no. 89, l. 29 ob.), though by this time she herself had doubts.

[54] Marriage in a woman's teens remained common in Russia through the early nineteenth century; Aleksandr Mikhailovich, in his *Agreement between Landlord and Peasant*, imagined eighteen to twenty as the right age. See Engel, *Women in Russia*, 30.

[55] See L. A. Bakunina to the Beyer sisters, letter of 1831 or 1832, IRLI f. 16, op. 4, no. 519, l. 1–2; for more on this conflict, see Kornilov, *Molodye gody*, 75–78.

[56] L. A. Bakunina to the Beyer sisters, letter of [1831?], IRLI f. 16, op. 4, no. 519, l. 1. Emphasis in the original. The quotation given is from François Malherbe's poem, "Consolation à Monsieur du Périer, gentilhomme d'Aix-en-Provence, sur la mort de sa fille." See Malherbe, *Poésies*, ed. Antoine Adam (Paris, 1971), 69–72.

In late 1832 Aleksandr Mikhailovich began to press Liubov hard to get married. His choice fell on Konstantin Renne, a baron from Courland who was serving as an officer in Tver. Liubov, however, did not want to marry him. Her father did not press the matter immediately, but he made his paternal preferences plain; soon, the matter became a sore subtext to all sorts of family occasions.

On December 18, 1832, for example, the family gathered for a celebration to send young Nikolai off to service. The Bakunin sisters prepared a charade, basing its plot on Bernadin de St. Pierre's sentimental classic *Paul et Virginie.* In the original story, Virginie, having been raised on a happy island idyll with her brother Paul, is summoned home to Paris by a wicked aunt, who seeks to marry her off to a rich man. Virginie refuses the engagement, but she perishes on the return voyage home. In the Bakunin sisters' version, however, the play has a happy ending. Seeing Virginie's ship sink, her brother Paul dives and saves her.

As she describes this domestic charade and its forced, happy ending to the Beyers, Liubov intercuts her picture of her family's pleasant routines with an uneasy sense that the only option open to her is indeed self-sacrifice. The problem, we see, is not so much the threat of Aleksandr Mikhailovich's patriarchal authority as the pressure of sentimental norms she feels compelled to obey: "I know that I am completely free in my choice, but this thought never leaves my head: *I must entrust myself blindly to my parents and believe that they desire only my happiness.*"[57] Her father's support of Renne placed her own internal judgment directly against the precepts that governed her family's idyll. On the one hand, she in theory had the right to follow her own desires. She could refuse Renne and reject her father's best judgment. To do so, however, was to question his reason and the assumption that he knew best. This was both proud and egotistical; it was also to bring into question the sentimental assumption that her parents' motives were in natural alignment with hers.

Liubov's solution to this dilemma, in the coming months, was more charades. She did not resist her parents' choice, but she acted in a way that she hoped would make her preferences plain. She threw hints; throughout the rituals of courtship, for example, she was cold to Renne in front of everyone, "polite and nothing more." But the plan backfired, as Liubov explained to the Beyers. Renne did not try to force things and thereby quietly succeeded: "Ap-

[57] L. A. Bakunina to the Beyer sisters, letter of December 18, 1832, IRLI f. 16, op. 4, no. 524, l. 1. Emphasis in the original.

proaching me very rarely, hardly speaking to me, all the while showing the greatest respect for my parents, he has managed to win the good graces of the whole household." By late February 1833, Liubov realized that she was the only one in her family who opposed him.[58]

In April, sensing Renne's proposal was coming any day, Liubov asked Natalia to tell her "what it is you believe that *la religion* bids me do."[59] Natalia replied that Liubov was her own best judge: "If you decide, despite everything your parents think to say to you in his favor, that this is a man who does not merit your love, or as you put it, that you cannot love this man, you would make yourself the victim for nothing by marrying him." By the time Natalia's letter reached Priamukhino, however, it was too late. "There is no longer any time to reflect, my dear friend," Liubov announced on May 2, 1833: "Le oui est prononcé." The engagement was on.[60]

Though she herself showed nothing but coldness to him, Renne had persisted. Finally, he spoke to her mother Varvara Aleksandrovna, asking for Liubov's hand in marriage. Renne received an oddly encouraging reply. Though clearly delighted, Varvara Aleksandrovna announced that while she was sure that Liubov would act as her parents wished—upon even a single word on their part—such a command would never be given. The decision was Liubov's to make. For Liubov, however, being offered the choice under such circumstances was as good as a command. To think otherwise was to belie the sentimental trust she was supposed to have in her parents' judgment. "Praying to God with great fervor," Liubov agreed to marry Renne. "The Baron returned the next day. I heard a carriage. I was trembling all over, I knew that mother was to speak to him. I was very embarrassed when I saw him. They had told him my response. He was as troubled as I."

Renne left immediately, without speaking to her directly, and awaited his own parents' permission.[61] Thus Liubov's engagement, when it came was a leap of faith that reflected no harmony or agreement within the Bakunin home but simply a moral determination on Liubov's part to be a good daughter.

From this point on, Liubov's letters describe her life at Priamukhino as a series of *tableaux vivants*, in which the actions represented belie hidden emotions, with no possible harmony between appearance and reality. The pressures to pretend Liubov felt in her role as daughter doubled in her role as

---

[58] L. A. Bakunina to the Beyer sisters, letter of 20 February 1833, IRLI f. 16, op. 4, no. 524, ll. 5–6.

[59] L. A. Bakunina to N. A Beyer, letter of 14 April 1833, IRLI f. 16, op. 4, no. 521, ll. 4–5.

[60] L. A. Bakunina to N. A. Beyer, letter of 2 May 1833, ibid., l. 6.

[61] L. A. Bakunina to N. A. Beyer, letter of May 2, 1833, ibid., ll. 6–7.

bride. If during her engagement she had hoped that her parents might read her mood and change their minds, now she had made a pledge and feared being revealed as a liar. Precisely at this moment, she declared, society subjected her to particular scrutiny: "I am, for the moment, the object of general curiosity; I am watched with searching eyes, they want to read my soul."[62] The most difficult scene, she explained, was the one she had to play with her fiancé, who began to speak of intimate things: "Yesterday we went for a ride on horseback. He profited by it to speak to me on a subject which we were both afraid to undertake. Finally this moment passed. I do not know how I managed to stay on my horse." Struggling through the encounter, she returned to the house, where "I found no solace until after many tears."[63]

Why didn't Liubov confess her true emotions to her parents, even at this late date? As Liubov herself claimed, "the source of all my thoughts, of all my actions, is the ardent desire to please my parents, to prove to them my love. . . . No, my dear Natalie, do not think me deceived in a decision I sense was inspired by God himself."[64] Her friends, however, interpreted her decision precisely as a case of exaltation. Liubov was taking on responsibilities to her husband—sexual as well as social—that it would be a sin to fulfill insincerely. "What will happen to you, dear friend?" Natalie exclaimed, saying that she doubted that Liubov loved the Baron as "one should *love.*" Aleksandra was more blunt: "Are you still seriously thinking of marrying the Baron?" she wrote to Liubov in October 1833, as the day of the wedding approached. "C'est de la démente!"[65]

"Why don't we live in the Middle Ages?" Aleksandra despaired, deciding nothing would change Liubov's mind. "I could send any number of knights ready to rescue a woman from a forced union!"[66] And indeed, without speculating too much, we may suggest a third, and perhaps fundamental, explanation for Liubov's decision to play out the drama of her engagement to Renne without confessing her true feelings to her parents—namely, a desire to transfer this burden to someone else. For as Liubov herself was well aware, the longer she remained silent, the more ugly secrets and half-truths accu-

---

[62] L. A. Bakunina to N. A. Beyer, letter of May 15, 1833, ibid., ll. 12–12 ob.

[63] L. A. Bakunina to N. A. Beyer, letter of May 6, ibid., l. 8.

[64] L. A. Bakunina to N. A. Beyer, letter of May 15, 1833, ibid., l. 12.

[65] "This is insanity!" See A. A. Beyer to L. A. Bakunina, letter of 12 October 1833, IRLI f. 16, op. 8, no. 66, l. 2; see also N. A. Beyer to L. A. Bakunina, letter of 23 [September?] 1833, IRLI f. 16, op. 8, no. 89, ll. 29–32 ob.

[66] A. A. Beyer to L. A. Bakunina, letter of 6 November [1833?], IRLI f. 16, op. 8, no. 40, l. 21 ob. Date established by reference to "the Baron" (Renne) and Liubov's engagement to him, which ended shortly thereafter.

mulated at Priamukhino, and the more family life—heretofore pictured as rational, open, and harmonious—took on the character of a facade, covering up an arbitrary, opaque, and unbalanced reality. Breaking faith with her family's idyll and questioning her parents' judgment was no doubt a burden she did not want to bear. The exaltation of deciding to go through with the charade—while revealing her sacrifice to her friends—at least offered the consolation of performing a heroic role of her own choosing. It also left open the possibility that someone else in the family would finally recognize her sacrifice for what it was and call an end to the play.

And indeed, this is more or less what happened. The knight-errant necessary to bring Liubov's tragedy to the surface finally arrived, in the form of her older brother, Mikhail, on leave from Artillery School in St. Petersburg.

Mikhail's visit to Priamukhino in August 1833 was his first for almost five years.[67] He knew about Liubov's engagement. But throughout the summer of 1833, he confessed irritation at receiving only "short, indecisive" letters about the situation.[68] Upon his arrival at Priamukhino, Mikhail later recalled, he was dismayed by what he saw. Liubov and Renne fought when together; Liubov was cold to the man in public (as she told the Beyers she intended to be); and on the night before Mikhail's return to St. Petersburg, a "terrible scene" broke out over dinner, during which both of his parents fell ill. Mikhail urged his sisters to drop any further resistance to the engagement: "Let us not have any will but theirs."[69]

To frame things in this manner, however, was already to violate Priamukhino's most basic premise: that familial relations rested on consent, not submission. Blind obedience was the stuff of the pagan, patriarchal mores of ancient Greece, whereas the Bakunins thought of themselves as an enlightened, Christian, modern household. "Let her die, but let her fulfill her duties!" Aleksandr Mikhailovich supposedly raged when the sisters confronted him with Liubov's private doubts. In the end, however, he could not play the role of the tyrannical father, which so strongly contradicted his sentimental image of himself as *père de famille.* He reluctantly agreed to let Liubov break off the engagement. "We do not want Iphigenia's sacrifice," Varvara Aleksandrovna wrote bitterly to Mikhail in St. Petersburg, denying that she or

---

[67] A fact noted by Liubov herself in a letter to Natalia Beyer. See IRLI f. 16, op. 4, no. 521, l. 15.

[68] Letter to his sisters, 20 May 1833 (Bakunin, *Sobranie,* I:104).

[69] See letters to his sisters, 28 September 1833 and September 1833 (Bakunin, *Sobranie,* I:114 and 112–13). In 1837, he recalled these scenes in a lengthy letter to his father of 15 December 1837 (*Sobranie,* II:110–14 and 123–28).

her husband wished Liubov to marry against her will. (Racine's Iphigénie was Varvara Aleksandrovna's favorite play when she herself was a disaffected young woman; little could she have suspected then that her daughter would later enact a version of it—to such devastating effect—in her own home.)[70]

Not knowing that the engagement had collapsed but haunted (he claimed) by visions of his sister's martyrdom, Mikhail wrote two long letters, one to Liubov and one to his father. In his letter to Liubov, he decried her decision as an "illusory ideal": "This is an exaltation that cannot last a lifetime and that will have the most terrible consequences for all." The second letter, to his father, came with an enclosure that brought Liubov's drama of alienation full circle. Mikhail sent Aleksandr Mikhailovich the letters Liubov had written to St. Petersburg, letters that described her distance from the household and her painful private decision to marry the baron against her will.[71] The old and increasingly blind Aleksandr Mikhailovich, for so long the primary author of his family's life, was undoubtedly shocked by what he read there.

Thereafter, the Bakunin family returned to its prior routines but with an awareness that something profound had shifted. ("A secret voice tells me that a decisive moment has arrived," Mikhail wrote to his sisters in September 1833, even before the final scandal over Liubov's engagement.)[72] As Aleksandr Kornilov rightly observes, Aleksandr Mikhailovich's authority within the family, "heretofore unquestionable, was of course necessarily shaken."[73] Mikhail, until this point a sentimental young man very much in his father's mold, underwent an "intellectual revolution" that January. He renounced his father's plans for his future and declared that he intended to become a scholar.[74]

Liubov and her sisters, meanwhile, returned to making the rounds between Tver and Moscow, drawing ever closer to the Beyers and through them to the equally idealistic students of Stankevich's circle. For the Beyers, the events in Priamukhino were an eye-opening experience: "Priamukhino is, as I now see, a part of this earth, this valley of sorrows and tears, and not at all the terrestrial paradise of which I dreamed and that I believed had finally been realized," Natalia wrote to her friend Liubov in late November

[70] See letter to L. A. Bakunina, fall 1833 (Bakunin, *Sobranie*, I:115–20).

[71] Letter to Liubov, fall 1833 (Bakunin, *Sobranie*, I:120, 115).

[72] Letter to his sisters of 28 September 1833 (Bakunin, *Sobranie*, I:115).

[73] See Kornilov, *Molodye gody*, 78.

[74] This "intellectual revolution" is described in much more detail in chapter 7. The phrase appears in his letter to his sisters of 25 January 1834 (Bakunin, *Sobranie*, I:122).

1833.[75] For those who had access to this internal drama, the family's reputation as a source of natural harmony was shaken.

Even so, Liubov and her sisters remained provincial noblewomen, subject to their parents' dictates even if they disagreed with their reasoning. A little more a year after the quarrel surrounding her engagement, the entire drama repeated itself. Aleksandr Mikhailovich continued to pressure Liubov to accept various suitors; she felt compelled to at least entertain the men. But this time someone else seized the main part. Late in the fall of 1834, sister Varvara accepted the proposal of Nikolai Diakov, an Ulan officer stationed in Tver. This sudden decision shocked the Beyers as well as her brother Mikhail, who suspected that Varvara was in the grips of some exaltation. Varvara's marriage to Diakov once again threw the house into confusion; and a mystery developed surrounding this sudden pairing, which did not settle itself for several years.[76]

⊗⁄⊱⊰⊗

Throughout the early 1830s, the Bakunin daughters sought a moral system that could guide them through the particular social and psychological challenges they faced as noblewomen. Some of the relentless self-analysis to which the Bakunins and the Beyers subjected themselves reflected the obsessions with feminine morality that swept across elite Russian society in the first part of the nineteenth century. Surrounded by a strange mix of adulation and anxiety, and "watched with searching eyes" by their contemporaries, the Bakunin sisters worried about the state of their own souls. The educational manuals that populated their family's library (and indeed the very novels they read) told them to be suspicious of the feminine mind and to see it as naturally predisposed to extremes of egoism and exaltation. The sisters hoped to correct these faults and find some other, less subjective, purpose behind their lives.

They did not, however, adhere to the sentimental strictures of their day. Instead, they found a model for self-perfection in the traditions of private devotion that their grandmother and aunts had helped make an important part of the Bakunin family's life in the countryside. They analyzed their souls, performed spiritual penances, and asked themselves what religion called them

---

[75] N. A. Beyer to L. A. Bakunina, letter of 13 October 1833, IRLI f. 16, op. 8, no. 89, ll. 39–40.

[76] See Kornilov, *Molodye gody*, 79–82.

to do. Over time, their correspondence with the Beyer sisters gave them a forum through which they could begin telling the story of family life as they experienced it. They rendered their judgments on the actions unfolding in their home and invited the Beyers to do the same. In the process, they made their own stormy entrance into adulthood the central text of Bakunin family life, displacing their father's idyllic vision. They also opened up the history of their family life as a moral theater of sorts, with an audience in the Beyer household. It was precisely this pursuit of moral independence that gradually brought the Bakunin sisters to the attention of Moscow's student Idealists, who would have lost sight of them had they married quickly in the early 1830s and disappeared from the Beyer salon.

Instead, as the Bakunins returned to Moscow in early 1834, a charismatic young student named Nikolai Stankevich began to track their appearances with ever-increasing attention.

CHAPTER SIX

A Few Moments from the Life of Nikolai Stankevich

At first, Stankevich saw Liubov, Varvara, Tatiana, and Aleksandra in a reflected and largely unflattering light. He disliked their cousin Praskovia Mikhailovna, a poet whom Stankevich privately ridiculed as pretentious; and he felt nothing but plain sympathy for Liubov until January 1834, when she came to Moscow to have an operation on her teeth.[1] Thereafter, however, his vision of the Bakunin sisters, and of Liubov in particular, began to change. "Rzhevsky is visiting the Bakunins, in their village!!!" Stankevich wrote to his best friend, Ianuarii Neverov, in April 1834, using three exclamation points to communicate how thunderously important a visit to the Bakunin estate seemed. Passing by Priamukhino himself that May, he fantasized about stopping in to express his admiration for the daughters' "high souls," a maneuver he hoped might "refreshen" his own spirit. (Claiming it would be awkward to visit the family unacquainted and lacking a clear role to play before it, he rode on.)[2] Finally, in late February 1835, when the Bakunins returned to Moscow, Stankevich placed himself squarely in front of Liubov. She seemed taken by his conversation; her close friends quietly claimed that she

---

[1] See Stankevich's letters to Ia. M. Neverov of 26 March 1833 in Stankevich, *Perepiska*, 215; 2 May 1833 (*Perepiska*, 216); and 15 January 1834 (*Perepiska*, 277). On Praskovia Mikhailovna Bakunina, the daughter of Aleksandr Mikhailovich's brother Mikhail, see N. I. Os'makova, "P. M. Bakunina," in *Russkie pisateli: Biograficheskii slovar'*, ed. V. N. Baskakov and V. E. Vatsuro, vol. 1 (Moscow: Sovetskaia entsiklopediia, 1989), 144–45.

[2] See Stankevich's letters to Neverov of 18 April 1834 (*Perepiska*, 285) and 11 May 1834 (*Perepiska*, 286).

might well love him; and Stankevich relished the thought that a new age had dawned. "These four days might be an entire epoch in my life," he wrote to Neverov. If Liubov indeed loved him, "a new life would begin for me. Oh, how I came to know Providence in the minute they told me this!"[3]

Born in 1813 to a wealthy and socially active noble family in the southern province of Voronezh, Nikolai Stankevich was exactly the sort of young man the Nicholaevan government was seeking to reach with its educational initiative of the early 1830s. He came to Moscow, contemporaries later remembered, a beautiful and cultured young man. "He had fine black hair, a sloping forehead, small dark eyes; his gaze was tender and joyful," his friend the writer Ivan Turgenev recalled. "In his whole being, in all his movements, there was a kind of graciousness, an unconscious *distinction*—as though he were the scion of kings but unaware of his origins."[4] Such a charismatic young nobleman, properly molded by the government's "administrative ideal," might well have been expected to become an exemplary Nicholaevan official. Yet Stankevich chose to remain an exemplary student, fulfilling an educational program of his own choosing. After completing his university studies in the summer of 1834, he served briefly as a school inspector in his home province. At that point his desire to continue studying delayed the onset of his official career. "The age of activity has arrived for me, but I see that there is much I do not know," he wrote to his good friend Ianuarii Neverov in October 1834. He thought it necessary to undertake a broad plan of philosophical and historical study before assuming an as-yet-unspecified role in society as an educator and enlightener. "I want to become still more convinced of man's dignity," Stankevich added a year later, "and then, I admit, I want to convince others and to awaken them to higher interests."[5]

---

[3] See Stankevich's letters to Neverov of 9–13 March 1835 (*Perepiska*, 314–16) and 27 March 1835 (*Perepiska*, 316–18).

[4] On Stankevich's early life, see P. V. Annenkov, *Nikolai Vladimirovich Stankevich: Perepiska ego i biografiia* (Moscow: Tipografiia Kat'kova, 1857), 13–15; Edward J. Brown, *Stankevich and His Moscow Circle* (Stanford: Stanford University Press, 1966), 6–8; Z. A. Kamenskii, *Moskovskii kruzhok liubomudrov* (Moscow: Izdatel'stvo Nauka, 1980), 188–94; and I. S. Turgenev, "Vospominaniia o N. V. Stankeviche," in *Sobranie sochinenii v dvenadtsati tomakh*, ed. M. P. Alekseev and G. A. Bialyi, vol. 12 (Moscow: Khudozhestvennaia literatura, 1979), 298. The word "distinction" in the original is in French.

[5] Stankevich's determination to avoid any immediate career and focus instead on self-education and self-preparation is a leitmotif of his letters from 1833 onward. We can see it as early as his determination to give up the writing of his dissertation in favor of more free-form and "living" interests (N. V. Stankevich to Ia. M. Neverov, letter of 18 May 1833, *Perepiska*, 221), as well as his frequent description of his reading lists in his letters to Neverov thereafter (see, e.g., his letter of 11 July 1833, *Perepiska*, 234–35). See also his letters to Neverov of 16 October 1834

It was during this somewhat willful age of preparation and self-education that Stankevich began his pursuit of Liubov Bakunina; and indeed, a close examination of his letters and preparatory projects of these years shows that he expected his love for Liubov to play a vital, transformative role for him. What explains this sudden educational conception of life and love by a young Russian nobleman? And why did Stankevich see Liubov Bakunina in particular as the proper object to place at the center of his affections? As they allowed Idealist approaches to dominate instruction at Moscow University, Nicholaevan officials hoped that the new German learning would create a class of disciplined individuals who would freely align themselves with the purposes of the state and the tenets of official nationality. What they got in Stankevich was a young man who strove to develop his own moral system and to align himself with the broader cause of humanity.

More than that, Stankevich's unique combination of noble distinction and Idealist principles created an electrifying example for his student comrades to follow. When they were in his presence, as Lydia Ginzburg perceptively observes, suddenly it seemed that "a historically effective spiritual life was possible even without a role, even without a set, recognized form."[6] They could be their own guides, learn their own truths, and enter history on their own terms by advancing the cause of progress in their society. In this way, Stankevich helped his contemporaries translate the central ambitions of post-Kantian philosophy (self-knowledge, autonomy, and progressive agency in society) into compelling Russian terms, creating new norms, practices, and narratives for modern Russian manhood in particular. Stankevich and his circle invented a new system of freedom to supplant the formulaic noble liberty of the eighteenth century, with its steady and set routine of official service and estate life. Once mediated by memoiristic writing and scholarship, this Idealist tradition won for Stankevich and his circle the reputation of being the founders of the Russian intelligentsia.[7]

(*Perepiska*, 232) and 2 December 1835 (*Perepiska*, 341). This self-educational ambition hardened into an increasingly specific itinerary of philosophical study in late 1835, during Stankevich's discussions with Mikhail Bakunin.

[6] See *On Psychological Prose*, trans. and ed. Judson Rosengrant (Princeton: Princeton University Press, 1991), 51.

[7] On the importance of student traditions in the general culture of the intelligentsia, see Yuri Slezkine, *The Jewish Century* (Princeton: Princeton University Press, 2004), 140, 142–43; Barbara Walker, "On Reading Soviet Memoirs: A History of the 'Contemporaries' Genre as an Institution of Russian Intelligentsia Culture from the 1790s to the 1970s," *Russian Review* 59, no. 3 (2000): 327–52; Susan K. Morrissey, *Heralds of Revolution: Russian Students and the Mythologies of Radicalism* (New York: Oxford University Press, 1998), 3–14, 118. For examples of leading in-

Stankevich's life and the way he lived it stood at the core of this informal culture of Idealism. Yet if others looked to him to be their guide, Stankevich himself looked to his romances with women, as his letters and draft philosophical projects show. He accorded particular importance to the bittersweet story of his love for Liubov Bakunina. Their secret courtship and eventual engagement stimulated the intergenerational conflict that was beginning to rage at Priamukhino, even as Stankevich and his student comrades decided that the Bakunin estate could help them realize their Idealist ambitions. For all these reasons, it makes sense to pause for a moment here to consider Stankevich and his interactions with the Bakunin family in more detail.

❀⸕⸎❀

Stankevich's personal papers were collected and published in the late nineteenth century by his family and friends, who sought to honor his memory.[8] His first biographer, Pavel Annenkov (1813–1887), established what is still the dominant paradigm for interpreting Stankevich's life and place in history. Stankevich achieved little public notoriety during his lifetime, Annenkov noted. He died abroad of tuberculosis in 1840, before he had finished his education or assumed any set position in Russian society; and as a result, he retired from life "without achievements in his service book [*v formuliarnom svoem*

---

tellectual voices rallying around Stankevich as a founding father of progressive personality in Russia, see Annenkov, *Stankevich*, 8–12; P. Miliukov, "Liubov' u 'idealistov tridtsatykh godov,'" in *Iz istorii russkoi intelligentsii: Sbornik statei* (St. Petersburg: Tipografiia A. E. Kolpinskogo, 1902), 73–75, 81. In the late 1850s, a series of famous authors embraced the traditions of the Stankevich circle, setting the stage for its acknowledgment (right or wrong) as one of the progenitors of the Russian intelligentsia. See N. G. Chernyshevskii, "Ocherki gogolevskogo perioda russkoi literatury," in *Polnoe sobranie sochinenii*, ed. V. Ia. Kirpotin, vol. 3 (Moscow: OGIZ Gosudarstvennoe izdatel'stvo khudozhestvennoi literatury, 1947), 196–98, 210–11; Alexander Herzen, *My Past and Thoughts*, ed. Dwight Macdonald, trans. Constance Garnett, intro. by Isaiah Berlin (Berkeley: University of California Press, 1973), 245–53 (in Russian, see Gertsen, *Sobranie*, IX:34–46); N. A. Dobroliubov, "Nikolai Vladimirovich Stankevich," in *Sobranie Sochinenii*, vol. 2 (St. Petersburg, 1911), 116–51.

[8] See N. V. Stankevich, *Stikhotvoreniia. Tragediia. Proza*. (Moscow: Tipografiia i slovolitnia O. O. Gerbeka, 1890), as well as N. V. Stankevich, *Perepiska Nikolaia Vladimirovicha Stankevicha*, ed. A. Stankevich (Moscow: Tipografiia A. I. Mamontova, 1914); in the twentieth century his poetry was collected and published in S. I. Mashinskii, ed., *Poety kruzhka N. V. Stankevicha* (Moscow-Leningrad: Sovetskii pisatel', 1964), 83–127. The best overall guide to the history of Stankevich's legacy after his death is Brown, *Stankevich and His Moscow Circle*, 32–44, passim. I discuss the history of the Bakunins' involvement in this process in my article, "'That Historical Family': The Bakunin Archive and the Intimate Theater of History in Imperial Russia, 1780–1925," *Russian Review* 63 (October 2004): 574–93, as well as below.

spiske]." But history cannot be limited to those with official résumés, Annenkov argued archly. Stankevich, he observed, had been the chief authority and soul of his student circle, a "living ideal of truth and justice" whose very being "acted charmingly on men his age."[9]

Annenkov hoped that Stankevich could operate as a similar inspirational norm for future generations. He therefore set out to reconstruct Stankevich's "personality and character" as an artifact of modern Russian history. "In the personae of select people," Annenkov wrote, "life offers from time to time a complete and miraculous example for each young generation to imitate, as it begins its social life." It was precisely as such a historical "model" (*obrazets*) or "index" (*ukazatel'*) that Annenkov decided to present Stankevich.[10] Though Annenkov agreed with those who argued that Stankevich had left behind no records of "real activity" (that is, public activity), he still believed that the young man's letters provide ample evidence to "describe his personality and character."[11] In this way, Annenkov presented Stankevich's personal papers as the accidental records of a historic personality rather than as products of self-conscious activity. He believed that the goal of scholarship should be to analyse Stankevich as an exemplary personality produced by his times, rather than as a distinct individual who acted on and accomplished certain ambitions. In particular, Annenkov singled out Stankevich's "romantic history" [*istoriia liubvi*] as characteristic of his generation's high demands of itself.[12]

Scholars since have generally worked within this framework, reading Stankevich's letters and the romantic history they contain as the expressions of a dreamily impractical character—the prototypical "Idealist of the 1830s," chasing after an ideal love.[13] In a frequently cited passage from his correspondence, Stankevich himself indeed once remarked, "I think about love, as Princess Eboli does." (Eboli is a character from Schiller's *Don Carlos*, who pines for a single, perfect love.) "If I can find my ideal, and she does not re-

---

[9] Annenkov, *Stankevich*, 11–13.

[10] Ibid.

[11] Ibid., 5.

[12] See ibid., 147–62, esp. 161.

[13] Besides Annenkov, the most basic accounts are: Miliukov, "Liubov' u 'idealistov tridtsatykh godov,'" 74–81; A. Kornilov, *Molodye gody Mikhaila Bakunina: Iz istorii russkogo romantizma* (Moscow: M. and S. Sabashnikov, 1915), 93–103; Brown, *Stankevich*, 69–70. Soviet scholarship of the 1960s and 1970s comes closer to the truth about Stankevich, as it presents him as an early radical ideologue, doggedly attempting to work out an "integral worldview [*tselostnoe mirovozzrenie*]." See S. Mashinskii, "Stankevich i ego kruzhok," *Voprosy Literatury* 5 (May 1964): 131–32; Kamenskii, *Moskovskii kruzhok liubomudrov*, 271–80. Though Stankevich's alienation and latent radicalism are often overstated in these works, they are correct in seeing him as a self-conscious system builder.

ject me, if her love will be equal to mine, then that woman alone will my love make happy, and make of this one a Goddess."[14]

Perhaps the most influential opinion about Stankevich—expressed best by Martin Malia—is that the exalted hopes he attached to his love life were, at their base, products of alienation and repression. Repelled by the public values of Nicholaevan Russia—and unable to find an outlet for his abilities in Russian society—Stankevich was simply a talented and idle Russian nobleman who gave into the "intrinsic utopianism of the romantic ideal of love." This attempt to find compensations in private life for "a world where all nongovernmental public activity was excluded" had revolutionary consequences, Malia argues. On the one hand, it stunted any hope men like Stankevich might have had for actual love by raising expectations no real person could ever meet. On the other hand, it imparted to their worldviews a utopian quality that was to remain characteristic of Russian social thought throughout the nineteenth century.[15]

There are, however, several problems with this way of thinking about Stankevich's life, some of which run back to Annenkov's initial conception of Stankevich's place in history. First, it is arbitrary to decide that Stankevich's personal letters are simply the material traces of his character rather than the products of real activity. (The desire to do so, it may be hypothesized, reflects Annenkov's own determination to define "real activity" as something that occurs outside such "natural" realms of human life as home and family.)[16] Stankevich is, in fact, quite clear throughout his correspondence that he driving his personal development according to a self-conscious (and self-determined) plan. Despite his one reference to Princess Eboli, nowhere is this goal-oriented attitude toward his own life clearer than in his statements about

[14] See N. V. Stankevich to Ia. M. Neverov, letter of 2 June 1833, *Perepiska*, 226. "If I can find my ideal" etc. is a paraphrase of Eboli's exclamation from act II, scene 3 of *Don Carlos*. Friedrich von Schiller, *Don Carlos, Infante of Spain*, trans. Charles E. Passage (New York: Frederick Ungar, 1959), 68.

[15] See Martin Malia, "Schiller and the Early Russian Left," *Harvard Slavic Studies* 4 (1957): 187–89, 199–200; a similar argument for Herzen is advanced in Malia's *Alexander Herzen and the Birth of Russian Socialism* (New York: Grosset & Dunlap, 1965), 44–46. Prerevolutionary historians read Stankevich's character less critically but nonetheless also saw trouble in his "excessively high demands" on private life. See Annenkov, *Stankevich*, 11–12, 161–63; Miliukov, "Liubov' u 'idealistov tridtsatykh godov,'" 74. For similar interpretations of Stankevich, his character, and his idealistic expectations of his private life, see Andrzej Walicki, *The Slavophile Controversy: History of a Conservative Utopia in Nineteenth-Century Russian Thought*, trans. Hilda Andrews-Rusiecka (Notre Dame: University of Notre Dame Press, 1975), 342–45; Brown, *Stankevich and His Moscow Circle*, 69–82.

[16] On this point, see Randolph, "'That Historical Family,'" 582–83, 591–93.

love, systematized in a philosophical tract that Stankevich prepared in 1833 and titled "My Metaphysics." Oddly ignored by most historians, this document presents love not as the pursuit of a set ideal but rather as a method for self-education and the generation of a mature worldview.[17] In this sense, Stankevich's primary conception of his private life during these years was frankly ideological rather than naively idealistic. His romantic history was a novel of his own making rather than an accidental diary of his thoughts. And since his primary goal was self-development rather than love, Stankevich was no frustrated Romantic. He actually achieved much of what he wanted, as we shall see.

Second, it is also arbitrary to assert that Stankevich's interest in using his private life as a vehicle for his own self-development was a sociopsychological symptom engendered by some combination of political oppression, intellectual alienation, and social backwardness. As has been shown earlier, the private life of the Russian nobility was opened up as a realm for cultural distinction and experimentation by imperial political initiatives of the eighteenth century rather than by oppression after 1825. Nor does a careful inspection of Stankevich's life or letters show much evidence of antipathy to the officially sponsored ideals of Nicholas I's reign. On the contrary, the main inspirations of Stankevich's quest for a personal moral system were the professors and texts to which he was exposed at the university; many of the ideals around which he sought to build his personal moral system were ones exalted by official ideologues. Among these, in particular, was a belief in the inspirational norms that educated men like himself could derive from family life and feminine virtue.

In what follows, then, Stankevich's letters and the love life they record will be interpreted as a consciously produced story of development, a bildungsroman. Stankevich's pursuit of Liubov Bakunina provided the perfect material for this bildungsroman, for three reasons. First, she and her family represented norms of femininity and domesticity around which he hoped to build his worldview. Second, the events surrounding their love provided the plot to his personal history and marked the "epochs" in his philosophical development when he analyzed them retrospectively with friends. Last, and not

---

[17] One account of Stankevich's life and thought that does deal in detail with "My Metaphysics" is Michael Gershenzon, *A History of Young Russia*, trans. and ed. James P. Scanlan (Irvine, Calif.: Charles Schlacks, 1986), 172–75. Berlin rightly emphasizes the self-educational aspects of Stankevich's thought in "A Remarkable Decade," in *Russian Thinkers*, ed. Henry Hardy and Aileen Kelly (London: Penguin, 1994), 141–44, without discussing how Stankevich translated this theory into practice.

least, the Bakunins' distinction combined with Stankevich's own to elevate this youthful affair in the eyes of their contemporaries and historians.[18] Placed in this frame, Stankevich's autobiographical scheme became an exemplary drama of his time. Priamukhino, in short, provided an orienting norm, a plot, and a stage for Stankevich's attempt to convert his life into a story of development. In doing so, it helped him confer the imprimatur of noble distinction onto the Idealist social tradition he was trying to create.

❀⋰☆⋱❀

Stankevich developed his ambitions in public educational institutions and under the mentorship of the professors there. By birth and background, he came from a cultural milieu not all that different from the Bakunin family's. Like the Bakunins, Stankevich's parents were wealthy in land and serfs (though they enjoyed the advantage of not having the Bakunins' tremendous debts). Also like the Bakunins, the Stankeviches had settled into lives as enlightened members of the provincial nobility. Both families lavished time and effort on their children's education, expanding their horizons and senses of self far beyond the limited requirements of landlord life. Unlike the Bakunins, however, the Stankeviches sent their son to a formal, public education at an early age, enrolling him in Ostrogozhsk's famous district school when he was ten years old. Thereafter, he completed a finishing school for noble boys in Voronezh (the provincial capital) before finally going to Moscow in 1830.[19]

While enrolled in Moscow University, Stankevich lived in the home of Mikhail Pavlov (1793–1840), a professor of physics, mineralogy, and agriculture. Pavlov prepared Stankevich for the university's entrance exams, which the young man passed; for the next four years, Stankevich was a student, completing a degree in philology in 1834. At the university, Stankevich earned the affection of his fellow students, for the most part nobles, who admired him for his composed, self-possessed character and lucid mind. In an already established tradition of Russian student life, a small circle of student-comrades formed around Stankevich (his status as first among equals was

---

[18] On the Bakunin family's effect on Stankevich's student comrades, see below and chapters 7–9; on Priamukhino's archival role in Stankevich's own life, see the conclusion.

[19] On Stankevich's early life, see Annenkov, *Stankevich*, 13–15; Brown, *Stankevich and His Moscow Circle*, 6–8; Kamenskii, *Moskovskii kruzhok liubomudrov*, 188–94. On Ostrogozhsk and its enlightened nobility, see Aleksandr Nikitenko, *Up from Serfdom: My Childhood and Youth in Russia, 1804–1824*, trans. Helen Saltz Jacobson (New Haven: Yale University Press, 2001), 107–8.

charismatic and unofficial rather than formal). Bound together by the codes of fraternal friendship, united by the experience of being under their professors' tutelage but determined to find a calling for themselves, these young men pursued their self-education and self-formation through art, theater, music, philosophy, and—just as important—discussions of love, friendship, and women. Sometimes they met at Pavlov's house, in Stankevich's quarters, where they soberly drank tea and smoked themselves into exaltation. At other times, they descended on the Beyers, where Stankevich met the Bakunins. Flirtation and conversation with women then served as grist for more late-night self-reflection over tobacco and tea.[20]

Throughout this time, Stankevich's primary mentors and role models were the older male academics under whom he studied, in particular Professor Pavlov and Professor Nikolai Nadezhdin (1804–1856). Both men came from a clerical, rather than noble, background. Whether for this or some other reason, they both embraced the post-Kantian vision of the scholar as a modern cleric of sorts, whose role in life was to stimulate society's enlightenment while helping to direct it through the production of firm knowledge and clear principles. Pavlov famously began his lectures on physics with excursions into the nature of knowledge. "You wish to know nature? But what is nature? What is 'to know'?" Aleksandr Herzen recalls Pavlov asking prospective students at the door (as a result, Herzen adds, "it was tricky to learn anything about physics at his lectures, and impossible to learn anything about agriculture").[21] Yet Nadezhdin, a professor of fine arts and archaeology, was the more charismatic and ambitious of the two and had a deeper influence on Stankevich and his friends. A bracing lecturer and energetic journalist, Nadezhdin was a recent arrival to the university and only a few years older than his students. He also was the organizer of several publishing ventures,

[20] On the formation and development of the Stankevich circle — and its close relationship with the Beyer household — see Brown, *Stankevich and His Moscow Circle*, 8–13; Mashinskii, "Stankevich i ego kruzhok"; K. S. Aksakov, "Vospominaniia studentstva 1832–1835 gg," in *Moskovskii universitet v vospominaniiakh sovremennikov (1755–1917)*, comp. Iu. N. Emel'ianov (Moscow: Sovremennik, 1989), 187–90; M. Aronson and S. Reiser, *Literaturnye kruzhki i salony*, ed. B. M. Eikhenbaum (Moscow: Agraf, 2001), 133–37, esp. 134–35. On the phenomenon of "circle culture" more generally during this time, contrast the classic picture drawn by Isaiah Berlin ("Remarkable Decade," 141–44) with more recent accounts such as Walker, "On Reading Soviet Memoirs," and Rebecca Friedman, "Romantic Friendship in the Nicholaevan University," *Russian Review* 62 (April 2003): 262–83.

[21] On Pavlov, see Z. A. Kamenskii, *Russkaia filosofiia nachala XIX veka i Shelling* (Moscow: Nauka, 1980), 158–268, esp. 160–61; P. N. Sakulin, *Iz istorii russkogo idealizma: Kniaz' V. F. Odoevskii, myslitel,' pisatel'*, vol. 1, pt. 1 (Moskva: Izdanie M. i S. Sabashnikovykh, 1913), 115–27.

including *Telescope*—"a journal of contemporary enlightenment"—in which many of Stankevich's friends participated as translators and authors. Stankevich himself kept and collated Nadezhdin's lecture notes; his letters make it plain that he read and followed *Telescope* closely.[22]

In his lectures and journalism, Nadezhdin unfolded a broad agenda for Russia's educated elite. First, Russians needed to abandon the empty quarrels of the previous decades over whether Russian culture should develop in a "classical" or "romantic" direction. Such abstract questions were impossibly premature and ahistorical. What was needed now, Nadezhdin argued, was an era of careful study and preparation. Russia needed to absorb the best and most vital currents of European philosophy (by this he meant in particular the German Idealists, from first to last), even as Russians gathered information about themselves and the empire. Schelling—Nadezhdin's own intellectual hero—presented nature as a living, organic whole, progressing along an evolutionary ladder toward full self-expression and perfection. Nadezhdin imagined the vast Russian Empire was itself an ideal example of such a whole, and he contended that the consciousness it would produce should be unprecedented in human history. Already the empire had made enormous strides: "Our life grows not by the century, but by the hour." If Russia had exited its Middle Ages and come within a hundred years of Europe in the century since Peter the Great, Nadezhdin asked, "Can it take long to catch her now?"[23]

[22] On Nadezhdin, *Telescope*, and Stankevich, see N. K. Kozmin, *Nikolai Ivanovich Nadezhdin: Zhizn' i Nauchno-Literaturnaia Deiatel'nost,' 1804–1836* (St. Petersburg: Tipografiia M. A. Aleksandrova, 1912), 35–457, esp. 91, 258, 350–52; see also Kamenskii, *Moskovskii kruzhok liubomudrov*, 194–97; Z. A. Kamenskii, *N. I. Nadezhdin* (Moscow: Iskusstvo, 1984), 37–71; P. I. Prozorov, "Belinskii i Moskovskii universitet v ego vremia (iz studencheskikh vospominanii)," in Emel'ianov, *Moskovskii universitet*, 110–11. For an analysis of the role of Russia's clergy in the origins of the intelligentsia, see Laurie Manchester, "The Secularization of the Search for Salvation: The Self-Fashioning of Orthodox Clergymen's Sons in Late Imperial Russia," *Slavic Review* 57, no. 1 (Spring 1998): 50–76. Manchester argues plausibly that the influx of clerics' sons into Russia's professional classes in the nineteenth century helped infuse Russian intellectual life with clerical values and a sense of vocation. Yet it should also be said that the ideal of the thinker as a modern cleric had broad roots in European Romantic culture and was also a basic conceit of post-Kantian philosophy. On this, see Ben Knights, *The Idea of the Clerisy in the Nineteenth Century* (Cambridge: Cambridge University Press, 1978); Anthony J. La Vopa, *Fichte: The Self and the Calling of Philosophy, 1762–1799* (Cambridge: Cambridge University Press, 2001), 226–30; Laurence Dickey, *Hegel: Religion, Economics, and the Politics of the Spirit, 1770–1807* (Cambridge: Cambridge University Press, 1987), 1–32. Fichte defined the true scholar as a "priest of truth." J. G. Fichte, "Some Lectures Concerning the Scholar's Vocation," in *Fichte: Early Philosophical Writings*, trans. and ed. Daniel Breazeale (Ithaca: Cornell University Press, 1988), 176. On this ideal and its implementation at Priamukhino, see chapter 7.

[23] See Nadezhdin's programmatic essay in the first issue of his journal, N. I. Nadezhdin,

Nadezhdin assigned Moscow—the "Russian Manchester"—and its university-trained men a central role in this historic and exhilarating process. According to Nadezhdin, Russia's Enlightenment would proceed from scholarly men, who could rise above the "whine of opinion" to show a reliable path toward progress.[24] He argued that Russia's learned elite should take their methodological cues Kant, who first forced the human spirit to "take an account of its own powers and learn to know itself—before undertaking any positive assertions in the realm of metaphysics."[25] Aligning himself with Schiller, Nadezhdin also encouraged educated Russians to see their lives as artistic productions, works of art: "We must create ourselves," he writes in an essay on aesthetic education in 1831.[26] In short, the project Nadezhdin sketched for his students was both critical and ideological. The task of Russia's educated classes was to help awaken and energize Russian society through the creation and diffusion of a contemporary worldview. But in order to do so, Russia's learned elite had to remake itself through a period of preparation, catching up with Europe and using Kantian methods to acquire a modern identity of its own.

Like any good student, Stankevich was both shaped by his professors and critical of them. He felt that Pavlov sometimes exploited his boarders, students who deserved more for the money they paid. Stankevich was harder still on Nadezhdin, whom he later judged to be lacking in both insight and conviction. "Nadezhdin's outbursts are so imprecise, so insincere, so estranged from life and importance (for the most part), that it is sad to look at

---

"Sovremennoe napravlenie prosveshcheniia," *Teleskop* 1 (1831): 45–46; see also Kozmin, *Nadezhdin*, 89, 374–83. Nadezhdin's Schellingian conviction that Russia had a unique role vis à vis modern civilization was not entirely new: it had both eighteenth-century forerunners and direct Schellingian antecedents among the so-called wisdom lovers: see Andrzej Walicki, *A History of Russian Thought from the Enlightenment to Marxism*, trans. Hilda Andrews-Rusiecka (Stanford: Stanford University Press, 1979), 74–80.

[24] See Nadezhdin, "Sovremennoe napravlenie," 3 ("whine"), for his description of Moscow and the diffusion of a new era of enlightenment in Russia, 43–44.

[25] See Nadezhdin, "Sovremennoe napravlenie," 18.

[26] See N. N. [Nikolai Nadezhdin], "Neobkhodimost', zhachenie, i sila esteticheskogo obrazovaniia," *Teleskop* 10 (1831): 132. In his essay, "Schiller and the Early Russian Left," 199–200, Martin Malia credits Schiller with leaving an "aesthetic" imprint on Russia's student Idealists of the 1830s by convincing them that life should be poetic and "beautiful." This seems correct, but it is important that Stankevich's professors associated themselves with Schiller's ideas. Thus, for example, Stankevich in his letters announces his desire to read Nadezhdin's 1831 essay on aesthetic education—whose opening inscription comes from Schiller. See N. V. Stankevich to Ia. M. Neverov, undated letter of the early 1830s, Stankevich, *Perepiska*, 210; see also Rebecca Friedman's discussion of Schiller and the Nicholaevan university in *Masculinity, Autocracy, and the Russian University, 1804–1863* (New York: Palgrave Macmillan, 2005), 79–81.

them," Stankevich wrote in 1836, increasingly dissatisfied with Nadezhdin's leadership of *Telescope*.[27] Yet the language of these criticisms testifies to Stankevich's embrace of his professors' values and ambitions. He criticized Nadezhdin for lacking the very things that Nadezhdin himself argued should be part of any educated man's life: an exacting method and firm conviction. In this sense, Stankevich paid his professors the ultimate tribute of trying to hold them to their own standards. In the meantime, as his time at Moscow University drew to a close, he began laying plans for his own future plan of study, with a personal philosophical system he created in 1833 and titled "My Metaphysics."[28]

"My Metaphysics" takes the form of a short philosophical letter, aimed at an unknown addressee. As its title implies, however, Stankevich clearly meant the document to reflect the basic propositions of his own worldview and (more important) the method by which he intended to learn how to live his life. Stankevich begins by positing that all of nature—and with it all of life—is an evolutionary process, leading toward understanding. This is true because life possesses a meaningful end toward which it is working. (Here, Stankevich gestures toward a supreme Providence ["Reason, the Creator"] who guarantees the existence of such an end; but he does not define this figure in more detail.) Life, Stankevich further argues, will someday achieve this end because it acts according to rational laws. Within this system—binding up all of creation into a whole—different beings have different roles to play. To man [*chelovek*] in particular Stankevich assigns the role of being the "crown of creation." To him will be given the gift of seeing the whole; and in so doing, he will complete the process by which creation comes to self-consciousness. In man, "life, as it becomes aware of itself as a whole, rational and free, will take the form of an individual life, becoming aware of its individual being, rational and free."[29]

That day for Stankevich, however, has not yet come. Life is not a finished phenomenon but rather a process of understanding; and in any event, hu-

---

[27] On Stankevich and Nadezhdin, see N. V. Stankevich to Ia. M. Neverov, letter of 11 February [1837?] (*Perepiska*, 371); to V. G. Belinsky, letter of 30 May 1836 (*Perepiska*, 414); and to M. A. Bakunin of 22 October 1836 (*Perepiska*, 619–20). At this point, it should be said, Stankevich and still more his friends were quite closely involved in *Telescope*'s production. Given Nadezhdin's constant and ultimately losing struggle with censorship, these judgments seem harsh, and Stankevich may well have regretted them. On Pavlov's improprieties, see Stankevich's letter to Neverov of 11 April 1834 (*Perepiska*, 281).

[28] N. V. Stankevich, "Moia metafizika," in *Stikhotvoreniia. Tragediia. Proza.* (Moscow: Tipografiia i slovolitnia O. O. Gerbeka, 1890), 149–55.

[29] Ibid., 149–50.

manity has been corrupted by the Fall. ("About this later," Stankevich notes, again leaving his religious convictions vague.) For this reason, humanity must cleanse itself of a host of imperfections that hinder the fulfillment of its destiny. Stankevich assures himself this is possible: "In man's every atom there are elements of a normal man [*cheloveka normal'nogo*], as well as baser properties." Indeed, self-instruction and self-perfection are humanity's most fundamental calling: "It is an undoubted, though hardly new truth: humanity's life is its education." But this raises an obvious and important question of method. "How should an individual man educate his being? What should he take as his model, his prototype? Where is it?" Stankevich's answer: love. "Life is love. To know it partially, to act in accordance with its laws, one has to love."[30]

Stankevich reasons as follows: Love is the process by which life reproduces itself. Through love, "the last link of creation is contiguous to its beginning." For this reason, love may be thought of as an "intermediary force" in creation, a form of "feedback" [*samovozvratnaia sila*] that links the universe together and makes it a true whole. Love therefore offers men a chance to participate in this "common life," which alone may serve as a proper and poetic frame of reference, governing their existence. "Man [*chelovek*] only understands everything when he loves—and he who loves, will act beautifully."[31] (Here and throughout his metaphysics, Stankevich uses the Russian word *chelovek*, more literally translated as "person," to describe the hero of his story. But given the personal nature of Stankevich's metaphysics—and given later statements that imagine women's love in quite different terms—it seems safer to use masculine terms here. It is doubtful that Stankevich ever expected women to pursue the sort of educative love he imagines here.)

In "My Metaphysics," then, Stankevich imagines love not as a set ideal but as a practice for deriving meaningful and indeed "beautiful" norms for masculine behavior. Through loving, men can draw close to that "common life" [*vseobshchaia zhizn'*] which alone can provide models for their self-education and give their lives the correct form and meaning. In this sense, love is the key to recovering men's "normal" state, the perfection and purity they knew before the Fall.

The interest of this project—written when Stankevich was twenty years old and still a student in Moscow University—does not lie in some major innovation in the history of philosophy. Stankevich's account of the world

---

[30] See Stankevich, "Moia metafizika," 154.
[31] Ibid., 153.

weaves together visions of love, nature, and progressive self-cultivation that thrived in Russian academic circles in the early 1830s. Its main source of inspiration no doubt lies in Schelling's system of *Naturphilosophie* (championed by his university mentors), though in letters Stankevich credits Johann Wolfgang von Goethe with the notion that the "fallen soul is cleansed by divine love." He also praises Schiller for showing him that love is life's "mainspring."[32] Nor should we even necessarily assume that Stankevich's determination to receive instruction from love came from lofty philosophical or literary sources. Official proclamations, poetic almanacs, educational handbooks, newspapers, and novels alike praised women as beacons of morality in the modern world. Without feminine guidance and inspiration, these same sources warned, men must invariably fall short of their own vocations. Emperor Nicholas himself represented his marriage as the moral core of his reign and the norm that tied him to his nation. From this official adulation of love to the normative vision of "My Metaphysics" is but a short step.[33] ("The Church, and the family as well," Stankevich's friend Konstantin Aksakov later recalled, "were for him holy places, that he did not allow others to disparage in his presence.")[34]

The exact sources of Stankevich's normative vision of love seem less important than his unusual determination to translate his personal discoveries

[32] See N. V. Stankevich to Ia. M. Neverov, letter of 24 July 1833 (*Perepiska*, 236) (Goethe); and again to Neverov, letter of 20 May 1833 (*Perepiska*, 224). The notion of love as a cleansing and unifying force, defeating egoism, is also present in Schiller's *Philosophical Letters* (see Malia, *Herzen*, 44–45). It should be said that though Stankevich credits these poets with crystallizing these notions, there is no reason to believe that he derived the ideas from them. The idea of love as the motive force behind wisdom is as old as Plato's *Symposium*, if not older. See Alexander Nehamas and Paul Woodruff, "Introduction," in *Symposium*, ed. and trans. Alexander Nehamas and Paul Woodruff (Indianapolis: Hackett, 1989), xix; see also David Pugh, *Dialectic of Love: Platonism in Schiller's Aesthetics* (Montreal: McGill-Queen's University Press, 1997), 4–38, 325–43. Kamenskii, *Moskovskii kruzhok liubomudrov*, 194–209, has the best discussion of the various Russian intellectual crosscurrents at play in "My Metaphysics." It is clear that Stankevich himself associated the basic ideas behind "My Metaphysics" with Schelling, at least later: without naming "My Metaphysics," he summarizes its main ideas as Schelling's in a letter to Mikhail Bakunin of 12 November 1835, Stankevich, *Perepiska*, 584–85.

[33] See Richard Stites, *The Women's Liberation Movement in Russia: Feminism, Nihilism, and Bolshevism, 1860–1930* (Princeton: Princeton University Press, 1978), 15–16; Robin Bisha et al., *Russian Women, 1698–1917: Experience and Expression* (Bloomington: Indiana University Press, 2002), 26–32; Barbara Alpern Engel, *Women in Russia, 1700–2000* (Cambridge: Cambridge University Press, 2004), 22–38; Richard Wortman, *Scenarios of Power: Myth and Ceremony in Russian Monarchy*, vol. 1, *From Peter the Great to Nicholas I* (Princeton: Princeton University Press, 1995), 322–32. On the role of domestic norms in university students' educations, see in particular Friedman, *Masculinity*, 99–124.

[34] See Aksakov, "Vospominaniia studentstva 1832–1835 gg," 189.

into the language of post-Kantian metaphysics . As a group, Germany's academic idealists from Kant to Hegel avoided the merger of personal and philosophical life. They imagined public scholarship and debate as the proper realm of their self-creating activity and contented themselves with philosophizing *about* love rather than *through* it. Hegel, for example, derisively dismissed informal, nonacademic forms of philosophy as mere *"Konversation."*[35] Stankevich, however, decided to push his metaphysics deep into his intimate relations, subjecting his loves to his ambitions for development and analyzing his progress in letters to his friends. In the process, he both innovated within the Idealist tradition and began to model for his student contemporaries how they could use their personal lives as a forum for the mastery of Idealist philosophy and the attainment of a mature worldview.

⊛⌖⊛

Stankevich began to work out this practice in the middle of 1833—as "My Metaphysics" was gestating. By this point his university days were almost up, but he had already decided to extend them by turning to his personal relationships as a means to continue his education. Expressing a disdain for finishing his proposed dissertation on old Russian literature, he reported to his friend Neverov that he had decided love and art were the most educational realms of experience: "This is the world, in which a man should live, if he does not want to descend to the level of animal! This is the salutary sphere, in which he should reside, in order to be worthy of himself! This is the flame, with which he should warm and cleanse his soul!"[36] In "My Metaphysics," Stankevich placed his final emphasis on love (rather than art) as the primal medium of human development. Still, it is interesting to note that in this passage Stankevich mixes metaphors somewhat. On the one hand, he claims that love is a "sphere"—a space—in which man resides and that makes his ennoblement possible. Yet on the other hand, he speaks of love as a force or flame that cleanses the soul from its imperfections. The implication, clearly, is that

[35] On the reluctance of leading post-Kantians to use their schemes in salon conversation or apply them in their relations with women, see La Vopa, *Fichte,* 161–62; Heidi Thomann Tewarson, *Rahel Levin Varnhagen: The Life and Work of a German Jewish Intellectual* (Lincoln: University of Nebraska Press, 1998), 210–11, 216; Terry Pinkard, *Hegel: A Biography* (Cambridge: Cambridge University Press, 2000), 294–304, 482. Goethe quipped that Kant's elaborately articulated but ultimately reticent and musty views on love were "typical of such an old Bachelor," who had never brought philosophy and love into contact. See Isabel V. Hull, *Sexuality, State, and Civil Society in Germany 1700–1815* (Ithaca: Cornell University Press, 1996), 313–23.

[36] See N. V. Stankevich to Ia. M. Neverov, letter of 18 May 1833 (*Perepiska,* 221).

some kinds intimate relationships offer potentially transformative experiences, while others offer opportunities to convert these experiences into learning through retrospective analysis.

As he developed his ambitions for self-education in these years, Stankevich indeed distinguished between two kinds of love and their distinct roles in his personal development. There was friendship, "the best and most sacred species of love," as he explained to Neverov.[37] For Stankevich, his friends — by whom he predominantly meant his current and former university comrades — were a small and intimate masculine public with whom he could share the results of his personal searching. Friendship offered the chance to express the results of one's aesthetic experiences: "[W]ith whom can one share the feeling, which art gives birth to, if not with a friend?"[38] Romantic love for a woman, however, was an instructive experience — a historical datum for philosophical consideration. In practice, young Stankevich treated his pursuit of noblewomen's love instrumentally, as the quest for educational experiences that he could then consummate by analyzing them in intimacy with his male friends. As he subjected his love life to Idealist categories, he maintained at least a notional separation between this feminized, experiential realm and a discursive and masculine realm of reason.

Stankevich first began to apply his metaphysics of love to his relations with noblewomen of his acquaintance in the summer of 1833. Sometimes this process has been presented as a matter of Stankevich's forsaking "the flower of enjoyment" in favor of a utopian ideal of love.[39] Yet it should not be assumed that Stankevich was a virgin at this time or that he abstained from sexual activity during the course of his educational romances. Years later, his good friend Vissarion Belinsky would remark that he and his fellow students, until they all read Schiller, did not think twice about "having" a lower-class girl. Eventually, such behavior began to seem unchivalrous — so they switched to prostitutes. Proud self-legislators, they also practiced the "liberal art" of masturbation (as Stankevich himself seems to have called it).[40] For this reason, neither this nor any other of Stankevich's analyzed loves — which were all with noblewomen — was a matter of ideal renunciation. Rather, these

[37] See ibid.

[38] Ibid. On the widely cultivated ideal of masculine friendship as the most open and perfect of relations, see Friedman, "Romantic Friendship," 270–72. See also Friedman, *Masculinity*, 75–99.

[39] See, e.g., Malia, "Schiller and the Early Russian Left," 180–81.

[40] See V. G. Belinsky to N. V. Stankevich, letter of 29 September–8 October 1839, in Belinskii, *PSS*, XI:386; V. Sazhin, "Ruka pobeditelia: Vybrannye mesta iz perepiski V. Belinskogo i M. Bakunina," *Literaturnoe Obozrenie* 11 (1991): 39–40.

romances represented a chance—as Stankevich admitted to Neverov after the first—"to bring my feelings into a formula."[41] In other words, in good Idealist form, he treated each as a chance to advance and develop his own worldview, using his experiences with a noblewoman as an occasion for self-analysis and self-narration in a letter to a friend.

Stankevich's first metaphysical love was with a married woman during his stay with his family in the countryside in August 1833. He had first met her when she was fourteen; after the passage of several years, he reported to Neverov in French, "Imagine for yourself a beautiful blonde, with blue eyes, half-closed, languished and languishing." The attraction was mutual; they embraced and kissed passionately during an intimate rendezvous, and "I loved her." Characteristically, Stankevich immediately turns to the task of rendering historical judgment on this affair. His passion, he decides, was provoked by a fantasy, not a woman. Though bright, his lover was all surface: "She does not have deep feelings." As a result it was necessary to end their relationship; but his encounter with her had left behind a "miraculous ideal" of love—which he would now keep. "Now two extreme metaphysical questions have been answered," Stankevich informs Neverov. "Was kann ich wissen, was darf ich hoffen"? [What can I know, what can I hope for?—J. R.]; now there remains a middle term: was soll ich thun? [What should I do?—J. R.]"[42] As Stankevich's sudden switch to German in this passage makes clear, he is attempting to translate his discoveries into the technical language of Idealist philosophy. Through loving, he has acquired a guiding norm (his miraculous ideal of love) and with it an ambition, without knowing (quite yet) how to accomplish them.

Returning to Moscow, Stankevich left this woman behind, feeling guilty that she still seemed quite infatuated with him. He remained in a metaphysical frame of mind, however, and sought further transformative encounters with love.

> Let its devastating flame pass along my entire, insignificant being, let it destroy those weak bonds, by which I am entangled, heal the wearying sadness and disperse the restless shadows, tempting me in spiritual darkness. I would be resurrected, I would come alive again! Even if this love was the most unhappy . . . still it seems I would be better for it.[43]

[41] See N. V. Stankevich to Ia. M. Neverov, letter of 23 August 1833 (*Perepiska*, 244).

[42] See N. V. Stankevich to Ia. M. Neverov, letter of 8 August 1833 (*Perepiska*, 239–43, esp. 243).

[43] N. V. Stankevich to Ia. M. Neverov, letter of 15 September 1833 (*Perepiska*, 249).

Such a romantic encounter was not long in coming. Going to the home of his university friend Aleksei Beyer, Stankevich soon discovered that Aleksei's sister Natalia had become infatuated with him. Natalia, Stankevich instantly recognized, could not be accused of being superficial. On the contrary, Stankevich observed that she too had a metaphysical conception of romance: "She loves, because she forms ideals and contemplates people in their secret light." Yet Stankevich felt no physical attraction to her, and physical beauty was very much a part of the "prototype woman [*prototip zhenshchiny*]" that had begun to form in his head after his first romance.[44] The situation, Stankevich himself remarked to Neverov, was perfectly, poetically, instructively ironic: "Just now I am breaking free from the embrace of an earthly, sensuous love, and I find myself in front of a gentle being, whose friendship could be so sweet — and I run!"[45]

The result, for Stankevich, was a catastrophe, since the Beyer household was one of the hubs of the social life he and his friends had carved out for themselves in Moscow. Fortunately, thinking and "feeling through" this experience in his correspondence with Neverov, Stankevich made "something of a system, under which I conduct myself."[46] Visiting the Beyer house less frequently for a while, he sought to normalize the situation. Relating to Natalia as a "brother to a sister," Stankevich steered clear of the gossip, widespread in their circles, about their romance. By December, he felt that his careful, systematic behavior had extricated himself from this awkward affair. More important, he decided that he himself had invented much of its drama after all. There had been no reason to worry so much: though Natalia "is a kind girl and has feelings," Stankevich observed somewhat condescendingly, she was strong and "will not die from love." The awkwardness that had descended onto their relationship was itself the product of his own fear of doing wrong, which he would now strive to regulate. "Everything I wrote about her was written during an attack of moral fanaticism, which puts us up on stilts, places on our eyes magnifying glasses, that magnify 1,000 times," he wrote to Neverov on December 1, 1833. Judging himself instructed and sobered by these experiences, he calculated — wrongly, as it happened — that it was possible to return to their prior relations, and again he began to visit the Beyers often when he was in Moscow.[47]

---

[44] See N. V. Stankevich, letter to Neverov of 19 October 1833 (*Perepiska*, 254–55). On the "prototype woman" left in his heart after his first romance see his letter to Neverov of 14 October 1834 (*Perepiska*, 252).

[45] *Perepiska*, 254–55.

[46] See N. V. Stankevich to Ia. M. Neverov, letter of 5 November 1836 (*Perepiska*, 255).

[47] See N. V. Stankevich to Ia. M. Neverov, letter of 1 December 1833 (*Perepiska*, 264).

This ended, for a time, Stankevich's interest in educating himself through love. He spent much of 1834 pursuing his studies in a more prosaic manner. He completed his university education that summer and then spent several months in his home district of Ostrogozhsk reading history and philosophy. He wrote some poetry and a short, illustrative story about a young man like him, titled "A Few Moments from the Life of Graf Z—."[48] It was at this time that his brief career in service as a school inspector began and ended. His personal educational plans seemed much more attractive, however, and he began to work through post-Kantian philosophy on his own, beginning with Schelling's *System of Transcendental Idealism*. This desire for serious study soon brought him back to Moscow, where he could work with his friends.[49] It was there, in early 1835, that his metaphysical interest in romance returned, placing Liubov Bakunina at the center of his attention.

By virtue of their splendid isolation at Priamukhino—rumored to be a "temple of happiness," according to Neverov—the Bakunin sisters had gradually become objects of fantasy for these young university men.[50] "Your sisters' names drifted obscurely and secretly around our circle, like the realization of life's mystery," Vissarion Belinsky recalled to Mikhail Bakunin in 1838.[51] When Liubov and Tatiana arrived in Moscow that March, Stankevich informed Neverov that his own moment of reckoning had arrived:

> These days have passed by joyfully. Without petty interest, one is drawn in by these girls, as by beautiful Divine creations; you look at them, listen to them, want to seize them and keep their angelic faces by your side, so that you can regard them when your spirit is heavy. And you also want respect from them—respect, more than any other feeling. You want them not to mix you up with the crowds of worthless people.

His encounter with these formidable "divine creations" instantly summoned up Stankevich's analytical impulse. "A desire has arisen within me to keep a

---

[48] See N. V. Stankevich, "Neskol'ko mgnovenii iz zhizni grafa Z***," in *Stikhotvoreniia. Tragediia. Proza.* (Moscow: Tipografiia i slovolitnia O. O. Gerbeka, 1890), 156–73; and also the poem "Two Lives" (*Dve zhizni*) (Mashinskii, *Poety kruzhka N. V. Stankevicha*, 120, 558), which portrays two metaphysical loves.

[49] See Stankevich's letters to Neverov of 19 September and 16 October 1834 (*Perepiska*, 289–94).

[50] Natalia Beyer reports Neverov's praise of Priamukhino in her letter to Liubov Bakunina of 25 September 1833, IRLI f. 16, op. 8, no. 89, l. 29 ob.; by this time Natalia herself knew this wasn't true.

[51] V. G. Belinsky to M. A. Bakunin, letter of [12–24 October?] 1838 (Belinskii, *PSS*, XI:329).

diary: my many feelings could be instructive for those, who might read it after me." He promised to work up his thoughts "artfully" (*khudozhnicheski*) for Neverov, preparing himself for a fateful encounter with love and through it, knowledge. When Liubov seemed to look on him with particular interest, he declared that a new "epoch" in his life was at hand.[52]

Unfortunately for Stankevich, it soon turned out that the drama at hand was being stage-managed by someone else this time. Natalia Beyer had invented her own scenario to govern events in her family's salon, a scenario in which she herself was the hero. It was she, Stankevich soon learned, who urged Liubov to "have a little fantasy" about him. In the process, Natalia hoped to "show her love with a kind deed and be my matchmaker." But when Stankevich seemed so ungracious as to actually be wooing another maiden's hand in the Beyers' own home, the atmosphere was immediately poisoned. Stankevich himself admitted that he could understand why the Beyers might "think it bad on my part to be seeking through their household—as she could easily think, even though it wasn't really a matter of seeking, but studying [*ne iskanie, a skoree issledovanie*]."[53] Meanwhile, both Liubov and Stankevich felt horribly guilty and withdrew from the scene. "How much happiness I expected, and how much sorrow came down all at once!" Stankevich exclaims in a letter written to Neverov on March 27, 1835.[54] The Beyers soon left Moscow, ending Stankevich's contact with the Bakunins.

Even so, Natalia's plans did not entirely disrupt Stankevich's own educational ambitions. Within a day of the scandal, he was already writing Neverov to deliver the results of his latest brush with love. Characteristically, he declared himself transformed and improved by the experience.

At least I have been released by my dream, my joyful dream, that chased me throughout all my studies; my sorrow has grown dull, and I can give myself fully to ordinary, quiet activity. Now I am going to study Jewish history. This people presents many questions, and I hope to write an outline of Jewish history, though I don't know if I will succeed.

Stankevich also entered into a contract with his fellow student Kliuchnikov, agreeing to meet once a week to study Schelling, "in order to see the limit to which human understanding can come across its long life."[55] In other words,

[52] See Stankevich's letter to Ia. M. Neverov, letter of 9–13 March 1835 (*Perepiska*, 314–16).
[53] N. V. Stankevich to Ia. M. Neverov, letter of 22 April [1835?] (*Perepiska*, 318).
[54] See N. V. Stankevich to Ia. M. Neverov, letter of 27 March 1835 (*Perepiska*, 317).
[55] N. V. Stankevich to Ia. M. Neverov, letter of 28 March 1835 (*Perepiska*, 317).

Stankevich—despite what seems to have been his genuine attraction to Liubov Bakunina—very quickly subordinated it to his educational conception of love. The day after he realized the possibility of romance was over, he somewhat forcedly made it a stage in his development toward knowledge and self-consciousness. He had seen that love had nothing more to offer him in the short run, and he was ready to press on to more stoic studies, such as Schelling and "Jewish history."

Stankevich's previous educational romances ended after such moments of reckoning, but in the months that followed, he found himself unable to get Liubov and her family entirely off his mind. In part, this was due to his increasingly cordial relationship with young Mikhail Bakunin, whom Stankevich met in the Beyer salon in March 1835. Mikhail had just been released from the military and was being groomed by his relatives for a position in civil service. Yet young Bakunin expressed a great admiration for Moscow's students and eagerly sought out their friendship. In the fall of 1835 Stankevich encouraged Mikhail to join him in the pursuit of an inspirational vocation in society through the study of post-Kantian philosophy. Much to Stankevich's delight, Mikhail accepted the challenge.[56]

Their friendship, however, was not the only thing that kept Priamukhino and the Bakunins on Stankevich's mind. Though Stankevich denied it—and despite the ease with which he had placed his previous romances behind him—his friends suspected that he had developed real feelings for Liubov Bakunina. "Do not make a face like Minerva, do not smile like Mephistopheles," Stankevich wrote to Neverov in September of 1835, as he and a friend named Aleksandr Efremov prepared to visit Priamukhino at Mikhail's invitation. "We are just going: Efremov as a close acquaintance and friend of the household, and I as a man, who desires a better acquaintance with this honorable family."[57] Yet he later confessed to romantic hopes that were cruelly disappointed during his stay. Liubov treated him coolly throughout his visit. During a lengthy conversation about love, she declared that his good friend Neverov combined "all the conditions necessary to be loved by a spirited woman." Yet she said nothing about Stankevich himself. He claimed to be crushed by the experience: "I am carrying away a heavy weight on my spirit from which nothing will ever save me."[58] Thanks to his budding friendship

[56] See Stankevich's letter to M. A. Bakunin, 25 September 1835 (Stankevich, Perepiska, 573–74); and his letter to Ia. M. Neverov, 10 November [1835?] (Stankevich, *Perepiska*, 338). I discuss this plan of study more thoroughly in chapter 7.

[57] Letter to Ia. M. Neverov, 28 September 1835 (Stankevich, *Perepiska*, 330).

[58] Letter to Ia. M. Neverov, 26 October 1836 (Stankevich, *Perepiska*, 334).

with Mikhail, he would have another chance to bring this particular romance to a more acceptable conclusion.

⊛⁄⊱⁊⊛

What made Stankevich take such a self-conscious, educational approach to love? Why did he assign it such an important, epochal role in his life? It is common to invoke Russia's wintry political climate and relative social underdevelopment as explanations for the readiness with which Stankevich and his fellow students sought to draw philosophical morals from their personal lives. Denied a proper public outlet for their intellectual ambitions, the argument goes, even such talented men as young Stankevich were forced to make odd and "excessive" demands of their private lives.[59] But Stankevich's personal glass can also be seen as half full. The fact is, Stankevich himself was in no hurry to begin his public activity. As a young and wealthy nobleman, he had the luxury of being able to pursue the Kantian ideal of self-preparation to the fullest and on his own terms. Far more common than his complaints about his lack of opportunity are moments when he turns away from such opportunities, calling them premature. He decided early to wait on his academic career, refused close participation in Nadezhdin's *Telescope* to have more time for his own studies, and in general regarded his various endeavors (translations, opera librettos, even the unfinished "My Metaphysics") as chances to learn rather than as projects to be completed.[60]

Nor was Stankevich as bound as others by the rules of propriety. Men from a poor or clerical background — even famous intellects like Fichte and Hegel — needed respectability to sustain their livelihoods as thinkers in the early nineteenth century. In Moscow, Stankevich's idol Professor Nadezhdin saw his reputation savaged in 1835, when he was accused of trifling with a young woman's affections.[61] Unlike these men, Stankevich could afford to take liberties with his love life. He had no career to ruin, and he had his own wealth and nobility to fall back on. Moreover, he was still quite young, in an age when the university itself was helping to make the student a new kind of

[59] See in particular Berlin, "Remarkable Decade," 141–44; Malia, "Schiller and the Early Russian Left," 180–81, 198–200.

[60] See Stankevich's letters to Ia. M. Neverov of 18 May 1833 (*Perepiska*, 221) (abandoned dissertation); 2 June 1833 (*Perepiska*, 226); 5 November 1833 (*Perepiska*, 261) (abandoned theatrical project); 1 June 1835 (*Perepiska*, 321) (reluctance to commit to *Telescope*).

[61] On Hegel's (and Fichte's) need to sustain respectability, see Pinkard, *Hegel*, 275–304; La Vopa, *Fichte*, 150–80; on the scandal that nearly killed Nadezhdin's career, see Kozmin, *Nadezhdin*, 457–507.

social hero. By "bringing his feelings into a formula," making a "system" for his behavior, and plotting his life according to "epochs" established by his romances, Stankevich's metaphysics of love helped him present his personal life as a free-form drama evolving toward the meaningful end his professors praised so highly: a mature, contemporary worldview and a vocation in society as a spokesman on behalf of reason and morality. Placed in proper context, Stankevich looks less like a dreamy young introvert, whose personality somehow expressed the frustrated social climate of his day, and more like an earnest young nobleman who sought to perform his class's most typical social function — that of exemplary behavior — according to the powerful new scripts provided by post-Kantian Idealism.

Stankevich's interactions with the Bakunins fostered this ambition on several levels. They helped him orient, develop, and distinguish the Russian Idealist tradition he was seeking to invent. Yet it is also true that his relations with the Bakunins gradually defied his expectations. His love for Liubov refused to resolve itself into a neat educational romance and instead became a prolonged courtship. Though he expected to find Priamukhino a "temple of happiness," his visit in October of 1835 made him party to the sadder, more disturbing drama going on behind the scenes: the tension within the family surrounding the Bakunin childrens' fates and sister Varvara's unhappy marriage to Nikolai Diakov in particular.[62] Perhaps most unexpected of all was the passion Stankevich's new friend Mikhail Bakunin showed for Idealist philosophy and Mikhail's eagerness to assume an inspirational role in society. Racing through Stankevich's careful program of study in early 1836, Mikhail declared that he was ready to start calling humanity to a freer and more conscious existence — and that he would begin by transforming his own family's exemplary life.

---

[62] Stankevich notes Varvara's troubles in a letter to Neverov of 26 October 1835 (Stankevich, *Perepiska*, 335).

CHAPTER SEVEN

Mikhail and the Invisible Church

Stankevich's example helped bestow distinction on the practice of Idealist philosophy in the mid-1830s, turning it into a charismatic romantic tradition. Under his inspiration, many of his most talented university comrades (and even a few outsiders) tried to acquire firm convictions and an inspirational vocation in society through the mastery of German Idealism. This included such varied figures as the literary critics Belinsky and Vasilii Botkin (1811–1869); the historian Timofei Granovsky (1813–1855); and the writer Ivan Turgenev (1818–1883). All of these men claimed that their youthful interest in Idealism was the educational foundation on which their mature activity in society was built.[1] In no case, however, was Idealist philosophy practiced so enthusiastically—or controversially—as by the young Mikhail Bakunin.

When Mikhail's sisters first introduced him to Moscow society in the mid-1830s, young Bakunin bore little resemblance to his later self: the hairy, corpulent anarchist of radical lore. A self-portrait from 1829—superimposed, in

---

[1] On the influence of Stankevich's Idealism on these men as a group, see S. Mashinskii, "Stankevich i ego kruzhok," *Voprosy Literatury* 5 (May 1964): 125–48; Edward J. Brown, *Stankevich and His Moscow Circle* (Stanford, Calif.: Stanford University Press, 1966), 3–31; Z. A. Kamenskii, *Moskovskii kruzhok liubomudrov* (Moscow: Izdatel'stvo Nauka, 1980), 270–78; Lydia Ginzburg analyzes Stankevich's role as a historic touchstone for this group in *On Psychological Prose*, trans. and ed. Judson Rosengrant (Princeton: Princeton University Press, 1991), 48–57; see also Jane Costlow's thoughtful analysis of the image of Idealism in Turgenev's works, in her *Worlds within Worlds: The Novels of Ivan Turgenev* (Princeton: Princeton University Press, 1990). For more on Belinsky, see below, chapter 9.

Mikhail Aleksandrovich Bakunin
(1814–1876), self-portrait. From N.
Pirumova, *Bakunin* (Moscow: Molodaia
gvardiia, 1970).

a curious economy of paper, over the head of a bull—shows a well-groomed
boy with tender lips and fine, close-cropped hair. By 1834, Mikhail had managed to disappoint his parents twice, first by taking his sister Liubov's side in
the quarrel over Renne and then by running so far afoul of his military superiors that they expelled him from the Artillery School. Yet after a few
months of punitive duty in the empire's western provinces, Mikhail won a release from the military and promised his father that he would take up gain-
ful employment in the imperial civil service. His political views, on those rare
occasions he expressed them, were patriotic and autocratic. ("Russians are
not Frenchmen, they love their fatherland," seventeen-year-old Mikhail declared at the time of the Polish Uprising in 1831. "They love their sovereign,
for them his word is law.")[2] The dominant theme of his early letters is his
abiding affection for his family and desire to return home. "What a child I
was, when I rejoiced at the thought of traveling to St. Petersburg," he wrote
to his sisters in early 1831. "I would give half my life for the chance to be in
Priamukhino even for a moment, to hug you and assure you of the depth of
my friendship."[3]

[2] Letter to his parents, 20 September 1831 (Bakunin, *Sobranie*, I:52).
[3] See letter to his sisters, spring 1831 (Bakunin, *Sobranie*, I:47). Arthur Mendel reproduces

Mikhail Bakunin (1860s). From N. Pirumova, *Bakunin* (Moscow: Molodaia gvardiia, 1970).

numerous examples of Mikhail's homesickness in his biography of Bakunin (*Michael Bakunin: Roots of Apocalypse* [New York: Praeger, 1981], 10–11). He argues that this redolent sentiment is evidence of Mikhail's "estrangement" from the culture of his day. But other than a certain understandable dislike for barracks life, there is little in this sentimental correspondence that breaks from the emotionalism expected of loyal sons and brothers during this time. On this, see Richard Wortman, *Scenarios of Power: Myth and Ceremony in Russian Monarchy*, vol. 1, *From Peter the Great to Nicholas I* (Princeton: Princeton University Press, 1995), 249–69. See also Rebecca Friedman, *Masculinity, Autocracy, and the Russian University, 1804–1863* (New York: Palgrave Macmillan, 2005), chap. 5.

Mikhail's contemporaries were shocked by the effect Idealist philosophy had on this conventional, sentimental artillery officer. All of a sudden (it seemed) this homesick young man became a restless philosophical prophet. "Stankevich perceived his talents and set him down to philosophy," Herzen recalled bemusedly in *Past and Thoughts.* "Bakunin learnt German from Kant and Fichte and then set down to work upon Hegel, whose method and logic he mastered to perfection — and to whom did he not preach it afterwards? To us and to Belinsky, to ladies and to Proudhon."[4] As Herzen suggests, two things in particular startled Mikhail's new comrades. The first was the tremendous enthusiasm he displayed for philosophy; the second was his odd indiscretion in practicing it. Defying the students' conventional distinction between their own intimacy (steeped in philosophical analysis) and the language they used with others, Mikhail felt free to "preach" the Idealist tradition to anyone — up to and including women, and most notoriously of all his sisters.[5] By the summer of 1836 — the summer following his acquaintance with Stankevich — his prophesies of what the practice of Idealist philosophy at Priamukhino might accomplish reached ecstatic and improbable heights. "We feel ourselves to be both divine and free," Mikhail wrote to his sisters in August 1836, describing the purified "inner life" they were fashioning through philosophy, "and destined to liberate enslaved humanity and the universe, still victim to the instinctual laws of unconscious existence."[6]

What explains Mikhail's unbounded enthusiasm for post-Kantian philosophy? What did he hope to accomplish by professing it so freely in private society, and how did his controversial example influence his contemporaries? The most insightful approach to answering these questions is that suggested by Lydia Ginzburg, in her book *On Psychological Prose.* She presents Mikhail's "domestic romantic messianism" as a conscious rhetorical performance, played out for his friends and sisters at Priamukhino and meant to inspire their participation in some grand purpose.[7] Yet Ginzburg has relatively little to say about what that purpose was, or what ambitions stood behind it. She prefers to present Mikhail as a cultural phenomenon rather than as a person,

---

[4] Alexander Herzen, *My Past and Thoughts,* ed. Dwight Macdonald, trans. Constance Garnett, intro. by Isaiah Berlin (Berkeley: University of California Press, 1973), 253; cf. Gertsen, *Sobranie,* IX:43.

[5] Ginzburg describes the controversies Bakunins' instruction of his sisters unleashed in *On Psychological Prose,* 43–45, 75–76; I will return to this theme in what follows, particularly in chapters 8 and 9.

[6] Letter to his sisters Tatiana and Varvara, 10 August 1836 (Bakunin, *Sobranie,* I:329).

[7] See Ginzburg, *Psychological Prose,* 33–44, esp. 42.

identifying him as "one of the last and most brilliant expressions of Russian Romanticism."[8]

Unfortunately, such superlatives abound in the vast scholarly literature surrounding Mikhail Bakunin. He is routinely described as a creature produced by the social or historical forces of his time. Most scholars portray Mikhail as an alienated intellectual empowered and radicalized by post-Kantian thought.[9] In a harshly critical biography, Aileen Kelly argues that he is best understood as "the epitome of the introspective intellectual *à la russe* — the superfluous man."[10] Yet even sympathetic observers tend to present him as a product of Romantic frustration. In *Roots of Revolution,* a classic postwar history of Russian populism, Franco Venturi calls Mikhail "a son of the age of Nicholas I and the atmosphere of fear and concealed enthusiasms which oppressed the thirties." He then contrasts Bakunin with Herzen, who Venturi claims "found in his own family and in the world of his early youth a direct link with the culture of the Enlightenment and the Decembrist Revolt."[11]

There is, it seems, something excessively romantic about this tradition of imagining Mikhail as a raw expression of his times. Such formulations obscure his personality and place in society and history, instead of explaining them. To begin with, Mikhail was the son of Aleksandr Bakunin, not Nicholas I. The dominant intellectual influence of his youth was his father's brand of domestic enlightenment and in particular Aleksandr Mikhailovich's belief in the power of reason to create a world in which "all private wills will agree." Mikhail seems to have retained this sentimental faith in both family and reason to the end of his days. His anarchist writings of the 1860s and 1870s, as one recent scholar has noted, rest on an optimistic belief that humanity — when the prejudices that corrupt its authentic nature are stripped away — is essentially rational, virtuous, and social.[12] In the end, this vision of the world is not that different from the idyll Aleksandr Mikhailovich sought to build at

---

[8] Ibid., 34.

[9] See in particular Martin Malia, *Alexander Herzen and the Birth of Russian Socialism* (New York: Grosset & Dunlap, 1965), 86–87; Isaiah Berlin, "A Remarkable Decade," in Hardy and Kelly, *Russian Thinkers,* 144–45; Andrzej Walicki, *The Slavophile Controversy: History of a Conservative Utopia in Nineteenth-Century Russian Thought,* trans. Hilda Andrews-Rusiecka (Notre Dame: University of Notre Dame Press, 1975), 368.

[10] Kelly, *Bakunin,* 1–2.

[11] Franco Venturi, *Roots of Revolution: A History of the Populist and Socialist Movements in Nineteenth Century Russia,* trans. Francis Haskell (New York: Grosset & Dunlap, 1960), 36.

[12] George Crowder, *Classical Anarchism: The Political Thought of Godwin, Proudhon, Bakunin, and Kropotkin* (Oxford: Clarendon Press, 1991), 10–13, 118–69.

Priamukhino. (One is reminded, for example, of the harmonious and happy community unleashed by reason in Aleksandr's 1799 poem, "The Stream.") And indeed, as Mikhail's anarchist biographer Max Nettlau once observed, the sentimental family remained Mikhail's favorite model for society until the end of his days.[13]

Just as important, young Bakunin was a nobleman and not an intellectual. Indeed, it was precisely his desire to trade his noble identity for a scholarly one that drove his theatrical embrace of philosophy in 1836. Mikhail entered the Stankevich circle preceded but also defined by his family's distinguished reputation. To them he was "their brother" (as Belinsky put it). Yet Mikhail's early letters show that he desired to become a university man. In January 1834, he announced to his parents that he wanted to trade his life in noble society—consumed by social occasions—for one of scholarship, rooted in intellectual activity.[14] This "intellectual revolution" (as he called it) did not—of course—mean that he was disenchanted with the Empire's existing public order. Imperial officials themselves helped to valorize Moscow's academics as "new models for Russian manhood."[15] Yet Mikhail's decision rebelled against his reputation as a filial young nobleman. It required justification in the eyes of his parents, sisters, and even his newfound friends, who as university students might well have taken him for a dilettante. (Such indeed was the nickname that haunted him in university circles thereafter.)[16]

Seeking to overcome these objections—and thereby trade one sort of distinction in society for another—Mikhail presented himself as a post-Kantian scholar-cleric operating on the stage of private life. He drew a script for what this new identity would look like from the first—and most ecstatic—philosopher he read under Stankevich's tutelage: Johann Gottlieb Fichte. In the process, he fashioned a vision of himself and his role in society that not only transcended university circles but informed his later anarchism. He began to present himself as a Fichtean "priest of truth," whose emancipatory calling

[13] Max Nettlau, "Mikhail Bakunin: A Biographical Sketch," in G. P. Maximoff, ed., *The Political Philosophy of Bakunin: Scientific Anarchism* (London: Free Press of Glencoe, 1953), 30.

[14] See Mikhail's letter to his sisters of 25 January 1834 (Bakunin, *Sobranie*, I:122–24); A. Kornilov, *Molodye gody Mikhaila Bakunina: Iz istorii russkogo romantizma* (Moscow: M. and S. Sabashnikov, 1915), 130–36.

[15] See Richard S. Wortman, *The Development of a Russian Legal Consciousness* (Chicago: University of Chicago Press, 1976), 223.

[16] Looking for a pseudonym to replace Mikhail's name in his 1857 biography of Stankevich, Annenkov picked "philosophical dilettante," a choice no doubt suggested to him by university lore, see P. V. Annenkov, *Nikolai Vladimirovich Stankevich: Perepiska ego i biografiia* (Moscow: Tipografiia Kat'kova, 1857), 155 and 159.

in society was to stimulate the moral development of others and thereby bring about the coming of a self-directed social world. Indeed, Belinsky himself —at the end of the summer of 1836—was moved to predict that a Fichtean clerisy of the sort Mikhail was imagining might bring about the end of external authorities altogether.[17]

Curiously enough, it seems that it was Mikhail's pursuit of this particularly ecstatic vision of the scholar's vocation that both motivated his unusual embrace of philosophy in the late 1830s and laid the foundation of his future radical persona and even his anarchist social vision. Before attempting to analyze his early Idealism any further, it may be useful to recall the whole of Mikhail's life briefly here. If nothing else, it will help us understand the degree to which Mikhail's controversial transition from nobleman to scholar helped shape his much more famous career in life as a revolutionary.

⊛⅍⅀⊛

Born at Priamukhino in 1814, sent into service in 1828, Mikhail remained an exemplary young nobleman until his first return home in late 1833.[18] During his five years in St. Petersburg, he studied fortification, German, and dance; wrote homesick letters to his family; worshipped a beautiful young girl; and ran up the first in a long line of debts.[19] He later contended that this early era in his life came to a dramatic end in the fall of 1833, when the horrible familial quarrels that surrounded Liubov's engagement to Renne shattered his youthful complacency.[20] Whether or not this is true, some three months later, in January of 1834, he underwent his self-described "intellectual revolution" and began to show interest in leading a more reflective life, as a scholar.[21]

As early as 1832, Mikhail displayed a certain self-consciousness before university men. He expressed jealousy when he heard that Aleksei Beyer had be-

---

[17] See below.
[18] The best and basic accounts of Mikhail Bakunin's life are Kornilov, *Molodye gody;* idem, *Gody stranstvii Mikhaila Bakunina* (Leningrad: Gosudarstvennoe izdatel'stvo, 1925); Iurii Steklov, *M. A. Bakunin: Ego zhizn' i deiatel'nost', 1814–1876,* vol. 1 (Moscow: Izdatel'stvo Kommunisticheskoi Akademii, 1926); E. H. Carr, *Michael Bakunin* (London: Macmillan, 1937); Aileen Kelly, *Mikhail Bakunin: A Study in the Psychology and Politics of Utopianism* (New Haven: Yale University Press, 1987). For an overview of Bakunin's role in the world anarchist movement, see James Joll, *The Anarchists,* 2nd ed. (Cambridge, Mass.: Harvard University Press, 1980).
[19] See Bakunin's early letters to his family, *Sobranie,* I:70–110.
[20] See his letter to his father of 15 December 1837 (ibid., II:109–10, 127–28).
[21] Kornilov describes this transformation in *Molodye gody,* 130–36.

come a Moscow University student, joking that his childhood friend "has risen too high to remember me, a poor artilleryman."[22] His "intellectual revolution" of 1834—grandly announced in a letter to his sisters that January—had little specific content. At its center stood a vague desire to replace his previous life of leisure with a studiously constructed "inner existence."[23] Yet his dedication to Artillery School dropped precipitously, and soon Mikhail's superiors banished him to garrisons near Minsk and Vilna. Oddly enough, this only contributed to his scholastic ambitions. He found himself in the company of a former Moscow University student named Krasnopolsky, who introduced him to the works of Idealism's Russian proponents and helped confirm his growing desire to become an "ideal man, living a spiritual life."[24]

In 1835, Mikhail quit military service, began intensive study of philosophy under Stankevich's tutelage, and rejected a position in provincial administration that his father had arranged for him. Fleeing Priamukhino for Moscow that December, he defiantly declared that his immediate goal was to pursue his philosophical studies and, beyond that, to go to Berlin, where he could undertake formal academic training.[25] For several years his parents resisted this ambition. This set off a series of domestic conflicts (described in more detail below). Each winter Mikhail shuttled off to Moscow to study with his friends; each summer he returned to Priamukhino; and then finally in 1840 his father and mother agreed to let him go to Berlin. Mikhail left that summer.

Shortly after his arrival, however, Mikhail entered nationalist and socialist literary circles, began to take an interest in politics, and soon renounced his planned career in philosophy for one in revolution. (The motivations behind this transformation, and its relationship to his previous Idealism, remain a subject of controversy.)[26] In 1842, he published a blistering radical manifesto titled "The Reaction in Germany (A Fragment by a Frenchman)," under the pseudonym Jules Elysard. It contained the bold claim that all progress begins with destruction, which it distilled into Bakunin's most famous revolutionary maxim: "The urge to destroy is also a creative urge."[27] Not fooled by his pseudonym for long, the Russian government ordered Mikhail to re-

---

[22] See his letter to his sisters, 17 September 1832 (Bakunin, *Sobranie,* I:66).

[23] Letter to his sisters, 25 January 1834 (Bakunin, *Sobranie,* I:123).

[24] See Mikhail's letter to S. N. Murav'ev, January 1835 (*Sobranie,* I:162–63).

[25] See Kornilov, *Molodye gody,* 139–42; and Mikhail's letter to his father, January 1836 (Bakunin, *Sobranie,* I:189).

[26] See Kelly, *Bakunin,* 89–101, as well as below.

[27] See "Die Reaction in Deutschland (Ein Fragment von einem Franzosen," *Deutsche Jahrbücher für Wissenschaft und Kunst* 5: 247–51 (October 17–21, 1842), 985–1002, esp. 1002.

turn home. When he understandably refused to do so, he was stripped of his noble title. Mikhail's independence and increasing notoriety as a renegade Russian gentleman lasted until 1849, when he was arrested by Saxon authorities for encouraging a revolt against their king.

Three monarchies then jostled for the right to punish Mikhail Bakunin. The Saxons sentenced him to death, and the Austrians wished to imprison him for life for his revolutionary plots against their empire. Yet in the end Mikhail was returned to St. Petersburg, where the Emperor Nicholas I threw him in the Peter-Paul Fortress and suggested that he write a confession. He did, but still no verdict followed. Mikhail rotted in prison for most of the 1850s, gradually losing his teeth to scurvy; it was only after the ascension of Emperor Aleksandr II in 1855 that the Bakunin family was able to intervene on his behalf and have his imprisonment commuted to permanent exile in Siberia. Once there, Mikhail married and seemed to settle down; but in 1861 he fled eastward, talking and sailing his way across the Pacific and Atlantic oceans to arrive on Herzen's doorstep in London.

This daring escape won Mikhail worldwide celebrity and launched the last and most famous phase of his revolutionary career. First, he sought to organize Russian support for the Polish Rebellion of 1863; when this failed, he landed in Italy, where he planned a series of secret revolutionary organizations and became one of the socialist movement's most charismatic and active polemicists. In the late 1860s, Mikhail led a group of his Geneva sympathizers into the International Working Men's Association. Soon thereafter, however, Karl Marx accused Mikhail of conspiring to seize control of that organization. He also alleged that Mikhail betrayed human decency by collaborating with a bloodthirsty young revolutionary named Sergei Nechaev.[28] Mikhail denied these accusations. Moreover, he mounted a fierce critique of Marx's insistence on radical political organization. He believed that the revolutionary party Marx favored would usher in new and more oppressive forms of statehood, should it ever come to power. (As Mikhail elaborated these views, he wrote a series of treatises—largely fragmentary—on which his anarchist reputation has rested since.)[29]

[28] This episode generated perhaps the most lively controversy of Bakunin's life: on it, see in particular Lehning, *Archives* IV; Michael Confino, *Violence dans la violence: le debat Bakounine-Necaev* (Paris: F. Maspero, 1973); and Kelly, *Bakunin,* 257–88.

[29] See in particular Lehning, *Archives* I–III; Michael Bakunin, *God and the State,* ed. Paul Avrich (New York: Dover, 1970); Robert M. Cutler, trans. and ed., *From Out of the Dustbin: Bakunin's Basic Writings, 1869–1871)* (Ann Arbor: Ardis, 1985); Michael Bakunin, *Statism and Anarchy,* trans. and ed. Marshall S. Shatz (Cambridge: Cambridge University Press, 1990).

The true role of revolutionaries, Mikhail argued, was to be the revolution's "invisible pilots," "fomenting, awakening, unleashing" popular radicalism by their words and deeds without presuming to take political power for themselves.[30] He claimed that federations of small, autonomous communes would provide the only organization people needed in this age of self-governance, since humanity's better instincts — heretofore oppressed and corrupted by the state — would be released by the revolution. Mikhail's vision, in the words of one scholar, was of a "shining era of freedom in which men would direct their own affairs without interference from any authority." (The gendered language here is not Bakunin's own, but on the whole he was not known for his feminism.)[31]

In 1872, Marx finally won their struggle within the First International, and he excluded Bakunin from that organization. Though Mikhail still had many supporters, his health began to fail, and he retired to a villa just outside of Lugano, Switzerland. (As throughout most of his life, he lived on credit.) "I never saw then or later such an ecstatic and selfless devotion," the socialist Aleksandra Weber writes in her memoirs, describing the parade of Italian professors, students, shoemakers, and coal heavers who daily came to see "the great Bakunin" as he lay dying: "This was the loving, romantic feeling of students for their teacher, a feeling, where devotion to an idea fuses with devotion to the personality who bears it. This, it seems, is how great artists once related to their pupils, how the founders of great religions related to their closest followers."[32] Weber imagined that if this broken man could only mount the tribune "before a crowd, he would have the same impact."[33] But Mikhail Bakunin died on July 1, 1876 (NS).

For most of his life, Mikhail liked to draw a firm dividing line in his biog-

---

[30] See Mikhail Bakunin's letter to Albert Richard of 1 April 1870 (Lehning, *Archives*, VI:280).

[31] Paul Avrich, introduction to the Dover edition in Bakunin, *God and the State*, xii. Critical evaluations of Bakunin's ideas have, of course, varied tremendously over time. Some regard him as a chaotic but consistent thinker, while Isaiah Berlin famously called his ideas "glib Hegelian claptrap." For a sample of attempts that try to view Bakunin as a coherent thinker, see Paul Avrich, "The Legacy of Bakunin," in *Anarchist Portraits* (Princeton: Princeton University Press, 1988), 5–15; George Crowder, *Classical Anarchism: The Political Thought of Godwin, Proudhon, Bakunin and Kropotkin* (Oxford: Clarendon Press, 1991), 16, 118–70, esp. 16, 125–30; Joll, *The Anarchists*, 88–96; Venturi, *Roots of Revolution*, 429–45. For more critical accounts, see Isaiah Berlin, "Herzen and Bakunin on Individual Liberty," in *Russian Thinkers*, ed. Henry Hardy and Aileen Kelly (London: Penguin, 1994), 82–113, esp. 107; Kelly, *Bakunin*, 184–256. I will comment further on Bakunin's ideas below.

[32] A. Bauler, "M. A. Bakunin nakanune smerti. Vospominaniia," *Byloe*, no. 7/19 (July 1907): 72.

[33] Ibid., 72–73.

raphy, placing his youthful infatuation with Idealism on one side and his career as a radical on the other. He described his early interest in philosophy as a decadent mindset, encouraged by the "spectral world" of privilege in which he had been raised; and he claimed that these delusions dissipated entirely in the early 1840s, when he entered Europe's bustling social world. "I finally conquered metaphysics and philosophy in myself," he wrote to his brother Pavel in 1845.[34]

Relatively few scholars have been willing to take this claim at face value, however. Some argue that Mikhail's study of Hegelian philosophy in the late 1830s—for which his studies with Stankevich prepared him—played a crucial role in his radicalization. Hegelian concepts, they point out, provided the lingua franca Mikhail spoke with radicals in Europe upon his emigration there in 1840. They also credit Hegel's writings with turning his attention away from the sphere of abstract thought toward a radical engagement with society, politics, and history.[35] Others claim that Idealism functioned in Mikhail's life like a modern form of mysticism, encouraging him to believe that he was guided by a higher, more rational reality.[36] Writing in this vein, Aileen Kelly argues that Mikhail found in Fichte in particular a "formula" that helped him sublimate his personal frustrations into an explosive cult of destruction. (She calls this millenial formula "self realization through self-destruction": the idea that those who surrender themselves to progress completely are assured of becoming its foremost servants.) "In a modified but still recognizable form," she concludes, this formula became "the basis of his political ideology."[37] Less critically, George Crowder contends that the Idealist tradition led Mikhail to believe that true freedom lies in "moral self-direc-

---

[34] See Bakunin's letters to his brother Pavel (17 OS/ 29 NS March 1845, *Sobranie*, III:246) and his family (9 October 1842, *Sobranie*, III:120–24). See also his abortive memoirs (*Sobranie*, I:25–37, esp. 26–27), where the contrast between his happy but somewhat delusory home and the social repression then reigning in Russia is established.

[35] See Venturi, *Roots of Revolution*, 10–16; Andrzej Walicki, *A History of Russian Thought from the Enlightenment to Marxism*, trans. Hilda Andrews-Rusiecka (Stanford: Stanford University Press, 1979), 119–21.

[36] See Berlin, "A Remarkable Decade," 144–45; idem, "Herzen and Bakunin on Individual Liberty," in *Russian Thinkers*, ed. Henry Hardy and Aileen Kelly (London: Penguin, 1994), 105–13; Malia, *Alexander Herzen*, 82–87, 98; Malia, "Schiller and the Early Russian Left," *Harvard Slavic Studies* 4 (1957), 188–89.

[37] Kelly, *Bakunin*, 1–2, 35–37, 293–94. Among the other interpretations of young Bakunin that stress his social isolation and frustration, see in particular Martin Malia, *Alexander Herzen and the Birth of Russian Socialism* (New York: Grosset & Dunlap, 1965), 86–87; Isaiah Berlin, "A Remarkable Decade," in Hardy and Kelly, *Russian Thinkers*, 144–45; Andrzej Walicki, *The Slavophile Controversy: History of a Conservative Utopia in Nineteenth-Century Russian Thought*, trans. Hilda Andrews-Rusiecka (Notre Dame: University of Notre Dame Press, 1975), 368.

tion": the conscious fulfillment, that is to say, of one's deepest, most authentic nature. (Crowder contrasts this "positive" definition of freedom as a state of fulfillment with the classical, "negative" definition of freedom as the lack of constraint.)[38]

There is, of course, no reason to expect that every turn of Mikhail's long and event-filled life was somehow present in embryo in his youth. It seems clear enough that Mikhail's conscious interest in radical politics began, as he insisted, in the 1840s—after his departure from Priamukhino. Nor is there time or space here to evaluate the full ideological impact of the post-Kantian tradition on his later radicalism, especially since both Idealism's political legacy and Mikhail's remain controversial. My question here is simpler: what sort of man did Mikhail seek to become in 1836, as he refined his sense of a scholar's vocation under Stankevich's tutelage? The answer, it seems, is someone very much like the man Weber remembered from "the great Bakunin's" deathbed in 1876: a charismatic teacher whose example could inspire his contemporaries and convince them they had a higher, moral calling to fulfill in life. To examine Mikhail's philosophical activities of the mid-1830s is to see how this understanding of his vocation in life first came to him.

❀⋇❀

Mikhail's pursuit of a scholar's vocation began in earnest under Stankevich's supervision in the fall of 1835. Herzen's claim that Stankevich started Mikhail's philosophical education is somewhat mythical.[39] Mikhail's interest in scholarship and philosophy preceded their encounter by several years. Yet Stankevich provided Mikhail access to the student world he admired. Stankevich also established the plan of study that guided Mikhail's development thereafter. Stankevich was meticulous in his attention to detail, as if he were grooming a young ward in his charge. He even advised Mikhail on how to create a good reading desk.[40]

More important, Stankevich sketched for Mikhail a bold new vision of what a scholar's life entailed—and how he might go about transforming himself into one. Stankevich argued that Russians needed to learn to think of themselves as part of a progressively developing society. Indeed, it was

---

[38] On the anarchist account of freedom as moral self-direction and Bakunin's development of this particular vision, see Crowder, *Classical Anarchism*, 7–16, 129–30.

[39] Kornilov first observed this in *Molodye gody*, 130–36.

[40] Stankevich mentions this design in a letter to M. A. Bakunin, 4 November 1835 (*Perepiska*, 578).

the vocation of young men such as themselves to help stimulate this social self-consciousness and with it an optimism about the future. "Why not promote the awakening of such internal necessity, such organic force?" Stankevich asked Mikhail, echoing ideals he himself had heard from Nadezhdin some years before. Instead of serving in the bureaucracy's "machine," "why shouldn't one worry about helping the people to begin thinking for themselves, to seek their own means to prosperity?"[41]

The calling in society Stankevich thus imagined for them was pedagogical and ideological, rather than theoretical. Their goal would be to stimulate Russia's social awakening through the advocacy of philosophical methods and truths. They could only prepare themselves for this inspirational calling, Stankevich further explained, by undertaking a systematic study of Kantian and post-Kantian philosophy. "By solving the question of the origins and possibility of human knowledge," Stankevich believed, Kant had shown humanity how to learn about its true nature, role, and destiny in the world. For this reason one had to begin with him. Yet since knowledge had advanced since the 1790s, one also had to examine the writings of Kant's illustrious successors, among whose number Stankevich singled out Fichte, Schelling, and Hegel.[42] "I want to understand, to what degree humanity has developed its understanding," Stankevich summarized, as he explained both the aim and the method of his plan of study to Mikhail in November of 1835. "And then I want to show people their worth and vocation, and to call them to good."[43]

What Stankevich offered Mikhail, in short, was a developmental itinerary leading to an active and truly contemporary life. By mastering the post-Kantian tradition, they could assume an inspirational role in Russian society as enlighteners and awakeners; perhaps just as important, they could become fully contemporary men. (Kant, Stankevich declared to his friend Neverov, held the keys for "anyone who wishes to be equal to the best ideas of our time.")[44] Soon, the young men began to talk grandly of going there to walk among their

---

[41] See letter to M. A. Bakunin, 25 September 1835 (Stankevich, Perepiska, 573–74).

[42] See letter to M. A. Bakunin, 12 November 1835 (Stankevich, *Perepiska*, 585–86). Hegel is not mentioned in this letter, but it is clear that Stankevich regarded him as the endpoint of modern philosophical learning and introduced him to Mikhail as such at about this time. For such references to Hegel, see letter to Ia. M. Neverov, 10 November 1835 (ibid., 338) and letter to M. A. Bakunin, 24 November 1835 (ibid., 595).

[43] This plan of study and its aims are outlined in a series of eight long letters Stankevich wrote to Mikhail in November of 1835 (see *Perepiska*, 576–96; for the quotation just given, see 594). Mikhail's endorsement of the plan is already clear from his subsequent letters to Efremov of November and December 1835 (see *Sobranie*, 1:179–88).

[44] Letter to Ia. M. Neverov, 10 November [1835?] (Stankevich, *Perepiska*, 338).

fellow students and receive the latest word of European science as it was being spoken. (Thereafter, it was assumed, they would return to Russia to preach it.)[45]

More immediately, Stankevich's itinerary encouraged Mikhail to uproot himself from his isolated desk at Priamukhino. In December 1835, he suddenly escaped to Moscow, where he moved into an apartment with two students—Aleksandr Efremov and Vasilii Krasov. He announced to his family that his career as a scholar was beginning (he would support himself as a math tutor) and that his larger goal was to go abroad. His father, who had spent the better part of the previous year pulling strings to get him a civil service post, was humiliated and angered by this flight from "Mecca to Medina," as Mikhail's friends jokingly called it. Father and son exchanged poisoned accusations by letter, with Mikhail concluding melodramatically, "We are not fated to see each other again, we have died for each other."[46]

Though neither Mikhail nor his father was, in fact, ready for a final breach at this point, Mikhail's sudden departure did unleash a fierce polemical discussion within his family over his determination to break with noble traditions in favor of scholarly ones. "Real philosophy consists not in dreamy theories and empty chatter," Aleksandr Mikhailovich wrote to his son, "but in the fulfillment of the familial, social, and civic duties of our way of life."[47] Mikhail, who like his student friends aspired to live according to his own, philosophically determined principles, could not accept such morality by external fiat. "I have acted according to my own convictions," Mikhail replied to his father, "without which I cannot understand either life, or human worth."[48] Yet his sisters also scolded him bitterly over his move, which they claimed showed an unbridled egoism utterly irreconcilable with religion. "'Je l'ai voulu, je l'ai fait,'" Tatiana mockingly described his new morality: "I wanted to, so I did it."[49] "You know we are capable of appreciating your ideas

[45] On Berlin, see letter to M. A. Bakunin, 7 November 1835 (Stankevich, *Perepiska*, 581); letter to A. P. Efremov, 14 November 1835 (Bakunin, *Sobranie*, I:180). Although the phrase "equal to the best ideas of our time" comes from Stankevich's letters to Neverov (ibid., 338) it is from this same time (November 1835), and the pathos of "catch-up" pervades Stankevich's letters to Mikhail (ibid., 576–600). Stankevich's claims they have no time to waste to study Kant, who "is necessary as an introduction to new systems" (598; see also 587)—"I'll begin today, even if only two hours remain for study!" (576). Throughout, Kant is presented as doorway to path leading through Fichte and Schelling (and, eventually, to Hegel).

[46] Quoted in Kornilov, *Molodye gody*, 89, 139–42; letter to his father, January 1836 (Bakunin, *Sobranie*, I:189).

[47] Kornilov, *Molodye gody*, 141n2.

[48] Letter to his father, January 1836 (Bakunin, *Sobranie*, I:190).

[49] T. A. Bakunina to M. A. Bakunin, letter of [January 1836?], IRLI f. 16, op. 4, no. 582, l.

of moral elevation," Varvara added from Tver in February 1836. "The sole point where our opinions differ is that you reject duties, while we believe in them."[50]

For Mikhail, however, this sole point was increasingly the only point that mattered. "Two lives live within you," he wrote bitterly to his sister Varvara that March, complaining about what he believed to be their quietism:

> One is human and divine: a life of love, holy fire, that contains within it all your most beautiful hopes, all your poetic visions, and all your souls' dreams. This life—so you say—is not of this world. But you have another life as well, a kind of artificial life: this is a life of dogmas, moral-ity-book formulas; a life of anti-Christian tracts about obligation, about how to adapt all that is high and beautiful to everyday life.[51]

In this way, Mikhail's relations with his family took on a sharp, philosophi-cal character by the middle of 1836, as he responded to their moral chal-lenges.

Though reinvigorated by Mikhail's flight to Moscow in 1836, this debate had actually been raging for years in the Bakunin household. Before his sister Varvara married Diakov in early 1835, Mikhail had announced to his family that he feared her decision was an act of "religioso-heroico-romantic selfless-ness." "Any marriage from obligation or convenience—and that is not sancti-fied by feeling and founded on love or at least friendship and mutual respect—is a crime against family, fatherland, and nature," he sternly instructed Varvara herself.[52] But Varvara, trusting her own judgment, ignored his advice, and throughout 1834 and 1835 his sisters chided him for what they believed to be his unwarranted faith in his own reason. There were, Tatiana assured him, pur-poses and designs human minds could not fathom, "which you yourself may feel Misha, despite the fact that cold reason, indignant about the limits that have been set to it, desires to overturn everything that is above it, that it is not ca-pable of understanding." "If man can conceive everything," Liubov wrote to the Beyers in September of 1835, reacting to Mikhail's Idealism, "if there is nothing hidden from man, would he not become a God himself?"[53]

---

13. More generally, see Tatiana's letters to him of these months, ibid., ll. 12–17, where she rep-rimands him about his ambition to go to Berlin, among other things.

[50] V. A. D'iakova to M. A. Bakunin, letter of [early 1836?], IRLI f. 16, op. 4, no. 458, ll. 1–2.

[51] Letter to his sister Varvara of 9 March 1836 (Bakunin, *Sobranie*, I:221).

[52] Letter to his sisters, 5 October 1834 (Bakunin, *Sobranie*, I:149–50; cf. *Oeuvres [CD-ROM]*, 4); see also his letter to his parents, 4 October 1834 (Bakunin, *Sobranie*, I:143).

[53] T. A. Bakunina to M. A. Bakunin, letter of [fall 1834?], IRLI f. 16, op. 4, no. 582, ll. 2–3.

As of early 1836, Mikhail had yet to answer these objections to his sisters' satisfaction. In essence, and each from his or her own perspective, they were accusing each other of mysticism: of living life according to some unreasoned faith, be it in religion or reason. It is curious to see the children at this time debating the very same question that their father had attempted to solve in the late eighteenth century, as he sought to use domestic conventions to map out reason's proper limits and function. Aleksandr Mikhailovich proposed that his paternal household represented a perfect model for a free and progressive form of society, by uniting diverse subjects into a harmonious community. Though his methods were empirical rather than abstract, his vision was not, in fact, that different from the social vision proposed by Immanuel Kant. Indeed, as Kant himself sought to imagine what a truly ethical community might look like — a "church invisible," as he called it, in which people were governed and united by conscious morality — Kant picked as his metaphor the holy family, governed by God. (Whether this was because Kant's system in itself was paternalist or whether Kant's social imagination simply gave in to the domestic ideology of his time remains a subject of scholarly dispute.)[54]

As Mikhail began to study the Idealist tradition in earnest, however, he was no longer trying to return to that particular home. More important to him than domestic tranquility was his desire to be the producer of his own morality and to become the sort of charismatic man his student comrades represented. Just at this time — when he was being peppered by angry letters from his family and fighting off their accusations of exaltation and egoism — he came to Fichte's writings. There, he found a ringing defense of his right to moral self-determination and an even grander vision of the scholar's vocation in society.

Isolated from his family — but free to develop his interests in Moscow — Mikhail spent the first few months of 1836 learning to think and speak in Fichte's proud idiom.

@⟨⟩⟨⟩

This letter is dated by reference to Diakov's upcoming arrival and expected proposal. See also L. A. Bakunina to the Beyer sisters, letter of 6 September 1835, IRLI f. 16, op. 4, no. 527, l. 18.

[54] On Kant's ideal of an "ethical community" — and his proposal of the paternal household as model — see Immanuel Kant, "Religion Within the Boundaries of Mere Reason," Religion and Rational Theology, trans. and Ed. Allen W. Wood and George di Giovanni (Cambridge: Cambridge University Press, 1996), 135–36; Terry Pinkard, *German Philosophy, 1760–1860: The Legacy of Idealism* (Cambridge: Cambridge University Press, 2002), 63–65; and Isabel V. Hull, *Sexuality, State, and Civil Society in Germany 1700–1815* (Ithaca: Cornell University Press, 1996), 301–14.

Born in 1762, the son of a village weaver, Fichte was among the most pug-
nacious and controversial of the many writers and philosophers who gathered at the University of Jena—the capital of the Kantian movement—in the
1790s.[55] (He was also the idol of Jena's students; one jokingly called him "the
Bonaparte of philosophy.")[56] Fichte's most famous contribution to philosophy—the inquiry that made many, including Stankevich, believe he was
Kant's worthiest immediate successor and the first of the Idealists—was his
attempt to build a new, scientific worldview from the principle that self-consciousness develops through action. In this way, Fichte sought to eliminate
some of the uncertainties that Kant had left surrounding the ultimate source
of human knowledge, by describing its production.[57]

At the core of his philosophy lies the belief that knowledge is not a thing,
but a process—an activity. Cognition necessarily begins, Fichte argued,
when the self first imagines its own existence—when it first learns to say I.
The immediate consequence of this action, Fichte announced romantically, is
pain. For to be is to be aware of one's own limits—of a world outside oneself,
full of necessity and obligation. This is a world in which we must learn to
live—gradually introducing our own reason into it—and the only way to do
so is through an endless cycle of assertion and limitation. Because the condition he was describing was irresolvable and difficult, Fichte himself called his
teaching a *Strebensphilosophie*—a philosophy of ceaseless striving and longing.

Yet Fichte's confidence in progress was absolute; he implied that the romance of our development would someday come to a successful conclusion;
and his portrayal of life as a self-directed quest toward a truer and happier
existence electrified his student audience. "Anyone who fails to learn to think
for himself under Fichte's direction will never learn to do so," another of his

[55] On Fichte generally and his place in modern philosophy, see Daniel Breazeale, "Fichte," in
The Cambridge Dictionary of Philosophy, 2nd ed., ed. Robert Audi (Cambridge: Cambridge University Press, 1999), 307–9; Anthony J. La Vopa, *Fichte: The Self and the Calling of Philosophy,
1762–1799* (Cambridge: Cambridge University Press, 2001), esp. 183–230; Frederick C. Beiser,
German Idealism: The Struggle against Subjectivism, 1781–1801 (Cambridge, Mass.: Harvard University Press, 2002), 217–345; Dieter Henrich, *Between Kant and Hegel: Lectures on German Idealism*, ed. David S. Pacini (Cambridge, Mass.: Harvard University Press, 2003), 157–276; these
views all contrast strongly with those of Isaiah Berlin, who regards Fichte primarily as a kind
of modern mystic, see "The Apotheosis of the Romantic Will," in *The Proper Study of Mankind: An
Anthology of Essays*, ed. Henry Hardy and Roger Hausheer (New York: Farrar, Straus, and
Giroux, 1997), 568–72.
[56] Daniel Breazeale quotes from Fichte's students in "Fichte in Jena," in *Fichte: Early Philosophical Writings*, trans. and ed. Daniel Breazeale (Ithaca: Cornell University Press, 1988), 1–49,
esp. 19–20.
[57] On this point, see especially Henrich, *Between Kant and Hegel*, 37–38; 168.

students recalled, remembering the theatrical force of his lectures. Another marveled at his self-assurance: "Whether standing or striding about upon his sturdy legs, he was always firmly planted in the earth upon which he stood, secure and immovable in the sense of his own strength."[58]

It is easy to understand why Mikhail would have found this kind of thinker so attractive at this juncture in his life, both as a philosopher and as a role model. At a time when Mikhail's family attacked his philosophical ambitions, Fichte argued that it was a moral imperative to act according to one's own, critically produced convictions. Fichte also offered the consoling thought that "a man who has not suffered, has not lived."[59]

It should not be presumed, however, that Mikhail actively sought him out for this reason. Rather, others encouraged his interest in the philosopher, which rapidly grew. In November 1835, Stankevich described Fichte to Mikhail as a necessary second stop on their philosophico-historical itinerary. (In a somewhat mythological formulation that was already becoming a textbook cliché, Stankevich presented Fichte as the evolutionary link between Kant and Schelling.)[60] People in Moscow were interested in discussing Fichte: the Beyers asked Mikhail to come to their house and read the philosopher with them.[61] Perhaps most important, in early 1836 Mikhail was asked to translate Fichte's famous 1794 series "Some Lectures Concerning the Scholar's Vocation" for Professor Nadezhdin's journal, *Telescope*. Mikhail's

---

[58] Quoted in Breazeale, "Fichte in Jena," 19–20.

[59] See Mikhail's letter to his sisters, 28 February 1836 (Bakunin, *Sobranie*, I:208), where this thought is thematically connected to Fichte by context. The virtues of suffering become a major theme of his correspondence thereafter. Both Aileen Kelly and Arthur Mendel attempt complex psychological readings of Mikhail's interest, arguing that he sought and found in Fichte a formula for the resolution of his growing frustrations as an "alienated" (or in Mendel's case, psychopathological) intellectual. See Kelly, *Bakunin*, 32–37; Mendel, *Bakunin*, 57–58. I would agree with the simpler reading advanced by Kornilov, *Molodye gody*, 149–50: Mikhail took up Fichte at Stankevich's suggestion and found there a defense of his moral ambitions and scholarly vocation.

[60] See letter to M. A. Bakunin, 12 November 1835 (Stankevich, *Perepiska*, 584–85), where he introduces Fichte as Kant's most immediate follower and link to Schelling; and 21 April 1836 (ibid., 605–6), where Fichte is the next step beyond Kant. Mimicking some of Stankevich's Fichtean formulations (e.g., "I=I"), Mikhail begins to speak Fichte in a letter to A. P. Efremov of 14 November 1835 (Bakunin, *Sobranie*, I:180). Mikhail speaks definitively of the evolution of German philosophy as leading "from Kant (Fichte, Schelling) through to Hegel" in a letter to Aleksandra Beyer of April 1836 (Bakunin, *Sobranie*, I:260). Seemingly about this time, Mikhail undertook to make an abstract of the second introduction to Fichte's most famous work, the so-called *Wissenschaftslehre*. Unfortunately, only a damaged manuscript remains, recently published for the first time: "Extrait de 'Zweite Einleitung in die Wissenschaftslehre' de Fichte" (*Oeuvres* [CD-ROM], under the category Various: Notes on Philosophy: 1835).

[61] Letter to the Beyers, February 1836 (Bakunin, *Sobranie*, I:204).

translation — and still more his remarkable talent for philosophical conversation, now demonstrated for the first time — soon combined to make Fichte the author of the day in the Stankevich circle and Mikhail his leading exponent.[62]

At the center of Fichte's lectures on the scholar's vocation is a vision of how a select group of young men can become skilled "priests of truth" — or "educators of mankind," as Fichte also calls them — and in the process help bring about a better, freer, more ethical society.[63] Like all Kantians, Fichte begins by considering with the problem of knowledge: how can we learn how to perfect ourselves morally? In "My Metaphysics," Stankevich rooted his answer to this question in a belief in nature, but for Fichte, society holds the key. Through a process of *"mutual action, mutual influence, mutual passivity and activity,"* Fichte argues, people can learn to believe in and direct themselves.[64] For by calling out to one another and receiving free responses, individuals can confirm that it is possible to be the kind of conscious, autonomous actors Fichte believed it was in their nature to be.[65] Human life in society is thus best conceived as a process of "communal perfection: my own through the independent action of others and theirs through my independent action."[66]

To lead and inspire this progressive sociability, Fichte called for a special clerisy of exemplary individuals — "priests of truth." Such a "priest's" duty in society was to be "be the best, most moral man of his time."[67] In particular, as Anthony J. La Vopa has shown, Fichte presented his "priest" not as a scientific authority but rather as a "an instrument of the revelatory moment" — a social performer whose rhetorical task was to "think before his readers," thereby stimulating their own moral awakenings and drive toward self-perfection.[68] On occasion, arrogant, paternal, and even implicitly authoritarian

[62] I. G. Fikhte, "O naznachenii uchenykh," *Teleskop: Zhurnal sovremennogo prosveshcheniia* 29 (1835): 3–57 (this is Mikhail's translation), reproduced as "Traduction de 'Über die Bestimmung des Gelehrten' de Fichte" in *Oeuvres [CD-ROM]*; see also J. G. Fichte, "Some Lectures Concerning the Scholar's Vocation," in Breazeale, *Fichte*, 137–84. In a letter to his sister Tatiana on 8 March 1836 (*Sobranie*, I:218) Mikhail reported with relish that he was hard at work on this translation. In a letter to the Beyers on 7 May 1836 (ibid., 301), he announced it would soon be published and that he and his friends were spending much time discussing Fichte.

[63] See Fichte, "Scholar's Vocation," 175–76; "priest of truth" is translated as *zhrets istiny* by Bakunin: see "Traduction de 'Über die Bestimmung des Gelehrten' de Fichte" (*Oeuvres [CD-ROM]*, 54).

[64] Ibid, 22; cf. Fichte, "Scholaz's Vocation," 158. Emphasis in the original.

[65] "Traduction," 19; cf. Fichte, "Scholar's Vocation," 156.

[66] Again, I quote from Bakunin's translation, "Traduction," 23; cf. Fichte, "Scholar's Vocation," 160.

[67] "Traduction," 53–54; cf. Fichte, "Scholar's Vocation," 176–77.

[68] La Vopa, *Fichte*, 116, 225–30.

notes sounded in Fichte's lectures.[69] He was clear that his scholarly priesthood would be made of men, and he claimed it would be their responsibility
to provide *"supreme supervision over the actual progress of humanity in all respects,
and continual inducement to perfection."*[70] But Fichte himself insisted that the
scholar "only has the right to act on others by moral means." His priesthood
should never use "coercive methods," only inspirational ones, because we
"teach—far more forcefully—by example."[71] Indeed, coercion contradicts
the final goal of society, Fichte believed. For in his view our most basic desire is to find in society models of the kind of people we long to be—"free, rational beings," not "slaves."[72]

At the heart of Fichte's ecstatic vision of the human future was not the individual but the collective. He shared in the Kantian ideal of an ethical or
purposeful community: a world composed of beings so harmonious, social,
and rational that society would lose the need for compulsion altogether,
ushering in a world without external authorities.[73] Like the idyll in which
Mikhail was raised, Fichte's ideal world was one where all private wills would
agree. But he believed that this agreement would be achieved through internal rather than external methods. Reason and sentiment would be harmo-
nized by mutual inspiration and moral self-perfection rather than by imposed
conformity to external, empirically determined laws. "Like all those human
institutions which are mere means, the state aims at abolishing itself," Fichte
announces with shocking optimism in his lectures. "There will certainly be a
point in the a priori foreordained career of the human species when all civic
bonds will become superfluous." This day will come because Idealism's scholarly "priests of truth"—through their ceaseless inspirational activity—will
have prepared humanity for a new era of self-governance.[74]

Needless to say, this bold prediction of society's self-directed future did

[69] A point made by La Vopa, *Fichte*, 228.

[70] "Traduction," 47. Emphasis in the original. Cf. Fichte, "Scholar's Vocation," 172.

[71] "Traduction," 52–53; cf. Fichte, "Scholar's Vocation," 175.

[72] See Fichte, "Scholar's Vocation," 158–59. Perhaps because of the reference to "slaves," this
passage is not translated in Bakunin's version, though its sense is captured in the quotation given
next.

[73] For Kant's ideal of the "ethical community," see Immanuel Kant, "Religion within the
Boundaries of Mere Reason," in *Religion and Rational Theology*, trans. and ed. Allen W. Wood and
George di Giovanni (Cambridge: Cambridge University Press, 1996), 133–36; Fichte's conception of "purposeful community" may be found in Fichte, "Scholar's Vocation," 156; Bakunin
translates this as *obshchestvo, soobraznoe s tseliiu* ("Traduction," 19). On the role of this ideal in
Kantian thought, see Terry Pinkard, *German Philosophy, 1760–1860: The Legacy of Idealism* (Cambridge: Cambridge University Press, 2002), 62–65.

[74] Fichte, "Scholar's Vocation," 156.

not make it into print in autocratic Russia. (Nor did any of Fichte's loose talk about the undesirability of "slaves.") Neither of these specific passages appears in Mikhail's translation, approved by Russian censors that May. It seems doubtful he or his friends were so foolhardy as to even try to publish this stateless vision of the future—at least not yet.[75]

It is clear, however, that Fichte's theatrical vision of the scholar's vocation in society crystallized Mikhail's scholastic ambitions as never before. Almost immediately, as Lydia Ginzburg has noted, Mikhail was "attracted by the affective and hortatory features of Fichte's doctrine and temperament," and began to speak of his inspirational, emancipatory mission in the world.[76] He debuted this role before the Beyer sisters, who were then struggling with twin frustrations, domestic and romantic. Aleksandra was so bothered by her mother's interference in her life that she threatened to go to a monastery. Natalia, dispirited by her several failures in love, wanted to withdraw from student society altogether ("I do not wish to live anymore *like a caricature,* as your excellent *maman* has said," she wrote to Liubov at the end of 1835.)[77]

In response, Mikhail offered to show them a new way of living their lives, adopting his new priestly voice:

> Alexandrine, the truth is so powerful, that there is no evil, that it cannot cure, no misfortune, that it cannot turn into absolute bliss. This truth is God, absolute love, the kind that never disowns its children, that always opens its arms to those longing for embrace. This God, this absolute love, is bliss. Alexandrine, I am called to be its priest, its instrument before you. Forget, Alexandrine, that you are speaking to a young man of your acquaintance, forget my personality and look at me as a being called to save you, to open before you the door to truth.

Mikhail adopts an overtly religious idiom in this appeal to establish a common language with his female friend and overcome the social conventions that separate them.[78] He tries to appear before Aleksandra not as a young

---

[75] Though dated 1835, this book of *Telescope* was approved by the censors in May 1836 (see Pustarnakov, "Idei Fikhte v neakademicheskoi filosofii," 121).

[76] Ginzburg, *On Psychological Prose,* 38.

[77] See N. A. Beyer to L. A. Bakunina, IRLI f. 16, op. 8, no. 66, l. 10; on conflicts in the Beyer household, see Kornilov, *Molodye gody,* 201–7. Emphasis in the original.

[78] Ginzburg analyzes the genesis of this philosophical-religious idiom in *Psychological Prose,* 37–43. It is based on Fichte's own attempt to translate his ideals to a lay and feminine audience, his 1806 *Guide toward the Blessed Life.* See Johann Gottlieb Fichte, *Die Anweisung zum seeligen Leben,* in *Werke 1806–1807,* ed. Richard Lauth and Hans Gliwitzky (Stuttgart-Bad Cannstatt: Friedrich Frommann Verlag, 1995).

man, but as a neutral being or "instrument," a "priest" called to bring her to an awareness of the truth. Such appeals to the Beyers were combined with injunctions to forget about the monastery, drop their despair, and act upon their innermost convictions. "To love and to want—that is our device!"[79]

The Beyers' mother, suspicious of such talk, finally demanded that Aleksandra make up her mind about marriage. Talked out of her plan to go to a monastery by Mikhail, Aleksandra instead sought refuge with Mikhail's sister Varvara in Tver, only to wear out her welcome there rather quickly. Aleksandra made no secret of the fact that she disapproved of the Diakov's marriage—a sentiment that was gaining force among the Bakunin children themselves at this time—and unable to remain as a guest in the house, returned to Moscow by May. Natalia, meanwhile, declared that she had fallen in love with Mikhail. When he failed to reciprocate, she abandoned Moscow for the country, leaving Mikhail abashed and guilty.[80] At this point, Mikhail's attempt to model himself as a Fichtean "priest of truth" might have died out entirely had not Varvara's humiliation at the hands of her husband suddenly given it new meaning at Priamukhino.

☸⚶☸

From the beginning, Mikhail had assumed that some mordant vision of martyrdom—rather than love—had fueled Varvara's agreement to marry Diakov. The reality, undoubtedly, was more complicated than that. At the time, as Kornilov observes, marriage was the main gateway to maturity and some modicum of independence from her parents for a young noblewoman like Varvara.[81] Though she had always spoken of wanting a religious vocation in life—her ambition to found some sort of religious community was well known to the younger Bakunins, and they thought her more likely to become a nun than an estate mistress—her one surviving letter to Mikhail from this time suggests that she looked forward to having children. "I will form their young souls for heaven," she wrote to him late in 1834.[82] (Needless to say, this was not the kind of optimistic formulation the men in his family favored.)

---

[79] Letter to Aleksandra Beyer, 6 April 1836 (Bakunin, *Sobranie*, I:253). More broadly, Mikhail's relations with the Beyers—in which this moral "mission" before them is continued—is detailed in his letters to them that spring (ibid., 278–304.

[80] Kornilov recounts all these events in *Molodye gody*, 201–7.

[81] Kornilov, *Molodye gody*, 80.

[82] V. A. Bakunina to M. A. Bakunin, letter of late 1834, IRLI f. 16, op. 4, no. 447, l. 3.

It is also possible she felt some attraction to Diakov: he was later remembered in the family as a simple and well-wishing man—an outdoorsman and a hunter who was kind when he wasn't angry.

Even so, Mikhail claimed that in June 1834 he, Varvara, and Aleksandra Beyer had gone walking by the mill pond, and Varvara confessed that she was marrying Diakov out of a sense of obligation to her parents. "As soon as possible after the engagement I will demand that we be married," Mikhail recalled her saying, "for if it takes too long, I'm afraid that I will change my mind and take my word back."[83] Kornilov discounts this recollection as fanciful, but Aleksandra Beyer's letters show that she understood Varvara's intentions the same way. In the fall of 1834, Aleksandra pleaded with Liubov to convince Varvara of the "horror of a marriage without love—the horror of which you know."[84] Failing in this attempt, Aleksandra hoped against hope that Varvara's sacrifice would turn out to be a miraculous deed. Varvara "was born to do something grand," she wrote to Tatiana in late 1834; perhaps this would be it. "Son oeuvre est belle, belle sera sa vie."[85]

The controversy surrounding the Diakovs' marriage died down during its first year, at the end of which Varvara gave birth to a son named Aleksandr. By early 1836, however, the couple was obviously unhappy and increasingly estranged. Sex, in particular, divided the Diakovs. Aleksandr's birth left Varvara ill; she now found that the physical presence—let alone the sexual advances—of her husband repelled her.[86] As a result, Varvara spent much of that winter with her parents in the provincial capital of Tver. Varvara increasingly distanced herself from Diakov and came to speak of her marriage as a terrible mistake, undertaken in a moment not of true religion but extravagant exaltation.[87] All along, her sisters felt much the same way. "I swear to you," wrote Tatiana in an undated letter no later than January 1836, "that I would have rather seen her [Varvara] in her tomb than at the altar pledging eternal love to Diakov."[88] Yet during the first year of the Diakovs' marriage they had felt an admiration for Varvara's decision to live according to

---

[83] Letter to his sisters, 5 October 1834 (Bakunin, *Sobranie*, I:150).

[84] See A. A. Beyer to L. A. Bakunina, letter of [fall 1834?], IRLI f. 16, op. 8, no. 40, ll. 19–20. See also Kornilov, *Molodye gody*, 80. At this point, it should be noted, Mikhail and the Beyers were not corresponding, so Aleksandra's protest was entirely her own.

[85] "Her deed is beautiful, her life will be beautiful." A. A. Beyer to T. A. Bakunina, letter of late 1834, IRLI f. 16, op. 8, no. 8, l. 7 ob.

[86] A point emphasized by Kornilov, *Molodye gody*, 324–25, 339; Carr, *Bakunin*, 53; and others.

[87] This process is convincingly described by Kornilov in *Molodye gody*, 324–25.

[88] Tat'iana to the Beyers, letter of [January 1836?], IRLI f. 16, op. 4, no. 629, l. 5.

her sense of duty.[89] After spending more time with the "ménage fortuné" in the spring of 1836, however, Tatiana came to a different conclusion. Swearing Mikhail to total secrecy, she confessed: "Varinka is not happy—you know that we cannot remain indifferent spectators to her sufferings."[90] Varvara's health and spirits seemed to be flagging, as she tired of life with Diakov. Quite independent of Mikhail, Tatiana thus came to a disturbing conclusion: "It would be a crime to abandon her alone with Nicholas."[91]

Already intending to come to Priamukhino for the summer—having made up with his father and lacking any way of fulfilling his plan to go to Berlin—Mikhail welcomed this concession to his way of thinking, even if it was under duress. In a letter of May 1836, he admitted as much: "Let us shake hands and make our peace. We love one another—of that there is no doubt. I do not know if we understand each other well—I doubt it. But this, too, will come, for those who love cannot fail, in the end, to understand one another."[92] Varvara, for her part, rejoiced at Mikhail's return, calling him her "guardian angel"—which he was, in a sense, because his visions of self-determination as well as his physical presence helped establish a buffer between her and her failed marriage. Horrified by her own mistake, Varvara found solace in Mikhail's Fichtean religion:

> Oh, never, never will all our love ever repay you for the happiness, the raptures, which your love gives us—we are only good little creatures who know nothing but how to love, and cry, and jump for joy—but we will be your glory, your crown, in the other world above.[93]

Rather than relate to her brother as a brother, in flesh or in spirit, she projected onto him the image of the Savior and onto herself the frailties of miserable humanity. We may assume this was itself a rhetorical performance of sorts: both an act of repentance for her exaltation and a plea for help at a very difficult time.

As a result, upon his return home, Mikhail's authority among Priamukhino's younger generation was unchallenged. Even his younger brothers,

---

[89] Ibid., where after expressing her regrets about the Diakovs' marriage, Tatiana expresses pride that Varvara has been able to "establish order in her home."

[90] Tat'iana to Mikhail, letter of early February 1836, IRLI f. 16, op. 4, no. 582, l. 17.

[91] Tat'iana to the Beyers, letter of March 1836, IRLI f. 16, op. 4, no. 535, l. 4.

[92] See letter to Varvara of late May 1836 (Bakunin, *Sobranie,* I:297). This letter appears to be in direct response to Varvara's, cited just above.

[93] Varvara to Mikhail, letter of [April 1836?], IRLI f. 16, op. 4, no. 661, ll. 13–14.

with whom he had considerably less contact and shared experience than with his sisters, rushed to make themselves ready for his teachings. Aleksandr Mikhailovich relented in his criticisms and made a truce with his son. With the Beyers at Popovo and the Bakunin sisters (including Varvara, now more or less permanently separated from her husband) at Priamukhino, Mikhail developed his philosophy of self-determination at will, unchecked by any obstacles. In this time of concentration, Mikhail announced, the way was being prepared for a new and more humane order, first in their little society of friends, then throughout the world. It would be an order based on real agreement between individuals and shared inner convictions, "a harmony of souls that understand and love one another."[94] "Absolute freedom and absolute love—that is our goal," he wrote to his sisters in August of 1836, "the emancipation of humanity and the entire world—that is our calling."[95]

Mikhail's use of this ecstatic language in his home was partly a result of the fact that Priamukhino had always been a space for philosophical debate. One vision of reason after another had been the subject of domestic controversies since the late eighteenth century. Yet he also was well aware of the distinction that surrounded his family's name in the Stankevich circle; and he hoped the example he set at Priamukhino would be taken up as a model by his friends. He invited Belinsky—already a well-known critic—to come to Priamukhino for a month-long visit that fall. Properly coached by the domestic dreams of his day, Belinsky himself imagined evenings spent singing in Priamukhino's parlor, gathered with the Bakunin family around the piano: "In these choruses I thought to hear perfected humanity's hymn of ecstasy and bliss."[96]

Seeking, as he later recalled, to impress the Bakunin sisters, Belinsky took it upon himself to promote Fichte's social vision in Nadezhdin's *Telescope*, using a review of a work by a minor theologian as an excuse. Belinsky called for the creation of a new "scholarly estate," based in the clergy, that would participate in the empire's gradual awakening and spiritual liberation. The goal would be Russia's internal, moral development until such time as the state itself would become unnecessary. Invoking the apostle Paul's famous declaration that humanity's future belonged to grace, not law, Belinsky sketched the stateless, purposeful community that had been omitted from Mikhail's earlier translation of Fichte's "Lectures."

---

[94] Letter to the Beyers, 24 May 1836 (Bakunin, *Sobranie*, I:305).
[95] Letter to his sisters, 10 August 1836 (Bakunin, *Sobranie*, 329).
[96] Letter to M. A. Bakunin of 16 August 1837 (Belinskii, *PSS*, XI:174–75).

Yes, it will come, this time of the kingdom of God, when there will be no poor and no rich, no slave, no master, neither the faithful nor the faithless, neither law nor crime: when there will be no moments of ecstasy but rather all of life will be one continuous moment of ecstasy, when the disharmony of individual consciousnesses resolves in a single full harmony of common consciousness.[97]

Belinsky read this ecstatic review aloud to the delight of his audience.

Professor Nadezhdin, however, was not so amused when he received the article in Moscow. "You have gone so deep into the kingdom of ideas, my dear sir, that you have forgotten about real circumstances," he wrote to Belinsky, announcing his intention to cut the piece drastically. Imperial censors worked over the remainder equally critically, and when the final, published version appeared, it did so without the Idealist vision of a world without external authorities. (Mikhail's sister Tatiana prepared a copy of the full version, however, which remained in the Bakunin family archive until the late 1960s, when it was published.)[98] Nadezhdin's discretion did not, however, save *Telescope*. In late October of 1836, Emperor Nicholas I ordered the journal shut down for the sin of having published Petr Chaadaev's "Philosophical Letter," an anxious assessment of Russia's past, present, and future. Since Belinsky assisted Nadezhdin with the journal, his apartment in Moscow was searched and all his papers were confiscated. For two weeks, Belinsky's friends hesitated over whether he should try to escape abroad or return to Moscow to face questioning. In mid-November, he chose the latter course and was delivered "directly from the town gate to the chief of police."[99]

Before *Telescope's* sudden closure brought the summer to a halt, however, Priamukhino's reputation reached its zenith among Moscow's students, due to its curious combination of the virtues of family life and philosophy. Stankevich, upon hearing of the successful progress of Belinsky's visit, wrote glowingly to his friend Neverov: "The Bakunin family is an ideal family, therefore you can imagine how it should act upon a soul, which is not immune to God's spark!" Stankevich added that he firmly believed in the familial ideal, "perhaps even

---

[97] I. T. Trofimova, "Stat'ia V. G. Belinskogo 'Opyt sistemy nravstvennoi filosofii. Sochinenie magistra Alekseia Drozdova,'" *Russkaia Literatura* 3 (1969): 125–46, esp. 144.

[98] On Nadezhdin's reaction and censorship of Belinsky's article, see ibid., 125–26.

[99] On the sequence of events before and after *Telescope's* closing, see Iu. G. Oksman, *Letopis' zhizni i tvorchestva V. G. Belinskogo* (Moscow: Gosudarstvennoe izdatel'stvo khudozhestvennoi literatury, 1958), 132–35, esp. 135. Trofimova, "Stat'ia Belinskogo," 125, claims Belinsky's friends destroyed his archive, but the basis of this claim is unclear.

too much." He returned to Priamukhino later that fall to declare his affections in secret to Liubov. The two began a clandestine correspondence and became engaged, without initially seeking their parents' formal approval.[100]

⊛⟿⊛

When Mikhail first began to study Fichte's writings in the winter of 1836, he did so with the assumption that the philosopher was but a way station on a much larger intellectual itinerary leading "from Kant (Fichte, Schelling) through to Hegel."[101] Stankevich encouraged him to see their passage through this itinerary as a method of self-development; and since the goal was to reach the end of this road and become "equal to the best ideas of our time" they never expected to tarry too long on any one philosopher. For Mikhail, however, Fichte's conception of a scholar's vocation arrived at an opportune time. It entered his life at precisely as he was looking for a scholarly role model. It helped him to defend himself from his family's skeptical objections, on the one hand, and to show himself to be the philosophical equal of his new student friends, on the other. Throughout 1836, Bakunin played this role with such success that he temporarily overcame his sisters' religious objections and even came close to convincing his student friends to forget their race with history and announce the coming of the millennium.

The closing of *Telescope* reminded everyone involved that the Russian government expected its educated subjects to align themselves with the state, not daydream about its eventual passing. That November, Mikhail's progress along Stankevich's philosophical itinerary resumed, as he turned his attention to the study of Hegel. Even so, Mikhail's Fichtean turn as a "priest of truth" on the stage of private life fixed itself in the memory of everyone involved. It established Mikhail as the most radical — in terms of his willingness to dispense with convention — of Russia's Idealists. It brought Idealist arguments into the center of the Bakunin family's life in a way that was mocked thereafter, as Belinsky and others began to reflect critically on the vision of "perfected humanity" Priamukhino offered. In this way, the summer of 1836 would serve as a highwater mark, of sorts, in the romance of Russian Idealism — the point at which the Stankevich circle passed through the stage of its greatest philosophical enthusiasm and began to recover from it.[102]

[100] Stankevich, *Perepiska*, 363. On Liubov's engagement to Stankevich, see Kornilov, *Molodye gody*, 292–322.

[101] Letter to Aleksandra Beyer, April 1836 (Bakunin, *Sobranie*, I:260).

[102] See below, chapter 9.

Fichte's vision of a scholar's vocation had a particularly strong impact on Mikhail Bakunin himself. First, it gave him a new, self-determined but still charismatic role he could play in society, replacing his older, exemplary role as a nobleman. Second, it proved flexible enough to survive Mikhail's interest in a scholarly career and inform his future radicalism. In the 1860s, he imagined the revolutionary vocation in Fichtean terms. He presented the ideal radical as a revelatory instrument of truth, whose task it was to use inspirational words and deeds to "foment, awaken, and unleash" popular liberty. He hoped, thereby, to finally stimulate that era of social harmony and enlightened self-governance, of which first his father and then he himself had once dreamed at Priamukhino.

For a glimpse of Mikhail's radical scholarly technique in action, we may return to Weber's memoir of his final days. As she observed this dying prophet, Weber was struck in particular by Bakunin's theatrical ability to use "*his entire being*" to inspire in his fellows a "thirst for justice and happiness." No one seemed outside of the reach of his charisma, which he carefully calibrated with each listener in mind.

> Observing Mikhail Aleksandrovich's relations with simple people I grew ever more amazed. Often, while explaining his philosophical views and retrospectively developing, so to speak, his own world-view, he would speak about Hegelianism and dispute it point by point. Only by straining could I follow the course of his logic. . . . Yet when I saw with what ease he entered into intellectual relations with people who were barely literate, people of a different class, a different race—my amazement only grew. After all, despite his simple life and surroundings, Bakunin remained a real Russian seigneur [*barin*] from head to toe.[103]

Here, as if through a stereoscope, we can see several layers of Mikhail Bakunin's character brought into sudden unison. To the end of his days, no one ever forgot Mikhail Bakunin was a nobleman. That distinction always lay at the basis of his charisma.[104] Yet Idealism gave him a story through which he

[103] See A. Bauler, "M. A. Bakunin nakanune smerti. Vospominaniia," *Byloe*, no. 7/19 (July 1907): 62–78, esp. 72–73.

[104] Shortly after his death, for example, in their preface to their edition of *God and the State*, Carlo Cafiero and Elisée Reclus present the following description of Bakunin: "A Russian gentleman related by marriage to the highest nobility of the empire, he was one of the first to enter that intrepid society of rebels who were able to release themselves from traditions, prejudices,

could describe his break from that existence and rebirth as a new and utterly modern kind of man. As always in the romance of Russian Idealism, this story ends with Hegel. But it is his Fichtean pedagogical skills that allow Mikhail to continue using this charismatic narrative far beyond its original audience in Imperial Russian society. Even in Lugano in 1876, Mikhail was still framing his life as a story of philosophical development through Idealism. Indeed, he was still calling others to join him in the practice of this romantic tradition.

---

race, and class interests, and set their own comfort at naught." Once again, the legend of Bakunin's noble birth survives his revolutionary transformation, and endows it with his prior distinction. See Carlo Cafiero and Elisée Reclus, "Preface to the First French Edition," in Michael Bakunin, *God and the State* (New York: Dover Press, 1970), 5.

CHAPTER EIGHT

Varvara's Liberation

By the fall of 1836, Mikhail's sister Varvara had been informally separated from her husband for nearly a year. Her position at Priamukhino was increasingly untenable. She lived as a grown woman in her parents' house, obliged to be a wife to her husband during his fairly regular visits yet unwilling to return to their married life on its previous terms. She also was subjected to polemics from all sides. Her parents insisted she reconcile with Diakov, while Mikhail urged her to renounce the man entirely. This she refused to do, in part because she continued to feel guilty about the marriage and in part because she had no real alternative. Mikhail could—and eventually did—leave home. In November of 1836, tiring of life at Priamukhino and eager to resume his studies with his student friends, he returned to Moscow. Varvara, however, could only choose between her family's house and her husband's home, a nearby estate called Ivanovskoe.[1]

Eventually, Varvara decided that her only choice was to reach a common understanding with her husband. She went to Ivanovskoe and sought to negotiate a new relationship with him, one in which they would share the raising of their son but cease sexual relations, living as "brother and sister," as she put it. Mikhail suspected that Varvara was merely giving in again to a

---

[1] On the conflicts inside the Bakunin home at this time and Mikhail's return to Moscow, see E. H. Carr, *Michael Bakunin* (London: Macmillan, 1937), 45–48; A. Kornilov, *Molodye gody Mikhaila Bakunina: Iz istorii russkogo romantizma* (Moscow: M. and S. Sabashnikov, 1915), 252–67. On his studies of Hegel in early 1837, see D. I. Chizhevsky, *Gegel' v Rossii* (Paris: Dom knigi i Sovremennye zapiski, 1939), 90–91.

false sense of duty.[2] Yet he also rather abruptly declared that he needed to make a definitive break from his home. "It is necessary that I be alone, and that I develop my forces in isolation," Mikhail wrote to Varvara in late March 1837.[3] It briefly seemed like Mikhail no longer wanted to take an active part in his family's or his sisters' affairs.

Instead, however, events at Priamukhino took a new and radical turn. By June of 1837, Mikhail began to recruit his friends into an elaborate plot to "liberate Varinka" by arranging for her to escape abroad. That summer, he surprised Varvara herself with the scheme, to which she agreed. Bitter intergenerational conflict at Priamukhino then followed, as Mikhail's parents and husband fought Mikhail's plans to "liberate Varinka," while his friends, sisters, and even a few relatives worked to bring it about. Reconstructed by the Bakunin family's historian Aleksandr Kornilov as "one of the brightest episodes in the history of Russian Romanticism," this plot to liberate Varvara caused a scandal at the time and has provoked much bemused historical commentary since.[4] Not long ago, when Tom Stoppard sought to bring the intimate dramas of Russia's romantics to the stage in his theatrical trilogy *The Coast of Utopia*, he chose Varvara's liberation as his plot for act one.[5]

Despite the attention that has been lavished on this affair, however, several basic questions about Varvara's liberation remain unanswered. First, it has never been particularly clear when, exactly, this odd domestic conspiracy started, or what Mikhail's own motives were in concocting it. Kornilov's diffuse and ultimately misleading account straddles several phases in Mikhail's intellectual development, making it difficult for later scholars to associate the scheme with any particular ambitions on his part. Nor have historians ever had a very good sense of what Varvara herself thought of the affair and the philosophical frame Mikhail sought to throw around it. Some scholars use Kornilov's evidence to portray Varvara as the instigator of her own liberation, while others portray her as an indecisive, vacillating woman, pushed into leaving her husband by her domineering brother.[6]

[2] See V. A. Diakova to M. A. Bakunin, letter of 22 January [1837?], IRLI f. 16, op. 4, no. 458, l. 14; and T. A. Bakunina to M. A. Bakunin, letter of 29 January 1837, IRLI f. 16, op. 4, no. 582, ll. 43–45. Kornilov discusses Varvara's attempts to "convert" Diakov, and Mikhail's objections to them, in Kornilov, *Molodye gody*, 340–41.

[3] Letter to his sister Varvara, 27 March 1837 (Bakunin, *Sobranie*, I:419) and also his letter to his parents of late March 1837 (ibid., 420–21).

[4] See Kornilov, *Molodye gody*, 323–72.

[5] Tom Stoppard, *Voyage: The Coast of Utopia, Part I* (London, Faber and Faber, 2002), esp. 28–49.

[6] Among the interpretations that stress Diakova's active participation her liberation, see Mar-

Fortunately, closer scrutiny of Varvara's own letters makes it possible to clarify both the chronology and the competing ambitions that surrounded her liberation. Not only did this odd domestic conspiracy coincide with Mikhail Bakunin's first fascination with Hegel, he himself presented it as a fruition of his mastery of Hegel's vision of the world. He encouraged his friends, family, and above all his sister Varvara herself to read her "liberation" as the decisive finale of their youth. Examining Varvara's letters also allows us to understand what she thought about the Hegelian vision of self at the heart of her brother's new radical identity. Under Hegel's influence, Mikhail imagined that history works through painful experience to break down humanity's illusions, preparing it for its real role in the world. As she considered this theory of the self, however, Varvara experienced some of the doubts that haunted women throughout the long nineteenth century and beyond. Was it possible for her to imagine her own intellectual development according to a scheme designed for a man? Did accepting the progressive philosophical justification her brother wished to place on her liberation mean affirming the justice of events to which she had not consented? In the hidden heart of this conspiracy, in short, we can see Varvara struggling with ethical questions that women's inequality posed to the progressive visions created by men in the nineteenth century. As such, it helps us expand our understanding of Hegel's role in the making of Russian radicalism by allowing us to explore the role played by sex and gender in this process.[7]

In a famous passage in his memoir *Past and Thoughts*, Herzen once praised Hegel's philosophy as the very "algebra of revolution." "It emancipates a man in an unusual way," he remarked, "and leaves not one stone upon another of the Christian world, of the world of tradition that has outlived itself."[8] By and large, historians have agreed that Hegel played the most decisive role in the intellectual genesis of Russian radicalism by convincing young men like

---

shall S. Shatz, "Mikhail Bakunin and the Priamukhino Circle: Love and Liberation in the Russian Intelligentsia of the 1830s," *Canadian-American Slavic Studies 33*, no. 1 (Spring 1999): 15–18; Edward J. Brown, *Stankevich and His Moscow Circle* (Stanford: Stanford University Press, 1966), 78–80; for accounts that emphasize Bakunin's driving ambitions, see Arthur Mendel, *Michael Bakunin: Roots of Apocalypse* (New York: Praeger, 1981), 97–104; Aileen Kelly, *Mikhail Bakunin: A Study in the Psychology and Politics of Utopianism* (New Haven: Yale University Press, 1982), 41–42; Carr, *Bakunin*, 52–58. All these interpretations are based on Kornilov's account.

[7] On woman's place in nineteenth century visions of progress and the ethical dilemmas they raised, see Carla Hesse, *The Other Enlightenment: How French Women Became Modern* (Princeton: Princeton University Press, 2001), 104; and Carol Pateman, *The Disorder of Women: Democracy, Feminism, and Political Theory* (Stanford: Stanford University Press, 1989), chapters 1 and 4.

[8] See Alexander Herzen, *My Past and Thoughts*, ed. Dwight Macdonald, trans. Constance Garnett (Berkeley: University of California Press, 1973), 237; cf. Gertsen, *Sobranie*, IX:23.

Mikhail that it was not only possible but necessary for them to take an active role in society as agents of progressive change. Hegel saw history as a rational process, famously arguing that the "rational is real"—meaning that reason is the only authentic, actual force in the world. Though Hegel himself had a reputation as a statist, his famous maxim could easily be understood as a demand that "reality should be made rational," and that people only become their real selves by serving this purpose. As educated Russians attempted to understand their lives according to Hegel's "algebra," Leszek Kołakowski and others have argued, they gradually acquired a potentially radical belief in their own duty to participate in society and politics on behalf of progress.[9]

Yet finding one's place in a Hegelian world clearly means grappling with Hegel's account of selfhood. Only a rational self, after all, can locate its role in a history that is organized by reason. And sex—both in the sense of gender and in the sense of sexual conduct—plays a visible role in Hegel's explanations of how the modern, rational self is made. Admittedly, Hegel's pronouncements on sex are perhaps the most controversial element of his system. Scholars to this day debate whether it is possible to detach Hegel's account of reason from his assumptions about male and female nature, or his claims about the nature and meaning of sexual acts.[10] Be that as it may, statements about how sex affects selfhood run like a red thread through Hegel's most famous writings. Men and women are described as having different na-

[9] See Leszek Kołakowski, *The Founders*, vol. 1 of *Main Currents of Marxism: Its Rise, Growth, and Dissolution*, trans. P. S. Falla (Oxford: Clarendon Press, 1978), 81–85; see also Andrzej Walicki, *A History of Russian Thought from the Enlightenment to Marxism*, trans. Hilda Andrews-Rusiecka (Stanford: Stanford University Press, 1979), 115–30. See also Chizhevsky, *Gegel' v Rossii*, 287–459; Kelly, *Bakunin*, 44–72; Martin Malia, *Alexander Herzen and the Birth of Russian Socialism* (New York: Grosset & Dunlap, 1965), 218–57. Though all of these deal with the anxieties of the "superfluous man," a classic Russian theme, none of them look more broadly at issues of gender and sexuality, and do not examine the place of sex in Russian understandings of Hegel. For an attempt to place gender in Russian intellectual life of the 1830s, see Rebecca Friedman, "Romantic Friendship in the Nicholaevan University," *The Russian Review* 62 (April 2003): 262–83.

[10] For critiques that see gender and sexuality as written in to Hegel's method, see e.g., Genevieve Lloyd, *The Man of Reason: "Male" and "Female" in Western Philosophy*, 2nd ed. (Minneapolis: University of Minnesota Press, 1984), 85–90; Benjamin R. Barber, "Spirit's Phoenix and History's Owl, or the Incoherence of Dialectics in Hegel's Account of Women," *Political Theory* 16, no. 1 (February 1988): 5–28; and Kelly Oliver, *Subjectivity Without Subjects: From Abject Fathers to Desiring Mothers* (Lanham: Rowman & Littlefield, 1998). For recent attempts to separate out Hegel's reason from a particular sexual system, see Jeffrey A. Gauthier, *Hegel and Feminist Social Criticism* (Albany: State University of New York Press, 1997); Terry Pinkard, *Hegel's Phenomenology: The Sociality of Reason* (Cambridge: Cambridge University Press, 1994), 307–8. Varieties of opinion on this issue are represented in Patricia Jagentowicz Mills, *Feminist Interpretations of G. W. F. Hegel* (University Park: Pennsylvania State University Press, 1996). See in particular the articles by Pateman, Krell, Mills, Irigaray, O'Brien, and Ravven.

tures (men are active like animals, according to the *Philosophy of Right,* while women are passive like plants).[11] These natures reach maturity in different spheres of life (thus women's calling is the "natural" society of the home, in the *Phenomenology of Spirit,* while men find themselves by going out into the world).[12] Procreative, heterosexual, married sex, meanwhile, occupies a crucial juncture in Hegel's account of the self-fulfillment of modern men and women. Such sex, he argues, allows for the fulfillment and conscious appropriation of instinctive desires — even as it realizes these desires through marriage, family life, and procreation. This "natural" domestic realm is then seen to be the ground from which larger and more conscious communities are built, up to and including the state. For all of these reasons, as Terry Pinkard has recently observed, "the family is in fact the basic way in which 'nature' becomes 'spirit'" in Hegel's account of history.[13]

No matter how one reads Hegel, then, it is clear that he is a philosopher who sees a relationship between gender, sexual behavior, and domestic institutions in the making of modern selfhood.[14] Even the most half-hearted attempt to use this algebra would have to account for sex as a variable; and Russian Idealists of the 1830s and 1840s are famous for the zeal with which applied philosophy to their own lives. (According to Herzen, there was not a paragraph in Hegel's philosophy which "had not been the subject of desperate disputes for several nights together.")[15] Yet how did sex fit into the calculations of Hegel's first Russian adherents, especially as they began to plot out radical new roles for themselves in life? Despite the revolutionary impact Hegel had on Russian social thought — liberals and radicals imagined themselves and their future in his terms for much of the following century — this is a question scholars have not yet asked, much less answered.

This is unfortunate on several levels. Most obviously, it deprives scholars today — locked in a debate over the role of sex in Hegel — of a chance to see how one set of nineteenth-century people lived through this issue. How did they read the status of gender and sexuality in a Hegelian world? In addition, losing track of sex in our histories of Hegelianism risks losing track of

---

[11] See T. M. Knox, trans., *Hegel's Philosophy of Right* (Oxford: Oxford University Press, 1967), 263–64, § 166.

[12] See G. W. F. Hegel, *Phenomenology of Spirit,* foreword by J. N. Findlay, trans. A. V. Miller (Oxford: Oxford University Press, 1977), 268–78, §§ 450–63.

[13] Pinkard, *Hegel's Phenomenology,* 303.

[14] Of course, whether this relationship is necessary to Hegel's system, or simply a contingency of the modern moment as he saw it, may be debated.

[15] Herzen, *My Past and Thoughts,* 232 (cf. Gertsen, *Sobranie,* IX:18).

the status of sex in the ideologies and identities to emerge from it. For example, most histories of Russian Hegelianism posit that it began conservatively—apologizing for the rationality of the existing state—before turning radical as young men like Mikhail seized upon its more revolutionary implications.[16] Can the same be said, however, of sexual politics—did a Hegelian embrace of the state, for example, go hand in hand with an acceptance of Hegel's paternalistic prescriptions for contemporary gender roles? Did Hegelian "radicalism" mean reversing them? Likewise, how do assessments of the meaning of sexual behavior fit on this scheme? In the end, there seems no reason to assume that Hegel's audience adhered to his conclusions about the meaning of sex in his system. On the contrary, they may have calculated the role of sex in the making of a rational world—and a rational self—in a very different way. Underneath a "conservative" position on the state may have lingered a new conception of the role of sexual behavior in selfhood; under a "radical" position—paternalistic gender norms.

The history of Varvara's liberation allows us to examine all these themes, not least from the point of view of Varvara herself. First, however, we need to come to a clearer understanding of the conspiracy's genesis.

❀❀❀

Just when and why Mikhail's opposition to Varvara's marriage coalesced into a plot for her "liberation" has never been particularly clear. In his fundamental biography, Kornilov portrays Mikhail's effort as a long and methodically waged "struggle," conducted over the course of several years and consisting of two phases. In the first, beginning in early 1836, Mikhail battled Varvara's own conscience, gradually convincing her that her marriage was a lie she must abandon. Having won this battle by the fall of 1836, he then proceeded to the second, "external" phase of the struggle. For the next two years he fought for Varvara's freedom, placating (if not deceiving) her parents and husband with the ruse of her illness and raising monies for her trip from a variety of sources. Along the way, Kornilov claims, Varvara wavered in her commitment to her escape, forcing Mikhail to make tactical retreats while he steadfastly "conducted his line."[17]

---

[16] See e.g., A. N. Pypin, *Belinskii, ego zhizn' i perepiska* (St. Petersburg: Tipografiia M. M. Stasiulevicha, 1876), 155–238; Chizhevsky, *Gegel' v Rossii,* 84–96. This is, of course, a common scheme for understanding the political development of Hegelianism more generally, from conservatism to radicalism: see Kołakowski as cited above.

[17] For Kornilov's chronology, see Kornilov, *Molodye gody,* 322–30, esp. 325 and 330.

This is not, however, how Varvara herself remembered the history of her emancipation. We know this from a letter she wrote to Mikhail on 27 November 1837 (at the height of the drama and well before her eventual escape). Playing the piano that morning, Varvara found herself overwhelmed by memories of "the first day of my liberation." She recalled

> that clear, blue sky which smiled to me so sweetly for the first time, that air in which I breathed so alive and free, and how you and I met in the garden — and our entire conversation — and the quivering and lively beating of my heart, as you spoke with me — and everything, everything came alive in my breast — Beethoven, Marbach, Schubert, his *Allmacht* in particular — brilliant evenings, picnics, trips to Kutuzov Hill, and the wonderful night before Langer and Pahl left — all this ran through my heart.

As can be seen, Varvara pictures her liberation not as a long campaign but as a sudden conversion, occurring on a historical "first day." Awakened, energized, and ultimately emancipated by her conversation with Mikhail, she finds an intimate public already gathered to celebrate the event with food, philosophy, and song. A burst of activity follows in the form of rollicking excursions around the landmarks of the Bakunin family estate. The hill where General Kutuzov himself was rumored to have planned Napoleon's defeat becomes the launching point for a new sort of domestic revolution: a plot for her physical escape, still ongoing when this recollection was written.[18]

Telltale details allow us to date these events to late June or early July of 1837 (a full year later than Kornilov imagines). First, there is the presence and participation of Langer and Pahl, two musicians from Moscow, who visited Priamukhino only once during Varvara's life there — precisely at this time. Second, there is the prominent mention of Beethoven and the poet Gotthart Oswald Marbach (1810–1890), two figures who became prominent in the Bakunin children's lives in the summer of 1837.[19] Mikhail was in fact present in Priamukhino at this time; he arrived from Moscow in June, bring-

---

[18] See V. A. Diakova to M. A. Bakunin, letter of 27–29 November [1837?], IRLI f. 16, op. 4, no. 460, ll. 40–41. Although this letter bears no year date, it can be dated by its reference to Bakunin's November 1837 departure to Moscow (and memories of that summer).

[19] Thus in Mikhail Bakunin's correspondence Beethoven and Marbach are mentioned for the first time in letters to the Beyer sisters, 24 June 1837 (Bakunin, *Sobranie*, II:22) and 2 July 1837 (ibid., 29).

ing Langer, Pahl, Beethoven, and Marbach with him.[20] Mikhail's correspondence supports this chronology perfectly. He mentions his plan to liberate his sister for the first time in a letter written on June 24, 1837, shortly after his arrival at Priamukhino.[21] Three weeks later, Mikhail writes that his sister has been "internally" liberated (through their garden conversation, one may suppose); at this point, he writes, only her "external liberation" remains.[22] Subsequent letters abound in conspiratorial detail, as Mikhail concocts a scheme to send Varvara to the spas at Karlsbad (in Bohemia), using her frail health as a ruse to extract her from her family's grasp. No such planning occurs before.[23]

In sum, all reliably dated evidence corroborates Varvara's recollection of her "liberation" as a plot that began in the summer of 1837.[24] This matters for two reasons. First, it sharpens our understanding of the character of this famous affair. Instead of being a long and single-minded struggle—waged by Mikhail over several years (and in no small part against Varvara herself)—Varvara's liberation was a conspiracy that came together quickly, lasted less than a year, and took wing with her enthusiastic assent.

Second, Varvara's letter allows us to see the tremendous theatricality of this conspiracy. In the scene Varvara describes, her brother becomes her liberator by directing her to read and perform her own life according to a new script. The sheer exaltation of this event—replete with musical, philosophical, and historical accompaniment—makes it plain that from the beginning

[20] On Langer and Pahl's arrival in Priamukhino, see Bakunin's letter to his sisters, 24 June 1837 (*Sobranie*, II:22); see also Kornilov, *Molodye gody*, 350.

[21] Letter to the Beyers, 24 June 1837 (Bakunin, *Sobranie*, II:23).

[22] See Bakunin's letter to the Beyer sisters, 13–16 July 1837 (*Sobranie*, II:37).

[23] The first mention of Diakova's trip to Karlsbad, for example, occurs in Bakunin's letter to the Beyers of 31 July 1837 (*Sobranie*, II:54).

[24] Kornilov cites two other letters by Diakova, dated by him as "late February or early March 1837" and "April 1837," that refer to a concrete scheme for her escape. The originals of these letters do not, however, bear dates. Kornilov neither mentions this fact nor explains his attribution. Comparison with reliably dated material suggests they were written much later, seemingly in early 1838. Thus, the "April 1837" letter refers to Marienbad, a destination that appears in Bakunin's letters only in December of 1837; while the "February or March" letter refers to a detailed plan for Varvara's escape months before it appears in the correspondence of its supposed architect, Bakunin. For the February or March letter, see Kornilov, *Molodye gody*, 342–43, and V. A. Diakova to M. A. Bakunin, undated letter, IRLI f. 16, op. 4, no. 460, ll. 60 ob.–60; for the April letter, see Kornilov, *Molodye gody*, 353–54, and V. A. Diakova to M. A. Bakunin, undated letter, IRLI f. 16, op. 4, no. 460, ll. 24–25. Other details argue against Kornilov's dating: both letters refer to Diakov's grudging acceptance of his wife's independence, something gotten only in late 1837; the April letter refers to the assistance of friends, only solicited later.

much more was at stake than Varvara's personal independence. The garden compact opens with the revelation of a new and providential horizon. It proceeds through a series of intimate celebrations, with Schubert's ultra-Romantic celebration of the ubiquitous Almighty as its hymn. "He speaks in the thundering storm, in the river's reverberant roar," "Die Allmacht" proclaims in crescendo, a verse likely sung by Varvara herself in her strong voice.[25] What sort of script, then, did he Mikhail place on her sister's liberation, as he encouraged her to feel "alive and free" for the first time?

Though none of Mikhail's biographers ignore Varinka's liberation, neither have they paid much attention to the philosophy behind it. Most claim it arose from Mikhail's Idealistic commitment to individual liberty; others see in it the first stirrings of women's emancipation in Russia, while still others say it reflects a compulsive desire on Mikhail's part to control his sisters' fates.[26] There is undoubtedly some truth to each of these explanations. In particular, Mikhail was always commanding in his personal relationships and jealous of his sisters' lives. It is difficult to ignore the amorous, even incestuous overtones of the romantic rendezvous Varvara describes.

Diagnosing Mikhail's subconscious motives, however, does not free us from the responsibility of understanding his explicit ambitions. Since we can be much more precise about the chronology of Varvara's liberation than Kornilov was, it is possible to be clearer about the ideals that framed the conspiracy. In particular, we can see that Mikhail's scheme for his sister's emancipation emerged as a response to Hegel's call to recognize the reason at work in one's personal history.

Throughout early 1837 (as his scheme began to form) Mikhail told anyone who would listen that "Hegel is giving me a completely new life."[27] From the time of his "intellectual revolution" in 1834, he had pursued the study of post-Kantian philosophy, planning to become a scholar. Traveling his itinerary that led from "Kant (Schelling, Fichte) through to Hegel," he variously

---

[25] See Richard Capell, *Schubert's Songs* (New York: Macmillan 1977), 212–14; on Diakova's musical interests and ability, see Kornilov, *Molodye gody*, 348.

[26] Of the biographical works cited earlier, Kornilov, Brown, and Shatz draw a close connection between Diakova's "liberation" and her brother's commitment to individual liberty, while Mendel, Carr, and Kelly focus on Bakunin's psychology. Shatz also describes the affair as a blow against patriarchy. Other examples of each of these views could be produced.

[27] Letter to his sisters of the beginning of May (Bakunin, *Sobranie*, I:428). On Bakunin's studies of Hegel and the philosopher's importance for him at this time, see Kornilov, *Molodye gody*, 373–411; Chizhevsky, *Gegel' v Rossii*, 90–94; Kelly, *Bakunin*, 46–60; Bakunin's 1837 notebooks on Hegel, reproduced in *Oeuvres [CD-ROM]*.

refined and re-created his own inner life.[28] Arriving at Hegel in early 1837, however, he learned that such self-cultivation was but one phase in his development and not the last. Maturity, according to Hegel, demanded a bracing encounter with the world. This encounter would cleanse him of his youthful delusions and prepare him for conscious and effective activity in the world. Youth's epoch of sentiment would come to an end, to be succeeded by an epoch of reality. He would become "truly a man," mature, active, and free.[29]

Mikhail had hit upon the ideal for which he would become famous in the literary circles of the 1830s and early 1840s: the call to reconcile oneself with reality and thereby become a "real man."[30] It was an ambition he translated with celebrated ease from technical German into Romantic Russian, projecting both himself and Hegel into the foreground of Russian thought for the first time. Yet the question remained where and how, in Russian terms, one might become a "real man." When Mikhail started to read Hegel in early 1837—very likely beginning with the *Phenomenology of Spirit* or a summary of it—his most immediate desire was to finish his education by going to Berlin. Correctly if conveniently, he read Hegel as requiring men to break with their homes.[31] "As Hegel says," Mikhail wrote to his sisters on 20 February 1837, *"the harmony that one takes from home is not yet a true harmony, it must be submitted to contradictions, storms,* terrible struggles, so as to be destroyed, so as to make man suffer, and oblige him to rehabilitate it by thought." Mikhail specifically contrasted his manly destiny to go out into "the world" with his sisters' vocation to realize themselves at home.[32] To become a real man, by contrast, he needed to act elsewhere.[33]

[28] Letter to A. A. Beyer of the beginning of April, 1836 (Bakunin, *Sobranie,* I:260).

[29] Bakunin outlines this scheme of development in a letter to his sisters of 20 February 1837 (Bakunin, *Sobranie,* I:407–8).

[30] Space prevents me from tracing here Bakunin's gradual and situational substitution of Hegelian terms of art *Wirklichkeit* and *deistvitel'nyi chelovek* for his first renderings, such as "the world" and "truly a man." The changing vocabulary reflects his increasing fluency with Hegel and his ability to acquaint his domestic audience with the new concepts and terminology as well. The basic narrative structure of encounter and transformation remains the same, however, as does the goal of finally, historically achieving one's real self. Compare the following letters to observe the pattern: to his sisters, 20 February 1837 (*Sobranie,* I:406–8); to the Beyer sisters, 27 July 1837 (ibid., II:45–48); and N. M. Ketcher, November 1837 (ibid., II:73–74).

[31] On Hegel and gender, see the work of Barber, Perrot, Martin-Fugier, and Mills cited earlier.

[32] See Bakunin's letter to his sisters, 20 February 1837 (*Sobranie,* I:406–9). Emphasis in the original.

[33] See Bakunin's letter to his sister Varvara, 27 March 1837 (*Sobranie,* I:418–19); his letter to his parents of late March 1837 (ibid., I:420–21) echoes similar themes.

Mikhail's skeptical parents refused to pay for his voyage abroad. This, in the end, is what brought him to Priamukhino in the summer of 1837.[34] By then, however, his vision of what it took to become a man had changed. He described himself as already tested and resolved, possessed of the maturity and activity Hegel envisioned. "I have been exposed to the most terrible storms the past half-year or so, but these storms have passed, and I have conquered true harmony, a harmony that is complete and full of reality," he wrote to his Moscow friends Aleksandra and Natalia Beyer in late June 1837. Steeled by this experience, he was able to look difficult facts "in the face, so as to place myself above them, and govern them according to my will." His goal would now be "to arrange the fate of my family." First and foremost, this meant addressing the plight of his sister Varvara. "Yes, I will liberate her," Mikhail concluded, noting that his resolution was a recent one.[35]

How had this change come about? What brought domestic affairs back into his vision as a legitimate sphere of his activity? At its root, Mikhail's exuberant "new life" was undoubtedly the product of rationalization. Committed to becoming "truly a man"—but frustrated in his attempts to realize this ambition on Hegel's gendered terms—Mikhail simply reinterpreted his personal struggles of the previous year as an adequate substitute for the decisive encounter with the world Hegel demanded.[36] His conflict with his parents, his moments of self-doubt, his misunderstandings with friends and sisters: all this was nothing less than "a struggle for life and death—but in the end life triumphed, and I found myself in a higher state of Being."[37] (The language here clearly mimics the famous passage in *The Phenomenology of Spirit*, where Hegel calls man to face "the danger and trial of death"—albeit by leaving his home and risking his life in the public realm.)[38]

Matured by his struggles within his own family, Mikhail claimed, he had become not merely a priest, but indeed a "fighter for Truth."[39] He had been stripped of all vestiges of youthful illusion (the spiritual adolescence Hegel

[34] Bakunin announced this change of plan to his sisters in a letter of 13 May 1837 (*Sobranie*, I:433).

[35] See Bakunin's letter to the Beyer sisters, 24 June 1837 (*Sobranie*, II:23–25).

[36] As Aileen Kelly rightly observes, Bakunin showed little regard for institutions in Hegel; with the exit of "the world," we may say that he lost sight of them altogether. See Kelly, *Bakunin*, 54–55.

[37] See Bakunin's letter to the Beyer sisters, 31 July 1837 (*Sobranie*, II:50). Bakunin here describes his mood just before his return to Priamukhino that June.

[38] G. W. F. Hegel, *Phenomenology of Spirit*, trans. A. V. Miller (Oxford: Oxford University Press, 1977), 278, § 463.

[39] Letter to the Beyer sisters, 31 July 1837 (Bakunin, *Sobranie*, II:50).

called *Schönseligkeit*)[40] and was now ready to perform Spirit's work wherever he found it.[41] In his letters to the Beyers — among the first intimates of his domestic conspiracy — Mikhail identified Varvara's liberation as one such cause. He called it a grand "combat" that pitted "the faithful of the old world" (Varvara's husband and parents) against the apostles of the new (himself, his siblings, and the others he made intimate to this domestic conspiracy).[42]

The meaning of Varvara's liberation for the making of Mikhail's new identity as a fighter for truth and real man was twofold. First, Mikhail used it as evidence that his life was indeed now vigorous and real. "I have entered into the true element of my life, and I have conquered it by internal and external revolutions," he wrote to the Beyers on 19 July 19 1837 after explaining that his domestic intervention was succeeding.[43] Second and more broadly speaking, the plot offered Mikhail an opportunity to reimagine Hegel's account of selfhood in terms that fit his own situation. His transformation had implicitly undone his first understanding of Hegel, which imagined that true men were made only by leaving the home. During Varvara's emancipation, by contrast, he argued that life itself was a "continuous," universal process of liberation: "liberation from spectrality, from limitation, and entrance into the sphere of Truth and freedom."[44]

In place of the proverbial separate spheres, Mikhail posited only one true reality: what he called the "sacred sphere." (Opposite this world he posited a life of meaningless circumstance, ultimately illusory.) In this ubiquitous realm, spanning both home and the world, reason worked in one and the same way: by punishing human illusions and forcing individuals to recognize the higher reality at work in their lives. This implied a blurring of the lines between public and private experience, as well as the notions of gender difference built around them. Mikhail invited women as well as men to see their lives in these terms, ignoring notions of discretion as he recruited friends and relatives, "insiders" and "outsiders," into the cause of his sister's liberation. For example, he urged his friends the Beyers to regard their individuality as "the temporary products of organization that will perish with that organization." Essential to this were not the "empty forms" of subjectivity but rather the "eternal Divine Content" of objective truth, of which it was humanity's vocation to be the vessel. (Hegel, who disdained discussion of philosophical

---

[40] Literally, the "condition of the beautiful soul."
[41] Letter to the Beyer sisters, 31 July 1837 (Bakunin, *Sobranie*, II:49–51).
[42] See Bakunin's letter to the Beyers, August 1837 (*Sobranie*, II:59); see also ibid., I:57–58.
[43] Letter to the Beyer sisters, 19 July 1837 (Bakunin, *Sobranie*, I:40).
[44] Letter to the Beyer sisters, 2 July 1837 (Bakunin, *Sobranie*, II:31).

themes with women as mere *Konversation*, would surely have been horrified
by such consciousness raising.)[45]

For women as well as men, then, in Mikhail's definition, reaching free, rational maturity meant finding one's place in this one, ubiquitous, supraindi-
vidual reality, as active at home in the countryside as out in the world. In this
sense it is no accident that Varvara's memories of the "first day of my liberation" were memories of awakening to a purposeful world theretofore hidden
in her family's garden. Nor is it accidental that Mikhail was so careful to
distinguish between his sister's internal and external emancipation. Never
narrowly concerned with her physical escape, Mikhail presented Varvara's
liberation in historical terms as an inevitable manifestation of her hard-won
maturity and freedom. "She is already free, since her mind has been liberated
from the prejudices that fettered its liberty," Mikhail announced to the Beyer
sisters as he turned to planning his sister's voyage in August 1837. "Once internal liberty has been really constituted, external freedom must follow as its
necessary consequence."[46] From its first day, in this sense, Varvara's liberation was meant to follow—and thereby vindicate—her brother's unorthodox
developmental scheme.

Over the long term, it did not escape contemporaries that Mikhail imagined himself as "real" only by discarding a great deal of what Hegel meant by
"man." Mikhail himself was derided by his critics as insufficiently masculine—as being, in fact, a "eunuch." While historians have often speculated
that this charge had physiological roots in some anatomical abnormality, in
Mikhail's transformation of Hegel we can see a radical philosophical indif-
ference to gender as well. Mikhail's intervention in family life was sharply
and mockingly critiqued by contemporaries as a willful subversion of normality and reality, as understood by both philosophy and common sense. To
the extent that they adopted Mikhail's philosophical language and sensibility, his sisters and the Beyers also became the subject of polemic and ridicule,
much of it centering on portraits of them as denatured *femmes savantes*.[47]

---

[45] Letter to the Beyer sisters, 31 July 1837 (Bakunin, *Sobranie*, II:52). Note that this letter
concludes with conspiratorial detail. This language of divine service entered into other intimates'
letters as well See Belinsky's letter to Bakunin, 1 November 1837 (*PSS*, XI:185–86).

[46] Letter to the Beyers, August 1837 (Bakunin, *Sobranie*, II:52).

[47] On the literary controversy surrounding Bakunin, see Marshall Shatz, "Bakunin, Turgenev, and Rudin," in *The Golden Age of Russian Literature and Thought*, ed. Derek Offord (New
York: St. Martin's, 1992), 103–14; Kelly, *Bakunin*, 67–72; Lydia Ginzburg, *On Psychological Prose*,
trans. and ed. Judson Rosengrant (Princeton: Princeton University Press, 1991), chaps. 1 and
2. On Bakunin's anatomy, see Marshall S. Shatz, "Michael Bakunin and His Biographers: The
Question of Bakunin's Sexual Impotence," in *Imperial Russia, 1900–1917: State, Society, Opposition*

Taken together, these critiques show that even when he called his fellow men to embrace "our beautiful Russian reality"—as he did in an essay aimed at students published in the *Moscow Observer* in 1838—Mikhail did so in terms that were subversive of common gender distinctions, including those accepted by Hegel himself.

But what of Varvara? What (if any) were her doubts about her emancipation and the Hegelian historical scheme that framed it?

⊛⅌⊷⊛

After the first day of her liberation, Varvara had a long time to think about it. The initial plan was for her to leave home almost immediately. Taking her son and sister Tatiana with her, she would go to Karlsbad, where she would live in the peace and anonymity of a spa town. Both her husband and her parents opposed this plan. The parents suspected it was the product of Mikhail's philosophical fantasy and would have nothing to do with it; Diakov, less resolutely, refused to provide his wife with money or his permission to travel (necessary under Russian law) unless he himself could accompany her abroad. The result was a stalemate that lasted several months. In November 1837—well before this conflict was resolved—Mikhail returned to Moscow to rejoin friends and continue his studies. He urged his sister to remain patient and keep him apprised of developments at Priamukhino.[48] From then until her eventual departure in June 1838, Varvara wrote him letter after letter. Carefully preserved in the Bakunin family archive, they provide a complete record of her thoughts about her liberation.[49]

These letters make it clear that Varvara greeted her brother's scheme with great enthusiasm. She does not seem to have hated Diakov, whom she regarded as a decent man (she reprimanded Mikhail whenever he disparaged her husband). Yet she felt she had made a grave mistake in marrying him, even if it had been under pressure from her parents. She wanted complete control over the education of their son; and she distrusted her husband's changing moods, marked by pleading, touching, and threats. Her husband's legal authority over her was more or less absolute, contingent on his whims.

(Essays in Honor of Marc Raeff), ed. Ezra Mendelsohn and Marshall S. Shatz (DeKalb: Northern Illinois University Press, 1988), 219–40.

[48] On the evolution of the plan and opposition to it, see letter to the Beyers, August 1837 (Bakunin, *Sobranie*, II:59–60); to his sisters, 22 December 1837 (ibid., 92–93); and to his sisters, 24 December 1837 (ibid., 93–94).

[49] None of what follows was used by Kornilov.

Divorce in Russia was so difficult that no one in her immediate circle knew for sure whether it was even possible.[50]

Varvara's letters show that she was also excited by the Hegelian philosophical frame her brother placed around her liberation, at least initially. There is little evidence that Varvara read Hegel. Neither, however, did some of the men who have gone down in history as "Russian Hegelians." (Like Belinsky, Varvara learned about Hegel primarily through Mikhail's interpretations.)[51] Mikhail went to great pains to translate modern philosophy into the religious idiom his sisters preferred (a mixture of Russian and spiritual French). In the case of Hegel, he used Gotthart Marbach's *On Modern Literature, in Letters to a Lady* as a primer of sorts. (Marbach's work, singled out in Varvara's memory as the text most closely associated with her liberation, was an attempt to explicate and defend the new philosophy before a female audience.)[52] There is no question that by the time Mikhail left for Moscow, Varvara was thoroughly conversant with the developmental framework her brother had constructed around her emancipation. Her reports from Priamukhino — often written in German — are studded with such Hegelian terms of art as *Wirklichkeit* ("reality") and *Schönseligkeit* ("the disease of the beautiful soul"). More important, they show Varvara attempting to think through her life in her brother's Hegelian terms.

Together they worked out a progressive history of her life that gradually lead from her childhood and adolescence to "the terrible epoch *die mich in die Wirklichkeit zurückbrachte.*"[53] According to this three-part scheme, Varvara's

[50] See N. V. Stankevich's query on the subject in his letter to A. P. Efremov, 23 NS /11 OS November 1837 (*Perepiska*, 425–26); Gregory L. Freeze, "Bringing Order to the Russian Family: Marriage and Divorce in Imperial Russia, 1760–1860," *Journal of Modern History* 62, no. 4 (December 1990): 709–46. On Diakov's broad authority over his wife and son, see William G. Wagner, *Marriage, Property, and the Law in Late Imperial Russia* (Oxford: Clarendon Press, 1994), chap. 1.

[51] On Bakunin's role as interpreter of Hegel for his contemporaries, including Belinsky, see Chizhevsky, *Gegel' v Rossii*, 84–85, 117. Note, however, that unlike Belinsky, Diakova knew German, a fact that caused Belinsky no small embarrassment when he visited Priamukhino and was teased by the Bakunins for this gap in his education. See V. G. Belinsky to M. A. Bakunin, letter of 16 August 1837 (*PSS*, XI:175).

[52] On Marbach, see Ruth-Ellen B. Joeres, "The Gutzkow-Menzel Tracts: A Critical Response to a Novel and an Era," *MLN* 88, no. 5 (October 1973): 1002. Bakunin's aborted translation of Marbach for his sisters is reproduced in *Oeuvres [CD-ROM]*.

[53] "[T]hat returned me to reality." See V. A. Diakova to M. A. Bakunin, letter of 27 November [1837?], IRLI f. 16, op. 4, no. 460, ll. 40–41. Bakunin uses this scheme in a famous letter to his father of 15 December 1837 (*Sobranie*, II:112–14). A fascinating and much-quoted autobiographical fragment by Diakova, published by Kornilov, is also written according to this interpretive scheme. He dates it 18 January 1837 (see *Molodye gody*, 331–35), but the original bears

childhood had been a blessed and harmonious era of religious feeling, full of faith and hope. Yet this harmony had been disrupted by the events of her adolescence. First, her parents sought to rein in her spiritual independence by subjecting her to a then fashionable mixture of Orthodox catechism and Catholic piety à la Saint Francis de Sales.[54] Then they tried to force her and her sisters to marry, becoming obsessed with this notion in the wake of Liubov's broken engagement. Disturbed and divided, Varvara had accepted marriage to Nikolai in a moment of exaltation, hoping to make her parents happy and to reduce the pressure on her sisters to marry.[55] Rooted in delusory notions of individual heroism and filial duty, this sacrifice had been ruthlessly and necessarily punished by the reality of her marriage (the "terrible epoch" of her life). Ruined, she had lived "without desire or hope" until the awakening of her liberation. This had restored her lost union with God by revealing the hand of reason in her life. She was thereby returned to the reality of her life and prepared for a mature and free existence. "The time of fantastic dreams is over for me," Varvara wrote to her brother shortly after his departure, noting that she was invigorated by this new understanding of her life. What remained was to realize her freedom by leaving her husband.[56]

At this point it may be useful to try to compare this narrative with Hegel's most famous statements on the role of sex and marriage in the life of a woman, made in his 1821 *Philosophy of Right*.[57] As numerous commentators have noted,

---

no year date. See V. A. Diakova to N. N. Diakov, letter of 18 January [undated], IRLI f. 16, op. 4, no. 492, ll. 3–6 ob. Again, this seems to be a case of misdating by Kornilov: the letter seems to have been written in early 1838. It refers to Diakov's journey to Moscow at that time and also shows Hegelian influence in its vocabulary and construction.

[54] On religious currents in Diakova's childhood, see A. N. Pypin, *Religioznye dvizheniia pri Aleksandre I*, Piksanov (Petrograd: Ogni, 1916), 83–155.

[55] Although Kornilov is no doubt right to claim that Varvara's real motives in getting married were more complex and less altruistic (*Molodye gody*, 81–82), there seems to be some truth to the notion that it was planned as a sacrifice. According to sister Tatiana, Varvara confessed her plan before heading to the altar (see Tatiana's undated letter of [early January 1838?] to Mikhail, IRLI f. 16, op. 4, no. 582, ll. 71–72.) The letter can be dated to early January by reference to Varvara's flight to her aunt's house at this time .

[56] See V. A. Dyakova to M. A. Bakunin, letter of 27 November [1837?], IRLI f. 16, op. 4, no. 460, ll. 40–41.

[57] I include this discussion for purposes of comparison only: it is unlikely that Bakunin read the *Philosophy of Right* before early 1838 (see Chizhevsky, *Gegel' v Rossii*, 91). The relevant sections of the *Philosophy of Right* are T. M. Knox, trans., *Hegel's Philosophy of Right* (Oxford: Oxford University Press, 1967), 111–16, §§ 161–69. Though these passages are used by many recent commentators as Hegel's definitive statements on sexuality, marriage, and gender, my purpose here is not to provide a definitive gloss of Hegel's views on this subject but rather one common reading of them.

both marriage and sex occupy paradoxical and perhaps contradictory positions in Hegel's understanding of femininity.[58] On the one hand, Hegel posits that women should be free to choose their spouses; he understands marriage as a moment of maturing liberation for both sexes, in that by following their particular passions (their romantic and sexual desires), both sexes realize themselves in a conscious and substantive union (marriage). Hegel specifically rules out compulsion in marriage and indeed posits that divorce must be allowed in cases of estrangement.[59]

On the other hand, Hegel constructs femininity so passively that it is difficult to understand where women derive the ability to make any choice independent of their spouses. It is also unclear what sort of liberty and prospects for future development they gain thereby.[60] Where Hegel imagined that men come to maturity, self-consciousness, and reality through struggle, he was famously evasive on the subject of feminine development. "Women are educated—who knows how?—as it were by breathing in ideas, by living rather than by acquiring knowledge," he writes in an addition to the *Philosophy of Right*.[61] As a result, women are supposed to move harmoniously from the realm of their birth family to their new lives with their husbands, with only one moment of conscious activity between: the point of their decision to marry. This decision, rooted in emotional, physical desires, paradoxically eliminates the meaningful role of sex in women's lives thereafter. After marriage, in Hegel's view, "physical passion sinks to the level of a physical moment, destined to vanish in its satisfaction."[62] Ideally, then, a woman's life in her new home marks the end as well as the beginning of her development. Instead of continuing to progress through her experiences within the home (sex preeminently being one of them), a woman becomes passive and unthinking again, yielding to the passions and development of her spouse.

[58] See, in particular, Terry Pinkard, *Hegel's Phenomenology: The Sociality of Reason* (Cambridge: Cambridge University Press, 1994), 305–6; Joan Landes, "Hegel's Conception of the Family," in *The Family in Political Thought*, ed. Jean Bethke Elshtain (Amherst: University of Massachusetts Press, 1982), 139; Oona Ceder, "The Family, the State, and Citizenship in Aristotle's, G. W. F. Hegel's, and J. S. Mill's Political Thought" (PhD diss., Stanford University, 2000), 10–11, 372, 397.

[59] See Knox, *Philosophy of Right*, 118, § 176, and its addition, 265–66.

[60] This point is made with particular clarity by Ceder, "The Family, the State, and Citizenship," 10–11.

[61] See Knox, *Philosophy of Right*, 263, § 166, and its addition on pages 263–64.

[62] Knox, *Philosophy of Right*, 112, § 163. See also Hegel's *Philosophy of Nature*, where he specifically rules out sex as a source of "theoretical intuition" and insists that during and after sex woman "remains in her undeveloped unity." See M. J. Petry, ed. and trans., *Hegel's Philosophy of Nature*, vol. 3, *Organics* (London: George Allen and Unwin, 1970), 173–75, § 368 and addition.

Though Hegel allows for divorce in cases of estrangement, he sees this as an accident that can only mark a step backward for a woman. Exiting her husband's home, she must return to her family's, resuming the life and role in society she possessed previously as daughter and sister. (It should also be said that though Hegel allowed for divorce, he felt that political and ecclesiastical authorities should regulate this procedure to make sure it complied with ethical standards and was not mere caprice.)[63]

Comparing the Hegelian narrative behind Varvara's liberation with Hegel's views in the *Philosophy of Right*, we can see that there are striking differences as well as similarities. Hegel did not believe in compulsion in marriage and thus like Mikhail and Varvara would have judged the Diakov marriage as invalid if compelled. But Russian law was much more restrictive about divorce than Hegel (not allowing, for example, divorce on grounds of estrangement).[64] Walking Varvara back to the position of dutiful daughter, living in her parents' home, was neither legally nor practically possible. In addition, Mikhail desired to awaken his sister to reality—in part, as suggested above, as proof of his own activity as a real man. For this reason, he posited her marriage not only as a moment of illusion and compulsion but as the beginning of a painful and profoundly conflictual process by which she was gradually brought to a more conscious understanding of her life. This understanding now pointed her away from both husband and family, abroad to some new, conscious existence that Hegel would not have understood or at least not have recognized as progressive or historical. In effect, Varvara's flawed marriage becomes the middle term in her development from unconscious member of her family to one of a new breed of conscious and "real" people—a breed born in conflict and strife Hegel believed women should never know. Perhaps the most important difference, then, between the narrative behind Varvara's liberation and Hegel's is that Mikhail's scheme makes his sister's development—and her experiences in private life—historical. Instead of having her entire freedom subsumed in the liberation of marriage, a brief moment that essentially makes no difference in her consciousness, Varvara's marriage becomes the beginning of her rise to reality.

There are striking differences as well between how Mikhail imagined his sister's new, self-conscious existence and Hegel's presumptions about femi-

---

[63] On these points, see Benjamin R. Barber, "Spirit's Phoenix and History's Owl, or the Incoherence of Dialectics in Hegel's Account of Women," *Political Theory* 16, no. 1 (February 1988): 5–28; Pinkard, *Hegel's Phenomenology*, 307–8; and Ceder, "The Family, the State, and Citizenship," 10–11.

[64] Wagner, *Marriage*, 67.

nine psychology and behavior. In his letters home, Mikhail time and again urged his sister to be firm ("Dear Varinka, you must be firm"; "Are you strong, Varinka?"; "In the name of heaven, have courage and firmness!").[65] This was because he imagined firmness to be the behavioral style of the real person. To be firm was to display a certain stoicism, a faith in Spirit combined with an equal faith in self ("Belief in God and firmness in our decisions: those are our devices!")[66] But in Hegel's world, such stoicism and the rational alienation from circumstance it implied were masculine virtues. Women's reason in Hegel is marked by immediate emotion, full commitment to the family, and unconscious passivity.[67] To be firm, by contrast, symbolized a conspiratorial withdrawal from circumstance into a world of indifferent logic. One acted not out of emotion, caprice, or credulousness, but from a sober assessment of the situation and with the end in mind.

Varvara's letters record her attempts to adopt a new firmness in her life. She reported that she was picking her fights with her parents and winning their acquiescence to her journey by force of conviction. She transcribed a lengthy conversation with her husband word for word, showing how she calmly defeated his hysterics point by point.[68] Sister Tatyana praised her letters to Diakov as "cleverly"—that is, calculatedly—written. "It's true, Misha," Varvara wrote as if surprising herself, "it seems to be no joke that I am starting to leave the stage of *Schönseligkeit*—it is time, long ago time, that I did!"[69]

Toward the end of December, however, Varvara's firmness began to crack and her doubts—about the philosophical frame her brother wanted to place around her life, at least—began to develop. She wavered about understanding her life in her brother's new terms even when things were going well. She was uncomfortable with the notion that her present redeemed her past ("No matter what you say, Misha, I cannot yet convince myself that much of my

[65] See Bakunin's letter to his sisters, 24 December 1837 (*Sobranie*, II:93); to his sisters, end of December 1837 (ibid., 128); and to his sisters, 25 December 1837 (ibid., 94).

[66] See Bakunin's letter to Varvara, 22 February 1838 (*Sobranie*, II:138).

[67] Here I follow Genevieve Lloyd in seeing Hegel as positing distinctive kinds of reason for men and women. See Lloyd, *The Man of Reason: "Male" and "Female" in Western Philosophy*, 2nd ed. (Minneapolis: University of Minnesota Press, 1984), 80–85.

[68] This fascinating letter in the form of a play is IRLI f. 16, op. 4, no. 460; begins ll. 61–62 and finishes ll. 58–59.

[69] V. A. Diakova to M. A. Bakunin, letter of [end of November–early December, 1837?], f. 16, op. 4, no. 460, ll. 36–37. Although this letter bears no date, it was clearly written after Bakunin's departure for Moscow but before receipt of news from him. Diakova also describes her firmness with her parents in a letter to Bakunin of 30 November [1837?], IRLI f. 16, op. 4, no. 661, l. 79 (again dated by reference to Bakunin's departure).

life has not been lost"). However logical, the Hegelian world of rational reality seemed cold and galling. It was upsetting for her to think that the only way to awaken to the truth of her life was "to march sweetly to negation, to see oneself stripped little by little of one's grandeur, of all of one's dignity and noble attributes, to be returned little by little to the sentiment of one's nullity--this is horrible."[70] Whereas the heroines of Varvara's youth were saints and martyrs—individuals who suffered for a cause they believed in—the model of personality her brother advanced called for a gradual and punishing surrender to reality's inhuman logic. One became real by accepting one's life as a progressively unfolding bildungsroman, in which painful experience gradually substituted a more powerful, objective content for weak and subjective feeling.

Yet there were days when her Hegelian firmness seemed no more empowering than her previous misery. December revealed that the household was full of vicious gossip against her and that her father was much more opposed to her departure than it had seemed. Diakov veered between anger and despair, each dangerous in its own way. "Take me from here when you can, Misha--only with my departure can all this end," Varvara wrote in late December. She asked why it was they could not rip their sisters "from this snake pit as well?"[71]

To Mikhail, at least, it was immediately clear that while Varvara's desire to leave home was not eroding, her faith in the higher logic he assigned to it was. He reminded Varvara to remain calm and alive to the logic at work in her life, especially at this crucial moment. "*Die Zeit der Verklärung ist schön da,*" he wrote in mid-December, "the sun of Truth has risen, let yourself look upon it. No more doubt, no more numbness."[72] This letter arrived, however, just as circumstances took a turn for the worse at Priamukhino. Their father began giving Diakov legal advice, informing his son-in-law that there were legal remedies for Varvara's recalcitrance. She could be compelled to live with him; alternatively, the courts could force her to give up her son. To calm her

---

[70] See V. A. Diakova to M. A. Bakunin, letter of [mid-December 1837?], f. 16, op. 4, no. 460, ll. 42–43. Letter dated by reference to struggles in Bakunin household at that time.

[71] See V. A. Diakova to M. A. Bakunin, letter of [late December, 1837?], IRLI f. 16, op. 4, no. 460, l. 2. Letter dated by reference to worsening situation in the Bakunin household, leading up to Varvara's flight to Kozytsino in early January.

[72] "The time of transfiguration has come" (the rest of the passage is also in German). See Bakunin's letter to Varvara, December 1837 (*Sobranie*, II:85). Though the exact date of this letter is unknown, it is clearly written in reference to Diakova's misgivings. See similar exhortations not to "fall into the sleep of limited subjectivity" in his letters to his sisters of 13 December 1837 (ibid., 86–87) and 14 December 1837 (*Oeuvres [CD-ROM]*, 2–3).

down, Mikhail reassured Varvara that Russia's enlightened government would never enforce such "ancient laws."[73] (One doubts she took much comfort from this.) By early 1838, Varvara was in such visible despair that Mikhail hurriedly returned home from Moscow to shore up her spirits and place her in the care of an aunt.[74]

By this time, however, Varvara had lost all firmness; indeed, she was visibly in despair. She expressed dismay that outsiders were interpreting her struggle as a "heroic action." Her marriage was her fault ("she blames herself entirely for her horrible situation," sister Tatiana noted), and she no longer saw it as illustrative of a greater principle.[75] To some, this guilt suggested a return to conventional thinking. Belinsky, reading her letters, was shocked by her despondency and began to wonder if she desired reconciliation with her husband. This suspicion was fanned by the fact that, feeling under siege within her family, Varvara considered taking refuge at her husband's estate, Ivanovskoe.[76]

Far from being reconciled to her life with Diakov, however, Varvara was becoming ever more horrified by it. At first glance, this may seem odd, because Diakov, a kind man when not angry, had finally agreed to her journey abroad. Mikhail triumphantly declared his brother-in-law to be a member of their camp and invited him to come to Moscow. But for Varvara, her husband's generosity only underscored the perversity of her condition. As a woman, she was bound to her husband's whims, which seemed to be guided not by some higher logic but rather by his all-too-human impulses. "*N*[ikolai] remains well-inclined," she wrote Mikhail,

> but who can say for sure. He remains, after all, but a good and weak creature (as you have finally recognized, to my great pleasure). My situation remains so awful. I cannot resist, even now he has every right to kiss me, to caress me—he can enter my room at any time, and say to me whatever he pleases—and I must be silent, and cannot forbid anything—you, Michel, as a man will not understand all the humiliation of

[73] See Bakunin's letters to his sisters, 24 and 25 December 1837 (*Sobranie*, II:92–95). Diakov's broad discretion over his wife was, in fact, not "ancient" but imperial. See Freeze, "Bringing Order."

[74] See Bakunin's letter to his sisters, 31 December 1837 (*Sobranie*, II:129–30); and Kornilov, *Molodye gody*, 362–66.

[75] Tatiana described her sister's graphic despair in a letter to Mikhail of [January 1838?], IRLI f. 16, op. 4, no. 582, ll. 71–72. Dated by reference to Varvara's escape to Kozytsino, her aunt's estate.

[76] See Belinsky's letter to M. A. Bakunin, 1 January 1838 (*PSS*, XI:226). These doubts, of course, bore their polemical fruit several months later.

this condition. I am nothing anymore for him, and required to put up with all his liberties. How hard this contradiction is only a woman's heart can feel. You will tell me that I should not allow it—but one cannot take everything away from him at once, and if I really did that, then all would be lost. Only I can give his decision force. If he distances himself from me even once everything is lost, he will fall into enemy hands, and then I will have nothing left to hope for.[77]

In effect, then, Varvara came to the humiliating realization that her emancipation required her prostitution. If she were to act cleverly enough to keep Diakov's loyalties and make her escape, she must submit to his caresses. As a married woman, she felt she had no other options. This was a side of reality no man would ever know: patriarchal subjugation under the law.

What was worse, the logic her brother assigned her liberation implied that Diakov's painful touch played a vital role in her rise to reality. Its function was to destroy her illusions and thereby open her eyes to true reality. Varvara could not accept this and regarded her sufferings as unjust. "Do not be angry at my great impatience to leave here," Varvara wrote to her brother in January or early February 1838.

My relations with N[ikolai] become more difficult every day, more intolerable, more degrading—his caresses soil me, and I cannot rid myself of them. That is the origin of my morbid impatience to be liberated from him. I am not afraid of suffering, but I am afraid of everything that stains me and casts a shadow on my spirit. You yourself said, Misha, that the soul is not separate from the body—that internal life is inseparable from external, thought from action—and I sense the justice of your words, and for that very reason, when he is here, I cannot be at peace, something always alarms and tortures me—my relations with him contradict the truth—and this contradiction oppresses and claws me—Liberate me as quickly as you can, Misha![78]

Conscious but not yet free, able to govern circumstance only through sacrificing her body, Varvara stood her brother's logic on its head. Her external

[77] V. A. Diakova to M. A. Bakunin, letter of [January 1837?], IRLI f. 16, op. 4, no. 458, l. 28. Dated by Nikolai's recent decision and Mikhail's recent departure. The "enemy hands" in question are those of her parents, still opposed to her journey.

[78] See V. A. Dyakova to M. A. Bakunin, undated letter of [late January–early February 1838?], f. 16, op. 4, no. 460, ll. 49–50. Dated by reference to the state of her liberation at that time: Diakov's tentative support and friendship with Mikhail.

liberty would have to be achieved before her internal life could develop. Before then, her dishonest and forced sexual relations with Diakov would not raise her consciousness and indeed were potentially scarring.

As Varvara knew he would, Mikhail responded to such letters by urging his sister yet again to be firm. If her husband's caresses were painful, she should simply refuse them, "although in no case should you compromise his dignity."[79] But Mikhail did not explain just how she was to manage the trick of respecting Diakov's dignity while maintaining some of her own. Varvara responded by declaring that she would "wake only under another sun":

> There are so many humiliating contradictions in my existence, my position now is so horrible, that I would have to go mad, if I did not have the prospect of a life that is free and truly human. All my efforts right now are directed toward seizing it, so much so that the present slips across me as a bad dream, of the sort that leaves with the rising sun. I will sleep, then, as long as it is possible to sleep. . . . I say to myself: sleep. Sleep, for if I awake, I will be lost. O, Michel, Michel, a sleep of this sort is reprehensible. But for me it is the only means of salvation. Thanks to this sleep, a thousand sensations pass one after another through my soul, and escape without leaving a trace there.[80]

A more complete reversal of the logic her brother assigned to her emancipation is hard to imagine. Rather than rising to consciousness through the painful force of reality, Varvara imagined that she must break out of her previous world entirely, keeping herself as numb as possible until then. As woman, it seemed to her, she had no other choice. To embrace her brother's vision of reality was to accept as necessary what seemed to her to be injustices. It was also to ignore the very real role that involuntary sex played in her life, as symbolized by her husband's right to enter her room and seize her.

By April 1838, the final arrangements for Varvara's journey were completed.[81] Her husband remained true to his decision, borrowing four thousand rubles from his brother to arrange for his wife's journey. Varvara's parents finally relented as well. In May the Diakovs left home together for

---

[79] See Bakunin's letter of the beginning of February 1838 (*Sobranie*, II:133).

[80] See V. A. Dyakova to M. A. Bakunin, undated letter of [mid-February, 1838?], IRLI f. 16, op. 4, no. 458, l. 27. Dated by Bakunin's response of the end of February 1838, regretting that Diakova feels she must "sleep" (see *Sobranie*, I:141).

[81] Bakunin relates this news to his sisters in a letter of 22 February 1838 (*Sobranie*, II:138); see also Kornilov, *Molodye gody*, 366–69.

St. Petersburg. Nikolai still planned to accompany his wife and son abroad, returning once they were settled there. When the couple reached the capital, however, he changed his mind and turned back home instead. After living a few uncomfortable weeks with relatives, Varvara and her son Aleksandr boarded a steamship for Lübeck, finally leaving Russia in the middle of June. Her brother Mikhail, who had left no stone unturned in trying to raise money to go with them, remained behind for another two years. In the end, Varvara settled not in Karlsbad but in Berlin. Her departure, as police reports would later testify, started a scandal that set tongues gossiping all across Tver Province.

⊛⫣⫤⊛

At first glance, Herzen's famous maxim that Hegel was his generation's "algebra of revolution" falls short of the mark, when applied to Mikhail Bakunin. The political views he developed under Hegel's influence in the late 1830s were archconservative: even as Varvara was preparing to go abroad, he published an article in the journal *Moscow Observer* that called on his contemporaries to embrace contemporary Russia as a rational product of Russia's historical evolution.[82] Behind this political conservatism, however, Mikhail's own embrace of "rational reality" led him to form his first conspiracy, a plot to undo his sister's subjection that was, in the end, quite successful in turning the Bakunin home upside down. For him, at least, Hegel's algebra was important not as an invitation to a certain political stance but as a call to imagine his own historical agency as expressed in deeds as well as words. Throughout his life thereafter, Mikhail would be known for his incredible appetite for forming such historical conspiracies, practicing again and again the skills he had first perfected during "Varinka's liberation."

Varvara, however, like many future members of Mikhail's conspiracies, had a bittersweet reaction to Hegel's algebra, at least as her brother construed it. Initially invigorated by this new philosophy of action and liberation, Varvara rethought its rationale over time. She had doubts about her brother's scheme, precisely because of its implications for her life as a woman. These doubts did not, however, make her less eager for her physical emancipation; nor was she reconciled to the paternal logic of her existing family life. Instead, Varvara's doubts about her liberation centered on the question of whether her painful marriage and struggle to leave it represented the fulfillment of

---

[82] For more on the *Moscow Observer* and Mikhail's participation in it, see chapter 9.

some higher idea. Despite her brother's persistent urgings, she refused to accept that some rational reality was at work in her life or that she should regard her painful experiences as a necessary process of maturation. She could not recognize the marital order to which she was subjected as being of her own making, even though she believed her marriage was a terrible mistake. Comfortable neither with a theory that ignored her gender nor with one that used gender to naturalize her sexual subjugation within the family, Varvara expressed doubts about both, even as the day of her departure for Europe approached. Mikhail largely ignored these doubts, by now convinced that his main aims had been achieved. Varvara's misgivings, however, were closely observed by another commentator, who soon mounted a fierce critique not only of Mikhail's claims of consciousness and maturity but of the noble domestic world in which they were developed.

CHAPTER NINE

Belinsky

When Mikhail returned to Moscow in November of 1837—several months before Varvara's liberation—he shared an apartment with his old friend Belinsky. As usual, Mikhail explained that his departure from home was necessary for the further development of his inner life. "Moscow is necessary for me, because there I can find far more means for my studies, and in particular for the study of that science which comprises my whole life's exclusive goal."[1] The truth of the matter was, however, that Mikhail had actually finished his romance with Idealism. Having sweated through Hegel's modern calculus, he declared himself a "real man." Though he continued to study while awaiting the opportunity to go abroad, he was eager to begin playing his role of awakener and emancipator on some broader stage outside the home. "Es ist Zeit zu sprechen," Mikhail wrote to the Beyer sisters in March 1838: "The time has come to speak."[2]

Fortunately, a golden opportunity seemed to be at hand. In early 1838, Vasilii Androsov, the editor of a journal called the *Moscow Observer*, offered to turn its editorial reins over to Belinsky. Ailing and isolated in Moscow's literary life, Androsov had seen his journal's subscription lists decline steadily. He hoped that a new and more vigorous editor—with the help of enthusias-

---

[1] Letter to his sisters from the beginning of December 1837 (Bakunin, *Sobranie*, II:75).

[2] Letter to the Beyer sisters of March 1838 (Bakunin, *Sobranie*, II:154; cf. *Oeuvres [CD-ROM]*, 1). On Mikhail's move to Moscow more generally, see A. Kornilov, *Molodye gody Mikhaila Bakunina: Iz istorii russkogo romantizma* (Moscow: M. and S. Sabashnikov, 1915), 414–17; and Iu. G. Oksman, *Letopis' zhizni i tvorchestva V. G. Belinskogo* (Moscow: Gosudarstvennoe izdatel'stvo khudozhestvennoi literatury, 1958), 151–52.

Vissarion Grigorevich Belinsky
(1811–1848). From Belinskii, *PSS*, II.

tic friends recruited from the ranks of Moscow's students — might be able to get the *Observer* going again. Belinsky jumped at the chance. Since the collapse of his previous employer, *Telescope*, he had been unable to find a replacement position and had been reduced to utter poverty. Mikhail instantly decided that the *Moscow Observer* was a perfect platform for "my first entrance into the literary profession."[3] This was especially true since he and Belinsky, after some philosophical disagreements in the previous year, had come to a common agreement that Hegel's philosophy — and more specifically, his notion that reality is rational — represented the last word in contemporary politics, society, and aesthetics.[4]

The first issue of *Moscow Observer* fully reflected this program. Belinsky's contribution, a lengthy review of *Hamlet* as performed by the famous Russian actor Mochalov, presented Shakespeare's most famous tragedy as a meditation on maturity and its painful acquisition. Life, the critic speculates, is given to two types of people: "some vegetate, others live." Those who wish to

---

[3] Letter to the Beyer sisters, 13 March 1838 (Bakunin, *Sobranie*, II:154).

[4] On the transfer of the *Observer* to Belinsky and its initial, Hegelian program, see V. S. Nechaeva, *V. G. Belinskii. Zhizn' i tvorchestvo, 1836–1841* (Moscow: Izdatel'stvo Akademii nauk SSSR, 1961), 99–108.

live—and make their life into a meaningful "deed"—must pass from their youth to adulthood. Yet "this internal enlightenment requires much struggle, much suffering, and for this many are called but few are chosen."[5] Mikhail, meanwhile, translated a series of speeches that Hegel had made while teaching at the Nuremberg Gymnasium in the first decade of the 1800s. Though Hegel's intent was to call his young charges to self-education (*Bildung*), Mikhail used a long preface to the work to call his generation to enter and work in the world, leaving behind its sentimental illusions. "We hope," wrote Bakunin confidently, "that the new generation will affiliate itself with our beautiful Russian reality, and abandoning all empty pretensions to genius will finally feel a need to become real Russian people."[6] Bakunin concluded by explaining how humanity, having left behind its infancy in the Middle Ages, was now suffering through a period of skepticism and abstraction, on the way to a more full-blooded maturity.[7]

The first issue of the *Moscow Observer* thus presented a bold, independent front, one that went out of its way to present its contributors as grown men, emancipated from the circumstances surrounding their youth and united by a common vision of reality. Behind the scenes, however, things were far from as simple as that. The youths Belinsky and Mikhail had lived through were, in fact, quite different. Increasingly, their sense of what was real differed as well. Though they agreed in regarding reality as a rational, maturing force, they came to disagree about just where and how this embodied reason expressed itself in Russian life. Mikhail was satisfied that he had already solved the problem, once and for all, with his application of Hegelian categories to the conflicts of his private life. He saw himself as the natural leader of Hegelianism in Russia and Belinsky as the pupil.[8] In a series of famous polemical letters written later that year, however, Belinsky threw off that yoke and insisted that he possessed a clearer understanding of reality. Furthermore, he critiqued Mikhail's self-presentation as a "fighter for truth" on the stage of private life as a grotesque comedy, a farce. Such an intellectualized

---

[5] V. G. Belinskii, "'Gamlet.' Drama Shekspira. Mochalov v roli Gamleta," in *PSS*, II:256–57.

[6] Mikhail Bakunin, "Gimnazicheskie rechi Gegelia. Predislovie perevodchika," in *Sobranie*, II:166. On Hegel's original speeches, see Terry Pinkard, *Hegel: A Biography* (Cambridge: Cambridge University Press, 2000), 275–305. See also Martine Del Giudice, "Bakunin's 'Preface to Hegel's "Gymnasium Lectures"': The Problem of Alienation and the Reconciliation with Reality," *Canadian-American Slavic Studies* 16, no. 2 (Summer 1982): 161–89.

[7] Both Bakunin and Belinsky refer to this three-stage narrative, which, though common to Idealism, is infused with themes of suffering and struggle taken from Fichte and Hegel.

[8] Though I describe this in more detail below, it has been established by prior biographers. See, e.g., Kornilov, *Molodye gody*, 417–22.

approach to domestic conflict was abnormal, Belinsky declared; it had had horrible consequences for the woman it was meant to save (Varvara), and it had only encouraged Mikhail to draw away from the actual reality of life. Through this critique, Belinsky laid his own claim to a title that Mikhail had so assiduously sought in the past year: the title of being the first man of his generation to fully assimilate the legacy of Idealism and thereby become a mature, real man.

Crucial to Belinsky's critique was his status as an outsider to the world of distinction and liberty that noble homes like Priamukhino represented. Indeed, Belinsky's claim to be the first real man of their cohort rested on his immersion, as a poor and relatively unfree individual, in the prose of everyday life. Yet there are several ironies—long observed, but never satisfactorily resolved—surrounding Belinsky's ambition to usher in a new and independent era in Russian social thought. Though he was indeed born outside the Bakunin's Arcadia, the new historical persona he crafted in his letters to Mikhail depended on it. What he saw and felt at Priamukhino became an integral part of Belinsky's influential story of development. His participation in the Bakunins' idealized domestic life gave him access to its world of distinction, while in his recollections he drew a withering portrait of estate life's limitations and flaws. All of this was meant to suggest that Belinsky, the historical man, was a new kind of Russian thinker, independent of the private realm of culture the Bakunins represented. Yet even though he was indeed a journalist living in Moscow, much of his historical reputation as a transitional figure in Russian life would depend on the historical impression he made at Priamukhino. To understand why this is so, we need to know a little more about Belinsky the man, the myth, and the myth maker.

⊛⁄⊁⊛

Belinsky's father was a naval doctor; his mother, the daughter of a ship captain. Belinsky himself was born near St. Petersburg in 1811, but the family soon moved to Chembar, a town in Penza Province, far to the south and east of Moscow, where Belinsky's father worked as a doctor, eventually earning hereditary membership in the Russian nobility in 1830. Belinsky, because of inadequate documentation, did not receive this status until 1847. Indeed, his social status throughout most of his life was somewhat indeterminate: poor but free, not a peasant or a burgher but neither a cleric nor a noble—a "man of miscellaneous background" [*raznochinets*], as the Imperial Russian expression had it. After completing grammar school in Chembar and studying for a few years at the Penza Gymnasium, young Belinsky in 1829 made the trip to Moscow, where he took a chance on the entrance examinations. His lack of proper identity papers held him up at first (as it would throughout his life). But in late 1829, he was accepted. "I expect that in *legendary* Chembar," he wrote to his parents, with a sarcasm aimed at his doubters, "people will be surprised that I have been admitted to the Imperial Moscow University as a *student*. However, I care little for the opinions of Chembarians. Though they couldn't appreciate me in *Chembar*, they have in Moscow! I think *everyone knows* that between Chembar and Moscow there is no small difference and between Chembar residents and Moscow professors there is also *a little distance*."[9]

Like many students, Belinsky hoped his admission to Moscow University would help him overcome the disadvantages of his birth—his poverty, his lack of distinction, and (perhaps most nagging of all) his sense of provincialism. Unfortunately for Belinsky, it was not as easy as all that. In 1832, he was thrown out of the university as a student of "limited abilities" (his protests against the treatment of state-supported students like him seems to have been the real reason). Then began a struggle to sustain himself as a journalist and literary critic that lasted the rest of his short life. For most of the 1830s he lived in Moscow, writing for a series of journals, such as *Telescope* and *Moscow Observer*. In October 1839, during a time of increasingly tense relations with his Moscow friends (and Mikhail in particular), Belinsky moved to St. Petersburg to take up an editorial position with the journal *Notes of the Fatherland*. He died there in May 1848, still impoverished but finally documented, having received confirmation of his nobility from Penza just a few months before.[10] Yet Belinsky destroyed his personal archive in February 1848, as his increasingly radical social views drew the attention of imperial authorities and he began to fear he would be searched and arrested.[11]

A tireless writer, Belinsky was one of the most prodigiously published and historically inclined journalists of his day. In essay after essay for a period of nearly two decades, he sought to place the development of Russian social consciousness into a historical frame. Yet despite this furious and detailed

---

[9] Letter to his parents of 9 October 1829 (Belinskii, *PSS*, XI:19). Emphasis in the original. On Belinsky's early biography and youth, see V. S. Nechaeva, *V. G. Belinskii. Uchenie v universitete i rabota v "Teleskope" i "Molve" 1829–1836* (Moscow: Izdatel'stvo Akademii nauk SSSR, 1954), 1–161; B. F. Egorov, "V. G. Belinskii," in *Russkie pisateli: Biograficheskii slovar'*, ed. V. N. Baskakov and V. E. Vatsuro, vol. 1 (Moscow: Sovetskaia entsiklopediia, 1989), 206–17; and Oksman, *Letopis'*.

[10] Belinskii, *PSS*, XII:474; Oksman, *Letopis'*, 544.

[11] Oksman, *Letopis'*, 548.

record of publication—or perhaps because of it—for much of the nineteenth century his legacy was difficult to interpret. Belinsky was among the first Russian writers who might with justice be called a public intellectual, as opposed to a cleric, court poet, or gentleman of letters. His essays, published periodically, tempted his readers to try to follow his intellectual evolution. This, however, was not an easy task. In the early 1830s, Belinsky spoke with a brash Schellingian voice, easily recognizable to those familiar with the intellectual tastes and scientific pretensions of his mentors, Moscow University's professors. Then in the late 1830s his writing grew ever more abstract and technical, sprouting Fichtean and Hegelian terms. Simultaneously, his political views became more pronounced, first leaning in a shockingly statist and apologetic direction. His move to St. Petersburg ushered in a new period of creativity, one marked at first by a certain mystical humility before the city and then by an increasing (and implicitly radical) engagement with sociological themes. Contemporaries presumed that censorship—and the still rickety nature of the platform provided by Russian journalism—explained why the famed critic had not made the reasoning behind his intellectual development clear. This still left open the question of what logic drove this philosophical odyssey. The answer, contemporaries believed, lay somewhere "*behind* his articles and expressions," in the life of Belinsky "the man" rather than Belinsky "the writer."[12]

Yet this was a much less visible figure, one about whom furious controversy also swirled. On the one hand, there was the Belinsky of radical lore, an individual of fierce, independent convictions who passionately loved truth. He was a social and intellectual outsider with the "spirit of a gladiator," who symbolized (by virtue of his very appearance) the dawning of a new, more democratic age in Russian literary life.[13] Yet there was another oral tradition about Belinsky as well: one that remembered him as an unpolished intellect gently mocked by Stankevich as "furious Vissarion" because of his

[12] See A. N. Pypin to P. V. Annenkov, letter of 1 February 1874, in T. Ukhmylova, "Materialy o Belinskom Iz Arkhiva A. N. Pypina," *Literaturnoe Nasledstvo* 57 (1951): 305 (emphasis in the original); and also S. Vengerov, "Pypin, Aleksandr Nikolaevich," in *Entsiklopedicheskii slovar'*, vol. 25(St. Petersburg: Tipo-litografiia I. A. Efrona, 1898), 892–94.

[13] The phrase "spirit of a gladiator" is Herzen's. See Alexander Herzen, *My Past and Thoughts*, ed. Dwight Macdonald, trans. Constance Garnett (Berkeley: University of California Press, 1973), 237–45, esp. 241 (cf. Gertsen, *Sobranie*, IX:31). For similar portraits, see also N. G. Chernyshevskii, "Ocherki gogolevskogo perioda russkoi literatury," in *Polnoe sobranie sochinenii*, ed. V. Ia. Kirpotin, vol. 3 (Moscow: OGIZ Gosudarstvennoe izdatel'stvo khudozhestvennoi literatury, 1947), 177–309; A. N. Pypin, *Belinsky, ego zhizn' i perepiska* (St. Petersburg: Tipografiia M. M. Stasiulevicha, 1876).

unsteady temperament. This tradition spoke in compassionate but condescending terms about a man who bore the marks of a "harsh, isolated upbringing," who was given to "distraction" and extremes and whose intellectual agenda had been set by a series of charismatic friends, among them Mikhail Bakunin.[14] Belinsky's defenders denounced this construction as a snobbish slander—the last gasp of noble pretension—while their critics accused his supporters of turning their flesh-and-blood hero into an idol. Taken together, these polemics generated enough heat to make Belinsky a legend shortly after his own time—"the greatest Russian myth," as Isaiah Berlin has written, "in the nineteenth century, detestable to the supporters of autocracy, the Orthodox church, and fervid nationalism, disturbing to the elegant and fastidious lovers of western classicism, and for the same reasons the idealised ancestor of both the reformers and the revolutionaries of the second half of the century."[15]

In the late 1800s—under circumstances described later—Belinsky's private letters began to be published. This made it possible for Russia's reading public to begin to try to reconcile Belinsky the man, the writer, and the myth. Much of the scholarship about Belinsky since then has tried to master the intricacies of his intellectual evolution, with varying degrees of success.[16] Only relatively recently have scholars—most notably Lydia Ginzburg and Marshall Shatz—begun to examine Belinsky the myth maker: the autobiographer and storyteller who once said of himself "I stand between two worlds." They have noted that Belinsky placed Priamukhino at the center of the conflict of his life, using a polemical correspondence with Mikhail Bakunin to articulate his own transition from Idealism to the mature, socially oriented world view for which he was famous.[17] But why was Belinsky's own Priamukhino romance so important to his self-invention? The key, it seems, to answering this

---

[14] See Edward J. Brown, *Stankevich and His Moscow Circle* (Stanford: Stanford University Press, 1966), 86–90; P. V. Annenkov, *Nikolai Vladimirovich Stankevich: Perepiska ego i biografiia* (Moscow: Tipografiia Kat'kova, 1857), 39–40, 126–32.

[15] Isaiah Berlin, "A Remarkable Decade," in *Russian Thinkers*, ed. Henry Hardy and Aileen Kelly (London: Penguin, 1994), 152.

[16] See, e.g., Herbert E. Bowman, *Vissarion Belinski, 1811–1848: A Study in the Origins of Social Criticism in Russia* (Cambridge: Harvard University Press, 1954); Victor Terras, *Belinskij and Russian Literary Criticism: The Heritage of Organic Aesthetics* (Madison: University of Wisconsin Press, 1974); and E. Iu. Tikhonova, *Mirovozzrenie molodogo Belinskogo* (Moscow: Rossiiskaia Akademiia nauk, Institut Rossiiskoi istorii, 1993).

[17] Lydia Ginzburg, *On Psychological Prose*, trans. and ed. Judson Rosengrant (Princeton: Princeton University Press, 1991), 58–107, esp. 81; Marshall Shatz, "Bakunin, Turgenev, and *Rudin*," in *The Golden Age of Russian Literature and Thought*, ed. Derek Offord (New York: St. Martin's, 1992), 103–14.

question lies in exploring the process by which Belinsky replaced a civilizing scenario designed for him by the Stankevich circle with a historical romance of his own invention.

⊛⁄₅⁊⊛

Belinsky first met Mikhail Bakunin in Stankevich's apartment in early 1835, though their substantive acquaintance really took place the following winter, when Mikhail was living in Moscow and studying Fichte.[18] When Stankevich left Moscow that spring, they became still closer friends. Belinsky came in the evenings to the apartment Mikhail shared with some other former students, and together they discussed Fichte's lectures on a scholar's vocation and talked about the calling still forming in their own heads. "Our hope, our plans for the future—these are the typical subjects of our conversations, always animated, during which every man says what he feels and thinks, not the things he feels obligated to feel and think," Mikhail wrote to the Beyer sisters in late May 1836.[19]

Stankevich and his friends valued Belinsky for his industry and talent. Alone among them, he was already beginning to make a name for himself in literature.[20] Yet Belinsky's bold criticism roiled the small literary world of Moscow, and Stankevich himself worried that Belinsky was wasting his natural gifts on undisciplined polemics.[21] Stankevich, of course, could afford to be more scholarly, since he did not have to earn a living by making a literary name for himself (or even, for that matter, to publish at all). Belinsky at the time was struggling to support himself and constantly having to borrow money, which he found degrading.

It was during this time—May 1836—that Mikhail Bakunin, as he was leaving Moscow, invited Belinsky to visit him in Priamukhino later that summer. At the thought of spending a month in the countryside with the Bakunins, Belinsky later recalled, "[M]y eyes grew dim and the earth burned beneath my feet. I couldn't imagine myself in that society, in that sacred and

---

[18] Oksman, *Letopis'*, 92, 117.

[19] Letter to the Beyer sisters of 7 May 1836 (Bakunin, *Sobranie*, I:301).

[20] See, e.g., "Nichto o nichem, ili otchet g. izdateliu 'Teleskopa' za poslednee polugodie (1835) russkoi literatury," in Belinskii, *PSS*, II:7–50. On Belinsky's equally controversial first essay, "Literaturnye mechtaniia," see Oksman, *Letopis'*, 73–88.

[21] See Stankevich's claims to this effect in his letter of 14 June 1835 to Neverov (*Perepiska*, 325). See also Brown, *Stankevich and His Moscow Circle*, 88–89.

mystery-filled atmosphere."[22] When Mikhail repeated this invitation in August by letter—and accompanied his invitation with seventy-five rubles to pay for Belinsky's trip—the critic thought again and decided to go.[23]

Belinsky's visit was surrounded by high expectations on all sides. Stankevich was sure that the Bakunins' civilized home life would smooth Belinsky's rough edges and give him an ideal around which to orient his behavior. "Belinsky is taking a rest from his wearisome, lonely life of drudgery [*burlatskaia zhizn'*]," he wrote to Neverov in September 1836,

> I am sure this trip will have a beneficial effect on him. A man of noble feeling, with a healthy, free mind and good conscience, he needs only one thing: to see life in its most noble sense—to experience it, and not just to imagine it—to know moral happiness, and that a harmony between the inner and outer worlds is possible—a harmony that to him has seemed inaccessible so far, but in which he now believes. How this pure sphere of mild, Christian family life can soften the soul![24]

Upon arrival, Belinsky desperately tried to fit in to the Bakunins' legendary life. In a feat of salon polish, he carefully copied several poems by Pushkin into Liubov's poetry album.[25]

Almost immediately, however, this carefully planned civilizing scenario flew off its rails. Belinsky felt uneasy in the manor house and in the company of noblewomen in particular, and so he raced restlessly up and down the stairs, secluding himself in his guest room whenever possible. Even so, embarrassment after embarrassment followed. At dinner, seeking to show his independence, he launched into an impromptu defense of the French Revolution; his hosts the Bakunin parents greeted the outburst with an awkward silence, while the younger generation giggled at Belinsky's indiscretion. More humiliation followed when Belinsky found himself unable to participate in group readings of German literature, since he did not know German. (Mikhail even had the indelicacy to poke fun at his ignorance. Belinsky instantly felt a "malice towards everyone, and even towards the innocent German language," which only served to remind him "of my deep humilia-

[22] Letter to Mikhail Bakunin of 12–24 October 1838 (Belinskii, *PSS:* XI:329).

[23] Ibid.

[24] Letter to Ia. M. Neverov of 21 September 1836 (Stankevich, *Perepiska,* 363).

[25] Belinsky's entries are IRLI f. 16, op. 6, no. 57, ll. 82–122.

"The Prophet" by Pushkin, as copied by Vissarion Belinsky into Liubov Bakunina's poetry album. From IRLI f. 16, op. 6, No. 57.

tion.")[26] The whole affair then came to a nightmarish halt in November 1836, when the scandal surrounding *Telescope* broke out.

In sum, Belinsky's visit to the Bakunin home in the fall of 1836 was an awkward disaster, a painful trial that defied the high expectations everyone

[26] See the painful recollections contained in Belinsky's subsequent, polemical correspondence with Mikhail: letter to M. A. Bakunin of 12–24 1838 (*PSS*, XI:320), and letter to M. A. Bakunin, 16 August 1837 (ibid., 173–76, esp. 175). See also Oksman, *Letopis'*, 133–35, esp. 135; Nechaeva, *Belinskii. Uchenie*, 397–404.

projected onto family life and resulted in Belinsky's humiliation rather than his inspiration. "I left Priamukhino still far from the man I thought I was: I was agitated, but still not reborn," Belinsky recalled.[27] The affair might well have been forgotten, had Belinsky not decided—suddenly and provocatively—to make it the subject of a blistering, polemical correspondence between him and Mikhail in the fall of 1838.

❀❀❀

In August 1838, two months after Varvara's emancipation, Liubov Bakunina died of tuberculosis after being severely ill for almost a year. Liubov's slow and painful death brought both grief and guilt. It was hard enough to see her die little by little, under the care of a series of doctors summoned from Moscow, who alternately raised and dashed the Bakunin family's hopes. But the younger Bakunins watched Liubov die in the guilty knowledge that a wide gulf of deception and mutual misunderstanding already separated them from this fading "heavenly angel." The hidden emotions surrounding her death heightened its tragedy.

For Liubov did not just die: she died abandoned by her ideal love, a love Mikhail and her sisters had conspired to help bring about. Stankevich, engaged secretly to Liubov in late 1836, had decided by early 1837 that he did not love her after all. Rethinking the whole affair through Hegelian lenses, he decided that he had committed the classic, youthful sin of falling in love with love. "Perhaps this horrible catastrophe was necessary to save my soul from its sickly *Schönseligkeit* and torpor, and to destroy my imaginary, spectral life and settle me in the real world," Stankevich wrote secretly to Mikhail. Unable to tell Liubov herself, Stankevich used his poor health to postpone the engagement and left for Europe in the summer of 1837.[28] Liubov's sisters tried to soften the blow, but no matter what face they put on it, the galling results of Stankevich's retreat seemed to vindicate their parents' suspicions. Liubov herself, still in love but hardly deceived, had neither the strength nor the restless willpower for "reconciling" contemplation. She withdrew from the younger generation's struggles and campaigns. "With the weakening of her [physical] forces, she has fallen morally," Tatiana wrote to Mikhail in late

---

[27] Letter to M. A. Bakunin, 16 August 1837 (Belinskii, *PSS*, IX:173).

[28] The most detailed examination of the evolution of Stankevich's feelings may be found in Brown, *Stankevich and His Moscow Circle*, 69–79. See also his confessional Hegelian letter to Mikhail of 31 May 1837, *Perepiska*, 625–29.

1837, expressing the uneasy pity the other children felt during Liubov's last months.[29] Afterwards, their consciences lacerated them for being so petty.

Death in fact transformed Liubov into a symbol of an almost saintlike stoicism, of a profound inner poise they had simply not been able to understand. "Our consciousnesses, our intentions, always divided us from her," Mikhail wrote to Varvara on 24 August 1838, "and only now are we able to completely measure the depth of our love for her."[30] Liubov's death similarly stunned the Bakunins' Moscow friends, for whom the sense of guilty awe was just as palpable. Grateful for having the chance to "commit to memory that pale, gentle, holy, beautiful face, a face that expressed a suffering, which had not yet conquered the spirit's power," Belinsky thanked the heavens that he had known Liubov Bakunina: "I knew life's great mystery, not as a presentiment, but as a wonderful, harmonious apparition."[31]

The question, however, immediately arose: why had Liubov's happiness failed so miserably? What could *she* have possibly done wrong? Even writing Stankevich about her death seemed awkward ("How could one possibly write him?" Belinsky asked Mikhail in his letter), because the burden of having been at fault for her sufferings seemed so large.[32] The Bakunins and their friends were reluctant to place the blame entirely on Stankevich, but a reason had to be found, not only for Liubov's sufferings but for the collapse of family life in the Bakunin home. If the younger Bakunins had succeeded in defying Priamukhino's sentimental dogmas, it was nonetheless obvious that no real accord had emerged to replace them, nor was likely to. After a few weeks' respite for mourning, Belinsky delivered his judgment of the reason behind Priamukhino's striking absence of harmony.

During the previous year, Belinsky had given Priamukhino careful thought. He recalled that the goal of his first visit to the Bakunin home had been to catch sight of perfection. Instead he had found preciousness and pretension. Secretly uncomfortable, Belinsky had been humiliated by Mikhail's high-handed treatment of him and his personal and financial misfortunes. Encouraged to fall in love with the youngest Bakunin daughter, Aleksandra, during a separate visit to Priamukhino in July of 1838, Belinsky felt similarly fooled. Not only did she not love him (she had already pledged herself, in fact, to Belinsky's good friend

[29] T. A. Bakunina to M. A. Bakunin, letter of 16 December 1837, IRLI f. 16, op. 4, no. 582, l. 76.

[30] Letter to Varvara, 24 August 1838 (Bakunin, *Sobranie*, II:199).

[31] Letter to M. A. Bakunin, 13–15 August 1838 (Belinskii, *PSS*, XI:268).

[32] Ibid., 270.

Vasilii Botkin), he discovered that he himself did not particularly care for her.[33] He slowly came to see Priamukhino as a beautiful but delusory place, where people ignored their real obligations and desires — the important (if seemingly trivial) "kopecks" of everyday existence — in the name of abstract ideals. The philosophical friendship that Belinsky shared with Mikhail gave way to a fierce, "polemical correspondence" (as Bakunin and Belinsky called it) about reality and the Bakunin family's relationship to it.[34]

Belinsky opened this polemical correspondence with a fiercely written letter dated 10 September 1838.[35] There were two kinds of men, Belinsky declared. On the one hand, there were those who possessed an instinctive grasp of "normalcy" (*normal'nost'*), men who, if they did not spend much time reasoning about reality, nonetheless conducted themselves with unerring simplicity. On the other hand, Belinsky continued, there were those who by their natures were ill suited to live in the real world, despite the fact that they had a perfect theoretical grasp of the way that world worked in principle. Mikhail belonged to this second category of hopelessly abstract intellects; Belinsky, though finding himself guilty of some dreamy-headedness, believed he belonged to the first.[36]

Belinsky insisted that he did not mean to be judgmental: whatever malice was in his voice, he declared, stemmed from his need to defend his own nature and logic from Mikhail's dominating influence. Every man (even Mikhail) possessed a right to have his own nature. With women, however, things stood somewhat differently. "A woman's development must above all occur in life, in living reality," Belinsky contended. "Thought possesses much less significance for her, although of course a certain amount is necessary as well." Since women in general possess such strong, powerful natures — "substances" — to limit them to a purely speculative life was to put them on a collision course with reality, with the essence of their own being, he claimed.[37]

In not understanding this, in lording his abstract intellect over his emotional sisters, Mikhail had committed a cardinal, almost unforgivable sin, Belinsky argued. He had turned these beautiful creatures into unrecognizable

---

[33] Oksman, *Letopis'*, 167–68; see also Belinsky's sad letter to M. A. Bakunin, 18–19 July 1838 (*PSS*, XI:252–56) and then his retrospective analyses of this romance in his letters to M. A. Bakunin, 10 September 1838 (ibid., 302–3) and to V. P. Botkin, 10–16 February 1838 (ibid., 359–60).

[34] Lydia Ginzburg provides the best analysis of Belinsky's quarrel with Bakunin in *On Psychological Prose*, 60–71.

[35] Letter from Belinsky to Mikhail Bakunin, 10 September 1838 (Belinskii, *PSS*, XI:281–305).

[36] Ibid., 288.

[37] Ibid., 287–88.

femmes savantes, philosophical oddities unsuited for any kind of normal existence. Mikhail had doomed his sisters because he had made them unsuitable for the one proper, meaningful sphere for woman in the society of the day: the family. For a woman, Belinsky declared,

> marriage is the only reasonable way to experience life and the only reality. Here, in Russia, this is especially the case. Among us, a girl is deprived of all freedom, and society regards her freedom as willfulness, which, if reprehensible in a man, is even more so in a girl. She is forbidden to go out, forbidden to go to the theater, into society, she is forbidden to give herself freely to any feeling, any thought: she constantly needs the aegis of her mother. Marriage for her is an emancipation, the beginning of her individuality [*samobytnost'*].

By the same token, a woman who never married was doomed to deformity, Belinsky continued. "No matter how she gives herself over to fantasies, society will take its due, and sooner or later she will feel its blows, and the result will either be an early death or a monstrous marriage."[38]

But this, Belinsky concluded, was what was now happening with the Bakunin sisters, because of their fascination with Mikhail's abstract philosophizing. Varvara's marriage to Diakov had proven as much.

Though Mikhail's inattention to "kopecks" came at little immediate cost to him, for his sisters the effect was disastrous. Mikhail had denied his sisters the chance to find their true selves through engagement with the one institution that could provide a meaningful framework for feminine personality in Russia. As an example of what happened to high-minded *femme savantes* who failed to anchor themselves to reality by marriage, Belinsky conjured up the image of the Beyers' tutor Maria Afanasevna, "a genius of a woman" once respected for her metaphysical wisdom but now universally mocked as a spinster and scarred by her unnatural "virginal old age": "I repeat, reality is a monster armed with steel claws and it will eat anyone who departs from it or tries to go against it."[39]

A sharp reassertion of society's normative assumptions about men, women, and the home thus anchored Belinsky's critique of Priamukhino and Mikhail as its faithful son. No longer did Belinsky believe in houses that were isolated oases of ideals, where some odd culture of intellection was practiced, if that

[38] Ibid.
[39] Ibid., 286–88, esp. 288.

meant that those same households ignored what Belinsky conceived to be the natural rhythms of home life. He still believed that life was ruled by a higher reason—this was a legacy of what he now began to call his "idealism"—but he did not believe that this rationality could be found anywhere else but in normalcy, that is, in the norms produced by society, rather than by deductive methods: "I think *exactly the same* about life, marriage, service, in a word, about all human and social relations as those 'practical people,' which not so long ago I despised and hated—even as I think about all this *completely differently* than they do."[40] From the perspective of his new theory, he felt, he could finally explain both Liubov's hopelessness and unreasoning affection for Stankevich and Varvara's demonstrative despair during her separation from Diakov. Liubov loved as a woman should: unthinkingly, emotionally, simply. Though Belinsky had despised such an unconscious love earlier while still in the grips of abstraction, "*only that* kind of love could satisfy me now," for this was the kind of love a woman could give and a man could properly desire. It was Stankevich, not Liubov, who had acted improperly.[41]

As for Varvara, toward the end of her liberation she had taken to calling herself a "*weak, fallen creature.*" Belinsky felt he finally understood what she meant.

> Now I comprehend this self-doubt, this modesty: this was the torturous striving for reality of a soul that felt outside of reality. Your thoughts did not give her strength; she was intimidated by them, but did not accept them—from this she was saved by her strong, individual nature and her involuntary presence in reality (and not in dreams and fantasies about reality). She is a mother, and has contemplated many things, about which our trite philosophy has not even dreamed. She has felt how there are ties which cannot be undone as easily as one throws shoes off one's feet.[42]

Even the noblest women were corrupted by a bad marriage, Belinsky felt, since marriage was the lifeblood of women's reality. But Varvara's prospects outside marriage were scarcely better, despite the fact that it was clear she could not live with Diakov. This, then, was the real source of her continuing misery, a misery Mikhail could never understand: Varvara's liberation was as an escape into spectrality, rather than reality. As she herself was well

[40] Ibid., 282. Emphasis in the original.
[41] Ibid., 303. Emphasis in the original.
[42] Ibid., 299. Emphasis in the original.

aware—he claimed—all her philosophy meant nothing because it contradicted her condition.

Throughout his letter, Belinsky insisted that he respected Mikhail's philosophical acumen. Coming only a month after Liubov's death, however, the letter could scarcely have been more painful or damning. Perhaps the most destructive implication of all was that Mikhail's great, speculative mind was destined to remain of no use to anyone. Mikhail, in confining his activities to Priamukhino's ideal world, had divorced his reason from necessary experience: "You will object, that you have experienced many tempests within the family; but, first of all, such a life is one-sided, and, second of all, you created many of these circumstances, thinking you were struggling with real ones."[43] The family might serve a necessary purpose, protecting tender natures in a difficult world. But refined home life could not provide a narrative for the rise of consciousness and the making of a better world, for reality would always remain much larger than merely the family. At best, family life was a refuge; at worst, it was a dream world in which the mind wandered fruitlessly among its own lyrical fantasies and subjective delusions.[44]

One effect of Belinsky's critique was to draw a sharp distinction between his own ability to critique the Bakunins' existence in retrospect—from his position outside the home—and any critique of Mikhail's Idealism that might have emerged from within Priamukhino. It is characteristic that even as Belinsky drew several important and seemingly sympathetic implications from Varvara's struggle, he did not attempt to link his critique with Varvara's doubts. Varvara herself, when she heard about Belinsky's "new theory of women" (as she called it) was appalled by the moral Belinsky had drawn from her story. "[I]t is painful and sad to me, when I think that Belinsky judges us and laughs at us," she wrote to Mikhail in December 1838.[45]

Although Belinsky did not blame the Bakunin sisters for their fate, neither did he spare any salt when he condemned them as women doomed by their defiance of social conventions in the years thereafter. In 1843, Belinsky confessed that he felt sorry for Varvara, "inasmuch as I know, from my own experience, what the plague of Germanism (*nemetchina*) can do, if it is inculcated from childhood—it's the same as being infected with syphilis in

[43] Ibid., 292.

[44] After receiving a sharp reply from Mikhail, Belinsky developed all these themes further in a gigantic letter, 12–24 October 1838, Belinskii, *PSS*, IX:307–47.

[45] V. A. Diakova to M. A. Bakunin, letter of 21 December 1838, IRLI f. 16, op. 4, no. 447, ll. 11–12.

childhood—you'll never recover."[46] After Botkin's courtship of Aleksandra Bakunina ended with Botkin feeling spurned, Belinsky consoled him by arguing that Aleksandra was a "damaged nature" broken by the same dreamy-headedness that gripped the rest of her family. "Her imagination lives in her head, which means that her head rules her heart—and this is worse than when a man's heart rules his head."[47]

In retrospect, we may say that the Bakunin sisters became an early attempt at the portrait of sickly Russian womanhood that Belinsky drew in his famous cycle of essays on Pushkin, written from 1843 to 1846.[48] Identifying overly-intellectual, "ideal maidens" as a particularly grotesque phenomenon of Russian reality, Belinsky's essay called them "sickly growths on the social body."[49] As he had with the Bakunin sisters, Belinsky argued that women given to "idealizing" will be destroyed by its pathology even if they give it up: like "the remnants of a poorly healed illness, it will poison their tranquility and happiness."[50] Belinsky argued that even the heroine of Pushkin's famous novel *Evgenii Onegin*—the lovely Tatiana Larina, a "brilliant nature" who Belinsky praises as the perfect example or "type" of contemporary Russian womanhood—suffered the fate of falling into this trap. Educated on romantic novels, unable to understand her love Onegin, she entered his library, only to be shocked and horrified by what she found there. Understanding Onegin with her mind—but still not her soul and body—she decides to let herself "be given" to a man of whom society approves and becomes a cold and forbidding aristocratic lady. "The life of a woman is concentrated in her heart," Belinsky concludes, again echoing the language he had used when critiquing the Bakunin sisters. "For her to love is to live." "This is the role for which nature made Tatiana," he notes sadly, "but society remade her."[51]

If Tatiana's library studies bore no fruit—because they contradicted her nature and eventually overwhelmed it—that need not be the final result of Pushkin's poem itself, Belinsky concludes with pathos. Despite being conceived in an "aristocratic time"—an era, Belinsky implies, that is rapidly passing—Pushkin's poem itself can become a maturing "act of consciousness" for Russian society at large, as its morals are revealed through critical thought

[46] Letter to Botkin of 31 March–3 April 1843 (Belinskii, *PSS*, XII:150).

[47] Letter to Botkin of 10–11 December 1840 (Belinskii, *PSS*, XI:571).

[48] See Belinsky's famous ninth essay on *Evgenii Onegin* (*PSS*, VII:473–504).

[49] Belinskii, *PSS*, VII:478–79.

[50] Ibid., 479.

[51] Ibid., 480–501, esp. 480, 501. That this rather harsh, naturalistic reading of Tatiana's fate is far from the only one is shown admirably by Olga Peters Hasty, *Pushkin's Tatiana* (Madison: University of Wisconsin Press, 1999).

and public discussion.[52] It was to the role of leading the critical dissection of Russia's aristocratic world that Belinsky himself pretended. By pushing back against the pretensions of the sphere of distinction Priamukhino symbolized, Belinsky presented himself as an outsider, aligned with a broader reality that was rapidly moving beyond the idealized but isolated realm of noble domesticity. Belinsky aspired to be society's tribune, rather than the scribe of some particular circle. Unlike Tatiana—or the Bakunin sisters for that matter—he could escape this past.

When Belinsky first came to Priamukhino, it was imagined that the Bakunins would civilize him. Instead, over time and as he told it, the romance of his Idealism was a story of how he overcame the distinction that surrounded elite life and saw the more problematic reality it concealed. He was a witness to Arcadia, had learned and could write its history, but it was not his home, and his consciousness was not trapped by its ideals. Belinsky achieved this portrait of himself through a sharp reassertion of domestic and gender norms that he felt the Bakunins' relentless intellection had violated. In so doing, he implied that the truly meaningful "acts of consciousness" took place somewhere other than the limited sphere of home life, a sphere he felt that women could not yet leave, because of the social and cultural conditions of his day. Still, thirty years later, it would be Priamukhino that would allow historians to resurrect Belinsky "the man" for history.

For a decade or so after Belinsky's death in 1848, censorship made it difficult to commemorate his memory or even to get his name in print. In the interlude, the rumors surrounding his life grew in intensity, with some idolizing him and others subjecting his legacy to ridicule. Ironically, Lazhechnikov's 1859 memoir—one of the first accounts to overcome the ban on Belinsky's name—served to broadcast the notion that some unnamed noble family had helped to soften and civilize Belinsky. In so doing, it told a story inspired more by ideals of noble distinction and elevation that still surrounded the Bakunin home, than by Belinsky's much more complex relationship to his experiences at Priamukhino.[53]

[52] Ibid., 502–3.

[53] See the introduction to this book for a discussion of Lazhechnikov's 1859 memoir, which is I. I. Lazhechnikov, "Zametki dlia biografii Belinskogo," in *Polnoe sobranie sochinenii*, vol. 12 (St. Petersburg: Tovarishchestvo M. O. Vol'f, 1900), 228–60, esp. 255–57. For a complete description of the nineteenth-century controversies surrounding Belinsky, see the introduction to V. S.

Finally, in the early 1870s, the esteemed historian Aleksandr Pypin determined to solve the mysteries surrounding Belinsky's name by creating a new
and scientific biography.[54] Pypin sympathized with Belinsky, but he was also
a scholarly positivist and quite possibly the best-read man in the empire. His
goal was to produce a definitive study of the many twists and turns in Belinsky's life, based on a thorough reading of all available materials. Yet Pypin,
like readers before him, found Belinsky's published works impossibly obscure, especially when it came to reconstructing the critic's "transition from
Moscow Idealism to a new point of view."[55] In the years 1836–1840, he felt,
the brash and bold Belinsky simply dissipated into a cloud of Fichtean abstraction before becoming (briefly) an appalling apologist for the Russian
state. It was only after this episode, when he moved to St. Petersburg, that
Belinsky had finally assumed what Pypin believed to be Belinsky's normal,
mature, and historic role in Russian society.

What had happened? Contacting Belinsky's friends and relatives through
the vast network of his university acquaintances, Pypin sought resolve this
mystery. In time, he turned to the Bakunins. At first the Bakunins expressed
reluctance to share their collection of Belinsky's correspondence with Pypin,
citing the essentially intimate character of these letters. Pypin responded with
a second appeal, in which he promised to abstract away from all "purely intimate" details toward "general considerations." This second try yielded a
stunning bounty, exceeding all expectations. The Bakunins replied with more
than four hundred pages of original correspondence by Belinsky, centering
on exactly the years that interested Pypin most.[56] The family's official representative in this matter, Mikhail Bakunin's brother Aleksandr Aleksandrovich Bakunin, placed few limitations on how Pypin could use these letters.
He simply requested that Belinsky's biographer exercise caution. In pulling out the "thread of Belinsky," Aleksandr Aleksandrovich asked, Pypin

---

Nechaeva, *V. G. Belinsky. Nachalo zhiznennogo puti i literaturnoi deiatel'nosti* (Moscow: Izdatel'stvo
Akademii nauk SSSR, 1949), 3–28.

[54] Pypin describes his intention to rescue Belinsky from historical oblivion in the preface to
his eventual work, see A. N. Pypin, *Belinskii, ego zhizn' i perepiska*, vol. 1 (St. Petersburg: Tipografiia M. M. Stasiulevicha, 1876), 1–5.

[55] Pypin notes his difficulties in his correspondence with his fellow journalist Pavel Annenkov.
See Ukhmylova, "Materialy," 305–7, esp. 307 (letter to Annenkov, 1 February 1874).

[56] Pypin's copies of Belinsky's letters are IRLI f. 250, op. 1, no. 253. From notations Pypin
made on these copies, we may be sure that he acquired all of Belinsky's correspondence with the
family directly from the Bakunins. For the Bakunins' initial reluctance but eventual cooperation, see the exchange between Pypin and the family reproduced in Ukhmylova, "Materialy,"
313.

should be careful to avoid "wounding, or at least wounding sharply, a family which has neither the right nor the obligation to open itself to the vision of strangers."[57]

The Bakunin letters allowed Pypin to solve the enigma of Belinsky's development. Previous commentators had blamed the influence of friends (most notably the notoriously didactic Mikhail Bakunin) for Belinsky's bouts of conservative abstraction. Though exculpatory, this explanation hardly did Belinsky any credit, as it suggested he was gullible. From letters Pypin edited and published, however, it became clear that Belinsky consistently rejected Bakunin's conception of the how reason worked in the world, seeing it as the sort of fantasy only a privileged nobleman could maintain. Belinsky worshipped existing reality, it turned out, precisely because he objected to Bakunin's disdain for Belinsky's own impoverished existence. Though politically shortsighted, Pypin believed, this attempt to wring meaning from circumstance pointed toward the critical realism for which Belinsky was so famous.[58]

For the first time, thanks to the Bakunin letters, the logic of this crucial turning point in Belinsky's development could be divined from the record of his life. More generally speaking, Pypin's *Belinsky, His Life and Correspondence* (published in 1876) was credited with effecting a revolution in the historical understanding of Belinsky. As the critic's private life was revealed, Belinsky emerged with heretofore hidden fury as a "fighter for his own ideas." In place of the old riddle, there suddenly appeared a man whom "it was impossible not to love more than Belinsky the writer."[59] Yet Pypin was constrained — both politically and by his own promises that he would protect the Bakunin family's privacy — as to what he could say about the domestic world that had preserved the memory of Belinsky the man. He used circumspect initials (the family "B-x") whenever he was describing the Bakunins. In his acknowledgments, he thanked the family only obscurely, as his "rural friends."[60]

As a result, the domestic context in which Belinsky imagined his transformation into a real man — the context that preserved this transformation despite censorship and the repeated destruction of Belinsky's own archive —

[57] See A. A. Bakunin's letter to Pypin of 10 March [1874?], in Ukhmylova, "Materialy," 313. The original of this letter is IRLI, f. 16, op. 3, no. 115, ll. 1–2.

[58] See Pypin, *Belinskii*, vol. 1, 221–37, esp. 224–25, 232–37.

[59] S. Vengerov, "Pypin, Aleksandr Nikolaevich," in *Entsiklopedicheskii slovar'* (St. Petersburg: Tipo-litografiia I. A. Efrona, 1898), 25:892–94. For Pypin's use of the Bakunin letters, see Pypin, *Belinskii*, 154–237, where he quotes the Bakunin archive on almost every page.

[60] Ibid., vii.

remained largely untouched by Pypin's history, a fact that would continue to characterize Russian biography until almost the end of the imperial era.

Even so, at Priamukhino today there is a marker remembering Belinsky as one of the Bakunin family's many guests. The tribute is quite fitting. Though Belinsky the writer opposed himself to the noble home, Belinsky the historical man was in many ways its native son.

Epilogue

In his biography of Belinsky, Pypin praised the Bakunin family for its hospitality and intelligence. "The family B.," he observed, "belonged to that small number of families who did not lead their everyday lives according to gentry custom but rather knew and valued intellectual and aesthetic interests. These families gave a warm welcome to that rising generation, from which came many of the most prominent actors of our enlightenment."[1] Though true enough in themselves, such formulations have a static and somewhat mythic character. They credit the Bakunin home with fostering intellectual development but explain little about how the Bakunin home acquired this particular power. What were the origins of the Bakunins' particular brand of domestic enlightenment? What sort of framework did domestic ideals, society, and practices offer for Russian social thought in the nineteenth century? In particular, how did home life shape and support the traditions surrounding the Stankevich circle? In this book I have tried to answer these questions. Before bringing my story to an end, let me first offer a few general conclusions here.

The home life for which the Bakunin family became famous was not, primarily, a product of idleness or alienation. Instead, it was inspired by a culture of domestic distinction promoted by the imperial government in the late

---

[1] A. N. Pypin, *Belinskii, ego zhizn' i perepiska,* vol. 1 (St. Petersburg: Tipografiia M. M. Stasiulevicha, 1876), 129–30. Similar formulations may be found in P. V. Annenkov, *Nikolai Vladimirovich Stankevich: Perepiska ego i biografiia* (Moscow: Tipografiia Kat'kova, 1857), 155, and elsewhere.

eighteenth century, as Russia's rulers sought to mobilize the full resources of Russian noble private life. During their time at Priamukhino the Bakunins developed many different ambitions and habits. Praskovia presented her family as an example to others; her mother and sisters devoted themselves to religious practice and inner life; her brother Aleksandr imagined his family's estate as a laboratory for enlightenment; while his wife Varvara kept track of Priamukhino's comings and goings in her *Memory Books*. Each of these efforts expanded the cultural range of home life and helped turn an unpretentious manor house into an expressive forum for intellectual activity. All along, however, Priamukhino possessed a distinction whose ultimate source was imperial power. In the late eighteenth century, Catherine II and her advisers had sought to rally noble families behind the civilization of the provinces. Under Nicholas I, domestic virtues were celebrated as unifying commonplaces of imperial life. In both cases, home life was elevated as a source of example and inspiration by imperial officialdom, in the hope that domesticity could provide productive and patriotic social norms.

It was this distinction that helped to draw the ambitious young men of the Stankevich circle to Priamukhino. They themselves were surrounded by a kind of charisma: namely, that of the academic world to which they belonged. At Priamukhino, however, they found the audience, ideals, and practices that assisted them in the creation of a new and freestanding tradition in Russian social thought. Inspired by the Kantian tradition, the Stankevich circle sought to accomplish that movement's central goals: moral self-determination and participation in the advancement of public reason.[2] They wished to make themselves the "equal to the best ideas of their time," as Stankevich put it, and they turned to private life as a forum for this activity. Priamukhino supported this process in three fundamental ways.

First, domestic ideals provided norms around which Stankevich and his friends sought to build their worldviews. They expected the Bakunins to be an ideal family and imagined that their time at Priamukhino would foster their intellectual development by showing them a vision of perfected humanity. Second, Priamukhino provided a productive forum for philosophical self-reflection — not least because the younger Bakunins eagerly participated in it. Placed into this distinguished frame, biographical events were easily re-

---

[2] Carla Hesse provides a stimulating discussion of these values and the conditions necessary for their realization in Carla Hesse, *The Other Enlightenment : How French Women Became Modern* (Princeton: Princeton University Press, 2001), xii. Above all, Hesse argues, Kantian visions of moral self-development require a "durable" space for self-reflection; in retrospect, one may say Priamukhino provided the Stankevich circle with just such a space.

cast as turning points in a historic quest to translate the latest word in European philosophy into compelling Russian terms. Last but not least, the Bakunin family's time-keeping habits archived these philosophical romances, so that the charismatic tradition of self-development the Stankevich circle created could be inspected, admired, and imitated by future generations. When Pypin, or before him Stankevich's biographer Annenkov, wished to document the intellectual history that stood behind the Idealists' development, the Bakunin family papers helped them to do so.[3]

The history of the Bakunin home opens a new perspective on the making of intellectual traditions in early nineteenth century Russia. It shows how the Idealists—whose labors have long been understood as an act of alienation—partook in the common, and quite official, domestic ideals of their day. More important, it helps document their participation in an imperial culture of distinction, whose resources they used to animate and archive the new social tradition they were trying to create: that of autonomous, self-determined, progressive Russian thinkers. In effect, the Bakunin family's life supported a new kind of ennoblement in Russian culture, one rooted in history rather than social caste. Though the Stankevich circle by and large belonged to Russia's well-born nobility, it was through their activities in private life that they were able to achieve recognition as "the best people of their time."[4] From this point of view, the romance surrounding Russian Idealism is both an offshoot of the Empire's existing traditions of charismatic authority—its court-sponsored "scenarios of power"—and an attempt to create a new, and freestanding, form of charisma, based in society at large.

A combination of censorship, privacy, and domestic conventions pre-

---

[3] On late nineteenth-century historians' historical consultations with the Bakunins, see John Randolph, "'That Historical Family': The Bakunin Archive and the Intimate Theater of History in Imperial Russia, 1780–1925," *Russian Review* 63 (October 2004): 580, 588–91. Among the major scholarly editions heavily dependent on the Bakunin archive are: N. V. Stankevich, *Perepiska Nikolaia Vladimirovicha Stankevicha*, ed. A. Stankevich (Moscow: Tipografiia A. I. Mamontova, 1914); E. A. Liatskii, ed., *Belinskii: Pis'ma*, vol. 1 (1829–1839) (St. Petersburg: Tipografiia M. M. Stasiulevicha, 1914); M. A. Bakunin, *Sobranie sochinenii i pisem*, vol. 1, *Dogegelianskii period, 1828–1837*, ed. Iu. M. Steklov (Moscow: Izdatel'stvo Vsesoiuznogo obshchestva politkatorzhan i ssyl'no-poselentsev, 1934). Note that the Bakunin archive also yielded papers by Vasily Botkin, Ivan Turgenev, and several other, lesser-known figures.

[4] See P. Miliukov, "Liubov' u 'idealistov tridtsatykh godov,'" in *Iz istorii russkoi intelligentsii: Sbornik statei* (St. Petersburg: Tipografiia A. E. Kolpinskogo, 1902), 73. It is worth mentioning in this context that much of Miliukov's famous essay was based on archival work he did at the Bakunin family's Crimean dacha, Gornaia Shchel' where much of the Priamukhino archive was located in the late nineteenth century. He thanks the Bakunins for this assistance (ibid., 82); see also Randolph, "'That Historical Family,'" 590–91.

vented the historical exploration of the Bakunin home until nearly the end of the imperial era.[5] Mikhail Bakunin's eventual infamy kept "the family B's" name out of print even as his friend Belinsky publicly expressed his distaste for the unnaturally intellectualized (as he saw it) femininity Priamukhino seemed to foster. The family cooperated with historians on the condition that as much of its intimate life be left out of the public eye as possible. As a result, much of the story just told was excluded from the purview of history. This includes the activity of the Bakunin grandparents and parents, who started to fashion an exemplary existence at Priamukhino in the late eighteenth century; the interests and agency of the Bakunin sisters, whose ambitions connected Priamukhino to the culture of student Idealism in the 1830s and whose archival labors in the home preserved its documents long thereafter; and not least, the history of noble home life itself, destroyed by revolution before it could be studied historically. When the Tver Scholarly Archaelogical Commission came looking for the Bakunin family papers after the family itself had fled in 1917, they found many documents "heaped in a mountain on the floor of the office."[6] Reconstructing the intellectual culture such family archives represent requires taking an interest in the domestic realm that produced them, before it was consumed by revolution.

By that point, of course, the Bakunin family's own home life at Priamukhino had ended as well. The estate's last master was Mikhail Alekseevich Bakunin (1880–1962), one of Mikhail Bakunin's nephews. Caught in Moscow at the time of the revolution, he fled south to the Crimea with his family and then fought on the White (and losing) side of the Civil War. After being evacuated with General Kutepov's army to Bulgaria, this branch of the Bakunin family settled in Belgium. By this time Priamukhino itself had been nationalized and turned into a school, although the heart of the house—the central wooden corpus, purchased by Liubov Petrovna in 1779—burned down shortly thereafter. Only one of the two stone wings added by Aleksandr Bakunin in the early nineteenth century still stands.[7]

It is hard not to feel a certain sense of poetic justice when one looks at these

---

[5] The exception being Kornilov's incomplete series on the Bakunin family: A. Kornilov, *Molodye gody Mikhaila Bakunina: Iz istorii russkogo romantizma* (Moscow: M. and S. Sabashnikov, 1915); and A. Kornilov, *Gody stranstvii Mikhaila Bakunina* (Leningrad-Moscow: Gosudarstvennoe izdatel'stvo, 1925).

[6] Vladimir Sysoev, *Bakuniny* (Tver: Sozvezdie, 2002), 279 This was only one part of the Bakunin family's papers, about which see John Randolph, "On the Biography of the Bakunin Family Archive," in *Archive Stories: Facts, Fictions, and the Writing of History*, ed. Antoinette Burton (Durham: Duke University Press, 2005), 209–31.

[7] Sysoev, *Bakuniny*, 228–32, 269–94.

ruins. Both the privilege families like the Bakunins represented—and the independent, sometimes radical social traditions they supported—helped inspire Russia's early twentieth-century revolutions. Indeed, at the end of the nineteenth century, some of Aleksandr's grandchildren and great-grandchildren participated in socialist groups. Varvara Diakova's son Aleksandr defended striking workers as a lawyer, while his son opened an illegal press at the Diakov estate Luganovo.[8] Yet for most of the nineteenth century, people who expected to find at Priamukhino a nest of radicalism—rather than a nest of country gentlefolk—were disappointed. In the 1860s a student named Vasily Lind wrote a novel "that began with a picture of life at Priamukhino and my relations with the Bakunins and ended with the seizure of Petersburg by the armies of revolution."[9] When he actually paid a visit to the Bakunin family, however, Lind came to think that their revolutionary reputation was "in essence totally inaccurate."[10] At Priamukhino, he writes, "life's goal took on a different hue," quite out of step with the materialism and social utilitarianism that characterized the 1860s. "It was no longer tied to the notion of sacrifice or imminent ruin, but with the notion of personal happiness, and without a guilty conscience, at that."[11]

The idyllic, paternal vision of family life that had enchanted Aleksandr Bakunin in the late eighteenth century still framed family life in the mid-1800s. By this time, Aleksandr himself was dead (he died in 1854, at the age of almost ninety), as was his wife Varvara, who died in 1864. Their sons, Nikolai, Pavel, Aleksandr, and Aleksei headed the household thereafter, living in and around Priamukhino and becoming leaders of the liberal party of the local nobility. Nikolai and Aleksei were arrested in 1862 for protesting the terms of the peasant emancipation of 1861. (The Bakunins felt this important reform, which ended serfdom in Russia, had been conducted too bureaucratically and demanded too little of Russia's nobility.)[12] Thereafter, Pavel

---

[8] Ibid., 267–69.

[9] V. N. Lind, "Vospominaniia," *Russkaia mysl'*, no. 6 (1916): 53.

[10] Ibid., no. 8 (1911): 37.

[11] Ibid., 63.

[12] On 5 February 1862, thirteen officials from Tver Province responsible for implementing the emancipation legislation abandoned their duties because they felt that the government's gestures toward civic involvement in the process were inadequate. Among these men, all of whom were arrested and taken to the Peter-Paul Fortress, were Nikolai and Aleksei Bakunin. For the best account of this affair, see Terence Emmons, *The Russian Landed Gentry and the Peasant Emancipation of 1861* (Cambridge: Cambridge University Press, 1968), 344–49. The officials' protest and documents relating to it were printed in the exile publication *Osvobozhdenie* in 1903 (see "Epizod iz istorii obshchestvennykh dvizhenii v Rossii," in *Osvobozhdenie*, ed. Petr Struve, vol. 1 [Stuttgart: Dietz, 1903], 17–23). Pavel Bakunin defends the legality of his brothers' actions in

and Aleksandr played prominent roles in Tver's new institution of local self-administration, the zemstvo.[13] A leader both at home and in public, Pavel in particular took pains to present himself as a "belated voice of the 1840s," and sought to preserve the Romantic traditions Priamukhino had spawned in the 1830s long after their original authors had moved on.[14]

Pavel's efforts, however, were already a self-conscious attempt to sustain a culture of Idealism that many believed had reached its historic fruition a generation earlier. Ivan Turgenev was the last young man of this first generation to come to Priamukhino in search of a romance to fire his moral education. He visited the Bakunins in May and October of 1841, where he pursued and won Tatiana's affections only to disappear over the horizon thereafter, leaving her with a few ultra-romantic poems as his parting gift. Tatiana herself complained of the scripted, over-determined quality of their relationship: "Why do these involuntary ruminations seize me in the very minutes when I wish to be closest to you?," she wrote to Turgenev, when his short-lived interest in their romance was clearly on the wane.[15] But by then, Turgenev had already moved on, and the next time he would return to Priamukhino it would be in his fiction. His friends and knowledgable critics instantly recognized in three separate works—Turgenev's early short story "Andrei Kolosov" (1844); a second story, "Tatiana Borisovna and her Nephew" (1848), later included in his *Sportsman's Sketches;* and his first novel, *Rudin* (1856)—plots, scenes, and characters from Priamukhino.[16]

In "Andrei Kolosov" Turgenev wrote about a hopeless, ideal romance, alternatingly construed as Stankevich's love for Liubov Bakunina or Turgenev's own affair with Tatiana. *Rudin* was read more consistently as a portrait

---

a draft "Memorandum on the 13 Peace Mediators," though it is unclear if this memorandum was ever sent. See IRLI f. 16, op. 6, no. 53. The Bakunin family archive also contains other collections of correspondence surrounding the affair: see IRLI f. 16, op. 6, nos. 46 and 49.

[13] It would take another book to describe the family's rich role in the so-called Era of Great Reforms. For now, see Emmons, *The Russian Landed Gentry,* 344–49; Sysoev, *Bakuniny,* 172–228; and N. M. Pirumova, *Zemskoe liberal'noe dvizhenie: Sotsial'nye korni i evoliutsiia do nachala XX v.* (Moscow: Nauka, 1977), esp. 101–4.

[14] See Pavel Bakunin, *Zapozdalyi golos sorokovykh godov: Po povodu zhenskogo voprosa* (St. Petersburg: Tipografiia V. Bezobrazova, 1881). See also N. S. Bakunina's correspondence with her future husband Pavel, where these values are discussed and become the basis of their future life together: IRLI f. 16, op. 5, no. 112, ll. 1–44.

[15] Tatiana's letters to Turgenev are published by Brodskii, "'Premukhinskii roman,'" 122–59; for this letter, of 15 June 1842, see 123.

[16] See I. S. Turgenev, "Andrei Kolosov," in *Polnoe sobranie sochinenie i pisem* vol. 4 (Moscow: Nauka, 1980), 7–33; idem, *Rudin* in *Polnoe sobranie sochinenii i pisem,* vol. 5 (Moscow: Nauka, 1980), 197–322; and idem, "Tat'iana Borisovna i ee plemiannik," in *Zapiski okhotnika,* ed. A. L. Grishunin et al. (Moscow: Nauka, 1991), 134–42.

of Mikhail, although critics disagreed as to whether Turgenev had succeeded
in capturing young Bakunin's true character. Finally, in "Tatiana Borisovna
and her Nephew," Turgenev portrayed his former love as an old maid, im-
prisoned by her own romantic illusions.[17] In each of these works, Turgenev
invited the Russian reading public to live through the romance of Russian
Idealism in a voyeuristic fashion. Even before memoirists and historians celebrated the lives of Russia's "Idealists of the 1830s," Turgenev's readers could
eavesdrop on this generation's intimate life and make judgments about its
ideals and historical significance.[18] In the process, these same readers became
participants in the charismatic intellectual tradition the Stankevich circle
had, quite consciously, sought to invent.

By the time Turgenev's *Rudin* appeared in 1856, Mikhail Bakunin had already spent several years in prison just outside St. Petersburg, after his
arrest by Saxon authorities in 1849. It was, needless to say, an odd and unwanted kind of homecoming. When he arranged Varvara's liberation in 1838,
Mikhail counted on being able to join her in Berlin more or less immediately.
Yet lacking his parents' permission (and still more their money), he remained
stuck in Russia for another two years. Varvara, meanwhile, wandered around
Europe in his absence, accompanied by her young son Sasha (Aleksandr).
She lived for a while in Berlin and then Switzerland, where she began a warm
and ultimately romantic correspondence with Stankevich, who was seeking
a cure for his tuberculosis under the advice of various doctors. In the spring
of 1840 they agreed to meet in Naples. Shortly thereafter, however, Stankevich's illness entered its final stage, and Varvara rushed to meet him outside
of Rome. Accompanied by an old student friend named Efremov, they traveled north toward the Swiss border. On the way, Stankevich died.[19]

Varvara returned to Berlin, where she shared an apartment with Mikhail.
They socialized with a broad circle of students, professors, writers, and Russian emigrés, making the acquaintance, among others, of the young Ivan Tur-

---

[17] N. L. Brodskii discusses the Bakunin theme in each of these works in his "'Premukhinskii
roman,'" in *I. S. Turgenev* Moscow: Gosudarstvennoe izdatel'stvo 1923), 107–21. See also Marshall Shatz, "Bakunin, Turgenev, and *Rudin*," in *The Golden Age of Russian Literature and Thought*,
ed. Derek Offord (New York: St. Martin's, 1992), 103–14, as well as Lydia Ginzburg, *On Psychological Prose*, trans. and ed. Judson Rosengrant (Princeton: Princeton University Press, 1991),
43–48.

[18] For a reading of Rudin as an attempt to overcome Romantic rhetoric, see Jane T. Costlow,
Worlds within Worlds: The Novels of Ivan Turgenev (Princeton: Princeton University Press, 1990),
11–29. It seems logical to think that Turgenev's readers retraced this process as well.

[19] See Edward J. Brown, *Stankevich and his Moscow Circle* (Stanford: Stanford University Press,
1966), 10, 80–1; Stankevich's letters to Varvara are Stankevich, *Perepiska*, 722–44.

genev, whom they eventually dispatched to Priamukhino. But by late 1841, relations between Mikhail and his sister had grown frosty. Mikhail failed to notice, Varvara wrote to Tatiana, how her position as a married woman separated from her husband subjected her to many humiliations. Though he could readily barter an existence from others in exchange for his company and ideas, she lived on increasingly tenuous lines of credit that eventually faded altogether. She also worried that her son Aleksandr was suffering from isolation.[20] Her husband, Diakov, meanwhile, promised to take her back without conditions: "I desire that your return to Priamukhino will allow you to know the happiness you deserve so well."[21]

In the summer of 1842 Varvara finally decided to return to her husband in Russia, having spent nearly four years abroad. Mikhail accused her of succumbing to what he called a "Lenten Idealism": an odd mixture of philosophical resignation and religious obligation.[22] Shortly thereafter, Varvara became pregnant again, leading Belinsky to quip sarcastically: "That's inner life for you!" (He believed her return showed that she had learned a lesson about the realities of life.)[23] In the end, however, Varvara's decision to return to Diakov seems to have been a practical one, made for reasons that had little to do with the philosophical significance other people wanted to assign it. She and her husband were later remembered as an amicable if not particularly well-suited couple, who by their middle age reached an agreement on how to get along. (Diakov himself died in a hunting accident in 1852.) Yet Varvara never seems to have reconciled herself to the progressive conception of "reality" that her brother and former friends embraced. In the early 1850s, she had a violent quarrel with her brother Pavel on the subject, rejecting his repeated insistence that human affairs expressed some overarching reason. "That which we call reality," she wrote, "is a sphere given over to eternal arbitrariness, foolishness, the most disconnected contradictions, the most brutal passions."[24] In this sense, Varvara overcame her Idealism more thoroughly than her male counterparts.

Varvara lived until 1866. Until the end of her days, she preserved Stankevich's letters as a special relic of her past.[25] Her sister Tatiana, meanwhile,

[20] See Varvara's letters to Tatiana from late 1841 and early 1842, IRLI f. 16, op. 4, no. 445, ll. 1–10 ob.
[21] For Diakov's letter to his wife, see IRLI f. 16, op. 5, no. 80.
[22] Letter to his relatives, 9 October 1842 (Bakunin, *Sobranie*, III:114–19).
[23] Letter to Botkin of March 1843 (Belinskii, *PSS*, XII:150).
[24] This diary is M. E. Saltykov-Shchedrin Tver State Regional Museum, f. 1056, 2nd notebook, ll. 21–22.
[25] See N. S. Bakunina to A. I. Stankevich, letter of 14 December 1902, State Historical Mu-

became known within the family as Priamukhino's first historian. As early as 1842, she started a history of family life, based on Priamukhino's correspondence; and while this project was never completed, she carefully stitched her family's letters into a series of notebooks. After her death in 1871, her sister-in-law Natalia Semenovna (Pavel's wife) became the guardian of this family archive, "sacredly preserved" (as she described it) by her sisters-in-law for future generations.[26] When historians began to approach the Bakunins in the second half of the nineteenth century, the family was thus well-prepared to help them. By the time Pypin first contacted the Bakunin family in 1874, for example, all four hundred pages of Belinsky's correspondence had already been carefully recopied into a notebook for preservation.[27]

In the early twentieth century, Natalia Semenova decided to send Stanke-vich's and Belinsky's letters to Moscow's Historical Museum. Priamukhino's "entire female personnel" protested this decision, she claimed, but she was firm in her belief that these letters belonged "more to Russian society than to a family" — "to the future generation, and not to a private home."[28] The philosophical romances these letters contained entered Russia's national archives in an organized fashion — ready to educate "future generations" — even as the private existence that inspired and sustained them came to an end.

---

seum (GIM) f. 351, op. 1, d. 3, ll. 68–69. Natalia Semenovna, Varvara's sister-in-law, here describes Varvara's efforts to preserve Stankevich's letters.

[26] One of Tatiana's nieces, Ekaterina Bakunina, describes "Auntie Tania's" role as historian in a letter to A. A. Kornilov, 13 January [1917], GARF, f. 5102, op. 1, d. 412, ll. 59–60. See also N. S. Bakunina to A. I. Stankevich, letter of 27 April 1902 in GIM f. 351, op. 1, d. 3, l. 63 ob.; and Kornilov, *Molodye gody,* vii–xii.

[27] This notebook, dated "Priamukhino 1871," is IRLI f. 16, op. 9, no. 542.

[28] For Natalia Semenovna's controversial decision to send Stankevich's and Belinsky's letters to the State Historical Museum, see her letters to A. I. Stankevich: 15 November 1903 (GIM f. 351, op. 1, no. 3, ll. 88–89; "more to Russian society"); 24 August 1903 (ibid., ll. 84–85; "to the future generation"); and also 2 February 1903 (ibid., ll. 74–75). She reports the protests of Priamukhino's "female personnel" in her letter of 14 December 1902 (ibid., ll. 68–69).

INDEX

Page numbers in italics refer to illustrations.